CW00832468

Collected Writings of
JOHN MURRAY

Collected Writings of

JOHN MURRAY

PROFESSOR OF SYSTEMATIC THEOLOGY
WESTMINSTER THEOLOGICAL SEMINARY
PHILADELPHIA, PENNSYLVANIA
1937–1966

Volume four
STUDIES IN THEOLOGY

REVIEWS

The Banner of Truth Trust

THE BANNER OF TRUTH TRUST
3 Murrayfield Road, Edinburgh EH12 6EL
PO Box 621 Carlisle, Pennsylvania 17013, USA

© 1982 Valerie Murray

This collection first published (Volume 4) 1982
ISBN 0 85151 340 9

Printed in Great Britain at
The Camelot Press Ltd, Southampton

Contents

v

Contents

Preface

WITH THE publication of these pages the hopes expressed in the Preface to the first volume of John Murray's *Collected Writings* in September 1976 are fulfilled. We do not doubt that the set as a whole will take its place among the finest theological writing of this or indeed of any other century. As with all true doctors of the church, among whom John Murray ranks, his purpose was broader and higher than the production of scholarship as such: he was jealous that the hearts and minds of his hearers and readers might be devoted to God. He aimed, to use his own phrase, at 'intelligent piety', and for that to occur he knew that meditation upon Scripture had to become a part of our being. 'Meditation', he wrote in a Foreword to a reprint of Charles Hodge's *Princeton Sermons* in 1957, 'is not detached dreaming. To be fruitful it requires intense application to the riches of truth deposited for us in God's Word. And the reward will be visions of the mountains of God. Rest of soul will then have reached the summit of its exercise, for we shall behold the majesty of the Lord.'

The contents of this volume, with one important exception, have originally appeared in various publications, most of which have been long out-of-print. The exception is the fourth chapter, 'Jesus the Son of God', which was the last major article to be prepared by Professor Murray. It is the only piece of his writing concerning which the present writer can ever recall him expressing the desire that it should be printed.

As most readers will be aware, a number of John Murray's notable works are not contained within these *Collected Writings*, their copyright being possessed by other publishers. In part to aid the reader to trace all his works a bibliography has been prepared for this final volume.

In this and in much else in the preparation for publication of Murray's *Collected Writings* my friend and colleague Dr Sinclair B. Ferguson has rendered invaluable aid. Mr S. M. Houghton of Abingdon, Oxfordshire, has provided the indexes and given other help.

For all the Banner of Truth Trust staff connected with the planning and production of these volumes the work has been a labour of love. The memory of John Murray's unremitting help and counsel, of his warm friendship, and, above all, of his example as a Christian we shall ever prize. We know that in years to come the testimony which he was enabled to give to biblical Christianity will continue to enrich the church until, it may well be, the day when those 'which sleep in Jesus will God bring with him'.

IAIN H. MURRAY
October, 1982

I

Studies in
Theology

1

Systematic Theology[1]

THE task of systematic theology is to set forth in orderly and coherent manner the truth respecting God and his relations to men and the world. This truth is derived from the data of revelation, and revelation comprises all those media by which God makes himself and his will known to us men. God reveals himself in all the works of his hand with which we men have any encounter. It could not be otherwise. It was of his sovereign will that God created the universe and made us men in his image. But since creation is the product of his will and power the imprint of his glory is necessarily impressed upon his handiwork, and since we are created in his image we cannot but be confronted with the display of that glory. Therefore what is called natural or general revelation comes within the scope of the data of revelation with which systematic theology deals. 'The heavens declare the glory of God; and the firmament showeth his handiwork' (Ps. 19:1). 'The heavens declare his righteousness, and all the peoples have seen his glory' (Ps. 97:6). God himself is invisible, but phenomenal reality discloses what is invisible, and so 'the invisible things of him since the creation of the world are clearly seen, being understood by the things which are made, even his eternal power and divinity' (Rom. 1:20). It is counter to the import of such passages to suppose that what the work of creation reveals is a God merely commensurate with what is finite. It is 'eternal power and divinity' that are clearly seen and it is for this reason that all men are unexcusable when they fail to worship God as God in the infinite and eternal majesty made known in the things that are seen.[2]

[1] This chapter originally appeared as two articles in *The Westminster Theological Journal*, Vol. XXV, 2 and Vol. XXVI, 1, 1963.
[2] Cf. Herman Bavinck: *Our Reasonable Faith*, Grand Rapids, 1956, pp. 40 f.

There is not only the creation externally visible; there is also the nature with which we are endowed and the work of the law written on our hearts (cf. Rom. 2:15). It would be a mistake, therefore, to think that these aspects of revelation are the domain of philosophy and the sciences but not of theology. As will be noted presently, the chief source of revelation for theology is the special revelation incorporated in Holy Scripture. But the latter comes to us in the life which we live in this world and therefore in a context which is filled with the manifestation of the glory of the same God who specially reveals himself to us in his Word. It would be an abstraction to suppose that we could deal with special revelation and ignore the revelatory data with which the context of our life is replete.

It is true that natural theology has been conceived of as a department of, or as a basis for, systematic theology, to be developed independently. This would be as much an abstraction as to deal with special revelation apart from general revelation. But excessive claims for natural theology or for an independent role assigned to it should not lead us to ignore the data of natural revelation or to think that it is not the province of systematic theology to deal with them. If we take the word 'natural' to designate the revelation given in the works of creation and general providence and in the constitution of our own being, then natural theology, properly conceived, would be the setting forth of the truth respecting God and his relations to men and to the world derived from these sources. It is in this light that the validity of such arguments as the cosmological and the teleological is to be maintained. To aver that they are invalid when construed as the necessary inferences to be drawn from the exhibition of God's glory in his observable handiwork is to succumb to the unbelief which Paul indicts in Romans 1:18–20.

The principal source of revelation is Holy Scripture. Systematic theology when true to its task must regard Scripture as that which Scripture claims for itself, namely, that it is the Word of God. It is a misuse of terms to say that Scripture is the Word of God if it is not itself revelation, if it is not revelatory word addressed to us. It is necessary to take issue with Emil Brunner, for example, when he says that the Scriptures are the witness to revelation but not revelation itself, possessing 'authority because they are the *primary witness* to the revelation of God in Jesus Christ'[1] so that 'critical reflection on the adequate-

[1] *The Christian Doctrine of God, Dogmatics,* Vol. I, Philadelphia, 1950, p. 45.

ness or inadequateness, of the Biblical doctrinal testimony for the revelation to which it bears witness, is not eliminated'.[1] The same position is stated with more clarity by Barth when, dealing with the same question, he says: 'there is a Word of God for the Church: in that it receives in the Bible the witness of divine revelation. . . . When we examine this statement more closely, we shall do well to pay attention to the particular determination in the fact that we have to call the Bible a witness of divine revelation. We have here an undoubted limitation: we distinguish the Bible as such from revelation. A witness is not absolutely identical with that to which it witnesses.'[2] In taking issue with this position it is not maintained that to speak of the witness or testimony of the Bible is improper. There is the witness of Scripture. The point of difference is that the witness of Scripture *is* revelatory and that God speaks to us *in* the witness of Scripture and not merely *through* the witness of Scripture. In other words, when we speak of the witness of Scripture, we mean the witness which Scripture is as revelatory witness of God to us: it is God's own witness to us, witness borne through the instrumentality of men but borne by such a unique mode that the witness of men is God's own witness. 'All scripture is God-breathed' (2 Tim. 3:16); 'as borne by the Holy Spirit men spoke from God' (2 Pet. 1:21).[3] This divergence in the estimate of what the Bible is is radical and it will have to be admitted that the theologies emanating from these opposing views of the witness of Scripture must be proportionately divergent.

When Scripture is viewed as revelatory and therefore as inscripturated revelation, this does not identify Scripture with God nor with Christ as the focal point of revelation. God confronts us in and with revelation and by revelation we come to know who God is and what he is. Again, Christ himself is the supreme revelation of God. He is the image of the invisible God, the effulgence of his glory and the transcript of his being (cf. Col. 1:15; Heb. 1:3). Scripture is not to be identified with him in this unique identity that is his. But it is apparent that we need more than the revelation which Christ is, and we can have no knowledge of, nor encounter with, the revelation that he is except through Scripture. It would be unnecessary to reflect on these matters

[1] *Ibid.*, p. 49.
[2] *Church Dogmatics* I/2, Edinburgh, 1956, p. 463.
[3] It is unnecessary to expound and defend the implications of these texts and the doctrine of Scripture here propounded. This has been done in numerous monographs in the last three decades as well as in older works.

in an essay of this kind were it not that the dialectic theology takes occasion in the discussion of this same theme to propound its view of the Bible as witness to revelation and insists upon the supremacy of the revelation in Jesus Christ himself to the prejudice of the revelatory character of Scripture as the Word of God written.[1]

When we properly weigh the proposition that the Scriptures are the deposit of special revelation, that they are the oracles of God, that in them God encounters and addresses us, discloses to us his incomprehensible majesty, summons us to the knowledge and fulfilment of his will, unveils to us the mystery of his counsel, and unfolds the purposes of his grace, then systematic theology, of all sciences and disciplines, is seen to be the most noble, not one of cold, impassioned reflection but one that stirs adoring wonder and claims the most consecrated exercise of all our powers. It is the most noble of all studies because its province is the whole counsel of God and seeks, as no other discipline, to set forth the riches of God's revelation in the orderly and embracive manner which is its peculiar method and function. All other departments of theological discipline contribute their findings to systematic theology and it brings all the wealth of knowledge derived from these disciplines to bear upon the more inclusive systemization which it undertakes.

Special revelation as deposited in Scripture is redemptive. It not only provides us with the history of God's redemptive accomplishments, not only does it interpret for us the meaning of these redemptive events; it is itself also an abiding and for us indispensable organ in the fulfilment of God's redemptive will. Without it we should have no encounter with redemptive revelation and therefore no experience of redemption. Without it the blindness arising from sin would so darken our understanding that in God's light we could not see light. This is the consideration that exposes the fallacy of attempting to interpret natural revelation in abstraction from the special revelation which the Bible provides. Natural theology is not an independent locus in systematic theology; far less is it an independent discipline.

Since special revelation is redemptive, there is another corollary of concern to systematic theology. It is that the theologian is unfitted for his undertaking unless he knows the power of the redemptive provision of which Scripture is the revelation and of the redemptive revelation that Scripture is. Without question, great contributions have been made and can be made to systematic theology by men who do not

[1] Cf. Emil Brunner: *op. cit.*, pp. 47, 49.

know this power. But it is a travesty for a man not knowing the power of revelation to pose as an expositor of it. This is just saying that the Scriptures cannot be properly interpreted without the illumination of the Holy Spirit nor can they be properly studied as God's revelation apart from the sealing witness of the Spirit by whom alone we can be convinced that they are the Word of God. The person who addresses himself to the interpretation and formulation of the truth conveyed to us by revelation is destitute of the prime requisite if he is not imbued with the humility and enlightenment which the indwelling of the Holy Spirit imparts.

Systematic theology is not itself revelation nor is it an addendum to revelation that is to be placed alongside of Scripture. It is always a duty, sometimes a necessity, which the fact of revelation places upon the church of God. It is an accomplishment which has grown out of Christianity as it followed its course in history. Systematic theology has been a development within the church of God. The church of the first century did not begin with it and many factors have to be taken into account if we are to explain and vindicate this evolution of what is often called dogmatics.[1] The paramount consideration, however, is the demand residing in the fact of revelation, namely, that the Word of God requires the most exacting attention so that we as individuals and as members in the solidaric unity of the church may be able to correlate the manifold data of revelation in our understanding and the more effectively apply this knowledge to all phases of our thinking and conduct.

The fact that systematic theology is a development which arose in the course of history within the sphere of the church reminds us that it should not be thought of as the product of a theologian or series of theologians. It is true that the greatest contributions have been made by theologians. We think of Athanasius, Augustine, and Calvin. But neither these men nor their work can be understood or assessed apart from the history in the context of which they lived and wrought, particularly the history of the church. We may not underestimate the influence exerted by these men upon subsequent history. But history conditioned their work also and it is only because they occupied a certain place in history that they were able to contribute so significantly to the superstructure which we call theology. Of more relevance,

[1] These factors are well summarized by Brunner in *op. cit.*, pp. 9 ff.

however, than this obvious fact of interaction and dependence is the doctrine of the presence and activity of the Holy Spirit. The Holy Spirit, in accordance with Christ's promise, had led the apostles into all truth (cf. John 16:13) in a way consonant with their unique commission and function. But he has also been present in the church in all the generations of the church's history, endowing the church in its organic unity as the body of Christ with gifts of understanding and expression. It is this ceaseless activity of the Holy Spirit that explains the development throughout the centuries of what we call Christian doctrine. Individual theologians are but the spokesmen of this accumulating understanding which the Spirit of truth has been granting to the church. Christ as Head of the church must not be thought of apart from the Spirit nor the Spirit apart from Christ. Hence it is to state the same truth in terms of Christ's presence when we say that he is walking in the midst of the churches and the angels of the churches are in his right hand. In him are hid all the treasures of wisdom and knowledge and from this fulness that resides in him he communicates to the church so that the church organically and corporately may increase and grow up into knowledge unto the measure of the stature of the fulness of Christ. It is this perspective that not only brings to view but also requires the progression by which systematic theology has been characterized. The history of doctrine demonstrates the progressive development and we may never think that this progression has ever reached a finale. Systematic theology is never a finished science nor is its task ever completed.

This progression does not mean that the advance has been uniformly continuous. There have been periods of theological decadence. Neither does it mean that the church as it exists in any one generation is characterized by the understanding, fidelity, zeal, or practice which its theological heritage deserves and demands. Lamentably, the professing church too often shows retrogression rather than progress and theological mission is to a large extent discarded. Instead of building upon foundations solidly laid the foundations are destroyed. 'They break down the carved work thereof at once with axes and hammers' (Ps. 74:6). But the unfaithfulness of the church in any one period or place does not suspend, far less does it make void, the constant progression which systematic theology is accorded by the oversight of the church's Lord and the enlightenment of his Spirit. This progression is a permanent deposit in the literature of the church and even in decadent periods there is a remnant in whose appreciation and consciousness that tradition is reflected. History likewise demonstrates how, after long neglect, the deposit of the past comes, in times of theological revival, to have renewed meaning and influence. Treasures that had suffered discard and relative oblivion are rediscovered by a new generation and the truth is again verified, 'other men laboured, and ye are entered into their labours' (John 4:38).

There have been the periods of epochal contribution and advance. The reformation of the sixteenth and seventeenth centuries is without question the most notable. It was then that the *opus magnum* of Christian theology was given to the church.[1] It was then that creedal formulation reached its zenith. The architectonic theologies of the Protestant churches witness to the vigour and devotion with which the study of theology had been pursued. It was the golden age of precision and formulation. The theology that does not build upon these constructions or pretends to ignore them places a premium upon retrogression and dishonours the Holy Spirit by whose endowments and grace these epochal strides in understanding and presentation have been taken.

The promulgation of heresy has exercised a profound influence upon the development of theology. It has always compelled the church to examine the deposit of revelation with more care, to set forth the truth in opposition to error and right to wrong, and to awaken the faithful to greater vigilance against the inroads of unbelief. It is futile to maintain that theology should be only positive and avoid negations. If there were no sin or liability to sin there would be no negatives. If there were no error there would be no need of controversy. Revelation is realistic and is thus directed against sin. Theology must likewise be realistic and oppose error. Perhaps the most fatal error the church ever encountered was the Arian. The first ecumenical creed was the official answer of the church to that which struck at its foundation. And who that has jealousy for the biblical witness to the deity of Christ does not recognize the debt of gratitude to the fathers of Nicaea for the *homoousion* clause of A.D. 325? The church's confession had been in the balance but the Head of the church guarded the interests of his honour.

However epochal have been the advances made at certain periods and however great the contributions of particular men we may not suppose that theological construction ever reaches definitive finality. There is the danger of a stagnant traditionalism and we must be alert

[1] The reference is to the definitive edition of Calvin's *Christianae Religionis Institutio*.

to this danger, on the one hand, as to that of discarding our historical moorings, on the other. Students of historical theology are acquainted with the furore which Calvin's insistence upon the self-existence of the Son as to his deity aroused at the time of the Reformation. Calvin was too much of a student of Scripture to be content to follow the lines of what had been regarded as Nicene orthodoxy on this particular issue. He was too jealous for the implications of the *homoousion* clause of the Nicene creed to be willing to accede to the interpretation which the Nicene fathers, including Athanasius, placed upon another expression in the same creed, namely, 'very God of very God' (θεὸν ἀληθινὸν ἐκ θεοῦ αληθινοῦ). No doubt this expression is repeated by orthodox people without any thought of suggesting what the evidence derived from the writings of the Nicene fathers would indicate the intent to have been. This evidence shows that the meaning intended is that the Son *derived* his deity from the Father and that the Son was not therefore αὐτόθεος.[1] It was precisely this position that Calvin controverted with vigour. He maintained that as respects personal distinction the Son was of the Father but as repects deity he was self-existent (*ex se ipso*).[2] This position ran counter to the Nicene tradition. Hence the indictments levelled against him. It is, however, to the credit of Calvin that he did not allow his own more sober thinking to be suppressed out of deference to an established pattern of thought when the latter did not commend itself by conformity to Scripture and was inimical to Christ's divine identity. This polemic on Calvin's part offers a prime example of the need to bring theological formulation to the test of Scripture as the only infallible norm. As it is true that *ecclesia reformata reformanda est* so also is it true that *theologia reformata reformanda est*. When any generation is content to rely upon its theological heritage and refuses to explore for itself the riches of divine revelation, then declension is already under way and heterodoxy will be the lot of the succeeding generation. The powers of darkness are never idle and in combating error each generation must fight its own battle in exposing and correcting the same. It is light that dispels darkness and in this sphere light consists in the enrichment which each generation contributes to the stores of theological knowledge.

[1] Cf., for example, Athanasius' *Expositio Fidei* where it is clearly stated that the Father has being from himself (τὸν ἔχοντα ἀφ' ἑαυτοῦ τὸ εἶναι) whereas the Son derives his Godhood from the Father (οὕτως ἡ ἐκ τοῦ πατρὸς εἰς τὸν Ὑιὸν θεότης ἀρρεύστως καὶ ἀδιαιρέτως τυγχάνει). See also his *De Decretis Nicaenae Synodi* §§ 3 and 19.
[2] Cf. *Inst.* I, xiii, 19–29.

Much of the pleading for adaptation of the gospel to the needs of this generation is suspect. For it is too often a plea for something other than the gospel. Far more important is the reminder that each generation must be adapted to the gospel. It is true, however, that the presentation of the gospel must be pointed to the needs of each generation. So is it with theology. A theology that does not build upon the past ignores our debt to history and naively overlooks the fact that the present is conditioned by history. A theology that relies upon the past evades the demands of the present.

The progressive correction and enrichment which theology undergoes is not the exclusive task of great theologians. It often falls to the lot of students with mediocre talent to discover the oversights and correct the errors of the masters. In the orthodox tradition we may never forget that there is yet much land to be possessed, and this is both the encouragement and the challenge to students of the wonderful works of God and particularly of his inscripturated Word to understand that all should address themselves to a deeper understanding of these unsearchable treasures of revelation to the end that God's glory may be made more fully manifest and his praises declared to all the earth.

Systematic theology is to be distinguished from the discipline that has come to be known as biblical theology. This does not mean that the latter is more biblical. It is true that systematic theology deals with the data of general revelation insofar as these data bear upon theology, and general revelation does not come within the province of biblical theology. But, since the principal source of revelation is Holy Scripture, systematic theology must be concerned to be biblical not one whit less than biblical theology. The difference is merely one of method.

Biblical theology deals with the data of special revelation from the standpoint of its history; systematic theology deals with the same in its totality as a finished product. The method of systematic theology is logical, that of biblical theology is historical. The definition of Geerhardus Vos puts this difference in focus. 'Biblical Theology is that branch of Exegetical Theology which deals with the process of the self-revelation of God deposited in the Bible.'[1] The pivotal term in this definition is the word 'process' as applied to God's special self-revelation. Or, as Vos says later, when taking account of the objections to the

[1] *Biblical Theology: Old and New Testaments*, Grand Rapids, 1948, p. 13.

term 'biblical theology', the name 'History of Special Revelation' is to be preferred.[1]

It cannot be denied that special revelation had a history. God did not reveal himself to man in one great and all-embracive disclosure. Since we are mainly concerned with the revelation that post-dates the fall of man and also to a great extent with redemptive revelation, it is apparent that this revelation began with the protevangelium to our first parents, was expanded more and more through successive generations and ages, and accumulated progressively until it reached its climax in the coming and accomplishments of the Son of God in the fulness of the time, the consummation of the ages. Our perspective is not biblical if we do not reckon with this history and with the process and progression which it involves. And our study of special revelation would not only be too restricted but it would also be dishonouring to God if it did not follow the lines of the plan which he himself pursued in giving us this revelation.

It is necessary to appreciate the terms of the definition of biblical theology. No phase of biblical studies enlists more interest or receives more attention at the present time than biblical theology. There is a reaction against what has been considered to be the religious and theological barrenness of the product that had been so largely devoted to literary and historical criticism, and this applies particularly to Old Testament studies. In the words of Gerhard von Rad, 'It is not so very long ago that a theology of the Old Testament could learn very little beyond questions of date and of this and that in matters of form from those introductory studies which were working mainly on the lines of literary criticism.'[2] But in the last twenty or thirty years there has been a marked change in 'the surprising convergence – indeed the mutual intersection – which has come about . . . between introductory studies and Biblical Theology'.[3] Or, to state the climate in the words of G. Ernest Wright, 'one of the most important tasks of the Church today is to lay hold upon a Biblically centred theology. To do so means that we must first take the faith of Israel seriously and by use of the scholarly

[1] *Ibid.*, p. 23; cf. also G. F. Oehler: *Theology of the Old Testament*, E. T., Edinburgh, 1874, Vol. I, pp. 7, 8, 20, 22.
[2] *Old Testament Theology*, E.T., New York, 1962, Vol. I, p. v. Walther Eichrodt is more emphatic and says: 'It is high time that the tyranny of historicism in OT studies was broken and the proper approach to our task re-discovered' (*Theology of the Old Testament*, E.T., Philadelphia, 1961, Vol. I, p. 31).
[3] von Rad: *idem.*

tools at our disposal seek to understand the theology of the Old Testament. But, secondly, as Christians we must press toward a *Biblical* theology, in which both Testaments are held together in an organic manner.'[1] And the realization of the fact that biblical faith is something 'radically different from all other faiths of mankind', he says, 'leads most Biblical scholars today to believe that far more unity exists in the Bible than was conceived fifty years ago. They are thus confident that a Biblical theology is possible which is something other than the history of the Bible's religious evolution.'[2]

It is not the purpose of this article to review the history of the distinctive discipline known as biblical theology from the work of Johann Philipp Gabler to the present time. But it is necessary to point out the radical divergences that exist between the viewpoint reflected in the definition by Vos, given above, and some of the representative exponents of biblical theology in the last two decades.

1. The most significant works in biblical theology at the present time are based on the assumptions of the literary and historical criticism which rejects the Bible's own representations. That is to say, the Bible is not regarded as providing us with 'the actual historical course of events'. There is, therefore, a reconstruction of biblical history in accordance with what are conceived to be the insights which scholarly research has afforded us. With respect to the framework, the period of the patriarchs, the oppression in Egypt, the Exodus, the Revelation at Sinai, the Wandering in the Wilderness, the Conquest, for example, von Rad says, this was 'not determined by the actual historical course of events, since that had long passed out of memory; its basis was rather a preconceived theological picture of the saving history already long established in the form of a cultic confession' and thus 'even the sequence of the main events conforms already to a canonical *schema* of a cultic nature'.[3] This position means the rejection of the truly historical character of the Old Testament. In this resides the basic divergence by which the work concerned has forfeited its right to be called *theology* of the Old Testament. The alleged history which provides the framework for this Old Testament 'theology' is a reconstructed history of which the Old Testament itself knows nothing. Even if

[1] *God Who Acts. Biblical Theology as Recital*, London, 1952, pp. 29 f.
[2] *Ibid.*, p. 35.
[3] *Op. cit.*, pp. 4 f. Cf. also Sigmund Mowinckel: *The Old Testament as Word of God*, E.T., New York, 1959, pp. 13, 15.

this viewpoint speaks of revelation and revelatory acts, the progressive revelation posited is not the process portrayed for us in the Old Testament. Biblical theology properly conceived and unfolded must follow the lines delineated for us in the Scriptures. To the extent to which these lines are abandoned or reconstructed, to that extent the theology ceases to be the *biblical* theology.

2. Representatives of the biblical theology being criticized show a radical divergence in respect of the unity which is indispensable to a proper view of revelation. In Sigmund Mowinckel's esteem, for example, 'The Old Testament is not a homogeneous entity', 'between "the Law" and "the Prophets" there is a huge cleft, an essential difference', so that the Old Testament 'bears the clear marks of a diverse human history with many cross-current lines'.[1] There is indeed the diversity and multiformity which accumulating divine self-disclosure involves. All of this belongs to the term 'process'. But to confuse diversity with heterogeneity is to relinquish the basic premise of biblical theology.

3. The almost exclusive emphasis upon revelatory *deeds* betokens a distinct deflection from the biblical witness. Again Mowinckel is representative. 'This idea of God as the God of history, and of history as the place of revelation, also clearly shows what the Bible means by revelation. It is not communication of knowledge, theoretical truths from and about God. Yes, it is too, but only secondarily and derivatively. Primarily and essentially *revelation is deed*; it is God's work of creating anew and of creating the future that is his revelation.'[2] 'As has been mentioned already, for the Old Testament, God's word is not utterances, not verbal expressions of ideas, concepts, and thoughts, but *deed*.'[3] With a total thrust that is more congenial G. Ernest Wright is perhaps the most pronounced advocate of this thesis. 'Biblical theology is *the confessional recital of the redemptive acts of God* in a particular history, because history is the chief medium of revelation.'[4] 'Biblical theology is first and foremost a theology of recital.'[5]

It is to be appreciated that Wright does not overlook the fact that God reveals himself in words.[6] Furthermore, many of the insights and

[1] *Ibid.*, pp. 16, 17, 19. Cf. also von Rad: *op. cit.*, pp. 6, 7, 8, 16.
[2] *Op. cit.*, p. 39.
[3] *Op. cit.*, p. 13.
[4] *Ibid.*, p. 28; cf. also pp. 38, 55, 59.
[5] *Ibid.*, p. 42.
[6] Cf. *ibid.*, pp. 23, 83, 103.

emphases in Wright's eloquent monograph are not only worthy of endorsement but are to be highly prized as contributions to Old Testament study.

It is not to be disputed that acts are central in God's redemptive accomplishment and that the cardinal message of the gospel is the proclamation of what God has done. Believing confession in both Testaments reflects these features. But the type of concentration upon *acts* as the media of revelation, exemplified in the biblical theology of the present, is subject to criticism for three reasons in particular. (a) Deeds are of themselves mute for us unless they are accompanied by word revelation respecting their significance.[1] This principle applies in a great variety of respects. If the acts are *God's* acts, they can only be understood for what they are in the context of knowledge respecting God, respecting his relation to the world in which the acts occur, and his relation to those who are the beneficiaries of these redemptive deeds. In a word, the interpretation of their meaning involves a concept of God derived from other revelatory data. Further, if they are acts of grace, the grace must be related to needs which make this grace relevant. Thus there are implications involved in the term 'deeds' which presuppose an understanding which the deeds themselves do not impart and the same applies to the confession respecting these deeds. (b) The concentration upon deeds is prejudicial to what occupies so large a place in the Scripture, namely, the verbal communication of truth respecting God and his will for man.[2] It is apparent that the

---

[1] It is not that G. Ernest Wright, for example, is oblivious of this fact. 'By means of human agents', he says, 'God provides each event with an accompanying Word of interpretation, so that the latter is an integral part of the former' (*ibid.*, p. 84). 'To confess God is to tell a story and then to expound its meaning' (*ibid.*, p. 85). It is that Wright and the other scholars concerned lay such emphasis upon revelation as consisting in 'acts' and on theology as recital that verbal communication is not accorded its place and as a result the concept of revelation is distorted. Cf. the succeeding footnote.

[2] James Barr, writing from a different theological standpoint from that of the present writer, has effectively drawn attention to this same feature of the biblical representation. In *The Princeton Seminary Bulletin* for May 1963 under the title, 'Revelation through History in the Old Testament and in Modern Theology' he sets forth some of the most cogent considerations in criticism of the viewpoint under consideration. Barr does not deny revelation through historical divine action but 'that it can be the principal organizing conceptual bracket which we use to view the material as a whole and to identify the common and essential features within its variety' (p. 8). With respect to the Exodus events and the texts bearing upon them, these texts, he says, 'far from representing the divine acts as the basis of all knowledge of God and all communication with him, they represent God as communicating freely with men,

reconstruction of Old Testament history adopted by the biblical theology in question goes hand in hand with the rejection of the authenticity of the Old Testament witness to this verbal communication. And the way in which biblical theology is distorted is due to a large extent to the suppression of this feature of the Old Testament itself. Again, this biblical theology is not a transcript of the Old Testament but of hypotheses which are alien to its representations. (c) The suppression of the revelatory word tends to discard or at least overlook the place which the communication of truth occupies in redemptive accomplishment. Redemption is the redemption of men in the whole compass of personality and in the whole realm of their relationships. Indispensable, therefore, is the enlightenment of the mind. How can redemption be effective in the whole range of personal life without the correction which truth conveyed imparts and the enlightenment which truth sheds abroad in heart and mind? The Bible in both Testaments is true to this need. It is true to this requirement because it is realistic, and the emphasis upon deeds to the suppression or neglect of verbal communication has come by a discount of the Bible's realism, a fallacy into which even orthodox apologetic has sometimes fallen when it says that Jesus came not to preach the gospel but that there might be a gospel to preach. Jesus came to do both.

4. The biblical theology representative of recent decades, in reconstructing biblical history, has deprived biblical theology of its foundations. Apart from the truncated and revised version of Mosaic and post-Mosaic history, of the Sinai transactions, of the wilderness journeys, of the conquest of Canaan, and of the events closely interrelated, it is characteristic to question, if not to deny, the authenticity of the patriarchal history as set forth in Genesis. Th. C. Vriezen, for example, 'takes the historical line to begin with Moses, not because', as he himself affirms, 'he denies the possibility of a pre-Mosaic revelation to Abraham, but because, in his opinion, a scholarly historical approach is possible to a certain extent with respect to Moses but not with respect to Abraham'.[1] And Walther Eichrodt, who rightly attaches primacy to the covenant relationship, does not go back farther

---

and particularly with Moses, before, during and after these events' (p. 7). Thus there are, he contends, other axes than that of 'acts' and the one he has particularly in mind is that of 'direct verbal communication between God and particular men on particular occasions' (p. 11).

[1] *An Outline of Old Testament Theology*, E.T., Oxford, 1958, p. 16, n. 1; cf. p. 30.

than Mosaic times to find this covenant concept.[1] The covenantal institution is basic to any construction of redemptive history and revelation. The Exodus cannot be biblically interpreted unless it is recognized to be in fulfilment of the patriarchal covenant (cf. Exod. 2:24, 25; 3:6–17). The Sinaitic covenant must be understood as an appendage to and extension of the Abrahamic (cf. Gal. 3:17–22). And the coming of Christ is in pursuance of the same (cf. Luke 1:72, 73). Christ is the seed in whom all the families of the earth are blessed (cf. Gen. 22:18; Acts 3:25; Gal. 3:8, 9, 16). It should be apparent how indispensable to biblical theology is the covenant concept and how far removed from the biblical data our theology must be if it is not oriented to the successive unfoldings of covenant grace and relationship. But the main interest of our present discussion is that the covenant history with which the Bible furnishes us is bereft of its foundation unless we go back to the origin of this history in the covenants made with Abraham (Gen. 15:8–21; 17:1–21). The theology which can dispense with this central feature of patriarchal history is not *biblical* theology.[2]

When biblical theology is conceived of as dealing with 'the process of the self-revelation of God deposited in the Bible', it must be understood that this specialized study of the Bible, so far from being inimical to the interests of systematic theology, is indispensable to the systematic theology that is faithful to the Bible. In some cases the present-day interest in biblical theology springs from or at least is related to an antipathy to systematics or, as it is sometimes called, dogmatics. The latter is charged with being abstract and philosophical and, therefore, devoid of the dynamic realism and force which ought to characterize any reproduction of the Bible's witness. This charge is not to be dismissed as without any ground or warrant. Systematic theologies have too often betrayed a cold formalism that has been prejudicial to their proper aim and have not for that reason and to that extent promoted encounter with the living Word of the living God. But two observa-

---

[1] *Op. cit.*, p. 36. Wright makes summary mention of 'the call of the Patriarchal fathers' (*op. cit.*, p. 76) as central in confessional recital, but the Abrahamic covenant does not give direction to his presentation of this recital.

[2] The significance of the Noahic covenants, pre-diluvian and post-diluvian, is not to be depreciated. They furnish us with the covenantal concept basic to all subsequent covenantal disclosures. But in terms of redemptive revelation we are bereft of the foundation of all subsequent disclosure if we fail to take full account of the Abrahamic covenants.

tions require to be made with reference to this charge and to the corresponding admission. First, there are certain phases of the truth with which systematic theology must deal and certain polemics which it must conduct that call for the type of treatment which to many people seems cold and formal. The painstaking analysis and exacting research which the pursuit of a faithful dogmatics requires must not be abandoned because some people have no interest in or patience with such studies. This would mean that areas of investigation necessary to the wide range of the theologian's mandate would be abandoned to the enemy. We must appreciate how diversified are the tasks and interests that come within the orbit of systematic theology. A biblical scholar's product may have to be sometimes as dry as dust. But dust has its place, especially when it is gold dust. Second, the charge, insofar as it is warranted, is not the fault of systematic theology, but of the theologian or of the milieu of which his product is the reflection. *Systematic* theology by its nature must have its logical divisions.[1] Not all theologies have the same sequence or the same structural schematism. But if we think of theology, anthropology, and soteriology, it is difficult to comprehend how any one sensitive to the governing message of Scripture can take exception to the exhibition of this message under such subdivisions as these exemplify. It is true, as Calvin reminded us at the beginning of his *Institutio*, that we cannot think properly of ourselves without thinking of God and we cannot think properly of God without also thinking of ourselves. But theology is teaching, exposition, communication, and it so happens that we cannot say everything all at once, nor can we think of everything that needs to be thought of God and of ourselves all at once. The observation all-important for the present is that there is nothing inherent in a logical mode of treatment that hinders, far less prevents, sustained confrontation with the living Word of the living God. Systematic structure is the application to the totality of revelation of the same method as the science of homiletics applies to the exposition of particular passages of Scripture.

Biblical theology is indispensable to systematic theology. This

---

[1] It is of interest that two recent noteworthy titles: Ludwig Köhler: *Old Testament Theology*, E.T., Philadelphia, 1957; Millar Burrows: *An Outline of Biblical Theology* adopt the method of topical presentation. It may not be legitimate to question the right of a scholar to choose his own title. But Burrows' work is not 'biblical theology' in the generally accepted use of the title. It is rather a systematic theology. And Ludwig Köhler does not follow the historico-genetic method of delineation.

proposition requires clarification. The main source of revelation is the Bible. Hence exposition of the Scripture is basic to systematic theology. Its task is not simply the exposition of particular passages. That is the task of exegesis. Systematics must coordinate the teaching of particular passages and systematize this teaching under the appropriate topics. There is thus a synthesis that belongs to systematics that does not belong to exegesis as such.[1] But to the extent to which systematic theology synthesizes the teaching of Scripture, and this is its main purpose, it is apparent how dependent it is upon the science of exegesis. It cannot coordinate and relate the teaching of particular passages without knowing what that teaching is. So exegesis is basic to its objective. This needs to be emphasized. Systematic theology has gravely suffered, indeed has deserted its vocation, when it has been divorced from meticulous attention to biblical exegesis. This is one reason why the charge mentioned above has so much to yield support to the indictment. Systematics becomes lifeless and fails in its mandate just to the extent to which it has become detached from exegesis. And the guarantee against a stereotyped dogmatics is that systematic theology be constantly enriched, deepened, and expanded by the treasures increasingly drawn from the Word of God. Exegesis keeps systematics not only in direct contact with the Word but it ever imparts to systematics the power which is derived from that Word. The Word is living and powerful.

What then of biblical theology? What function does it perform in this process? Biblical theology recognizes that special revelation did not come from God in one mass at one particular time. Special revelation came by process. It came progressively in history throughout ages and generations. Mankind has never lacked special revelation. Man's life had been regulated from the outset by specially revealed ordinances and commandments. When our first parents had fallen from their original integrity, special revelation with redemptive import supervened upon their sin and misery to inspire faith and regulate life in the new context which their sin had created. Thus began the process of redemptive revelation to the progressive unfolding of which the Bible bears witness. This process was not, however, one of uniform

---

[1] The principle known as the analogy of Scripture is indispensable to exegesis for 'the infallible rule of interpretation of Scripture is the Scripture itself'. But the analogy of Scripture is not to be equated with the synthesis which is the specific task of systematic theology.

progression. The Bible does not provide us with a complete history of special revelation (cf. John 20:30, 31; 21:25). But we must believe that the pattern found in the Scripture reflects the pattern followed in the history of revelation as a whole. This pattern which Scripture discloses shows that special revelation and the redemptive accomplishments correlative with it have their marked epochs. It is undeniable that the flood and the institutions related thereto, the Abrahamic revelations, the Exodus from Egypt, the Davidic period, the coming of Christ mark outstanding epochs in the history of revelation. The science concerned with the history of special revelation must take account of this epochal character and it would be an artificial biblical theology that did not adhere to the lines which this epochal feature prescribes. Redemption, as Geerhardus Vos observes, 'does not proceed with uniform motion, but rather is "epochal" in its onward stride. We can observe that where great epoch-making redemptive acts accumulate, there the movement of revelation is correspondingly accelerated and its volume increased.'[1] The divisions which biblical theology recognizes and in terms of which it conducts its study are not, therefore, arbitrary, but are demanded by the characteristics of redemptive and revelation history. The Bible is itself conscious of the distinct periods into which the history of revelation falls. Although there could be more detailed subdivision within certain periods, it could not be contested that the Bible itself marks off the distinguishing character and momentous significance of the creation of man, the fall of man, the flood, the call of Abraham, the Exodus, the advent of Christ. Hence the periods, the creation to the fall, the fall to the flood, the flood to the call of Abraham, the call of Abraham to the Exodus, and the Exodus to Christ.[2] are so well-defined that this structure must be adhered to in the discipline, biblical theology.

If biblical theology deals with the *history* of revelation it must follow the progression which this history dictates. This is to say it must study the data of revelation given in each period in terms of the stage to which God's self-revelation progressed at that particular time. To be

[1] *Op. cit.*, p. 16.
[2] The period from the Exodus to Christ would obviously require sub-division. But there is also good reason for recognizing a unity corresponding to that of the other periods. The New Testament era is, of course, the consummatory era in this structure. Redemption and revelation will be resumed at Christ's second coming. But the new revelatory acts associated with the second advent do not come within the province of biblical theology.

18

concrete, we may not import into one period the data of revelation which belong to a later period. When we do this we violate the conditions which define the distinctiveness of this study.[1] And not only so. We do violence to revelation itself, because the history of revelation and the progressiveness which characterized it belong to the activity of God by which revelation has come to us, and the error is not merely a violation of the science of biblical theology but a distortion of the history which must ever be borne in mind and prized as that apart from which redemptive revelation does not exist.

This is a subject worthy of considerable expansion. But, in relation to our present interest, it is this principle that bears directly upon exegesis. Exegesis is the interpretation of particular passages. This is just to say the interpretation of particular revelatory data. But these revelatory data occur within a particular period of revelation and the principle which guides biblical theology must also be applied in exegesis. Thus biblical theology is regulative of exegesis.

Systematic theology is tied to exegesis. It coordinates and synthesizes the whole witness of Scripture on the various topics with which it deals. But systematic theology will fail of its task to the extent to which it discards its rootage in biblical theology as properly conceived and developed. It might seem that an undue limitation is placed upon systematic theology by requiring that the exegesis with which it is so intimately concerned should be regulated by the principle of biblical theology. And it might seem to be contrary to the canon so important

---

[1] There are several questions that arise in connection with this principle. It is not the purpose of this article to discuss these. Suffice it to say that the abuses must be avoided. We are not prevented thereby from using the data of later periods of revelation in determining the precise import and purport of earlier data, their import and purport, however, in the precise context in which they were given. And we are certainly not to overlook the witness borne by the New Testament, for example, to the intent and scope of Old Testament data. We may not accede to the tendency so common to underestimate the richness of Old Testament revelation, the vigour of the faith of Old Testament saints, or the relevance of its institutions.

We should also keep in view the distinction that must be maintained in certain instances between the revelation given in particular periods and the inscripturation of that revelation. This is specially important in the pre-Mosaic periods. It is inscripturation that provides us with the data and assures us of their authenticity. Furthermore, inscripturation is a mode of revelation and so with inscripturation there are revelatory data that belong only to the inscripturation itself. Inscripturation does not merely provide us with a record of revelations previously given by other modes; Scripture is itself revelation.

to both exegesis and systematics, namely, the analogy of Scripture. These appearances do not correspond to reality. The fact is that only when systematic theology is rooted in biblical theology does it exemplify its true function and achieve its purpose. Two respects in which this is illustrated may be mentioned.

1. Systematic theology deals with special revelation as a finished product incorporated for us in Holy Scripture. But special revelation in its totality is never properly conceived of apart from the history by which it became a finished product. As we think of, study, appreciate, appropriate, and apply the revelation put in our possession by inscripturation, we do not properly engage in any of these exercises except as the panorama of God's movements in history comes within our vision or at least forms the background of our thought. In other words, redemptive and revelatory history conditions our thought at every point or stage of our study of Scripture revelation. Therefore, what is the special interest of biblical theology is never divorced from our thought when we study any part of Scripture and seek to bring its treasures of truth to bear upon the synthesis which systematic theology aims to accomplish. Furthermore, the tendency to abstraction which ever lurks for systematic theology is hereby counteracted. The various data are interpreted not only in their scriptural context but also in their historical context and therefore, as Vos says, 'in the milieu of the historical life of a people'[1] because God has caused his revelation to be given in that milieu.

2. Perhaps the greatest enrichment of systematic theology, when it is oriented to biblical theology, is the perspective that is gained for the unity and continuity of special revelation. Orthodox systematic theology rests on the premise of the unity of Scripture, the consent of all its parts. It is this unity that makes valid the hermeneutical principle, the analogy of Scripture. A systematic theology that is faithful to this attribute of Scripture and seeks earnestly to apply it cannot totally fail of its function. But when systematic theology is consciously undertaken with the claims and results of biblical theology in view, then the perspective gained is more than that merely of unity. It is the unity of a growing organism that attains its fruition in the New Testament and in the everlasting covenant ratified and sealed by the blood of Christ. Revelation is seen to be an organism and the discrete parts, or prefer-

[1] *Op. cit.*, p. 17.

ably phases, are perceived to be not sporadic, unrelated, and disjointed oracles, far less heterogeneous and contradictory elements, but the multiform aspects of God's intervention and self-disclosure, organically knit together and compacted, expressive not only of his marvellous grace but of the order which supreme wisdom designed. Thus the various passages drawn from the whole compass of Scripture and woven into the texture of systematic theology are not cited as mere proof texts or wrested from the scriptural and historical context to which they belong, but, understood in a way appropriate to the place they occupy in this unfolding process, are applied with that particular relevance to the topic under consideration. Texts will not thus be forced to bear a meaning they do not possess nor forced into a service they cannot perform. But in the locus to which they belong and by the import they do possess they will contribute to the sum-total of revelatory evidence by which biblical doctrine is established. We may never forget that systematic theology is the arrangement under appropriate divisions of the total witness of revelation to the truth respecting God and his relations to us men and to the world. Since the Bible is the principal source of revelation and since the Bible is the Word of God, systematics is the discipline which more than any other aims to confront us men with God's own witness so that in its totality it may make that impact upon our hearts and minds by which we shall be conformed to his image in knowledge, righteousness, and holiness of the truth.

2

Inspiration and Inerrancy[1]

We may properly use the term 'Christianity' to designate that order of things in the unfolding of God's redemptive purpose, which began with the advent of the Son of God in the flesh. It is a fact which we are too prone to overlook that Christianity never existed apart from the inscripturated Word of God. When Christianity took its origin this Word was embodied in the Old Testament. For our present interest the important consideration is that for Jesus the Word of God was that which was *written* and that, for him, that which was written was infallible. It is not irrelevant to appeal in this connection to such well-known texts as: 'The Scripture cannot be broken' (John 10:35) and 'Till heaven and earth pass away, one jot or one tittle shall in no wise pass away from the law, till all things be accomplished' (Matt. 5:18). These are texts which expressly affirm the irrefragable character of what was *written*.

But it is not only express assertion that is to be taken into account as indicating our Lord's attitude to Scripture. It is also the copious evidence which shows that, for him, Scripture merited and constrained absolute reliance. There is something desperate about the supposition that in reference to Scripture Jesus accommodated himself to current Jewish conviction. It is impossible to adjust the total attitude to Scripture reflected in the Gospel records to any such view of accommodation. If we think, for example, of the temptation in the wilderness, it is to be remembered that our Lord was in deathly encounter with the arch-enemy. Satan's assaults had as their intent the defeat of that purpose

[1] On this subject see also the author's major treatment, 'The Attestation of Scripture' in *The Infallible Word*, a Symposium by members of the Faculty of Westminster Theological Seminary (1946), revised edition 1967.

for which the Son of God came into the world. Only the verity and finality of an infallible Word could have provided the wherewithal to resist temptations which themselves had been buttressed by Scripture misused. 'Man shall not live by bread alone, but by every word that proceedeth out of the mouth of God' (Matt. 4:4). And when Jesus quotes two other words from the Old Testament the only possible interpretation is that he relied upon these words because he recognized that they *proceeded out of the mouth of God*. That is Jesus' concept of what was *written*; that is the definition of Scripture which alone explains the confidence of Jesus' appeal to it. Scripture is God-breathed.

And what shall we say of another occasion on which Jesus appealed to what was written? 'The Son of man goeth even as it is written of him: but woe unto that man by whom the Son of man is betrayed' (Matt. 26:22). Jesus was face to face with the indescribable ordeal of agony that lay before him and with the unspeakable tragedy of Judas' betrayal. Our Lord could contemplate neither without agony of spirit. When he says 'The Son of man goeth' he is thinking of the abyss of woe with respect to which he was later on to pray, 'O my Father, if it be possible, let this cup pass from me' (Matt. 26:39). And with respect to Judas it was the outcome of irreparable woe that engages our Lord's thought. These are circumstances that called for an immovable foundation on which to rest his feet. Can we escape the significance of the words 'as it is written?' If we have a modicum of sensitivity to the demands placed upon our Lord in this situation we can tolerate only one thesis, that of what was *written* there was no gainsaying, and from it there was no retreat. In what was *written* Jesus deciphered God's determinate counsel and the certainty of its accomplishment. Nothing less than the intrinsic certitude of the *written* Word is engraven on this appeal to Scripture.

If we think of Christianity as the movement associated with the life and ministry of Jesus in the days of his flesh – centred, of course, in Jesus himself but exemplified in the company of disciples whom Jesus had chosen – we must take account of the fact that it never existed apart from another infallible word. It is not in this instance the inscripturated word but the spoken word of the Word incarnate. That Jesus was infallible in all that he spoke and taught is the indispensable premise of all Christian thought. To put it negatively, the supposition that he was fallible in any word he spoke is ever, as suggestion, one to which the Christian must offer the instantaneous recoil of vehement dissent. Infallible is the correlate of his being God with us. 'Heaven and earth shall pass away, but my words shall not pass away' (Matt. 24:35).

We have thus two respects in which infallible word determined, conditioned, and directed Christianity from its inception. And it needs to be reiterated with all emphasis that Christianity never existed apart from these two norms and sources of infallible revelation. It is futile to maintain that Christianity can be abstracted from inspiration. For inspiration means simply God-breathed word. And if the testimony of Jesus is our norm, Old Testament Scripture 'proceeds out of the mouth of God', and his own words are as irrefragable as the Scripture itself.

Space will not permit us to pursue this same line of evidence and of thought as it applies to Christianity subsequent to the ascension of our Lord. Suffice it to say that the promises of Jesus, particularly the promise of the Holy Spirit, and his appointment of the apostles as his authoritative witnesses, are the guarantees that, when Jesus ascended on high, Christianity was not deprived of that authoritative and infallible word required by and appropriate to that stage in the unfolding of God's redemptive purpose which was signalized by the session of Jesus at God's right hand and the outpouring of the Holy Spirit at Pentecost, an infallible word in due time embodied for the church perpetual in the documents of the New Testament.

It is a strange phenomenon therefore, that the doctrine of the infallibility of Scripture should evoke so much opposition within the pale of evangelical Christianity. One cannot but indict this opposition with failure to reckon with the facts of Jesus' own witness as well as with the facts of the origin and early history of Christianity. And it is likewise strange that the term 'verbal inspiration' should evoke so much dissent if not scorn. When we speak of the inspiration of Scripture we refer to Scripture as *written*; otherwise we should not be speaking of *Scripture*. But there is no Scripture without words, and, if we are to speak of the inspiration of Scripture at all, we cannot dispense with the inspiration of words. Or if we are thinking of revelation in word, revelatory word, we cannot think of revelation apart from words, nor of the inspiration which guarantees the veracity and supplies the content of that revelation apart from words.

No word of our Lord offers more evidence of the esteem with which he regarded the Old Testament than that quoted already: 'One jot or one tittle shall in no wise pass away from the law, till all things be accomplished' (Matt. 5:18). It shows that he posited for the minutiae of the law an inspiration which guaranteed their divine character and veracity. In a word, he is speaking of jot and tittle inspiration. We are not to suppose that Jesus is speaking of these details in themselves apart from the words and clauses and sentences in which they appear. He is not speaking of jot and tittle in abstraction, for the simple reason that what represents a jot is no longer a jot if it exists in abstraction. And the same holds true of a tittle. Jesus is thinking of jot and tittle in construction and combination with relevant words, clauses, and sentences. In these relations they have the greatest significance, for to change one jot changes the meaning of the whole. And inspiration, of course, extends to the jots and tittles because it extends to the combinations of which they are integral elements. It is easy to see the force of what Jesus said. If there is inspiration at all it must take care of the smallest details which are indispensable to the conveyance of the truth enunciated. In like manner, when we speak of verbal inspiration we are not thinking of the words in abstraction and independence. Such words are not inspired because they do not exist in the Scripture. But words in relevant relationship must be inspired if that in which they have relevance is inspired. Inspiration must extend to the words if it extends to the truth which the words in construction and combination convey. It is impossible, therefore, to think of inspiration without *verbal* inspiration.

To predicate verbal inspiration and infallibility of the Scripture is the same as to speak of its inerrancy. Something cannot be infallible if it contains error of judgment or representation.

We are not to suppose that some such syllogism as the following – God's word is inerrant; the Bible is God's Word; therefore the Bible is inerrant – is necessarily *a priori* and arbitrary, or that it involves our imposing upon Scripture preconceived canons and determines beforehand what is possible or impossible for God. The syllogism is based upon certain presuppositions which are derived from the Scripture, respecting God, the Bible, and God's Word. The fundamental presupposition of the syllogism is that God is truth and that he cannot lie. Who is to say that such a tenet is arbitrarily *a priori*?

But however much of truth there is in the syllogism, it is not an adequate way of settling the question. For the syllogism, as has been indicated, presupposes a great deal, and one thing it presupposes is the meaning of the term 'inerrant'. It is precisely with that question that a great deal of the Christian apologetic is concerned. In maintaining and defending biblical inerrancy it is necessary to bear in mind that our concept of inerrancy is to be derived from the Scripture itself. A similar necessity appears in connection with the criteria of truth and of right. We may not impose upon the Bible our own standards of truthfulness or our own notions of right and wrong. It is easy for the proponents of inerrancy to set up certain canons of inerrancy which are arbitrarily conceived and which prejudice the whole question from the outset. And it is still easier for the opponents of inerrancy to set up certain criteria in terms of which the Bible could readily be shown to be in error. Both attempts must be resisted. This is just saying that we must think of inerrancy concretely, and our criterion of inerrancy must be divested of the *a priori* and often mechanical notions with which it is associated in the minds of many people, particularly of those who are hostile to the doctrine.

In all questions pertinent to the doctrine of Scripture it is to be borne in mind that the sense of Scripture is Scripture; it is what Scripture means that constitutes Scripture teaching. We cannot deal, therefore, with the inerrancy of Scripture apart from hermeneutics. In connection tion with any text we must ensure that it is the intended import that is brought into consideration and not some import which it may, at first sight, appear to convey, or an import which we arbitrarily attach to it.

In like manner, the analogy of Scripture, as one of the first principles of the science of interpretation, must be kept in view. It is a commonplace that we cannot think of everything at once. But it is not superfluous to be reminded of it in this connection. God cannot tell us everything we may know or need to know all at once; it would be contrary to the limitations inherent in our nature. God cannot deal with us as if we were divine. Hence, 'here a little and there a little'. In dealing with any subject which Scripture brings to our attention we must take into account all the relevant data made known to us, and since these data are not all concentrated in one place, we must address ourselves to the task of correlating all the data drawn from various parts of Scripture. Too often we find what we think to be discrepancy because we have left out of account, it may be, only *one* significant datum. Furthermore, we must recognize that oftentimes we are ignorant of significant data relevant to a particular subject, and we must be humble enough to admit the limitations under which we labour.

A few examples will illustrate the application of these foregoing principles and show the fallacy of applying to Scripture artificial and pedantic canons of errancy or inerrancy.

Three evangelists tell us that when Jesus fed the five thousand with five loaves and two fishes there were *about* five thousand *men* (Matt. 14:21; Luke 9:14; John 6:10). Jesus himself in referring to this incident says : 'Do ye not understand, neither remember, the five loaves of the five thousand and how many baskets ye took up' (Matt. 16:9; cf. Mark 9:18). If we come to these passages with an artificial canon of interpretation, we could argue that there was error of computation. If there were *about* five thousand, could it be said that there were five thousand? And if there were about five thousand *men*, could the incident be referred to by Jesus himself as the five loaves of the five thousand? We can readily detect that by such reasoning we are impos-ing a pedantic requirement which language of this kind was never intended to bear. In such a case the terms were not intended to express an exact enumeration of the number of people fed and we have no right to demand that when Jesus said 'five thousand' he intended to supply us with the exact numerical statistics. If that were so, the evangelists would not have been required to speak of *about* five thou-sand. The doctrine of inerrancy does not involve the absurd pedantry which would dictate this kind of precision in this case. Inerrancy is the inerrancy that operates with certain well-established and obviously recognized forms of expression.

There is apparent discrepancy between Acts 9:7 and Acts 22:9. In the former Luke tells us respecting Paul's experience on the road to Damascus: 'And the men who journeyed with him stood speechless, hearing the voice but seeing no man'; in the latter, Luke reports Paul as saying: 'And those who were with me saw indeed the light, but they did not hear the voice of him who spoke to me.' If the expression 'to hear the voice' must mean precisely the same thing in both verses then there is contradiction and, if contradiction, error.

The supposition that there is error here rests upon the assumption that words have one meaning and only one shade of meaning, an assumption that is patently untenable. Expressions which are, for all practical purposes, identical in form may have totally different meanings in different contexts. Dean Alford, though not subscribing to verbal inspiration, gives as good an explanation as need be, namely, that in 9:7 there is reference to 'the sound of the voice', which the men heard, and in 22:9 to 'the words spoken and their meaning' (Comm. *ad* Acts 9:7). He appeals to the analogy of John 12:29.

The apparent discrepancy in Acts 9:7; 22:9 points up the necessity of observing what was stated above in connection with verbal inspiration. If words in abstraction are inspired, then here we have contradiction. But since it is not with words in abstraction that we are concerned, but with words in relationship, then the word 'voice' may reflect on one fact in one context and relationship, and on another closely related fact in another context and relationship. Neither verbal inspiration nor inerrancy is in the least prejudiced by this variation, but must allow for it.

When Matthew 27:5–8 and Acts 1:18, 19 are compared there are two respects in which discrepancy appears. Matthew tells us that the priests bought the potter's field with the thirty pieces of silver, Luke that Judas obtained a field with the reward of iniquity. Matthew tells us that Judas went and hanged himself; Luke that Judas falling headlong burst asunder in the midst and all his bowels gushed out. The former appears more formidable and we may reflect on it.

On the basis of Matthew's account we must believe that the priests bought the field. How then could it be said that Judas obtained it? It is a rule frequently exemplified in the usage of Scripture that he who does something by another does it himself (cf. 1 Sam. 1:15, 16; 4:10). The rule that applies in this case is somewhat similar. Acts 1:18, viewed in this light, is seen to be not only true but signally eloquent. The priests actually bought the field. But it was with the money which Judas had secured as the reward of his iniquity. It was Judas' money. Judas was the instrument and his money the means by which the field was purchased. While it is true that the priests were not acting as Judas' agents, yet Judas' betrayal and its reward provided the wherewithal of the purchase. Who is to say that Peter or Luke (possibly this is Luke's parenthesis) could not have reflected on these facts, and upon the tragedy which the purchase of the field signalizes, by using the device of such rhetorical expression? It would be to deny to Peter or Luke the right to avail himself of one of the most eloquent ways of bringing the purchase of the field into relation to the iniquity of Judas in order that the relevant facts might point up the indictment against him. Acts 1:18 is seen thus to be a model of literary art and moral judgment. And it is the more detailed narrative of Matthew 27:5–18 that supplies the information in terms of which we are able to interpret Acts 1:18.

In Hebrews 9:7 we are told that into the holiest of all the high priest went alone *once in the year*. We know that the high priest went in on two distinct occasions on the great day of atonement. If the expression *once in the year* cannot with propriety be used to express the fact that it was only on the occasion of the great day of atonement that the high priest went into the holiest of all, and that this day of atonement came only once in the year, then Hebrews 9:7 is in error. It is surely patent, however, that Hebrews 9:7 is not reflecting upon the number of times the high priest went into the most holy place on the great day of atonement but on the other fact, namely, that on no other day but the annual day of atonement did he enter the most holy place. In respect of that fact Hebrews 9:7 is perfectly correct. But if we were to impose upon a text a requirement in terms of another consideration beyond its scope and intent, then Hebrews 9:7 could easily be shown to be in error.

Inerrancy in reference to Scripture is the inerrancy that accepts certain well-established and obviously recognized literary or verbal *usus loquendi*. It makes full allowance for the variety of literary devices which preserves language from stereotyped uniformity and monotony. And we must not allow the inerrancy which is implicit in the plenary inspiration of Scripture to be prejudiced by patterns of thought which are prescribed by pedantry rather than by sober judgment.

3

The Inspiration of the Scripture[1]

Mr President and members of the Board of Trustees, I must take this opportunity of expressing my deep appreciation to the Faculty of this Institution for having nominated me to the Board of Trustees for the position of Professor of Systematic Theology and of expressing to the Board of Trustees my deep gratitude for the privilege they have conferred upon me when they elected me to and installed me in this office. While intimating my appreciation of this honour and privilege I cannot refrain from hastening to voice in the very same breath my keen sense of unworthiness. The department of Systematic Theology in Westminster Seminary is intended to continue a great tradition, that tradition associated with names second to none in the theological firmament of the last hundred years. The memory of the names of Hodge and Warfield, predecessors in this tradition, truly fills me with what I can only call a humiliating astonishment which tends to make it appear presumption on my part even to think of assuming a position which follows in the train of their illustrious and devoted service to God and his kingdom.

But I have been prevented from succumbing entirely to the temptation arising from this humiliating sense of inadequacy by one consideration, the sense of Divine call and responsibility. In assuming this obligation I have been upheld and propelled, not by the hope that I shall ever be able to discharge the office with the devotion, erudition, and distinction of those who have gone before in this noble tradition,

[1] This article is taken from *The Westminster Theological Journal*, Vol. II, 2, 1940. It is a slightly altered form of the author's inaugural address as Professor of Systematic Theology, delivered at Westminster Theological Seminary on November 16, 1939.

but only by the conviction that, for the present at least, it is my calling, and therefore I can plead God's wisdom and grace in the pursuance of a task which though humbling in its demands is yet glorious in its opportunity.

I am going to address you tonight on the topic, 'The Inspiration of the Scripture'. It is a subject on which much has been written, particularly during the last hundred years. It is furthermore even a topic on which inaugural addresses have been given in the past by very distinguished and competent scholars. Nevertheless I think you will agree that it is a subject of paramount importance, importance increased rather than diminished by the movements of theological thought which are our legacy, and in the context of which we live the life that we live. At Westminster Seminary we claim that the reason for our existence as an Institution is the exposition and defence of the Holy Scriptures. It is our humble boast that all our work centres around the Bible as the Word of God, the only infallible rule of faith and practice. It is obvious, therefore, that our work and purpose are determined by our conception of what the Bible is. And what the Bible is, is just the question of its inspiration.

In view of the extensive treatment accorded the subject, and particularly the copious literature in defence of that view of the Bible which we at Westminster Seminary hold, there is scarcely anything new that I can say in elucidation and defence of the historic Christian position. Furthermore, it will be impossible to deal with the various theories of inspiration which have constituted divergence from or attack upon the biblical concept itself.

The systematic reconstructions which characterized the 19th century were entirely inhospitable and even inimical to the historic doctrine of plenary inspiration. Theologically speaking, the 19th century was largely dominated by the systems of Friedrich Schleiermacher and Albrecht Ritschl. Schleiermacher's depreciation of the Old Testament is a well-known fact. He utterly failed to appreciate the organic unity of both Testaments. But even if he had appreciated the organic unity and continuity of both Testaments, his theological presuppositions would have prevented him from reaching any true estimate of what that organic unity really is. For Schleiermacher Christianity consisted in the redemptive and potent God-consciousness exhibited by Jesus of Nazareth. This religious self-consciousness emanating from Jesus Christ is continued in the Christian church and as such it is the self-proclamation of Christ. His appeal to Scripture is simply for the purpose of ascertaining what that religious self-consciousness was. We ascertain thereby what was the religious experience of the first disciples, and so we may test our own experience as to its Christian character. The New Testament then is but the classic precipitate of Christian religious experience and only in that sense the norm of faith and the source of Christian theology.

Albrecht Ritschl avows that Christian doctrine is to be drawn alone from Holy Scripture, but only because Holy Scripture provides us with the classic documents of Christian beginnings. Ritschl had no doubt a deeper appreciation of history than did Schleiermacher. I take it that the centrum of Ritschl's theology is the overwhelming sense we have of the reality and presence of God in the person of Jesus of Nazareth. The New Testament documents confront us, he would say, with this Jesus of Nazareth as he conceived this Jesus to be. As such they are unique. They are the classic documents of Christianity because they are the documents that stand nearest to him. They reproduce most accurately the impression produced by Jesus upon those who came directly into contact with him. But to the doctrine of inspiration Ritschl not only offers rejection but, as James Orr says, shows a positive repugnance.[1]

I do not intend, however, to orient this address by the views of Schleiermacher and Ritschl. There are three other views of the Bible I shall select. These have no doubt affinities with those of Schleiermacher and Ritschl, but into these genetic relations we shall not enter. Neither do I propose to offer any detailed examination or refutation of them. But by showing very summarily their character we shall be able more intelligently to understand the nature of the biblical witness, and in our analysis of that witness detect how these views diverge from the biblical doctrine.

The selection of these three views may appear arbitrary. To a certain extent this is true. Yet the reason will become apparent as we proceed. It is, in brief, that any treatment of inspiration must also deal with the concept of revelation. These three views, taking their starting-point from revelation, make capital of that concept to do prejudice to the historic doctrine of inspiration. It will be our aim to show, to some extent at least, that the fact of revelation can provide no escape from plenary inspiration, and that a concept of revelation that is true to the

[1] Cf. *The Ritschlian Theology*, London, 1897, p. 96.

biblical witness is a concept that embraces inspiration as a mode of revelation.

(1) The first is that view of inspiration which regards an infallible superintendence or direction of the Spirit of God as extending to those parts of Scripture that are the product of revelation from God, while no such superintendence or direction extends to those parts that could be composed by the exercise of men's natural faculties upon sources of information available to them and which required simply the ordinary methods of research, compilation and systematization for their production.

I am aware that this particular way of stating the matter is but one modification of a more general point of view known as that of partial inspiration by which degrees of inspiration are posited. This theory of degrees of inspiration, it is thought, can readily be used to explain the various phenomena in Scripture and particularly the marks of human imperfection and fallibility which are considered to be inherent in it. But because we cannot deal with every particular modification of this general viewpoint we may keep that particular form more distinctly before our minds. To express this form more fully I might avail myself of the words of William Cunningham. 'The general principle upon which the advocates of this view proceed is this, that we must not admit of any divine agency, of any immediate and supernatural interposition of God in effecting or producing anything which could possibly have been effected without it, and they then quietly set up human reason, i.e. themselves, or their own notions, as competent and adequate judges of whether or not, in a particular case, any immediate divine interposition was necessary. With these principles they come to examine the Bible, take the different books of which it is composed, and the different subjects of which it treats, and set themselves to consider in regard to each book, and each subject, or class of subjects, whether mere men, unaided by any special divine assistance, could not possibly have given us such information as is there presented to us; and whenever there is any plausible ground for the allegation that men might possibly have communicated to us the information conveyed, they forthwith conclude that no divine inspiration was granted, that no special divine agency was exerted in guiding and directing them.'[1]

(2) The second is that view of inspiration which regards the inspiration of the Bible as consisting in a certain elevation of spirit

[1] *Theological Lectures*, pp. 296 f.

possessed by the writers of Scripture. This viewpoint has probably taken much of its stimulus from Coleridge's *Confessions of an Inquiring Spirit*. Coleridge, while admitting miraculous communication in the writing of part of Scripture, yet refers the writing of the rest of Scripture to the highest degree of that gracious influence of the Spirit common to all believers.[1] Christianity, it is claimed, is a supernatural religion grounded and settled on supernatural facts and doctrines, and the Bible is the precipitate of that supernatural revelation. The Bible is inspired because the men who wrote the Bible were inspired by the truth of the great supernatural and redemptive acts of God. The truth of Christianity taking possession of their hearts and minds caused a quickening and exaltation of spirit, and because written under that afflatus or exaltation of spirit the Bible is the product of inspiration. In the words of William Newton Clarke, 'Inspiration to write was not different in kind from the general inspiration of the divine Spirit. The writing of the Scripture was one of the higher and finer fruits of the influence of God upon the whole body of believing and receptive people. No promise can be cited of a divine influence differing from all other, given on purpose to prepare men to write; nor is there any claim in Scripture that the whole class of writers, as writers, were wrought upon differently from other sons of men. Men wrote from inward impulse. They wrote because they were impressed by truth from God, and were so affected by its power and value that they could write it in abiding forms.'[2] Or, perhaps with some margin of difference, it might be stated in the words of William Sanday: 'Just as one particular branch of one particular stock was chosen to be in a general sense the recipient of a clearer revelation than was vouchsafed to others, so within that branch certain individuals were chosen to have their hearts and minds moved in a manner more penetrating and more effective than their fellows, with the result that their written words convey to us truths about the nature of God and His dealings with man which other writings

[1] Coleridge says that there is a chasm of difference between the miraculous communication and 'inspired revelation' that is illustrated in the Law and the Prophets, 'no jot or tittle of which can pass unfulfilled', and the inspiration which he calls 'the highest degree of that grace and communion with the Spirit, which the Church under all circumstances, and every regenerate member of the Church of Christ, is permitted to hope, and instructed to pray, for'. This difference, he thinks, 'has in every generation been rendered evident to as many as read these Scriptures under the gracious influence of the Spirit in which they were written'. See *Confessions of an Inquiring Spirit*, Boston, 1841, pp. 120 f.
[2] *An Outline of Christian Theology*, New York, 1909, p. 43.

do not convey with equal fulness, power, and purity. We say that this special moving is due to the action upon those hearts and minds of the Holy Spirit. And we call that action Inspiration.'[1] We should naturally expect that this action of the Spirit should differ according to the nature of the content, and that is exactly what we find Sanday affirming. 'At the same time we cannot be surprised if, in this process of the application to life and worship of the central truths of the religion, there are some parts which are more distant from the centre than others, and proportionately influenced in less degree by the principles which are most fundamental. The glowing mass which sends forth light and heat loses both by radiation.' And so 'there are some books in which the Divine element is at the *maximum* and others in which it is at the *minimum*'.[2] At the best then, on this view, inspiration is that action of the Holy Spirit in the hearts and minds of the writers of Holy Writ whereby they had a more penetrative and effective perception of truth and in virtue of which the truth they wrote received 'classical expression, both as a model to after-ages and as a school of devout feeling'.[3] Inspiration then really respects the writers of Scripture and may be applied to Scripture only in so far as it is the product of men writing under that influence of the truth upon their hearts and minds.

(3) The third view is that of the Dialectic Theology, associated with the name of Karl Barth.[4] Barth claims that the written word, the Bible, is normative and authoritative. The Bible constitutes itself the canon. This self-imposition consists in the fact that the prophetic and apostolic word is the witness and proclamation of Jesus Christ. In the fulness of time the Word became flesh; in Jesus Christ *Deus dixit*. That is the absolute of the Bible, for it is *that* revelation that is attested in the Bible. As the Biblical writers are faithful to this centre they are carriers of the eternal Word.

The Bible itself, however, cannot strictly be said to be revelation and it cannot in itself as an objective reality be spoken of as the Word of God. Revelation comes to us through the mediacy of the Bible as it also comes to us through the medium of church proclamation. It is only because the Bible attests revelation given in the past and is the

---

[1] *Inspiration*, London, 1903, p. 127.

[2] *id.*, pp. 397 f.

[3] *id.*, p. 396.

[4] See Karl Barth, *Die Kirchliche Dogmatik, Die Lehre vom Wort Gottes*, Erster Halbband, München, 1932, pp. 89-261. English Translation by G. T. Thomson, *The Doctrine of the Word of God*, Edinburgh, 1936, pp. 98-283.

medium through which in a concrete confrontation revelation comes to us here and now that it may be called the Word of God. That the Bible may be the Word of God it must continue to confront the church as a free and living Word. This confrontation is God's free act, it is an act of God's grace and is the result of a divine decision. God from time to time speaks in the human word of the Bible, and in this event, which is a divine act of revelation and in which the Bible imposes itself, the Bible *becomes* God's Word. Man's word in the Bible becomes here and now true in us and for us.

The Bible is God's Word then by *becoming* from time to time God's Word to us. So we can speak, therefore, of the content of the Word of God only as that Word is constantly repeated in fresh divine utterance. God reveals himself in propositions, even in human language, since from time to time a word spoken by prophets or apostles becomes God's Word to us. That is the content of the Word of God.

The sole way we know it as the Word of God is that it comes straight home to us, it is directed to us, and that in a concrete confrontation as a divine *concretissimum* in a genuine and inescapable encounter. In this inescapable encounter a ruling divine power invades us and we stand in a crisis. It is a crisis in which an act of God, in this way and in no other, to this particular person and to no other, confronts him with choice, the choice of obedience or disobedience together with their resultant correlates of blessedness or damnation. Because of this the Word of God is never to be conceived of by us or reproduced by us as a general truth. However accurately the revelation may have been attested by the biblical writers it is never for that reason the Word of God to us. Only as there is the ever-recurring human crisis and divine decision does it become the Word of God.

Since, however, the absolute of the Bible is the witness to Jesus Christ the past revelation becomes contemporary. The time of Christ is made contemporary with the time of the prophets and apostles, and all in turn becomes contemporary with us. A particular *illic et tunc* (there and then) becomes a particular *hic et nunc* (here and now).

Since we are now dealing with inspiration it interests us to inquire a little more particularly what is the relation of this event of revelation – which is the Word of God in a concrete situation, in a crisis for us of life or death – to the written text of the Bible. Barth tells us that when the Word of God becomes an event, then revelation and the Bible are one in fact. But he warns us that we must not identify the Bible with this revelation. For in the Bible we have but human attempts to repeat and reproduce in human thoughts and expressions the Word of God. And so the Bible is not the Word of God until in a definite situation it becomes the medium of the Word of God to a particular person, not until by a concrete act of God repeated anew it becomes to that person the Word of God. For not until then does it have the personal character, the divine authority and the ruling power of the Word of God. Not until then can it be said that *Deus dixit* (God spoke), only that *Paulus dixit* (Paul spoke). And indeed God is not bound to the verbal form of Holy Scripture. He can use a verbal form beyond that of Scripture.

It has surely become clear then that the Bible, according to Barth, is not the Word of God by reason of a past activity of God, not the Word of God because, by a specific divine influence upon the writers, it possesses inherently in itself divine quality and character. It is not as a book written, not as an existing and abiding entity, not as a permanent deposit of divine truth, the Word of God. Apart from a *hic et nunc* personal act of God signalized in an event, it is never the Word of God. It is but the human witness to past revelation except as concrete parts of it, in concrete crises, become by a recurring act of divine revelation the Word of God to an individual soul.

The concepts of revelation held by these three views are not of course to be identified. Yet, in accordance with their respective presuppositions they all hold to supernatural revelation. The first two regard this supernatural revelation as a finished activity of God, the third demands that it be regarded as a continuous or at least ever-recurring act of God. In the matter of inspiration, the first holds to supernatural inspiration limited in extent or scope, the second holds to inspiration not specifically supernatural, but in kind common with the influence of the Spirit enjoyed by all believers, while the third can virtually dispense with inspiration altogether in favour of what is propounded to be the ever-present revelatory action of the Holy Spirit. It will have been seen how in each case the concept of revelation has been used to support the claim that the Bible is the Word of God, and yet has been used to eliminate the need and fact of plenary inspiration. Any presentation of the doctrine of inspiration that would be formulated or defended in opposition to these theories must, if it is to clarify and maintain itself, proceed along the line of defining these concepts and their relation the one to the other.

It must be appreciated that there is a distinction that may quite properly be drawn between revelation and inspiration. In this present discussion we are, of course, confining ourselves to *supernatural* revelation as it relates to inspiration. Revelation in this limited sense may be used with reference to the divine activity or to the product of that divine activity. In the narrowest and strictest sense the content of such revelation is the truth immediately communicated by God. Inspiration on the other hand refers to that influence of the Spirit of God brought to bear upon the writers of Holy Scripture whereby Scripture itself in its whole extent and every part is divine in origin, character and authority. Or, if we are thinking of Scripture as a finished product, we may use the word 'inspiration' to designate the quality of Scripture as divine by reason of that supernatural influence of the Holy Spirit under which it was produced.

Now as we study the content of Scripture it becomes obvious that much that is contained in Scripture is the product of supernatural revelation in this its strictest sense, the product of immediate communication from God to the mind of man. By various modes God disclosed to men knowledge that could be derived, not only from no other source, but also by no other method than that of immediate communication. And the Bible is the depository of that kind or type of knowledge.

But it is just as obvious that the Bible also contains much that was not derived from such supernatural communications. There is much material of varied character of which the writers were eyewitnesses or which they could have derived in the use of their natural faculties from extant sources of information. It must at least be conceded that there is much within the pages of Holy Writ that did not require for its knowledge on the part of the writers any supernatural revelation. And so it is apparent that there are at least two distinct kinds of content within the pages of Scripture.

Recognizing this distinction as regards content, how does it affect the question at issue, namely, that of inspiration? The moment we have asked that question it becomes necessary to make another distinction, a distinction necessitated by the consideration that we are dealing now with the influences brought to bear upon the writers of Scripture. It must be allowed that the writers of Scripture were themselves sometimes the recipients of supernatural revelations in the strictest sense. In such instances what they wrote was communicated to them by this strictly supernatural mode. But on other occasions, while the content of what they wrote is itself the product of supernatural revelation, that is, of immediate divine communication, we have no reason to suppose that the mode of communication to them as writers was that of supernatural communication. Peter, James and John were on the holy mount recipients of supernatural revelation, but we have no reason to suppose that Luke, in recording for us the information as to what Peter, James and John heard from heaven on that occasion, was the recipient of a supernatural revelation to that effect. We have good reason to believe that he learned it from Peter, James or John, or from sources of information emanating from the testimony of Peter, James and John. So that while oftentimes the data with which the inspired writer is dealing are data of a strictly supernatural character come to the knowledge of man by a strictly supernatural mode of communication, the mode of knowledge on the part of the writer is not in the strict sense supernatural.

We are not supposing that we have by any means exhausted the various categories into which the truth-content of Scripture would have to be placed, nor the various modes by which the writers of Scripture came to the knowledge of that truth-content they have conveyed to us. Far less have we been presuming to be able to determine in every case what were the modes by which the writers of Scripture were equipped to be the conveyors of the truth to us. But we have gone far enough in our analysis to appreciate the question: How does inspiration, whether we are regarding it as a divine influence or a divine quality, divine influence in producing Scripture or divine quality resident in Scripture, relate itself to the diverse kinds of truth-content embodied in Scripture?

There are various ways in which we may put this question, according as we are thinking of the various views of the nature of Scripture. If we are thinking, for example, of the Barthian view of Scripture, are we to suppose that the writers of Scripture, when engaged in their task of writing the diverse types of truth-content, were left to the infirmities and imperfections characteristic of human nature and characteristic of other human writers? Are we to suppose that they, though on occasions dealing with the Word of God in the most absolute sense of the word and though themselves even on occasion recipients of revelation, that is to say, in Barthian terms confronted in concrete crises with the Word of God in its authoritative and ruling power, yet give to us in the word they have written a merely human witness to that Word? Are we for that reason to suppose that the word of Scripture cannot itself be said to be the Word of God, but rather that ever and anon, now and here, in concrete situations by divine action and decision, it becomes the Word of God? Is that the way in which we may discover Christ and his apostles to have dealt with the then existing corpus of Scripture?

Or, having still another view of Scripture in mind, are we to believe that the inspiration of the writers was that elevation of spirit that came to them because of the supernaturalness of the revelation-content with which they were dealing?

Or, again, are we to suppose that a supernatural divine influence superintended, directed and controlled the writers of Scripture when they were writing what is revelatory in character, while no such influence was exerted upon them when they were dealing simply with the facts of nature and history or even dealing with those matters that required only the exercise of their natural faculties?

The thesis we maintain is that an examination of the biblical witness as to its character will show that a supernatural influence was exerted on the writers of Scripture, that this influence was all-pervasive, extending to every part of Scripture, that amidst the diversity of ways in which the content of Scripture was communicated to men, and amidst the diversity of ways in which the content of Scripture became the possession of its writers so that they might communicate it to us, there are no exceptions to, or degrees of, that supernatural influence we call 'inspiration', and no exceptions to, or degrees of, that 'inspiration' whereby Scriptures regarded as a product is rendered wholly divine in its origin, character, truth and authority.[1]

In view of this all-pervasive supernatural activity by which we contend Scripture is rendered wholly divine in character, we are required to recognize that the distinction between revelation and inspiration, though proper and necessary within certain well-defined limits, is not a distinction that can be applied with any absoluteness.

[1] It is deemed unnecessary to enter into any exposure of that gross caricature of the doctrine here stated that it involves the placing of the Divine imprimatur upon everything that Scripture records as having been said or done by fallen angels or men. The doctrine of plenary inspiration does not, of course, imply divine approval of the sins in thought, word and deed of which Satan, men and demons are represented as guilty. The writer would credit his readers with sufficient knowledge of the doctrine of inspiration to make such labour superfluous.

The fact of revelation in the strictest sense cannot be pleaded as an excuse for denying the pervasive activity or quality we call inspiration. Far less can revelation, when conceived of as a continuous or ever-recurring activity of God, be intruded as a substitute for that inspiration by which Scripture is constituted the Word of God.

The absoluteness with which the distinction is drawn in the interest of doing prejudice to that supernatural influence whereby Scripture in its entirety is invested with divine quality would have to be resisted for this reason, if for no other, namely, that the strictly revelation material cannot be abstracted from the historical, geographical and physical context in which it was given originally and in the context of which, as inscripturated, it is conveyed to us. God progressively disclosed and accomplished his redemptive plan in certain historical and geographical conditions; he revealed himself in word and deed in the sphere of a providence that includes as its necessary environment the world of nature. Revelation, though itself supernatural and therefore not given through the processes of nature, was given in the environment of the world of nature. Revelation does not consist of a series of abstract disclosures nor of disconnected disclosures. There is what Dr Vos calls the 'practical adaptability' of revelation. 'He has caused His revelation to take place in the milieu of the historical life of a people . . . All that God disclosed of Himself has come in response to the practical religious needs of His people as these emerged in the course of history.'[1] Revelation as an organism is therefore interwoven with the historical context, we may even say the natural context, in which it was given. Consequently the transmission of it to us must come in that context. It must not be abstracted. Any divergence from truth in the historical context must in the nature of the case disturb and distort the revelation itself. It becomes apparent then how prejudicial to the authenticity of the revelation material itself must be the attempt to drive a line of cleavage between the divine influence that guarded the transmission of the revelation content and the merely human agency by which the historical and geographical context of that revelation is transmitted.

But the most cogent reason why the absoluteness of the distinction between revelation and inspiration must be resisted is that Scripture not only records revelation; not only is it the inscripturation of

[1] Mimeographed Lectures on Old Testament Biblical Theology, p. 5. (Later published as *Biblical Theology*, Grand Rapids, 1948. Banner of Truth ed., 1975, pp. 8–9.)

revelation; it is as such in its entirety revelation. The Bible is much more than a living record of divine action and revelation. It is more than even a living reproduction and interpretation of the revelation of God in history. It is itself, as a written fact, *revelation*. In other words, it is not simply a history of revelation, not simply the vessel or vehicle of revelation, indeed not simply revelation history. It is, as *written word*, in itself revelation *fact*. It is *God* speaking to us men and, because so, it is, as a written product, in all its extent and detail, of divine origin and character and therefore divinely authoritative. It is itself, no less than the movements of God in history that it records, normative and determinative. That is just saying that inspiration is a mode of revelation. The Scriptures, as Dr Warfield says, cannot 'be degraded into the mere human record of revelation. They are themselves a substantial part of God's revelation; one form which his revealing activity chose for itself; and that its final and complete form, adopted as such for the very purpose of making God's revealed will the permanent and universal possession of man. Among the manifold methods of God's revelation, revelation through 'inspiration' thus takes its natural place; and the Scriptures, as the product of this 'inspiration', become thus the work of God; not only a substantial part of revelation, but, along with the rest of revelation, a substantial part of his redemptive work . . . But it is much more than a record of past revelations. It is itself the final revelation of God, completing the whole disclosure of his unfathomable love to lost sinners, the whole proclamation of his purposes of grace, and the whole exhibition of his gracious provisions for their salvation.'[1]

But we must proceed to ask: Does this view of inspiration we have presented stand the test of scrutiny? The moment we have said scrutiny we are required to ask, scrutiny of what? Is it the scrutiny of experience, or of history, or of scientific investigation? We would not disparage or dismiss with abuse the questions raised by these, nor would we underestimate the quota of evidence that might properly be elicited from them. But in the ultimate the norm is that which we have throughout suggested, the norm of Scripture itself. What is that view of Scripture entertained by itself? In other words, what is the biblical notion of inspiration? We may confine the inquiry to the question: What is the view entertained of Scripture by our Lord and his apostles? We do not claim that the inquiry more comprehensively treated

[1] *Revelation and Inspiration*, pp. 47 f.

should thus be delimited. But for our present purposes we may legitimately confine the question to these limits. We can, however, even within these limits do little more than give a few examples of the witness on the part of our Lord and his apostles to that view and use of Scripture which they held.

Perhaps the most significant utterance in the apostolic witness is that of Paul in 2 Timothy 3:16, a text that has been subjected to the most searching exegesis, particularly since the Reformation.[1]

There might be some reasonable doubt as to whether Scriptures of the New Testament canon were included in the scope of the πᾶσα γραφή of which Paul here speaks. Some able and cautious expositors are disposed to regard Paul as comprehending within the scope of Scripture all that could be called by that name. But Paul in the preceding context speaks of the ἱερὰ γράμματα which Timothy had known from a child. These sacred writings can be none other than the Scriptures of the Old Testament. Whether Paul had in mind a wider application by which other Scriptures were to be added and to which the same predicate could be ascribed, it may be difficult to say. But in any case the denotation cannot be any less than the Scriptures of the Jewish canon. This defines for us the denotation of that which Paul had in mind when in the succeeding context he affirms, 'All Scripture is inspired of God'.

I think that we may rather summarily dismiss what may be called the Socinian interpretation which reads the text as if Paul were making a distinction between inspired Scripture and uninspired Scripture, and which regards the ὠφέλιμος as the only predicate of the sentence, in which case it should read, 'Every Scripture that is God-inspired is profitable for doctrine'. Suffice it to say with Robert Watts that 'it cannot be for a moment imagined that, after passing such high eulogium upon the Holy Scriptures which Timothy, and his mother, and grandmother, had held in such veneration, the Apostle would at once proceed to inculcate an indefinite theory of inspiration, which, from its indefiniteness, could serve no other end than to perplex those who

---

[1] I must express here my deep indebtedness to Dr B. B. Warfield for the exact and massive scholarship he has brought to bear upon this whole subject and upon this text in particular. I would refer especially to his articles, 'The Inspiration of the Bible', 'The Biblical Idea of Inspiration', 'The Real Problem of Inspiration' and 'God-Inspired Scripture' in the volume cited above, *Revelation and Inspiration*. This volume is composed of articles written by Dr Warfield in several publications. They were published in book form after his death by the Oxford University Press, American Branch, in 1927.

would attempt to apply it, and must, in the end, lead to sceptical views on the whole subject of the claims of the sacred record'.[1]

It is immaterial whether we translate πᾶσα γραφή as 'all Scripture' or 'every Scripture', that is to say whether Paul conceives of Scripture collectively or distributively. If the former, then he means that Scripture in its entire mass as a unit is inspired of God. If the latter, then he means that Scripture in its every part is inspired of God. The result is the same. If Scripture in its whole extent is given by inspiration of God, then every part which goes to the making up of that total is inspired of God. And if Scripture is in every part given by inspiration of God, then Scripture in its total extent and content, which is the aggregation of its several parts, is given by inspiration of God. Scripture as such, whether viewed in its component parts or in its total mass, is given by divine inspiration.

What then is this quality that Paul predicates of Scripture? The word which we have so far translated as 'given by inspiration of God' or 'inspired of God' is very much more significant than our English translation might suggest. Paul is not here speaking of an inbreathing on the part of God into Holy Scripture. Nor is Paul speaking of an inbreathing into the writers of Holy Scripture. The term lends no support whatsoever to the notion that a human product or human witness is so inspired by God that it is by a here-and-now action of the personal God converted into or made to become the divine Word. Far less does it lend any support to the view that the writers of Holy Scripture were so inspired by the supernatural revelations they were honoured to record or communicate to us that a unique quality both as to content and character resides in the word they wrote. What Paul says is that 'All Scripture is God-breathed' or 'All Scripture, being God-breathed, is as well profitable'. What Paul affirms, therefore, is that Scripture, in Warfield's words, 'is the product of the creative breath of God, and, because of this its Divine origination, is of supreme value for all holy purposes'.[2] Or again, 'What is θεόπνευστος is "God-breathed", ... the product of Divine inspiration, the creation of that Spirit who is in all spheres of the Divine activity the executive of the Godhead'.[3] Paul's terse emphatic affirmation is that Scripture, the minimum denotation of which is placed beyond question by the

[1] *The Rule of Faith and the Doctrine of Inspiration*, p. 142.
[2] *Revelation and Inspiration*, p. 80.
[3] *id.*, p. 280.

context, is just precisely this kind of product. It is God's mouth, God's breath, God's oracle. He makes no qualifications and no reservations. He does not discriminate. He does not speak of degrees of inspiration. But what he does say is that 'every Scripture' or 'all Scripture' is God-breathed. All Scripture, since it is God-breathed, is also for that reason profitable for doctrine, for reproof, for correction, for instruction in righteousness, that the man of God may be perfect, thoroughly furnished unto every good work.

Paul is not here telling us anything about the human writers, nor of the way in which a divine product came to us through human instrumentality. He is, of course, well aware of the fact that God used human instruments, that he prepared and equipped these naturally, providentially, supernaturally, that certain modes of divine activity were operative in and through these human instruments to the end of giving us a γραφὴ θεόπνευστος. But the question of the human instrumentality is not within the purview of his thought here. He is now laying down with tremendous insistence the datum that Scripture is of divine origin and authorship, and by manifest implication that it is therefore of divine character and authority. It is the oracular Word of God. This is the tremendous *Pauline concretissimum*.

Perhaps the most significant utterance in the apostolic teaching beside this one of the Apostle Paul is that of Peter in his second Epistle: 'For we did not follow cunningly devised fables, when we made known unto you the power and coming of our Lord Jesus Christ, but we were eyewitnesses of his majesty. For he received from God the Father honour and glory, when there was borne such a voice to him by the Majestic Glory, This is my beloved Son, in whom I am well pleased: and this voice we ourselves heard borne out of heaven, when we were with him in the holy mount. And we have the word of prophecy made more sure: whereunto ye do well that ye take heed, as unto a lamp shining in a dark place, until the day dawn, and the day-star arise in your hearts: knowing this first, that no prophecy of scripture is of private interpretation. For no prophecy ever came by the will of man: but men spake from God, being moved by the Holy Spirit.'[1]

It was a very great privilege that Peter and the other two disciples enjoyed when they were with Jesus on the mount of transfiguration. They heard the eternal Father in audible speech bear witness to the

[1] 2 Pet. 1:16–21, A.R.V.

eternal Son, as the well-beloved Son on whom *his* good pleasure had come to rest. No wonder he relates the experience in such magnificent terms, 'We were eyewitnesses of his majesty. For he received from God the Father honour and glory when there was borne to him such a voice by the excellent glory.' No wonder he calls the scene the holy mount. But the astounding fact for our purposes is that he does not place that voice which came from heaven on a higher plane, as regards divinity, authority and stability, than the written Scripture. No indeed; he says the very opposite. 'We have also a more steadfast word of prophecy whereunto ye do well that ye take heed as unto a light that shineth in a dark place until the day dawn and the day-star arise in your hearts.' The written Word, whether he refers to the whole of Scripture or to that part specifically prophetic, gives ground for stronger and more stable assurance than the very word spoken on that occasion. It was not that Peter entertained any doubt as to the veracity and security of the heavenly voice that spake on the holy mount. But he advances a series of reasons why the Scripture affords us a more stable ground of confidence. These reasons are both negative and positive.

1. 'No prophecy of Scripture is of private interpretation.' The negative, it will be noted, is universal. In every case private interpretation is excluded. It is not the product of individual reflection or imagination. It is not merely the product of the writer's testimony to a fact or event witnessed by him.

2. 'No prophecy was ever brought by the will of man.' It does not owe its origin to human volition, determination, or initiative. Again the negative is universal.

3. 'Men spake from God.' The human instrumentality is recognized, and so any false inferences from the foregoing emphatic negatives – inferences calculated to do prejudice to the ostensible facts of the human authorship – Peter curtly obviates by the simple statement that men spake. They spake, however, from God, and it is that modification that supplies the ground for the negations of private interpretation and the will of man.

4. 'As borne by the Holy Spirit men spake from God.' This phrase 'borne by the Holy Spirit' has the position of emphasis in the sentence. It is, as Warfield observes, 'a very specific one. It is not to be confounded with guiding, or directing, or controlling, or even leading in the full sense of that word. It goes beyond all such terms, in assigning the effect produced specifically to the active agent. What is "borne" is

taken up by the "bearer", and conveyed by the "bearer's" power, not its own, to the "bearer's" goal, not its own. The men who spake from God are here declared, therefore, to have been taken up by the Holy Spirit and brought by His power to the goal of His choosing. The things which they spoke under this operation of the Spirit were therefore His things, not theirs. And that is the reason which is assigned why the "prophetic word" is so sure.'[1]

It is the absolute trustworthiness of Scripture that is being affirmed, and it is being affirmed expressly for the reason that it is not, in the last analysis, human testimony to a divine disclosure or revelation, not the product of human inspiration in recording the content of divine communications, but because it is itself divine testimony. The reason why he affirms this greater stability is just the fact that it is Scripture. Peter and his readers have not simply a word spoken on a particular occasion but the Word of God that has received, because it is Scripture, permanent embodiment and authentication.

When we turn to the testimony of our Lord himself, we find that his attitude to Scripture falls perfectly into line with those examples we have given of apostolic witness. Perhaps it would be more accurate and reverent to state the case in reverse order. We find that the apostolic witness breathes in the very same atmosphere as that attitude of meticulous acceptance and reverence exhibited by our Lord. The apostles had learned of Christ and they were baptized with his Spirit. It was none other than Jesus who said, 'Think not that I came to destroy the law or the prophets: I came not to destroy but to fulfil. For verily I say unto you, Till heaven and earth pass away, one jot or one tittle shall in no wise pass from the law till all things be fulfilled' (Matt. 5:17, 18). And it was he who said with a similar asseveration with respect to himself, 'Heaven and earth shall pass away, but my words shall not pass away' (Matt. 24:35). In the teaching of our Lord we are presented with the astounding fact that his attitude of meticulous acceptance and reverence proceeds from his recognition of the simple fact that it is written. We find no evidence that he sharply distinguished between the Word of God borne to us by Scripture as its vessel and vehicle and the written Word itself. No! The inescapable fact supported by an amazing mass of direct and indirect statement is that the Scripture, just because it was *Scripture*, just because it was *written*, just because it fell

[1] *Revelation and Inspiration*, p. 83.

within the denotation '*it is written*', was a finality in all questions. And the only explanation of such an attitude is that what Scripture said, God said, that it was God's Word just because it was Scripture, with which goes the corollary that it became Scripture because it was God's Word.

There are three episodes in the life and teaching of our Lord which we may adduce as illustrative of the thesis we have stated, namely, that the uniform attitude of our Lord was one of meticulous acceptance of Scripture in its entirety as the Word of God.

(1) The first is that of John 10:33–36. Jesus had just claimed equality with God the Father. He said, 'I and the Father are one', and the Jews rightly interpreted this as placing himself on an equality with God. Accordingly, they took up stones to stone him and accused him of blasphemy, a charge perfectly proper if the claim was not true. The charge, be it observed, was a tremendously serious one. It did two things: it denied his Deity and it denied his veracity, both of which were the basis of his mission and work. Validate the charge the Jews brought against him, and Jesus was the greatest of impostors.

It was a charge of just that kind that Jesus had to answer. Effective rebuttal, if ever necessary, was indispensable now. And it was by appeal to Scripture he met the charge. 'Jesus answered them, Is it not written in your law, I said ye are gods? If he called them gods unto whom the word of God came (and the Scripture cannot be broken), say ye of him whom the Father sanctified and sent into the world, Thou blasphemest, because I said I am the Son of God!' He staked his argument for the overthrow of the most serious allegation that could be levelled against him upon a statement of the 82nd Psalm, a statement too which does not appear in the Psalm as a word of God but as the word of the psalmist himself. Does he not do this precisely because he is convinced that in the Scriptures he is possessed of an unassailable instrument of defence? 'The Scripture cannot be broken.'

It is well for us to note the force of the brief parenthetical phrase, 'The Scripture cannot be broken'. It might be argued that Jesus in this reply to his adversaries was simply taking advantage of an *ad hominem* argument. 'Is it not written in your law?' And so no inference as to his own attitude to Scripture could be based upon his appeal to the 82nd Psalm. Jesus' parenthetical remark, 'The Scripture cannot be broken', silences any such objection, for there he expresses, not simply the attitude of the Jews to Scripture, but makes a categorical statement with respect to the inviolability of Scripture as such. It is not only because an appeal to Scripture is a finality for his opponents but because an appeal to Scripture is really and intrinsically a finality in itself. And for that reason an argument *a minori ad majus*, on the basis of one brief statement from the Old Testament, he regards as sufficient answer to the most potent kind of attack upon his person, veracity and mission. In the words of Robert Watts, 'Now the question here is not whether our Saviour's argument were cogent or pertinent. This is to be assumed if His personal rank be admitted. The sole question is, What, according to the language employed by Him, was His estimate of the Old Testament Scripture? It will be observed that He does not single out the passage on which He bases His argument, and testify of it that it is unbreakable, making its infallibility depend upon His own authority. Stated formally His argument is as follows:

'Major – The Scripture cannot be broken.

'Minor – I said, Ye are gods, is written in your law, which is Scripture.

'Conclusion – "I said, Ye are gods," cannot be broken. Such is unquestionably our Saviour's argument, and it assumes and affirms the unbreakableness and infallibility of all that was recognized by the Jews of His day as Scripture – the infallibility of the entire Jewish Bible; for He argues the infallibility of the clause on which He founds His argument, from the infallibility of the record in which it occurs. According to His infallible estimate, it was sufficient proof of the infallibility of any sentence, or clause of a sentence, or phrase of a clause, to show that it constituted a portion of what the Jews called ($\dot{\eta}$ $\gamma\rho\alpha\phi\dot{\eta}$) the Scripture. In this argument our Lord ignores and, by implication, invalidates all the distinctions of the later Rabbis, and their followers among modern Biblical critics, in regard to diversity of degrees of Inspiration among different books of Scripture . . . He argues the infallibility of the law itself and the clause embraced in it, from the infallibility of the Scripture, of which the law was but a part.[1] According to our Saviour's teaching, therefore, the entire set of writings designated Scripture by the Jews, was infallibly inspired.'[2]

(2) The second episode to which I shall refer is that recorded in Matthew 26:53, 54. The scene is the garden of Gethsemane, when

---

[1] It is questionable if Jesus in this passage in the use of the phrase 'your law' is referring to any particular part of Scripture. The present writer is disposed to think that 'your law' here is a designation of the entire Old Testament. But any difference of judgment with Dr Watts on that subsidiary detail does not in any way affect our judgment as to the cogency of his argument for the infallibility of Scripture.

[2] *The Rule of Faith and the Doctrine of Inspiration*, pp. 139 f.

Jesus was being apprehended by the servants of the high priest and rulers of the people. One of Jesus' disciples in his anger and excitement drew his sword and cut off the ear of one of the high priest's servants. Jesus remonstrates with his disciple, 'Put up thy sword into its place. For all those who take the sword will perish by the sword. Or thinkest thou that I cannot pray to my Father, and he will send me even now more than twelve legions of angels? How then should the Scriptures be fulfilled, that thus it must come to pass?'

In dealing with this impulsive disciple he could have used many forceful arguments. He could have said, 'It is the will and purpose of my Father that thus it should be, and that purpose cannot be frustrated.' He could have said, 'Your eternal security is bound up with this ordeal, and thus it must be. Invincible love of redemptive purpose constrains to this ordeal.' Such arguments could have been used with full sincerity and perfect validity. But such arguments he did not use. The argument he did use in this supremely critical hour of his earthly work was no more and no less than this, 'How then should the Scriptures be fulfilled?' I venture to say that the underlying presupposition of his resolution and argument – one that belonged to the ineradicable bent of his mind and will – was that the veracity of God was so bound up with the truth of Scripture, that, once thwart the fulfilment of Scripture, and you make God a liar. Could we find more demonstrable evidence of the supreme concern our Lord had for the unerring truth of the Old Testament, a concern amounting to crude fanaticism if it were not right and holy and true.

(3) The third instance I shall adduce is that from Luke 24:25–27, 44–47. It might with some degree of plausibility be argued that with the resurrection from the dead so momentous a change had occurred in the divine administration of his redemptive plan, so sharp a cleavage between the Old Testament dispensation and the New signalized, that the appeal to the past and in particular to the Old Testament Scriptures would have given place to, or at least be overshadowed by, the exposition of the new economy. The remarkable fact is that when our Lord after his resurrection is opening up to the disciples the redemptive significance for the world of his death and resurrection – opening up to them what Paul calls 'the mystery hid from ages and from generations' that there is no longer Jew nor Gentile, male nor female, bond nor free, but that Christ is all and in all – he made the very same characteristic appeal to the Old Testament. And his appeal is, if any-

thing, more emphatic and illuminating. He himself and his work is no doubt the centre of discourse and exposition. But the text for exposition of his own person and work is just precisely the Old Testament, as the embodiment of divine revelation with respect to his person and work and of the future programme of the kingdom of God upon earth. 'O fools', he says to the two disciples, 'and slow of heart to believe all that the prophets have spoken! Ought not Christ to suffer these things and to enter into his glory? And having begun from Moses and all the prophets he expounded unto them in all the Scriptures the things concerning himself.'

The question forces itself upon us, however: Does not this mass of testimony from our Lord and his Apostles, a tithe of which we have not given, confine itself to the Old Testament? It must be conceded that it is the Old Testament Scriptures Paul had in mind when he said to Timothy that from a child he had known the Holy Scriptures. It must be recognized that it was the Old Testament our Lord had in mind when he used as his final argument 'It is written' and said that 'the Scripture cannot be broken'. We not only recognize it but rejoice in the fact that to our Old Testament, so irreverently maligned by the scholarly and unscholarly world, we have the signature of him who is the image of the invisible God, the way, the truth and the life. We are not, of course, saying that the testimony of our Lord imparts inspiration to the Old Testament. It was inspired before he, the incarnate Son, accorded his testimony to it. His witness rather confirms and seals to us a divine character and authority antecedently and permanently belonging to it.

But does this fact not leave the New Testament Scriptures in a precarious position as regards the testimony to their inspiration? It must be acknowledged that we do not have precisely similar testimony from our Lord. He passed from this earthly scene before the New Testament was written. We do not have from the writers of the New Testament as copious a mass of testimony to the inspiration of the New as we have to that of the Old. But what we do have is adequate testimony, a line of testimony that constitutes the ground of faith. There is a threefold argument which I propose to advance.

1. *The first argument* is that drawn from analogy. It is just this. The New Testament economy is set forth in Scripture as even more glorious than that of the Old. That is just saying that it is signalized by a fuller

and more glorious disclosure of the divine character and will. The Epistle to the Hebrews enunciates the reason for this, and that which constitutes it, when it says, 'God, who at sundry times and in divers manners spake in time past unto the fathers by the prophets, hath in these last days spoken unto us by his Son, whom he hath appointed heir of all things, by whom also he made the worlds, who being the brightness of his glory and the express image of his substance, and upholding all things by the word of his power, when he had by himself purged our sins, sat down on the right hand of the Majesty on high' (1:1–3). And the Apostle Paul intimates a similar contrast with respect to the Mosaic economy when he says, 'For verily that which hath been made glorious hath not been made glorious in this respect, by reason of the glory that excelleth. For if that which passeth away was with glory, much more that which remaineth is with glory' (2 Cor. 3:10, 11). Now it is that revelation at sundry times and in divers manners, and that economy, which Paul says was passing away, that the Old Testament enshrines, the Old Testament to which we have such an amazing mass of testimony from our Lord and his apostles. Is it reasonable or tolerable to suppose that the Scripture which enshrines and communicates to us the content of that new and better covenant established upon better promises – the kingdom which cannot be moved, through which we come, not to the mount that burned with fire, but unto mount Zion, the city of the living God, the heavenly Jerusalem, and to an innumerable company of angels, to the general assembly and church of the firstborn which is written in heaven, and to God the Judge of all, and to the spirits of just men made perfect, and to Jesus the mediator of the new covenant, and to the blood of sprinkling that speaketh better things than that of Abel – should be less inspired, less God-breathed? If the older economy had an inspiration whereby Jesus could say, 'The Scripture cannot be broken', whereby Paul could say, 'All Scripture is God-breathed', and Peter, 'As borne by the Holy Spirit, men spake from God', are we to believe that the new covenant and economy signalized by all the implications of Pentecost was participant of a lesser gift? I cannot believe it. We find ourselves in a situation in which the promise of our Lord comes to bear with peculiar significance, 'It is expedient for you that I go away. For if I go not away, the Comforter will not come unto you, but if I depart I will send him unto you … He will guide you into all the truth' (John 16:7, 13).

2. *The second argument* I shall plead is that drawn from the divine authority the New Testament writers were conscious of possessing. As we read the New Testament one of its most impressive and pervasive features is the note of incisive and decisive authority, a note that does not confine itself to the apostolic preaching that lay back of the apostolic writings but belongs also to the writings themselves.

In the First Epistle to the Corinthians, for example, the apostle Paul devotes a considerable part of his discussion to the treatment of the spiritual gifts given to the apostolic church, the gifts of tongues, of prophesying, of miracles, of the interpretation of tongues. He enjoins that these gifts are to be exercised in compliance with principles of decency and good order. At the conclusion of that treatment he animadverts on the status and place of women in the public assemblies of worship. 'As in all churches of the saints', he says, 'let the women keep silence in the churches, for it is not permitted unto them to speak, but let them be in subjection, as also saith the law . . . For it is a shame for a woman to speak in the church. What? Was it from you that the word of God went out, or hath it come unto you alone?' (I Cor. 14:33–36). He enjoins silence upon women in the church by appeal to the universal custom of the churches of Christ. The Corinthians were not to be a law unto themselves in this matter, for the Word of God did not proceed from them and it was not given exclusively to them. They were to conform to a uniform practice enforced by the Word of God, and in accordance even with the law of the Old Testament. And then Paul, to clinch his whole argument, not only with respect to the place of women, but also with respect to the proper conduct of worship and the proper exercise of spiritual gifts and perhaps also the whole preceding part of his Epistle so far as it is regulative for the conduct of the Christian community, says, 'If any man thinketh himself to be a prophet or spiritual' – that is to say, if any one reckons himself to be possessed of the gift of revelation or possessed of the Holy Spirit – 'let him acknowledge that the things I write unto you are the commandment of the Lord. And if any is ignorant, let him be ignorant' (I Cor. 14:37, 38). The force of this for the topic we have in hand is that Paul reckons his own written word to be invested with the sanction and authority of God. He makes no qualification in his appeal to the Holy Spirit himself that the things he writes are the commandment of the Lord.

We have a similar note in 2 Thessalonians 3:12–14. In the immediate context Paul is dealing with those who had in their wanton, or even supposedly pious, idleness become busybodies. 'For we hear of some who walk among you disorderly, working not at all, but are busybodies. Now them that are such we command and exhort in the Lord Jesus Christ that with quietness they work and eat their own bread' (vv. 11, 12). And then in concluding he says, 'And if any man obey not our word by this epistle, note that man, that ye have no company with him, in order that he may be ashamed'. Could Paul have expressed himself with such imperious imperative and corrective if he had not been deeply aware of the divinely authoritative contents of his Epistle, divinely authoritative, let it be remembered, not only in the more sublime phases of its teaching, but also in the most practical of its details?

In the First Epistle to the Corinthians again he informs us as to the source of this authority. In the second chapter he is dealing with the transcendent wisdom of God, the wisdom which none of the princes of this world knew, the things which eye hath not seen nor ear heard, neither have entered into the heart of man. 'For', he proceeds, 'God hath revealed them unto us through the Spirit. For the Spirit searcheth all things, yea, the deep things of God ... Which things also we speak, not in words which man's wisdom teacheth, but which the Spirit teacheth, combining spiritual things with spiritual' (1 Cor. 2:10-13). The source, not only of the divine wisdom Paul is teaching, but of the very words he uses to teach it, is the Holy Spirit. Spirit-taught things and Spirit-taught words! That is the explanation and the only feasible explanation of the apostle's imperious authority.

3. *The third argument* is that derived from the fact that the New Testament writers themselves on occasion refer to one another's writings as they would to the inspired writings of the Old Testament or to the authoritative words of our Lord.

The only example I shall adduce is perhaps the most striking one. It is that of 2 Peter 3:10-16. Peter is dealing with the momentous facts and issues of the last day, the consummation of the world. He is answering the unbelief of those who say, 'Where is the promise of his coming? For since the fathers fell asleep all things continue as they were from the beginning of the creation'. He answers by appeal to the promise and veracity of the Lord. 'One day is with the Lord as a thousand years, and a thousand years as one day. The Lord is not slack concerning his promise as some men count slackness.' And so he asseverates, 'But the day of the Lord will come as a thief, in the which the heavens shall pass away with a great noise, and the elements shall melt with fervent heat. Nevertheless we, according to his promise, look for new heavens and a new earth, wherein dwelleth righteousness.' As we read these words we feel that the atmosphere is charged with the deepest solemnity. Peter is writing on a theme that required the most explicit divine utterances for the support of every statement made. Accordingly his appeal to the divine promise. 'The Lord is not slack concerning his promise.' 'We according to his promise look for new heavens and a new earth.' The reality of it all is staked upon the divine veracity and faithfulness. But mark the sequence. It is just in that context, as he draws lessons from these momentous facts, that he says, 'Account that the longsuffering of our Lord is salvation, even as our beloved brother Paul also, according to the wisdom given to him, hath written unto you, as also in all his epistles speaking in them of these things, in which are some things hard to be understood, which they that are unlearned and unstable wrest, as they do also the other Scriptures, unto their own destruction'. In a context of the profoundest solemnity and in one in which his argument is staked upon the divine veracity he appeals to the epistles of Paul, and in the most express way places the epistles of Paul on a plane of authority equal to that of the other Scriptures. This correlation of the Pauline epistles with other Scriptures he would not have dared to make unless it were the settled conviction of his mind that what could be said of other Scriptures could also be said of the epistles of Paul. It is Peter who said of other Scriptures in this same epistle that 'the Scripture is not of any private interpretation, for the Scripture came not of old time by the will of man, but as borne by the Holy Spirit men spake from God'. The inference is direct and inescapable that it was only because he would have said the same thing of the epistles of Paul that he placed them on a par with other Scriptures.

Now on the basis of such evidence we can surely say with intelligent and well-grounded assurance that the view which the Bible, considered as a unit consisting of both Testaments, entertains of itself is that 'All Scripture is God-breathed and profitable for doctrine, for reproof, for correction, for instruction in righteousness'. This we can affirm whatever may have been the denotation of Scripture directly in the purview of Paul when he penned these words.

If we reject the testimony of Scripture with respect to its own character can we validly or properly plead the authority of Scripture on any other topic? Are we not driven to the conclusion that if the testimony of Scripture on the doctrine of Scripture is not authentic and trustworthy, then the finality of Scripture as the absolute norm of faith is irretrievably undermined? Now, I am not saying that Scripture in that case would be useless. I am not saying that in that case it would entirely cease to be profitable. But what I am saying is that it would in that case no longer as *Scripture*, and for the reason that it is *Scripture*, constitute the final court of appeal in all matters of faith and practice. It might still be an invaluable witness, but no longer could we appeal to its final authority as residing in the fact that it is Scripture. For only as we accept the integrity of its witness can we accept any of its witness simply and finally because it is *its* witness. Much more is at stake in this matter than the doctrine of inspiration. The question at stake is the place of Scripture as the canon of faith. It is the question of the integrity of its witness, and the finality of its authority. More particularly it is the regulative authority of apostolic witness that is at stake. Most particularly it is the very integrity of our Lord himself.

The line of thought in this text we have quoted is to be very distinctly marked. Much thinking on this subject proceeds in the opposite direction from that of the apostle. Paul grounds the profitableness or utility of Scripture upon its divine origin. At least the preface and precondition of the purposes enumerated for which it is profitable is the fact that it is a divine product. It is divinity that validates its utility. In that, Paul very simply and directly cuts athwart any pragmatic grounding of the inspired character of Scripture. If we take our point of departure from utility and make utility our standard of judgment, then we have relinquished the divine order of truth and knowledge. To put it mildly, we have deserted the standing ground of a divine absolute and universal for that of a relative human particular that tosses itself on the uncharted, harbourless ocean of endless surmising.

'All scripture is God-breathed and profitable . . . for instruction, which is in righteousness.' It will surely be conceded without argument that the fundamental need of the individual and of society in any age is *righteousness*. It is righteousness that lies at the basis of, and is the end procured for us by, what is the cardinal doctrine of our faith. 'Whom God hath set forth', says Paul, 'to be a propitiation through faith in his blood; to declare his righteousness . . . that he might be just and the justifier of him who hath faith in Jesus' (Rom. 3:25, 26). As sin hath reigned unto death, so hath grace reigned through *righteousness* unto eternal life through Jesus Christ our Lord (cf. Rom. 5:21). 'What the law could not do, in that it was weak through the flesh, God sending his own Son in the likeness of sinful flesh, and for sin, condemned sin in the flesh: that the righteousness of the law might be fulfilled in us, who walk not after the flesh, but after the Spirit' (Rom. 8:3). Righteousness the basis and righteousness the end!

But what is the righteousness that is to be fulfilled in us? What is its content or norm? There is but one answer for the Christian – it is inspired Scripture alone that is the infallible and sufficient rule of faith and manners. Oh, my friends, how precious it is that in this world of sin with its vagaries of unbelief, its fluctuating philosophies, its dim light which is darkness, and its wisdom which is foolishness with God, its bewilderment and despair, we have a sure word of prophecy, whereunto we do well in taking heed as unto a light that shineth in a dark place until the day dawn and the day-star arise in our hearts! How precious that we have a word divine, infallible and sufficient for the individual, for the family, for the church, for society, for the commonwealth and even for the world! That is the implication of the apostle's word, 'instruction which is in righteousness, that the man of God may be perfect, thoroughly furnished unto every good work'. There is no circumstance in which man may be placed, no office he may be called upon to fill, no department of life in all its complexity and detail, for which Holy Scripture is not the infallible and sufficient guide. 'The law of the Lord is perfect, converting the soul: the testimony of the Lord is sure, making wise the simple. The statutes of the Lord are right, rejoicing the heart: the commandment of the Lord is pure, enlightening the eyes. The fear of the Lord is clean, enduring for ever: the judgments of the Lord are true and righteous altogether. More to be desired are they than gold, yea, than much fine gold: sweeter also than honey and the honeycomb. Moreover by them is thy servant warned: and in keeping of them there is great reward' (Ps. 19:7–11).

4

Jesus the Son of God

PETER's confession at Caesarea Philippi marks one of the most notable incidents in the public ministry of our Lord. In answer to Jesus' question: 'But whom say ye that I am?' Peter replied: 'Thou art the Christ, the Son of the living God' (Matt. 16:15, 16). The significance of both question and answer is pointed up by three considerations. First, there is the benedictory endorsement of the confession: 'Blessed art thou, Simon Bar-jona: for flesh and blood hath not revealed it to thee, but my Father who is in heaven' (v. 17). Second, there is the announcement, in its specific character without parallel in the recorded teaching of our Lord, respecting the building of his church and apostolic investiture (vv. 18, 19). Third, the incident marked an epoch in Jesus' teaching regarding the impending events that were pivotal in his messianic commission. 'From that time forth began Jesus to shew unto his disciples, how that he must go unto Jerusalem, and suffer many things of the elders and chief priests and scribes, and be killed, and be raised again the third day' (v. 21).

The epochal place occupied by the confession at Caesarea Philippi in the teaching of our Lord advertises of itself the significance that must be attached to the title 'the Son of God' in the identity that belongs to Jesus and in the faith which his identity demands. In this respect, however, Caesarea Philippi only exemplifies a fact that is pervasive in the witness of the New Testament. A survey of this witness is necessary in order that we may appreciate the extent to which the identity specified by the title enters into the witness borne to Jesus and determines the faith that is directed to him. I fear that even in orthodox circles the implications of this designation are too frequently overlooked and that the faith of Jesus as 'the Son of God' has suffered an eclipse that dishonours the Saviour and gravely impoverishes faith itself.

In the New Testament record of events it is not often that the voice of God the Father is mentioned as heard from heaven. There are only a few occasions. The two most notable occasions are: Jesus' baptism at Jordan and his transfiguration on the holy mount. No witness is fraught with more meaning than that uttered directly from heaven by God the Father (John 5:31, 37). Peter, the spokesman at Caesarea Philippi, reflects his sense of privilege when, with reference to the latter occasion, he writes later on: 'For we have not followed cunningly devised fables when we made known to you the power and coming of the Lord Jesus Christ, but were eyewitnesses of his majesty. For he received from God the Father honour and glory when there was borne to him such a voice by the majestic glory.' (2 Pet. 1:16, 17).

What then was the witness on these occasions? 'This is my beloved Son, in whom I am well pleased' (Matt. 3:17, 17:5; 2 Pet. 3:17; cf. Mark 1:11; 9:7; Luke 3:22; 9:35). The dignity of the ascription is underlined at the transfiguration by the addition: 'hear ye him'. (Matt. 17:5; Mark 9:7). The story unfolded in the New Testament is to the effect that this witness, given to Jesus' divine Sonship on the occasion of his baptism at Jordan, conditioned and captivated the faith of his disciples from the outset. John the Baptist's testimony is the corroboration of this fact: 'And I knew him not:' he says, 'but he who sent me to baptize with water, he said to me, Upon whom thou shalt see the Spirit descending, and abiding upon him, this is he who baptizes with the Holy Spirit. And I have seen and bear witness that this is the Son of God' (John 1:33, 34).

The confession at Caesarea Philippi is rightly recorded the significance that belongs to it in the development of our Lord's teaching and in the faith of the disciples. But we are not to suppose that the confession bespeaks a new discovery on the disciples' part of Jesus' divine Sonship. The confession harks back to the heavenly voice at Jesus' baptism and to the witness of the Baptist.

It would not be reasonable to exclude Andrew from John's audience when he bore witness that Jesus was the Son of God (John 1:33–40). It is altogether reasonable to conclude that the faith of Jesus in that identity conditioned his thinking when Andrew found his brother Simon and said: 'We have found the Messias' (John 1:41). But though a question may remain as regards Andrew in this respect, there can be no question in the case of Nathanael at the very inception of Christ's public ministry. There are several features of Jesus' encounter with Nathanael that are intriguing for us and they invite our interest. But what is of prime importance for our present study is Nathanael's confession: 'Rabbi, thou art the Son of God, thou art the King of Israel' (John 1:49). This is conclusive evidence that within the circle of Jesus' disciples from the onset the faith of Jesus as Son of God was integral to their evaluation of him as the Messiah.

Another instance in Jesus' public ministry showing that the confession at Caesarea Philippi was not novel in the faith of the disciples, is the worship of the disciples on the occasion of Jesus' walking on the water and stilling the storm. 'They worshipped him saying, Truly thou art God's Son' (Matt. 14:33).

In our survey of the New Testament witness to the divine Sonship of Jesus we may not overlook what is even prior to any of the instances so far considered. In view are the two occasions on which the angel Gabriel used this ascription in his address to Mary in connection with Jesus' begetting, conception and birth. 'He shall be great', said the angel, 'and will be called the Son of the Highest' (Luke 1:32). We cannot tell to what extent this information regarding the divine Sonship had been conveyed by Mary to the believing community. But two things are apparent. First, in the earliest announcement of Jesus' actual advent in the begetting of the Holy Spirit and conception by the virgin, the identity of the child had been defined in terms of the title 'Son of God', thus certifying the jealousy with which God insured that the conception entertained of him would not at any time be framed apart from this filial relation to God. Second, the earliest community of faith received revelation on the basis of which the divine Sonship would determine the evaluation of Jesus' person. In terms of revelation the community of faith had never been permitted to conceive of him as other than that which his divine Sonship made him to be.

As we peruse the New Testament we find copious evidence of the place occupied by Christ's divine Sonship in the confession of faith. In answer to Jesus' question to Martha if she believed that every one who believed in him would never die she answered: 'Yea, Lord: I believe that thou art the Christ the Son of God who comes into the world' (John 11:27). That this should have been spoken by Martha in spontaneous response to Jesus' challenging question, and spoken in the form of what is virtually protestation, indicates that the elements of her confession had become the staple of those who were his followers. The close parallel to Peter's confession and to that of others at earlier stages of Jesus' earthly ministry evinces that the recognition of his divine Sonship had not been reserved for occasional mountain-top experiences and visions of his glory, but was foundational in believing apprehension.

In pursuance of our present enquiry nothing could be more significant than what we find in the history and writings of the apostle Paul. As the sequel to his conversion we read: 'And immediately in the synagogue he preached Jesus, that he was the Son of God' (Acts 9:20). The import is, plainly, that to preach Jesus is to proclaim that he is the Son of God. Hence, when Paul later on refers to his conversion, we find the same centrality of the divine Sonship in his own description of what his conversion entailed. 'But when it pleased God, who separated me from my mother's womb, and called me by his grace, to reveal his Son in me, that I might preach him among the Gentiles, immediately I conferred not with flesh and blood' (Gal. 1:15, 16). 'To reveal his Son in me' is an unusual expression. Perhaps for this reason we are all the more constrained to recognize what is true in any case, that the revelation of Christ as God's Son is that to which the good pleasure of God the Father was directed in order that thereby the gospel of Christ might be preached among the Gentiles.

In Paul's epistles likewise, as he defines the gospel, we find this same priority in respect of Christ's Sonship. The gospel of God, he says, is that 'concerning his Son who was made of the seed of David according to the flesh, who was constituted the Son of God with power according to the Spirit of holiness by the resurrection from the dead, Jesus Christ our Lord' (Rom. 1:3, 4; cf. 1:9). Later in this Epistle the uniqueness of Jesus' divine Sonship is brought to our attention on two occasions, in the designation God's 'own Son' (Rom. 8:3, 32). In both verses Paul is dealing with what is central in the provisions of redemptive grace, the sending of the Son in the likeness of sinful flesh, and the non-sparing of the Son as the supreme manifestation of the Father's love. The title God's 'own Son' serves to accentuate the marvel of grace and the security accruing from the sacrifice involved. The same emphases are present in Galatians 4:4, 5: 'When the fulness of the time had come, God sent forth his Son . . . to redeem them that were under the law.'

Before passing on to another closely related aspect of New Testament teaching, it is appropriate to observe that the demons recognized Jesus in this identity and addressed him accordingly (cf. Matt. 8:29; Mark 3:11; 5:7; Luke 4:41; 8:28). And we need not doubt that when Satan in the wilderness addressed Jesus with the words, 'If thou art the Son of God' (Matt. 4:3; Luke 4:3, 9), there was the same recognition.

In view of the evidence establishing the centrality of his divine Sonship in the evaluation and confession of Jesus, we should expect that the identity involved would be given comparable prominence in the exercises of faith at the inception and in the continuance of the Christian life. This is what we actually find. It is exemplified by our Lord himself in the text which is probably the best known in Scripture. 'For God so loved the world, that he gave the only begotten Son, that whoever believes in him should not perish but have everlasting life' (John 3:16). It is surely implied that the faith that saves and issues in eternal life is the faith directed to Christ in his character as the only begotten Son. Support for this inference is derived from verse 18: 'He who believes not is condemned already, because he has not believed in the name of the only-begotten Son of God'. The 'name' stands for the person in his revealed character and, since faith is said to be in the name, it is in the specific identity of only-begotten Son that the Saviour becomes the object of faith. The same thought appears in John 3:36; 'He that believes on the Son hath everlasting life; and he that believes not the Son will not see life, but the wrath of God abides on him'. One other text from this Gospel should suffice to demonstrate this observation. Referring to the signs he had recorded in his Gospel John says: 'These are written that ye may believe that Jesus is the Christ the Son of God, and that believing ye may have life in his name' (John 20:31).

With the decisiveness and incisiveness characteristic of his Epistles, John writes to the same effect: 'Everyone who denies the Son hath not the Father: he who confesses the Son hath the Father also' (1 John 2:23); 'And this is his commandment, that we should believe on the name of his Son Jesus Christ and love one another' (1 John 3:23 cf. 4:15; 5:5, 12, 13; 2 John 9).

The faith by which the believer lives has this same character. 'The life I now live in the flesh', wrote Paul, 'I live by the faith of the Son of God who loved me and gave himself for me' (Gal. 2:20). And it is 'in the unity of the faith and of the knowledge of the Son of God' that believers attain to a 'perfect man to the measure of the stature of the fulness of Christ' (Eph. 4:13). If faith at its inception takes in the character impressed on it by Jesus' divine Sonship, so the faith by which believers are kept and persevere cannot dispense with the specific character belonging to Jesus as the Son of God.

The foregoing mass of evidence bearing upon the faith of Jesus as the Son of God compels an indictment. It can be stated in the form of a question: To what extent has our faith in Jesus been constituted and governed by that which is so pervasive in the witness of the New Testament? This constrains the further question: Has the proclamation of the gospel by the church been characterized by an emphasis that measures up to what this witness demands? There is much reason to fear that in the faith of believers and in the proclamation of the church there has been a lamentable hiatus in respect of that to which the gospel itself accords such prominence. The rudiment of faith in Jesus as Lord and Saviour is that he is the Son of God. His Sonship belongs to his identity, and a faith or confession or proclamation that is not conditioned by what he is in this specific character falls short at its centre and thereby robs the Saviour of the honour that is intrinsically his.

This survey has shown the centrality in the faith and confession of Jesus of that which is denoted by the title, 'The Son of God'. It is now necessary to inquire: What is the identity expressed by the title? If we go back to the confession of Peter, it would be plausible to argue that the title 'Son of God' stands in apposition to that which immediately precedes, namely, 'the Christ', and that it is no more than a messianic title, another way of specifying his messianic character and office. In that event the same could be true in other notable instances (cf. John 1:49; 11:27; 20:31; Acts 9:20). And, as far as Caesarea Philippi is concerned, this interpretation would appear to derive support from the parallel accounts in Mark and Luke where the confession is stated simply in terms of Messiahship (Mark 8:29; Luke 9:20). It is not our interest, for the present, at least, to call in question what has been called the messianic Sonship. But the thesis, required by the evidence upon which now attention will be focused, is that the title 'Son of God' is one predicated of our Lord in virtue of his pretemporal, ontological, intertrinitarian identity and relationship. The evidence will be discussed under two subdivisions.

I THE FATHERHOOD OF GOD

Divine Fatherhood is involved in the divine Sonship in whatever way the latter is understood. But we are concerned now with the Fatherhood that is intrinsic and eternal. There are several considerations.

1. There are the numerous instances in which this person of the Godhead is designated 'the Father'. This appears frequently in the discourses of our Lord himself (cf. Matt. 11:27; 28:18; Luke 9:26; 10:22; John 3:35; 4:21; 5:19, 21, 22, 26; 6:46; 10:17; 12:26; 14:6, 9, 31; 18:11; Acts 1:4, 7) and in the usage of the other New Testament witnesses (cf. John 1:14; Acts 2:33; Rom. 6:4; Eph. 2:18; 1 Pet. 1:17; 1 John 1:2; 3; 2:1, 14, 15, 16; 2 John 4). It is the absolute use of this title that is fraught with significance. The frequency of occurrences in the case of our Lord and of others admits of no other conclusion than that this is the name by which he is identified and distinguished intrinsically. This conclusion derives additional support from the fact that in a considerable number of instances the title is conjoined with the other title 'God' (cf. John 6:27; 1 Cor. 8:6; 15:24; Gal. 1:1; Eph. 4:6; 6:23; Phil. 2:11; Col. 3:17; 1 Thess. 1:1; 1 Tim. 1:2; James 1:27; 1 Pet. 1:2; 2 Pet. 1:17; Jude 1). This surely means that in his divine identity he is the Father, that Fatherhood and deity in the first person of the Godhead are correlative, and that we can no more dissociate Fatherhood from his person than we can deity.

2. When our Lord speaks of being sent or of coming into the world, he speaks in terms of being sent by and coming out from the Father (cf. John 5:23, 36, 37; 6:57; 10:36; 16:28; 20:21). As will be noted later, in connection with the sending or giving of the Son, it is unreasonable to think that it was by sending that the Father came to sustain the relationship denoted by the title. The implication is that when Jesus was sent it was by the Father and that he acted as the Father in the act of sending. Perhaps even more apparent in this respect is the implication of Jesus' word: 'I came out from the Father'. The thought is surely that he came out from the Father in the specific identity denoted by the name 'Father', and that, therefore, this identity was his antecedently.

3. Closely related to the preceding consideration is the prayer of our Lord on the eve of his crucifixion: 'And now, Father, glorify thou me with thyself with the glory which I had with thee before the world was' (John 17:5). To suppose that the pre-temporal glory enjoyed alongside of the Father could be dissociated from the relationship involved in the title 'Father' would require a disjunction that is exegetically untenable. Jesus prays to be glorified with the Father *himself* and, therefore, with the Father in that precise character. But then this, he

says, is the glory he had with the Father before the world was. So what belongs to the anticipated glory must also have belonged to the pre-temporal glory, namely, glory with the Father as Father.

These considerations point to the pre-temporal, intrinsic, ontological Fatherhood of him who bears the name 'God the Father'. The question necessarily arises: In virtue of what relationship does he bear this name? There is the Fatherhood that belongs to God in relation to creation. He is 'the Father of spirits' (Heb. 12:9); he is 'the Father of lights' (James 1:17); as responsible beings we are said to be the 'offspring of God' (Acts 17:29); by reason of redemption and adoption the Father specifically is said to be he 'of whom the whole family in heaven and earth is named' (Eph. 3:14). There are, however, two reasons why these relationships of paternal character cannot be considered as the reason for the Fatherhood that is intrinsic and eternal.

(i) The Fatherhood involved is not intrinsic and eternal; it belongs to the economics of creation and redemption. However much we emphasize the eternal counsel in pursuance of which these economies have come to be, they cannot themselves be placed in the pre-temporal and eternal realm. And to conceive of them as constituting an intrinsic relationship predicable of God is to destroy the distinction between what God is in himself necessarily, essentially and eternally, and what comes to be by the counsel of his will.

(ii) The usage of our Lord and of his apostles is the certain index to the reason for the intrinsic and eternal Fatherhood of God the Father. We have found that our Lord and other New Testament witnesses speak of God the Father as 'the Father' absolutely, without further specification, and we have already drawn from this the necessary inferences.

But our Lord not only speaks of 'the Father', but also, frequently, both in direct allocution and in discourse to others, he speaks of 'my Father' and 'my Father who is in heaven' (cf. Matt. 7:21; 16:17; 18:10, 35; 20:23; 26:29, 39; Luke 2:49; 22:29; 24:49; John 2:16; 5:17; 6:32; 8:19, 54; 10-18; 14:2, 20, 21; 15:1, 8, 10; 20:17). And the apostles likewise speak of the Father as 'the God and Father of our Lord Jesus Christ' (cf. Rom. 15:6; 2 Cor. 11:31; Eph. 1:3; Col. 1:3; 1 Pet. 1:3; see also 1 John 1:3; 2 John 3). This Fatherhood must be given the priority on all accounts and it alone can be the reason for and explanation of the intrinsic and pre-temporal Fatherhood. The conclusion is inevitable. To Fatherhood corresponds Sonship. And if the Father is eternal Father, the Son must be eternal Son. In a word, Fatherhood and Sonship are correlative, and in the Godhead they are eternally correlative.

The argument for the eternal Fatherhood and for its correlate the eternal Sonship must be extended one further step. There is what may be called the theological consideration. The doctrine of the Trinity is concerned with the differentiation within the Godhead that is necessary, intrinsic, and eternal. If there is Trinity there must be the distinction of persons and therefore the distinguishing property of each person, a property that is incommunicable. We must assume that the revelation God has given us of himself provides the index to these distinctions. In reference to the two persons with whom we are now concerned the Scripture offers no datum for intrinsic distinction that compares in relevance and frequency of occurrence with Fatherhood and its corresponding Sonship. Trinity requires that faith in the living God must be directed to all three persons in the ways appropriate to each in their respective distinctness. And worship must be characterized by the same differentiation. We worship the first person in the particularity that is his as the God and Father of our Lord Jesus Christ. We worship the second in the particularity that belongs to him as the Son of the Father.

It may not be amiss to note the way in which John in the prologue to his Gospel exhibits this truth. In John 1:1, 2 we have the distinction from God and identity with God; distinction in the words, 'the Word was with God' and 'was in the beginning with God', identity in the words, 'And the Word was God'. In verses 14 and 18 the differentiation answering the question of distinction is provided in the titles 'only begotten from the Father' and 'only begotten Son' (or 'only begotten God').

II THE ETERNAL SONSHIP

No more evidence for the eternal Sonship is really necessary than that which is implicit in the eternal Fatherhood. But it is appropriate to focus attention now upon the evidence derived from the New Testament witness to the Sonship of our Lord and Saviour Jesus Christ. It is necessary to do this not only to confirm the conclusions elicited from eternal Fatherhood but also to discover the implications of the divine Sonship and thus attempt to determine its true character.

1 *The Uniqueness of the Son*

No characterization bears out the fact of uniqueness more than the title 'Only-begotten'. Only in John's Gospel and First Epistle is this name used with reference to Christ (John 1:14, 18, 3:16, 18; 1 John 4:9). Whatever significance belongs to the latter part of the compound, it is impossible to overlook what is implicit in the first, namely, that to him alone belong the character and relation denoted.[1] In three of the instances the name qualifies Son – 'the only begotten Son' (John 3:16, 18; 1 John 4:9). This is highly significant. It is in his identity as Son that he is only-begotten and, therefore, in that relationship to God he stands alone. Since it is in relation to the Father that he is Son, we must conclude that the same is true in respect of his being the only-begotten. John 1:14 indicates this more specifically. For John says: 'We beheld his glory, glory as of an only-begotten from the Father'. The relevance to the Father obtains whether we interpret 'from the Father' as referring to the Son's existence as only-begotten in the intimacy of fellowship alongside the Father or to his coming from the Father when he became flesh.

The apostle Paul has his own way of expressing the uniqueness of Jesus' Sonship. He speaks of God's 'own Son' (Rom. 8:3, 32). This mode of expression is not without its parallel in the Gospel of John. The Jews were seeking to kill Jesus, we are told, 'because not only was he breaking the Sabbath, but was also calling God his own Father' (John 5:18). There must have been in Jesus' reference to God as his Father (cf. v. 17) a note of exclusiveness reflecting the uniqueness of his filial identity. It was upon this claim on the part of Jesus that the Jews laid hold when they alleged, and alleged correctly, that he called God his own Father. If we regard John 3:16, 18 as words spoken by Jesus himself, a view that has much to commend it, then, of course, the uniqueness involved in the title 'only-begotten' appears in the words of Jesus himself. But John 5:17, 18 is of particular interest in this respect that, even if John 3:16, 18 were not Jesus' own words, the uniqueness of being only-begotten is shown to have its analogue in the language of Jesus himself.

The textual variant in John 1:18 should not be overlooked. If 'only-begotten God' is the genuine reading, then the title 'only-begotten' is brought into conjunction with the predicate of John 1:1c: 'and the Word was God'. Without question we encounter difficulty here. If

[1] Cf. Geerhardus Vos, *The Self-Disclosure of Jesus*, New York, 1926.

'only-begotten Son' points to the uniqueness of his Sonship, are we now to suppose that 'only-begotten God' asserts the uniqueness of his Godhood? One thing must be said at the outset, that no toning down of his Godhood is possible in Johannine conception. The title 'God' here, as in John 1:1, admits of no qualification in respect of deity. I would, therefore, submit that the title 'only-begotten' in this instance, in combination with the name 'God', serves the twofold purpose of identifying the revealer as none other than he who in verse 14 is called 'the only-begotten from the Father', and at the same time reasserting his unqualified Godhood in accord with John 1:1c; in other words, that we have what might be called appositional construction.

2. *Transcendent Sonship*

What is in view now is the evidence in support of the eternal Sonship derived from those passages that deal more specifically with the Son himself and indicate the character of the filiation presupposed in them.

(i) *The Giving of the Son.* Foremost in this category is John 3:16. God 'gave his only-begotten Son'. The governing thought of the text is the greatness of the Father's love. The intensity is shown by the fact that he gave his only Son.[1] There are two considerations pertinent to our present interests. The first is what is involved in the *giving* of the Son. The giving must have inclusive reference and embrace, therefore, the incarnation from the point of its inception. In other words, it cannot be restricted so as to refer only to what transpired subsequent to the event of becoming incarnate. In the actual incarnation the person given was the Son and so the identity denoted by the term 'Son' was his prior to the incarnation. It could not be said that God gave the Son if he gave him to be the Son. If we think of messianic Sonship, this Sonship was pursuant to the giving and the result of it. Hence it could be that it was in his messianic identity that he was given, but that he was given for all that was involved in this messianic identity. The order of thought is reversed if we give to the designation 'only-begotten Son' any connotation other than that which is pre-messianic and, therefore, pre-existent. Having before us, then, what is implied in the giving, we derive some corroboration from what is the leading

---

[1] The greatness of the love is commensurate with and evidenced by the greatness of the gift.

thought of the text, namely, the greatness of the Father's love. If the Son is conceived of in the transcendent relationship of intra-divine Sonship, this is consonant with the main emphasis of the text. If we give to the title 'Son' a lower connotation, then we lose something that is germane, if not necessary, to the stress placed upon the greatness of the Father's love.

Romans 8:32 does not of itself offer the considerations drawn from John 3:16. But if we keep in view what has already been shown regarding the expression 'his own Son', then the thought is similar to that of John 3:16. In this case, however, it is the certainty of continued grace, guaranteed to the predestinated and called by the greatest of all gifts, the non-sparing and delivering up of the Son.

(ii) *The Sending of the Son.* It is admitted that the mere fact of sending to do a work, perform a mission, or execute an office does not of itself establish any transcendent identity. The prophets were sent. Jesus sent his disciples. Of John it is said that he was 'a man sent from God', (John 1:6). The thesis now being presented does not rest, therefore upon the thought of mission but upon other considerations that are peculiar to God's sending of the Son.

Jesus spoke frequently of being sent by God and, more specifically, of being sent by the Father (cf. Matt. 10:40; 21:37; Mark 12:6; Luke 20:13; John 4:34; 5:23, 36, 37, 38; 6:57; 7:28, 29; 8:16, 18; 11:42; 17:3; 20:21). We cannot properly interpret this frequent appeal on Jesus' part without taking into account co-ordinate statements on his own part. He was sent into the world (cf. John 3:17; 10:36; 17:18). The counterpart of being sent is that *he came* into the world (cf. John 1:9; 3:19; 9:39; 12:46; 16:28; 18:37; see also 6:14; 11:27). This coming was from above and from heaven (cf. John 3:31) and a coming out from the Father (cf. John 8:42; 13:3; 16:27, 28; 17:8). When he left the world into which he came, he returned to the Father (cf. John 7:33; 16:5, 10, 17; cf. 17:5). Although Jesus also spoke of sending the disciples into the world (John 17:18; 20:21), yet the distinctiveness of Jesus' mission is clearly borne out by these co-ordinate descriptions.

Since he came from above, from heaven, from the Father, it was in the identity that was his in heaven and with the Father prior to his coming that he came and was sent. This identity is distinctly specified as that of Son and only-begotten (cf. John 3:17-19; 17:1, 5, 8, 18). Hence this filial identity is pre-existent, pre-temporal, and transcendent.

When we turn to the apostolic witness, this inference becomes even more apparent (cf. Rom. 8:3; Gal. 4:4; 1 John 3:8; 4:9, 10; 5:20). In Romans 8:3 the words 'in the likeness of sinful flesh' are surely intended to define for us the mode, and 'for sin' the purpose of the sending. If the Son was sent in that mode, he is conceived of in the identity of God's own Son when he became human and, furthermore, it is the dignity belonging to him in that relationship to the Father that enables him to meet the exigency created by the impotence of the law. In Galatians 4:4 the language is reminiscent of our Lord's own word that he came out from the Father. But, even apart from this analogy of expression, the terms 'God sent forth his Son' admit of no other natural construction but that when Christ came into the world he came as the Son whom he antecedently was. As in Romans 8:3 the mode is defined for us and, in this instance, in terms that embrace the incarnation from its inception – 'made of a woman, made under law'. This intimates again that when he entered the realm into which he was sent it was as the Son he entered and thus as Son in the realm from which he came. In 1 John 3:8 we cannot suppress the significance of the term 'manifest'. In usage elsewhere it points to the making known of what previously existed (cf. John 1:31; Rom. 16:26; 1 Cor. 4:5; 1 John 1:2). In 1 John 4:9, 10 the thought is similar to John 3:16. The magnitude of God's love is shown in the fact that he sent 'the only-begotten Son', an identity presupposed in the sending, and certifying for that reason the incomparable greatness of the Father's love.

These various considerations have to be taken into account not discretely but in their cumulative effect. When combined they constitute conclusive evidence that when Jesus Christ is conceived of as the only-begotten Son given by the Father, sent into the world, coming forth from the Father, and coming into the world, the Sonship predicated of him in these connections is the intrinsic and pre-temporal Sonship.

The evidence surveyed establishes the fact of intra-divine and eternal Sonship. But once this Sonship is recognized, its character as intrinsic, transcendent, and eternal requires the conclusion that in respect of the title 'Son' as predicated of our Lord it is this intra-divine identity that always has the priority. For that reason the title when applied to him can never be conceived of apart from the transcendent identity involved in it. This must be the case in the various respects in which the predication occurs.

As we think of the Father's own witness at the baptism and trans-figuration, it is not possible to think of the allocation, 'Thou art my beloved Son', or of the witness to others, 'This is my beloved Son' as asserting anything short of the transcendent filiation. And when we think of the quotation of Psalm 2:7 in Hebrews 1:5 (cf. 5:5), 'Thou art my Son', although the context is replete with messianic references and the latter part of verse 5 quotes 2 Samuel 7:14 which has distinctly messianic import, yet the allocations in terms of deity and of specifically divine activity in verses 8, 10 and 12, as well as the characterization in verse 3, 'the brightness of his glory and the express image of his being', carry such transcendent implications that the corresponding implica-tions of the title 'Son' cannot be suppressed in the allocation of verse 5 or in the designation of verses 2 and 8.

For the same reason, namely, that the transcendent Sonship is prior and basic, it would not be possible to think of it as absent in the case of our Lord's own self-designation. There are the instances in which the transcendent Sonship lies on the face of the text. This is notably con-spicuous in Matthew 11:27; Luke 10:22. When Jesus says that 'no one knows the Father but the Son' and institutes the parallel with the co-ordinate knowledge of the Father that 'no one knows the Son but the Father', he claims for himself an exclusive and intensive knowledge predictable only of deity. And the most significant consideration for our present interest is that it is in his identity as Son that he possesses this knowledge. The Sonship, therefore, is that in virtue of which he knows the Father as the Father knows him, and the intra-divine character of the Sonship belonging to him is no less patent than the intra-divine character of the Fatherhood pertaining to the Father. Scarcely less apparent in this respect is Matthew 28:19. The co-ordina-tion of Father, Son and Holy Spirit as conjointly participants of the one name and as conjointly the source of covenant blessing and the object of covenantal devotion requires that equivalence of divine dignity be accorded to each person. And so the title 'Son' must be construed as itself expressing the dignity that places him on an equality with the Father and the Holy Spirit. Only intra-divine Sonship possesses this quality.

The conclusiveness of these two passages and the fact that the intra-divine Sonship is always prior and basic in the title 'Son' compel us to suspect that in other passages in which our Lord identifies himself as the Son this same identity is in view. We think, for example, of John

17:1: 'Glorify thy Son, that the Son also may glorify thee', a suspicion confirmed by what we have found already as to the implications of verse 5. Again we think of John 5:23: 'That all may honour the Son, even as they honour the Father' (cf. also John 6:40; 8:35, 36; 14:13). It would not be possible, in terms of the worship and devotion involved, for our Lord to claim for himself honour comparable to that given to the Father if the title by which he denominates himself were not indicative of transcendent identity. We find the same to be true in the witness of others in the New Testament. If we revert to Peter's confession (Matt. 16:16), there are overwhelming reasons for regarding the expression 'Son of the living God' as super-messianic.[1] If we think of the confession of the Baptist (John 1:34) and of Nathanael (John 1:49), we cannot but conclude that the import of the heavenly witness at Jesus' baptism shaped the understanding of both John and Nathanael. With reference to Matthew 14:33 no lower conception than that entertained by Peter at Caesarea Philippi can reasonably be attributed to the exclamation elicited by the manifestation of Jesus' supernatural power: 'Truly of God thou art the Son'. In view of the well-established intra-divine import of the title in the circle of disciples going back to the Father's voice from heaven at Jordan and reiterated in the teaching of Jesus' himself, we cannot interpret Martha's confession (John 11:27) in lower terms. And when we examine the later apostolic use of the title 'Son of God', we find contextual indications that the same transcendent conception is entertained. In Romans 1:3–4 (cf. v. 9), we cannot regard Paul in this summary definition of the gospel as conceiving of Jesus' Sonship in any lower category than is apparent in Romans 8:3, 32; Galatians 4:4 (cf. Acts 9:20; Rom. 5:10). In 1 Corinthians 1:9 the call of the Father into the fellowship of his Son suggests, to say the least, that the grace is exhibited in the transcendent dignity of the person into whose fellowship the saints are called (cf. Gal. 1:16). In 1 John 1:3 the co-ordination of Father and Son indicates that the Sonship in view is correlative with the Fatherhood of the first person. In 1 John 3:23; 4:15; 5:5, 9, 10, 11, 12, surely the same conception of Sonship obtains as we found already in 1 John 3:8; 4:9, 10 (cf. 4:14; 5:20). These are but a selection from many instances (cf. Mark 1:1; 2 Cor. 1:19; Gal. 2:20; Eph. 4:13; Col. 1:13; Heb. 6:6; 10:29; 1 John 2:22–24; 2 John 3, 9).

To sum up then, the thesis is as follows. The eternal, intra-divine,

[1] Cf. G. Vos: *The Self-Disclosure of Jesus*, pp. 180–182.

ontological Sonship is primary and basic in the title 'Son' as predicated of our Lord. Since it is primary and basic the identity and relationship involved must be conceived of as primary and basic in the witness of the Father to Jesus' Sonship, in the witness of our Lord when he addresses God as Father or refers to him as the Father and designates himself as the Son, and in the witness of disciples and apostles when they identify him by this title. This is corroborated in numerous passages by the considerations, sometimes explicit and at other times implicit, which evince that the intra-divine relationship is contemplated.

Some observations relevant to the subject of Jesus' Sonship are necessary. First; the title 'Son of God' with its distinctly ontological import occurs in contexts in which our Lord's messianic office, commission, prerogative, and functions occupy a prominent place. In Matthew 11:27 (cf. Luke 10:22) – where, as we found, the ontological Sonship is distinctly in view as that which alone explains the knowledge claimed by Jesus – messianic investiture, function, and prerogative are clearly intimated; investiture in the words, 'all things have been delivered unto me by my Father', function in the words, 'he to whomsoever the Son willeth to reveal him', and prerogative in the words, 'come unto me'. Hence in respect of designation the ontological Father–Son relationship is distinctly in view when Messianic commitment and activity are the actions specified – it is the Father who commits and it is the Son who reveals. The same is true in Matthew 28:18, 19. The authority given in heaven and in earth is messianic commitment. But the Father–Son relationship, as found already, is intra-divine. In John 3:16, for the reasons adduced earlier, the Sonship contemplated in the giving is the ontological. But the giving is unto messianic undertaking and sacrifice (cf. 1 John 3:8; 4:9, 10). In Romans 1:3, 4 the being made of the seed of David according to the flesh and constituted the Son of God with power are messianic in character. But Jesus as the Son is conceived of in his intra-divine identity. Finally, no passage points up this observation more clearly than Matthew 16:16 in which we have the co-ordination of the two titles, 'the Christ' and 'the Son of the living God', the one overtly messianic and the other ontological (cf. also John 1:49; 11:27). We are thus provided with copious examples of identification in terms of ontological Sonship when messianic commitment and the corresponding implications are envisioned.

The second observation is that the transcendent identity involved in the title 'Son' serves to place in relief the humiliation involved in the messianic commission. This is patent in several notable instances (cf. John 3:16; 17:1, 4, 5; Rom. 8:3, 32; 1 John 4:9, 10). It is the transcendent dignity belonging to him as Son that demonstrates the inimitable depth of the humiliation and the greatness of the love that prompted it. Hence, so far from being incompatible with humiliation, his being conceived of as the eternal Son is indispensable to the proper understanding and assessment of the humiliation, and consonant with this consideration is his identification as transcendent Son in the context where humiliation is most in evidence. It would detract from the character of the humiliation to think of his Sonship on any lower plane than that belonging to him as the eternal Son.

The third observation concerns what is implicit in the humiliation, namely, limitation. As incarnate there are the limitations inseparable from human nature. But there were also limitations to which he was subject in terms of his commission. As in the case of humiliation we should expect that the dignity of his intrinsic Sonship would not be suppressed when these limitations are brought into the foreground, but rather that identification in terms of this Sonship would serve to accentuate the reality and meaning of these limitations. For it is only as limitations imposed upon the eternal Son and willingly assumed by him that we can properly assess their significance and purpose. A few examples from the witness of the Gospels may here be adduced. Restriction in subservience to the Father's will is apparent in the agonizing prayers in Gethsemane (Matt. 26:39, 42; Mark 14:36, 39; Luke 22:42, 44). But in addressing the Father as 'my Father' or 'abba, Father' it is impossible to exclude the intra–divine filial relation from the scope of his conscience. The same holds true in a later episode in Gethsemane when he said: 'Thinkest thou that I cannot appeal to my Father, and he will now provide me with more than twelve legions of angels?' (Matt. 26:53; cf. John 12:27).

It is necessary in this connection to discuss those passages in which dependence upon and subordination to the Father are asserted when at the same time our Lord identifies himself as Son (cf. Matt. 24:36; Mark 13:32; John 5:19, 20, 26). Correlative with these are other passages in which Jesus speaks of the Father and his own filial relation is implied (cf. John 6:57; 10:17, 18; 12:49; 14:28, 31; 15:10). It is apparent that it is in respect of his messianic identity, office and commission that this dependence on and subordination to the Father obtain. It is easy to assume, therefore, that the Sonship in view in these instances cannot be the intrinsic and ontological Sonship but the messianic. It is this assumption that I call in question. As we found in other cases, we must distinguish between the distinctly messianic predications and the identifying designation. To speak in theological terms, the person may be identified in terms of what he is as divine when what is predicated of him is true only in virtue of what he is as human. Hence even in such an instance as Matthew 24:36 (Mark 13:32) the not knowing the day or the hour of his coming is a not knowing that can be applied to him only within the sphere of his messianic cognition. But it by no means follows that the title 'Son' by which he identifies himself is to be construed as messianic. In John 5:26 giving of life on the part of the Father must be regarded as communication to him in his dependent, messianic relation to the Father; in other words, communication that is economical. But Jesus' self-designation as the Son need not be interpreted as the Messianic Son. Or, to take one other example, when Jesus says, 'the Son can do nothing of himself, but what he sees the Father doing' (John 5:19), we have his complete messianic dependence in the realm of doing, a dependence integral to messianic commission, but nevertheless a dependence which in no way suspends his intra-divine identity and equality as the Son. And so it is consonant with and appropriate to all that belongs to the mystery of his person and commission that he should designate himself in terms of his intrinsic and transcendent Sonship.

In all of this, as it concerns our Lord's messianic dependence and subordination, we can discern again that it is only in the perspective of the dignity that belongs to him as the intra-divine Son that we can properly assess the messianic subordination. And we should, therefore, have no difficulty in finding the intrinsic Sonship in immediate conjunction with the most notable acknowledgements of messianic dependence. In Hebrews 5:8, 9, I think we have an enlightening corroboration. The learning obedience from the things he suffered and being made perfect as the author of salvation are distinctly messianic and could apply to him only in that capacity. The concessive clause, 'Son though he was', envisions the contrast between his identity as the Son and the necessity of learning obedience. The thought of his transcendent Sonship is required in order to give adequate force to this contrast. For if we give to the title 'Son' no more than messianic reference the contrast is deprived of the very consideration that makes it valid, namely, the discrepancy between what he was intrinsically and the conditions belonging to his messianic commission.

The thesis I am propounding, or at least proposing for serious consideration is, therefore, that in numerous instances where the title 'Son' might readily be interpreted as signifying messianic Sonship, and has been thus interpreted, there is not sufficient warrant for this interpretation and in several of these instances the considerations preponderate in favour of the conclusion that it is the ontological Sonship that is denoted by the title 'Son'.

There are a few passages in which, admittedly, it would seem necessary to conceive of the Sonship messianically. There is Hebrews 1:5b, 'I will be to him a Father, and he will be to me a Son'. This quotation is from 2 Samuel 7:14, which applied in the first instance to Solomon as the type of the greater King to come 'upon the throne of David and upon his kingdom to order it, and to establish it with judgment and with justice' (Isa. 9:7; cf. Luke 1:32, 33). Since transcendent Sonship did not belong to Solomon, it may seem necessary to regard the Sonship predicated of Christ in this instance as the extension and perfection of that which applied to Solomon, and therefore Sonship on the level of appointment and investiture as distinct from what is intrinsic and ontological. But even here the plausible is not conclusive. We must keep in mind that in typology the ultimate fulfilment or realization far transcends what pertained to the type. This is true of personal as well as of non-personal types. Even on the economic plane Christ far surpassed what was true of Solomon. Messianic Sonship did not apply to him. Hence, as pertaining to Christ, the transcendent plus that obtains may be carried a step farther and conceived of in terms of what is ontological and transcendent. Besides, we must remember that in redemptive typology the ultimate and perfect realization, what is sometimes called the antitype, is in idea and design antecedent to the type. The type or pattern, though historically prior, has validity and meaning only because of the ultimate realization in Christ. A good example is Matthew 2:15: 'Out of Egypt have I called my son'. In Hosea 11:1 (cf. Numb. 24:8) this refers to the emancipation of Israel from Egypt. But in the New Testament it is referred to Christ, and properly so because the deliverance of Israel found its basis and reason in what was fulfilled in Christ, and in this respect the calling of Christ out of Egypt has primacy. In other words, the type is derived from the antitype and not *vice versa*. So with Solomon and 2 Samuel 7:14

(cf. 1 Chron. 23:9, 10) Solomon's sonship is secondary and the significance is altogether dependent upon what is archetypal, transcendent, and heavenly. When Hebrews 1:5b and its counterpart in the Old Testament is viewed in this perspective, not only is the intra-divine Sonship of Christ allowable as the Sonship contemplated, but this Sonship is most appropriate as that which points up the transcendent character of him in whom 2 Samuel 7:14 is realized to perfection.

Similar conclusions apply to Hebrews 5:5, when the writer quotes Psalm 2:7 in connection with Christ's investiture with the high priestly office. The latter is, of course, messianic. But the purpose of the quotation, 'Thou art my Son, today I have begotten thee', is to identify the Father as the one who called and appointed him to the office of high priest. In the allocation 'Thou art my Son' it is not possible to exclude the intra-divine relationship which has primacy in the title 'Son' and appears in so many other instances with this import. If it should be necessary for exegetical reasons to find in the quotation not only identification of the persons involved, namely, Father and Son, but also reference to the act of investiture, this can not only be found in the second clause, 'Today I have begotten thee', but the same is most reasonably interpreted in that way (cf. Acts 13:33, 34). So, again, there is not sufficient warrant for discovering messianic Sonship and, since it is necessary to find intra-divine Sonship, we cannot insist that the address 'Thou art my Son' comprises more than the intra-divine identity denoted by the title 'Son'.

The thesis propounded is not that there are no occasions in which Sonship in messianic terms appears in the Scripture. There are instances in which I am not prepared to argue otherwise (cf. 1 Cor. 15:28; Heb. 3:6). Furthermore, in Luke 1:35 Sonship would appear to be predicated of Jesus in virtue of his supernatural begetting by the Holy Spirit and has been called his nativistic Sonship. The thesis is that the intra-divine Sonship is preponderant in the New Testament, and that a goodly number of instances in which messianic Sonship has been regarded as evident do not necessarily have this reference, but, instead, lend themselves readily to the interpretation submitted in the foregoing discussion. The result is of theological and practical significance. As we shall see presently the title 'Son' is charged with deity and it is that import that gives character to the confession of Jesus as the Son of God. The title 'Son' is far too liable to convey to our minds the thought of derivation, and with that the idea of his being secondary and subordinate in his intrinsic being and station. This liability arises because our thinking is not framed by the biblical concept of Jesus' Sonship but by transference to his Sonship of notions belonging to sonship as it obtains among men.

In John 5:17–31 we have events recorded, and sayings of Jesus, which provide explicit witness to the import of Jesus' Sonship. The pivot of the passage is the charge that 'not only was he breaking the sabbath but also calling God his own Father, making himself equal with God' (v. 18). This charge was based upon Jesus' own statement in defence of his healing on the sabbath day: 'My Father is working until now and I am working' (v. 17).

It might seem to us unreasonable to infer from Jesus' filial claim that he was thereby making himself equal with God. Was it not the teaching of the Old Testament that Israel sustained a filial relation to God and God a fatherly relation to Israel (cf. Exod. 4:22, 23; Deut. 14:1, 2; 32:5, 6, 20; Is. 43:6; cf. 1:2; 63:16; Hosea 11:1; Mal. 1:6; 2:10; Rom. 9:4)? The answer resides in the possessive 'My Father' and in the co-ordination of his own working with that of the Father. The possessive in the words of Jesus must be construed as implying the uniqueness expressed by the term 'his own Father' in the corresponding allegation on the part of the Jews (cf. Rom. 8:3, 32). And what the Jews considered to be the blasphemy of calling God his own Father was in their esteem aggravated by placing his own working in the same category as that of the Father. The all-important consideration is that in the ensuing discourse Jesus proceeds to reassert and confirm the two elements of the statement that aroused the resentment of the Jews and gave ground for their charge that he made himself equal with God. He proceeds to speak in the most sustained way of the Father–Son relationship (vv. 19, 20, 21, 22, 23, 25, 26). He unfolds in detail the co-ordination of his own working and that of the Father (vv. 19, 20, 21, 23, 26, 30). In the midst of this he makes the stupendous claim that, because of investiture with the prerogative of judgment, all men should honour the Son as they honour the Father (v. 23) – a claim to equality in respect of worship, and one which would be blasphemy on any other assumption than the inference the Jews derived from his original statement. Jesus did not deny the inference but rather vindicated the implications which the Jews properly discovered in Jesus' words.

This incident shows that in Jewish conception to claim to be the Son of God was tantamount to a claim to be equal with God (cf. John 19:7). This inference Jesus himself did not controvert or deny. On the contrary he adduced the prerogatives possessed and exercised by himself, prerogatives of such a character as God alone could possess and discharge.

To the same effect is John 10:28–39. The pivot in this instance, as in John 5:17–31, is the charge of the Jews: 'For a good work we stone thee not, but for blasphemy, and that thou being a man makest thyself God' (v. 33). The preceding context is similar to what we find in John 5:17. Jesus repeatedly spoke of God as his Father (vv. 25, 29) and of his oneness with the Father (v. 30), a oneness which in terms of verse 38 must be interpreted as the unity of reciprocal or mutual indwelling – 'the Father is in me and I am in the Father'. From the preceding context and from Jesus' question, 'Do ye say, Thou blasphemest, because I said, I am the Son of God?' (v. 36), we must conclude that it was his claim to be the Son of God that gave ground for the charge that he made himself God (v. 33). The line of thought is the same as in John 5:17, 18 with the variation that in this case the charge is that he made himself God, rather, than making himself equal with God. It is admittedly difficult to determine the precise character of Jesus' argument drawn from Psalm 82:6. It is not necessary for the present to discuss the question. It is sufficient to observe that Jesus defended himself against the charge of blasphemy and did not contest the inference which the Jews derived from his claim to divine Sonship.

These two passages illumine for us the basic import of the title 'Son of God'. It is the index to his transcendent deity. It is this that explains and validates the central place accorded to his Sonship in the confession of faith. It is because it connotes deity in being, station, and prerogative that the accent falls in the total witness of the New Testament on the Sonship as intrinsic, intra-divine, and eternal. For it is only an intrinsic Sonship that could constitute equality and identity with God. It is John again who at the conclusion of his First Epistle draws our attention to this correlation and coordination: 'We know that the Son of God is come, and hath given us an understanding, that we may know him that is true: and we are in him that is true, in his Son Jesus Christ. This is the true God and eternal life' (1 John 5:20). Here is the precipitate of the total witness of the New Testament.

There is, however, another implication for the faith and confession of Jesus as the Son of God. It is that faith in him as the Son of God involves more than the faith of Jesus. If faith is directed to him in his specific identity as Son of God, this identity is meaningless except as he of whom he is the Son comes within the compass of faith. This is but to say that the faith of Jesus implies the faith of the Father. Far be it from me to underestimate the truly Christological in the faith and confession of Jesus and the centrality of the Christological in biblical revelation. But I am convinced that a great deal of the emphasis upon the Christological in the theology of the present-day is gravely prejudicial to what is implicit in the confession of Jesus as the Son of God. In other words this is to say that the faith of Jesus with its corresponding confession that is not conditioned by the faith of God as trinity, and by the intra-divine and intrinsic relations involved in Jesus' identity as the eternal Son, does not provide the Christology the biblical revelation demands. The true Christology is one that has its starting point and finds its basis in Christ's intrinsic Sonship and therefore in its trinitarian correlatives. 'Every one who denies the Son, the same hath not the Father: he that acknowledges the Son hath the Father also' (1 John 2:23).

A third consideration is that the faith of Jesus is faith in him as the sent of the Father in his identity as the Son. Faith and confession may never be abstracted from the economy of salvation and this economy is the economy of intertrinitarian operation and cooperation. Faith in Jesus is faith in him as the sent of the Father and therefore is also faith in the Father as the one sending. It is our Lord himself who taught us: 'Verily, verily I say to you, he who hears my word and believes on him who sent me hath everlasting life' (John 5:24); 'Jesus cried and said, He that believes in me does not believe in me but in him who sent me, and he who sees me sees him who sent me' (John 12:44, 45); 'The words which thou gavest me I have given them, and they have received them and have known truly that I came out from thee, and they have believed that thou didst send me' (John 17:8).

As we think of the climactic demand of Jesus' commission, obedience unto death even the death of the cross, what is here brought into focus is the sending by the Father of the only-begotten and beloved Son in the identity that is intrinsically his as the Son for all that was entailed in the agony of Gethsemane and the abandonment of Calvary. The Son came. Let us not forget it. But he came because he was sent. Jesus laid down his life. Let us not forget it. But he did so in pursuance of the Father's commandment. What our Lord's words teach us to ponder is the marvel of the Father's love, the marvel before which we become lost in intelligent and holy wonderment. And his words remind us that to believe that the Father sent the Son is an indispensable ingredient of faith.

5

Who Raised Up Jesus?[1]

THE cardinal position the resurrection of Christ occupies in the Christian Faith cannot be more forcefully expressed than in the words of the Apostle, 'If Christ hath not been raised, your faith is vain; ye are yet in your sins' (1 Cor. 15:17). But who raised up Jesus?

The answer to this question appears so obviously in the New Testament that it might seem superfluous labour to devote any space to elaboration of it. For surely it was God who raised Jesus from the dead. But to leave the answer, thus simply and truly stated, without further analysis or enquiry, is to miss the richness and fulness of meaning that resides in the question. When we say that God raised our Lord from the dead we must remember that our conception of God is trinitarian, and so there are inherent in the question additional questions. When we say God raised Jesus, are we using the name God in the more absolute and indefinite sense of the Godhead, or are we using the name more specifically of the Father or of the Son or of the Holy Spirit? Since the Father is God and the Son is God and the Holy Spirit is God, and since the Father, the Son and the Spirit are distinct persons, it instantly becomes apparent that the simple answer, 'God raised Jesus from the dead', does not of itself answer these further questions. It is, therefore, to the question more specifically asked that we now address ourselves.

The preponderant usage of the New Testament is that Jesus *was raised* from the dead. That is just saying that in the resurrection Jesus is represented as having been the *subject* of an act of divine and omnipotent power. The two verbs most frequently used in this connection

[1] This chapter first appeared in *The Westminster Theological Journal*, Vol. III, 1, 1941.

are ἐγείρω and ἀνίστημι. Both verbs are used actively. In the case of ἐγείρω the usage is well illustrated by two passages in the Acts of the Apostles – ὃν ὁ Θεὸς ἤγειρεν ἐκ νεκρῶν (Acts 4:10), ὁ Θεὸς τῶν πατέρων ἡμῶν ἤγειρεν Ἰησοῦν (Acts 5:30). God raised Jesus. Likewise in the case of ἀνίστημι this usage is also well illustrated in the following passages – ὃν ὁ Θεὸς ἀνέστησεν λύσας τὰς ὠδῖνας τοῦ θανάτου (Acts 2:24), τοῦτον τὸν Ἰησοῦν ἀνέστησεν ὁ Θεός (Acts 2:32; cf. Acts 13:33, 34; 17:31).

When we ask the question as to the identity of the name ὁ Θεός in such passages, we are inevitably constrained under the direction of such passages as Romans 8:11, Galatians 1:1 and Ephesians 1:20 to regard the ὁ Θεός as the personal name of the Father. In Romans 8:11 Paul says, 'But if the Spirit of him that raised up Jesus from the dead dwell in you, he that raised up Christ Jesus from the dead shall also quicken your mortal bodies through his Spirit that dwelleth in you.' Here it cannot be doubted but the primary agent in the resurrection of Jesus is stated to be the person of the Godhead who is distinguished both from Christ Jesus and the Spirit, namely, the Father. In Galatians 1:1 the reference to the Father is direct, 'Paul an apostle, not from men nor through man, but through Jesus Christ, and God the Father who raised him from the dead'. In Ephesians 1:20 the subject of the action expressed in the clause, 'when he raised him from the dead', is given in verse 17, 'the God of our Lord Jesus Christ, the Father of glory'. With these might readily be co-ordinated Romans 6:4, 'As Christ was raised from the dead through the glory of the Father', though the aorist passive here (ἠγέρθη), as we shall see later on, may be rendered 'rose' as well as 'was raised'.

There can, then, be no question but that the Father as the first person of the Trinity is represented as the agent in the resurrection of Christ. The Father is the agent and Christ is the subject – God the Father, by the exceeding greatness of his power, raised up his Son Jesus.

When ἐγείρω is used with reference to the resurrection of Christ in the passive voice the problem of the agency contemplated is more complicated. This difficulty proceeds from the fact that the passive of ἐγείρω may be rendered as the passive of the transitive verb 'to raise', or it may express the intransitive verb 'to rise' or 'to arise'.

In the active voice ἐγείρω, with the exception of the present active imperative (ἔγειρε), appears to be uniformly used transitively, and so, when applied to the resurrection of Christ, always bears the meaning 'raise'. In every instance of the occurrence of the active voice except

John 2:19, 20, to which we shall presently allude, Jesus is the object and not the subject of the verb.

When, however, we turn to the passive of ἐγείρω, the case is very different. Here the intransitive meaning of the verb comes into distinct prominence. It must not, of course, be supposed that the transitive meaning disappears. In Matthew 11:5 – καὶ νεκροὶ ἐγείρονται, Luke 7:22 – νεκροὶ ἐγείρονται and Luke 20:37 – ἐγείρονται, οἱ νεκροί[1] (cf., also, 1 Cor. 15:15, 16, 29, 32, 35, 42, 43, 44, 52), the rendering 'raise' is surely distinctly to be preferred to the rendering 'rise', even though the latter is not impossible grammatically. When we come to the usage as it respects the resurrection of Christ, it would appear that the transitive meaning 'raise' is, to say the very least, distinctly possibly in the following passages: Romans 4:25; 6:4, 9; 7:4; 8:34; 1 Corinthians 15:4, 12, 13, 14, 16, 17, 20. It would admittedly be very difficult to decide with any conclusiveness which would be the preferable rendering in some of these cases. But the context would in some of them distinctly favour the rendering of our English transitive passive. In some of the cases just cited, on the other hand, it may very well be that the intransitive verb 'rise' or 'arise' is less awkward and therefore more felicitous and accurate.

There are other cases, however, where the preponderant usage of the New Testament in the use of the passive of ἐγείρω appears entirely natural and preferable. That the preponderant, if not uniform, meaning of the passive of ἐγείρω in non-resurrection passages is the intransitive, the most cursory examination of the numerous instances will disclose. Citation of examples would be quite superfluous. This usage in non-resurrection passages would naturally create a strong presumption for the same intransitive force in strictly resurrection passages, whether it be the resurrection of Jesus or of others. While for the reasons given already it would not be feasible to apply this force of the passive universally (for there are those passages where the transitive force must be allowed and indeed preferred), yet in many cases which directly refer to the resurrection, mostly, of course, to that of Jesus, but, in a few cases to that of others, the intransitive force is the distinctly natural. In Matthew 8:15 the ἠγέρθη does not refer to the resurrection of Peter's wife's

---

[1] ἐγείρονται, so far as form is concerned, might be present indicative middle. In such a case it would be intransitive. The reasons for regarding it as present indicative passive need not now be argued. Neither is it necessary in this article to discuss the use of the middle of ἐγείρω.

mother, for she had not died. But there is rather close similarity in that Jesus performed a miracle. The ἠγέρθη obviously does not mean 'was raised', but, parallel to the idea of the other co-ordinate verb (διηκόνει), means 'arose'. In Matthew 9:25 we have the raising of the damsel – καὶ ἠγέρθη τὸ κοράσιον. Surely, the obvious meaning is, 'And the damsel arose' rather than, 'And the damsel was raised' (cf. Matt. 14:2; Mark 6:14, 16; Luke 9:7). In Luke 7:14 when Jesus says, Νεανίσκε, σοὶ λέγω, ἐγέρθητι, again the natural rendering is 'arise' rather than 'be raised'. It is apparent, then, that in the usage as it bears upon the resurrection of Christ it becomes distinctly possible to adopt this intransitive rendering. In the judgment of the present writer this rendering is to be preferred in certain passages. The following will serve as examples: Matthew 27:63, 64; 28:6, 7; Mark 14:28; 16:6; Luke 24:6, 34; John 21:14; 2 Cor. 5:15; 2 Tim. 2:8. It would, at least, require rather artificial handling of a goodly number of these examples to try to impose the transitive rendering upon them. Consequently, in view of the preponderant meaning of the passive of ἐγείρω in non-resurrection usage, and in view of the same meaning as the natural and preferable one in several passages that deal directly with the resurrection of Jesus, we have to conclude that the mere use of the passive of ἐγείρω does not of itself imply that Jesus in his resurrection is viewed as the subject of action by another. So there is the distinct possibility that even in passages where the passive of ἐγείρω is used, Jesus' own activity in his resurrection is contemplated or expressed.

To *insist*, however, that there is reflection upon the agency of Christ in his own resurrection, in such usage as we have now been discussing, is not warranted. The mere fact that the same intransitive use of ἐγείρω appears in connection with the resurrection of others, who could not have been resurrected by the exercise of their own agency or power, prevents us from any such insistence. All we can say is that the possibility of Jesus' own agency is present, and that the mere use of the passive must not be taken as excluding the exercise of his own agency.

With respect to the verb ἀνίστημι the question is in several respects similar to that which we have just found in the case of ἐγείρω. The verb ἀνίστημι is also used both transitively and intransitively. It is used with reference to the resurrection of Christ in the following passages: transitively in the active voice – Acts 2:24, 32; 13:32, 34; 17:31,[1]

[1] In Acts 3:26 it might possibly be argued that there is reference to the resurrection. The present writer does not, however, think so. In Acts 13:32 it might be argued that

intransitively – Mark 8:31; 9:9, 10, 31; 10:34; Luke 18:33; 24:7, 46; John 20:9; Acts 10:41; 17:3; 1 Thessalonians 4:14. There are a few other cases where there are variant readings. But even if, in these few cases, we adopted the variant which reads ἀνίστημι, there would be no change in the facts, so far as our present enquiry is concerned. It will be noted that in all five cases where the transitive meaning appears, God is said to be the agent and Christ the subject of the resurrection. In each case Christ is the object of the verb. In the instances of intransitive use, it will be noted that, except in Mark 9:10, Jesus is in every case the subject of the clause. The four parts of the verb used are ἀναστῆναι (second aorist infinitive), ἀναστήσεται (future middle), ἀναστῇ (second aorist subjunctive active) and ἀνέστη (second aorist indicative active), in all of which cases ἀνίστημι is used in the intransitive sense 'to rise' or 'to arise'.

Now, as we already found in the case of the intransitive use of ἐγείρω, this intransitive use of ἀνίστημι may denote the activity of Jesus himself. The usage in other cases clearly establishes this as a distinct possibility in the use of ἀνίστημι as it applies to Jesus' resurrection. In some instances the present writer is disposed to think that this is the probable meaning, that is to say, that the activity of Jesus is distinctly contemplated. But again insistence on such an import is impossible, for the simple reason that the very same parts of the verb are used in the case of the resurrection of others who could not have risen by the exercise of their own agency or power, as, for example, Mark 5:42; Luke 16:31; John 11:23, 24; Acts 9:40; Ephesians 5:14; 1 Thessalonians 4:16.[1]

We have found, then, that the resurrection of Christ is distinctly referred to the agency of the Father, that Jesus is repeatedly represented as being the subject of resurrection power exerted upon him. We have also found that, while, in the intransitive use of the passive of ἐγείρω

---

the reference is not to the resurrection but to the incarnation. The context and particularly the sequence in relation to verse 34, where allusion to the resurrection is explicit, lead the writer to conclude that ἀνίστημι in verse 32 also refers to the resurrection. In Mark 14:58 ἀναστήσω rather than οἰκοδομήσω occurs in some manuscripts. But if we should even read ἀναστήσω here we should not be justified in basing much argument upon it. All the truth that underlies this statement of the false witnesses is embraced in John 2:19-22, which will be discussed later.

[1] ζάω is used of Christ's resurrection in Romans 14:9, and ζωοποιέω may have reference to the resurrection in 1 Peter 3:18. But nothing determinative regarding our present enquiry can be elicited from these passages.

and in the intransitive use of ἀνίστημι there is the distinct possibility, in some instances perhaps probability, that Jesus is regarded as active in his own resurrection, yet there is no conclusive evidence that there is allusion to the activity of Jesus in these cases of the use of either of these two verbs. The question then remains: Is there any support for the position that Jesus rose from the dead by the exercise of his own power? Or, in other words, are we justified in believing that Jesus was active in his own resurrection? To that question the answer is emphatically in the affirmative.[1]

There are two explicit statements to this effect from the lips of our Lord himself, recorded for us by John. They are John 2:19–22 and John 10:17, 18. These two passages, since they are explicit, afford us strong presumption in favour of regarding other passages, to which we have already referred but which are not in themselves conclusive, as reflecting on the activity of Jesus himself in his resurrection.

In the former passage Jesus says, 'Destroy this temple and in three days I will raise it' (ἐγερῶ αὐτόν). John's comment is to the effect that, 'He spake of the temple of his body' (περί τοῦ ναοῦ τοῦ σώματος αὐτοῦ) and that, 'When he was risen from the dead, his disciples remembered that he spake this, and they believed the scripture and the word that Jesus had spoken.' (It is probably to this occasion that we have allusion in Mark 14:58.) The directness of Jesus' claim and the obvious allusion to the resurrection cannot be doubted. This passage takes on the added significance that it was at the earliest stage of his earthly ministry that this disclosure was made, and so it witnesses to the fact that Jesus from the outset of his ministry was aware of his death and of his possession of that transcendent power by which he would in his own case break the bonds of death and raise from the dead the temple of his body.

The second passage, that of John 10:17, 18, bears features that are altogether unique. It contains not only the information that Jesus was active in his resurrection but also the most pregnant disclosure of the relation that that act of his own power and authority bore to his Messianic death and mission. To the analysis of its teaching we shall now proceed.

(i) Jesus says, 'I lay down my life, in order that I may take it again'. Here we are apprised of a relationship that exists between his death and resurrection that too often escapes our attention. It is that the

---

[1] There is, no doubt, the agency of the Holy Spirit in the resurrection of Christ. But discussion of that subject would require the treatment of a distinct line of evidence.

laying down of his life was to the end that he might take it again, that his death was to the end of his resurrection. We are, no doubt, quite familiar with the fact that the resurrection of Jesus was the *actual* sequel to his death. We are, no doubt, familiar with the fact that the resurrection was the *necessary* sequel to his death – God raised him up, having loosed the pains of death, because it was not possible that he should be holden of it. And perhaps we are also familiar with the truth that the resurrection is the *vindicatory* sequel to his death – God the Father glorified his servant Jesus in that he raised him from the dead and thus gave open demonstration to his righteousness. But on the truth here enunciated, that he died *in order that* he might rise again, our minds do not so familiarly dwell. And by it we should be reminded of the following facts.

(a) The death of Christ is not an end in itself. It is subordinate to a great purpose that can be achieved only through resurrection.

(b) The death and resurrection of Christ must never be separated; they are not only factually inseparable, they are causally inseparable. They stand related in such a way that they must together be regarded as the conjoint sources of our redemption.

(c) To be a Saviour, Christ had to pass through resurrection. It was an integral part of the experience and task assigned to him in the economy of redemption. The resurrection power exercised by the Father in the raising of Jesus, and the resurrection power with which, in virtue of that fact, Jesus is endowed are necessary facts in the plan of salvation. But if so, there needed to be death. For without death resurrection has neither existence nor meaning.

Our minds more commonly and quite properly move in a somewhat reverse direction, namely, that the resurrection was necessary in order to give meaning and efficacy to the redemptive fact of Jesus' death. In other words, the resurrection was the indispensable sequel to the redemptive efficacy wrought and secured by his vicarious death. But fulness of interpretation and of statement requires that our minds move in the direction of appreciating that the resurrection is also a redemptive fact. And so Jesus laid down his life in order that he might take it again. It is an impoverished doctrine of the resurrection that fails to take cognisance of this truth.

(ii) Jesus says, 'This commandment have I received from my Father'. The laying down of his life in order that he might take it again was wrought in pursuance of the Father's commandment. The commandment to which Jesus refers cannot be restricted to the laying down of his life nor to the taking of it again. It covers both, and that in the causal relationship which they are stated to sustain to each other.

But what we are particularly interested in now is that the very resurrection of Jesus by the exercise of his own power is an act of obedience to the Father. It is this aspect of Jesus' teaching in this passage that is too infrequently noted or appreciated. The expression of Paul in Philippians 2:8, 'obedient unto death', might seem to intimate that Jesus' death was the terminus of his obedience. This is, however, a mistaken exegesis. This phrase in Paul does not mean simply that Jesus was obedient up to the time of his death. It points rather to the extent or intensiveness of his obedience. He was obedient even to the extent of giving his life in death. His death was the supreme act or consummate manifestation of his obedience. But while it is intended to show the extent to which his obedience led him, we are not by any means required or allowed to regard the obedience that he rendered as the Messiah as having terminated with his death on the cross. It must not be interpreted in a way that will exclude, or do prejudice to, what Jesus says in our text, namely, that the exercise of his authority, executed in pursuance of the Father's commandment, extends even to the raising of himself from the dead. For Jesus says not only, 'Therefore doth my Father love me, because I lay down my life in order that I may take it again', but he also says, 'This commandment have I received of my Father'.

(iii) Jesus says, 'I have authority to lay it down, and I have authority to take it again'. As in John 5:27 and 17:2, surely the 'authority' of which Jesus here speaks is the Messianic authority that is committed to him in terms of the economy of redemption. If this is so, then it was in the exercise of power and authority bestowed upon him as the God-man, to the end and in the exercise of his Messianic task, that he raised himself from the dead. Truly it was only as divine that he could assume the Messianic task, it was only as divine that he could be invested with the correspondent authority, and truly it was divine power alone that could accomplish resurrection. But it was divine power strictly bestowed and strictly exercised in his Messianic capacity as the God-man.

We must not then regard the Messianic office or functions as suspended during the period of death and burial. Though dead, he was still the God-man Messiah, and it was in the exercise of such an office that he broke the bands of death and took his life again. The Messianic authority that he exercised during the period of death and in the act of resurrection was indeed affected and determined by the fact that he had died. The reality of death determined the conditions under which that authority was to be exercised and the very ends contemplated in the exercise of it, yet it was truly Messianic power, and Messianic power exercised, let it be remembered, in the accomplishment of no less a part of his redemptive work than that of resurrection from the dead. It was precisely that transcendent miracle that was wrought by his own authority.

(iv) Jesus says, 'Therefore doth my Father love me, because I lay down my life that I may take it again'. Our attention is hereby drawn to a striking example of trinitarian concurrence in the economy of redemption. We are perhaps surprised to find the laying down of his life and the taking of it again stated to be the ground upon which, or reason for which, the Father loves him. For is not the Son the object of an infinite and unchangeable love by reason of the eternal and intra-divine relation as the Only-begotten? Can anything that the Son does in time be a reason for the outflow of the Father's love?

While there is an outflow of eternal love that can never be spoken of as grounded in, or caused by, the work that Christ performed as Messiah, and therefore a love that can receive no increase from, nor find any condition in, any *ad extra* relation, yet this text points us to those new relations that the persons of the Godhead come to sustain the one to the other in the economy of redemption, relations which do not by any means obtain in the eternal and immanent relations of the persons to one another. The particular aspect of these economical relations stated here is that of the outflow of the love of the Father to the Son on the basis of the Son's discharge of the Messianic task. In all its infinitude and immutability, and to the full attainment of its satis-faction, a satisfaction that must be realized if the economy of redemp-tion is to achieve its purpose, the love of the Father comes to rest upon the Son, because he, the Son, lays down his life in order that he may take it again.

The leading thought, we must again remind ourselves, is the resur-rection of Jesus. And so we are compelled to appreciate the truth, the truth upon which our minds are not perhaps accustomed to dwell, that the resurrection from the dead by the agency of Christ himself in the exercise of the authority given to him as the Messiah, is the ground of the Father's love with reference to the Son.

We found at the outset of our study that the Father raised up Jesus. It was the *vindication* accorded to Jesus by the Father. It was the proof that the Father's love found full satisfaction in the redeeming work of Christ. It was the *seal* that the Father's eternal purpose of love with respect to men had been realized in their redemption through Jesus' blood. But that same resurrection was also the reason or ground of the Father's love. Here we have an example of that convergence or concurrence whereby the manifold wisdom of God is revealed and commended, and there is opened to us an avenue by which we may gain some added insight into the Apostle's word, 'That in the ages to come he might shew forth the exceeding riches of his grace in lovingkindness to us in Christ Jesus' (Eph. 2:7).

6

The Reconciliation[1]

THE term 'reconciliation' occurs in the New Testament four times (Rom. 5:11; 11:15; 2 Cor. 5:18, 19).[2] In Romans 5 and 2 Corinthians 5 it obviously refers to that which is spoken of in the contexts by means of the corresponding verb 'reconcile' (Rom. 5:10; 2 Cor. 5:18, 19, 20).[3] The verb used by Paul in other passages (Eph. 2:16; Col. 1:20, 22) is to the same effect though the form is slightly different.[4] In speaking of 'the reconciliation', therefore, we must take into account that which is denoted by both substantive and verb in the usage of the New Testament. The term, thus understood and applied, may be used actively or passively according as we think of the act of reconciling or of the status resulting from the accomplished action. When Paul says: 'God was in Christ reconciling the world to himself' (2 Cor. 5:19), he refers to the action or process involved (cf. Rom. 5:10). When he says: 'we have received the reconciliation' (Rom. 5:11), what is particularly in view is the relation established and bestowed in virtue of the reconciling action. These observations respecting the active and passive denotations, though necessary and helpful, do not resolve the questions that arise respecting what is involved in the reconciling action or in the resulting status and, more specifically, the questions pertaining to the relation of the objective, once-for-all action to the application and subjective realization of that which was once for all wrought in the death of Christ. It would be over-simplification to say, for example, that when the verb is used in terms of action, it refers exclusively to the historical,

[1] This chapter was first printed in *The Westminster Theological Journal*, Vol. XXIX, 1, 1966.
[2] The term is καταλλαγή.
[3] καταλλάσσω.
[4] ἀποκαταλλάσσω.

finished accomplishment wrought through the cross of Christ, even though there can be no doubt that this finished work is frequently in the forefront in such instances.

One of the questions that arises in connection with the biblical teaching is the scope or extent of the reconciliation. This question applies to the debate respecting limited or unlimited atonement, particular or universal redemption. But it is not restricted to the intent of the reconciliation in reference to mankind. One text is sufficient to remind us that the reconciliation may have much broader proportions. In Paul's word again we read: 'it pleased the Father that in him [Christ] all the fulness should dwell and through him to reconcile all things unto himself . . . through him whether they be things upon the earth or things in the heavens' (Col. 1:19, 20). The more inclusive scope of the 'all things' reconciled is suggested, to say the least, by the additional specification, 'the things upon the earth' and 'the things in the heavens'. Furthermore, in the preceding context the scope of these 'things' is indicated by the extent of Christ's agency in creation and providence and by the pre-eminence that belongs to him in the economy of redemption. 'By him were all things created in the heavens and upon the earth, the visible and the invisible' (v. 16). 'And he is before all things and in him all things consist' (v. 17). He 'is the beginning, the firstbegotten from the dead, in order that in all things he might be pre-eminent' (v. 18). It is with this perspective that the apostle proceeds forthwith to speak of God's reconciling action through Christ. And since this action embraces 'all things . . . whether they be things upon the earth or the things in the heavens' (v. 20), we could scarcely think of these 'things' as less inclusive than the 'all things in the heavens and upon the earth' referred to in verse 16 as the things created by Christ. We are compelled to ask: how can the cosmos be conceived of as the object of the reconciliation?

No one passage in Scripture throws light on this subject more than Romans 8:18-23. When Paul here speaks of 'the creation' (vv. 19, 20, 21) and 'the whole creation' (v. 22), he is using the term in the cosmic sense. It is obvious, however, that not all of created reality is included. There is delimitation by the terms of the passage itself.[1] It is of non-rational creation, animate and inanimate, that the apostle speaks. Thus the material heavens and earth are one day to be 'delivered from the

---

[1] Cf. *The Epistle to the Romans* (Grand Rapids, 1959), Vol. I, pp. 301 f., by the present writer.

bondage of corruption into the liberty of the glory of the children of God' (v. 21). It is of the same prospect that Peter writes: 'We, according to his promise, look for new heavens and a new earth in which dwells righteousness' (2 Pet. 3:13). Our interest now is the relation of the reconciliation wrought by Christ to this cosmic regeneration and restoration.

It should be apparent that the vanity to which the creation was subjected (Rom. 8:20) is the result of sin and corresponds in more cosmic proportions to the curse pronounced upon the ground in connection with Adam's sin (Gen. 3:17–19). Vanity and the bondage of corruption are the way or ways in which the estrangement introduced by sin is reflected in that creation which is man's habitation and of which he is the crown. The gravity of man's sin as revolt against God is hereby emphasized. Sin cannot be isolated in its effect; it is the contradiction of God and the wrath it must evoke has its cosmic repercussions. For this reason release from the curse and from the bondage of corruption cannot be wrought, any more than can sin itself be remitted, by an act of mere sovereignty. It is only the removal of sin that can release from the consequences emanating from it. We thus see how integrally related to the reconciliation accomplished by Christ is the hope even of the creation. In the reconciliation Christ dealt with sin and, more particularly, with the *alienation* which sin entails. Reconciliation as action and result brings within its scope the furthest reaches of the curse and so 'the creation itself also will be delivered'.

The cosmic relations of the reconciliation require us to pursue the question of scope still further. There is no difficulty in discovering how the reconciliation bears upon the removal of the vanity, the bondage of corruption, and the curse to which the heavens and the earth, viewed in terms of Romans 8:18–23; 2 Peter 3:13, are subjected because of man's sin. But do not the 'all things . . . whether they be things upon the earth or things in the heavens' (Col. 1:20) include more than the material heavens and earth? The preceding context, in defining 'all things in the heavens and upon the earth', mentions 'things visible and invisible, whether they be thrones, or dominions, or principalities, or powers' (v. 16). And must we not, therefore, bring the invisible principalities within the embrace of the reconciliation?

It may be difficult to conceive of the holy angels as becoming the beneficiaries of fruits accruing from the reconciliation and in this way embraced in the 'all things' reconciled. These angels have not sinned and in the strict sense in which the reconciliation is applicable to men they have no need of reconciliation. Yet it is not impossible to think of the angelic host as being affected by the liabilities devolving upon men particularly and also upon the created order because of man's sin. According to Scripture angels have played and still play an important role in God's manifold ministrations to men. This ministry of angels brings them into contact with sin and its evil effects. If, as Peter says, 'the angels desire to look into' the sufferings of Christ and the glories that were to follow (1 Pet. 1:11, 12), it is surely reasonable to believe that they look forward to the consummation of this glory when their ministry will no longer require this contact with sin and its evil consequences, when no longer will it be necessary for them to guard the heirs of salvation in the assaults of the hosts of darkness. We do not know what all the occupations of angels are. But in their ministry to men the sphere is one conditioned by sin and evil. From the necessity of ministering in such a sphere they will finally be released. It is the consummation proceeding from the reconciliation once accomplished that will provide this release. Surely this will be consummated bliss for the angelic host as well as for the saints. But, as indicated, it is the fruit of the reconciliation. Thus there are lines of thought that may properly be entertained whereby even the holy angels may be brought within the scope of the reconciliation.

Furthermore, though the term 'to sum up' in Ephesians 1:10 is difficult to interpret and is perhaps not definable, yet the action denoted is effected in Christ and is embracive of 'all things . . . which are in heaven and upon the earth'. These must include the angelic host just as the exaltation of Christ in the heavenly places is one 'far above all principality and authority and power and lordship and every name that is named, not only in this age but also in the one to come' (Eph. 1:21). But this summing up in Christ and the exalted lordship over all which he exercises are the result of his redemptive accomplishment (cf. Phil. 2:8–11) and this is but another way of referring to his reconciling action. So again the final status of angels is conditioned by the reconciliation.

If the relevance of the reconciliation to the holy angels is intelligible along such lines as have been proposed, what of the principalities of iniquity, 'the spiritual hosts of wickedness in the heavenlies' (Eph. 6:12)? These must be included in the principalities and authorities, powers and dominions over which Jesus is highly exalted (Eph. 1:21). Otherwise he would not be exalted above every name that is named both in this age and the age to come. And, to say the least, it would be difficult to exclude these powers from 'the things in the heavens and upon the earth' of Ephesians 1:10, or from the scope of the virtually synonymous expression in Colossians 1:20, and it would be impossible to exclude them from the 'all things in the heavens and upon the earth' of Ephesians 1:16. How could the evil angels be included in the reconciliation? Does not reconciliation have soteric import? Are we to posit the restoration of the fallen angels?

The reconciliation is that which has been wrought by the cross of Christ. This is common in all the Pauline passages (cf. Rom. 5:8–11; 2 Cor. 5:18–21; Eph. 2:11–17; Col. 1:20). It is significant and particularly germane to our present question that, when Paul speaks of God as reconciling all things upon the earth and in the heavens, he proceeds to state the relationship which that same cross of Christ sustains to the principalities and the powers of evil. 'Having despoiled the principalities and the powers, he made a show of them openly, triumphing over them in it' (Col. 2:15).[1] This is the language of conquest and subjugation. It might be argued that conquest and subjection are not incompatible with a saving result. It should be borne in mind, however, that reconciliation when soterically conceived has always in view the harmonious fellowship resulting, the removal of enmity and the establishment of peace with God. Any suggestion of such an outcome for the fallen spirits is wholly absent from Paul's teaching. His assessment of their role in the present age is in the opposite direction. In the companion epistle he writes: 'For our wrestling is not against flesh and blood, but against the principalities, against the powers, against the world-rulers of this darkness, against the spiritual hosts of wickedness in the heavenlies' (Eph. 6:12). Their role is one of unrelenting hostility to the kingdom of God and therefore affording no omen or promise of soteric reconciliation. And when Paul reflects on ultimate destiny their identity is still that of *enemies* and their end that of being brought to nought and placed under Christ's feet. 'Then the end, when he delivers over the kingdom to God and the Father, when he will bring to nought all principality and all authority and power. For he must reign until he places all the enemies under his feet' (1 Cor.

[1] Cf., for discussion of this verse and reference to relevant literature, F. F. Bruce: *Commentary on the Epistle to the Colossians* (Grand Rapids, 1957), pp. 239 f., n. 68.

15:24, 25). It is then that the victory of the cross (Col. 2:15) and the lordship inaugurated by the resurrection and ascension (Eph. 1:20–23) will be consummated in the final subjugation of all alien powers.

To this outlook the rest of the New Testament offers no dissident witness. The place of woe to which the impenitent are consigned is, according to our Lord's verdict, 'the everlasting fire prepared for the devil and his angels' (Matt. 25:41). Jude tells us that 'angels that kept not their own principality, but left their proper habitation he, [the Lord] hath kept in everlasting bonds under darkness unto the judgment of the great day' (Jude 6; cf. Rev. 20:10).[1]

If, therefore, the New Testament and Paul in particular give no support to the thesis of restitution for fallen angels and, on the other hand, teach the opposite, how are we to interpret Colossians 1:20? Must we conclude that the 'all things' upon the earth and in the heavens said to be reconciled are to be understood in a restrictive sense so as to exclude the fallen angels? It is a well-established canon that universalistic expressions do not always imply distributive universalism; they are to be understood restrictively in terms of the context, or in terms of the universe of discourse, or in accord with the analogy of Scripture. If this principle were applied in this case, there could be no objection from the standpoint of general hermeneutics. The argument might be that since 'reconciliation', when denoting the action of God through Christ, has distinctly soteric connotation and since this meaning cannot belong to the fallen angels, therefore they do not come within the scope of Colossians 1:20.

This solution does not, however, commend itself in terms of the context and of closely related passages. We cannot overlook the inclusiveness of the preceding context, especially of verse 16. The angels that kept not their first estate, though now fallen from their original integrity, must be included in the 'all things in the heavens and upon the earth' created by Christ. They must likewise belong to the 'all things' that consist in him (v. 17). They are among the 'all things' which find their final goal in Christ (v. 16). They are embraced in the 'all things' over which Christ is preeminent (v. 18) and over which he is head to his body the church (Eph. 1:22). Likewise, the summing up of all things in Christ, the things in the heavens and upon the earth (Eph. 1:10), is all-inclusive. We are thus led to the conclusion that the reconciliation referred to in Colossians 1:20 must be regarded as

[1] Cf., on this subject, F. F. Bruce: *ibid.*, pp. 209 f.

inclusive of the fallen spirits and that the bringing to nought and subjugation of these (1 Cor. 15:24, 25) must be conceived of as an aspect of 'the reconciliation'.

We cannot think of the summing up of all things in Christ and the attainment of the goal that all things were created for him apart from the final triumph over all enemies. The latter is an essential ingredient of the final end. But the summing up belongs to the economy of the fulness of the times (Col. 1:18). This economy is redemptively conditioned and oriented; it is the economy of redemption. This is but to say that only in virtue of all that Christ achieved in fulfilment of his redemptive mission and commission will the final goal appointed for him be realized. This helps us to understand how in the passage with which we are concerned the subjugation of evil principalities and power can be represented as an aspect of the reconciliation.

Reconciliation is one of the categories in which the atonement is to be defined, coordinate with obedience, expiation, propitiation, and redemption. We may well ask: why is the subjugation of enemies brought within the scope of the reconciliation when it is not brought within the scope of the others? It is easy to detect the discrepancy if we tried to construe such subjugation under obedience, or expiation, or propitiation; there would be no congruity. With redemption it could be said that it involves redemption from our enemies and subjugation of enemies is the way of insuring deliverance. But even here redemption is not appropriately applied to the subjugation so that the latter might be regarded as an aspect of redemption; redemption must be defined as release by the payment of a price. Release in no sense applies to the subjugation of the powers of darkness. This points up all the more forcefully the question respecting reconciliation. How can this category be applied to the subjugation of alien principalities?

If we were not able to answer the question or suggest the line along which the answer might be sought, we should be content to leave it unanswered without denying the premise that provokes the question. We cannot answer all questions which the teaching of Scripture or even its language may prompt. In this case, however, the situation that reconciliation presupposes and that imparts meaning to it is such that it may not be improper to find in the specific character of reconciliation the justification for its use in the text concerned (Col. 1:20). Reconciliation presupposes enmity. The other categories of the atonement have particularly in view other aspects from which the liability of sin is to be viewed. But what creates the need for reconciliation and determines its meaning is our alienation from God. What is brought into focus is our enmity against God and, as consequence, his holy alienation from us. No indictment exposes the true character of sin more than that 'the carnal mind is enmity against God' (Rom. 8:7). The essence of sin is to be against God and the liability of sin is no more adequately expressed than in the fact that God is, therefore, against us. The marvel of grace is that God removes this 'against'. It is by and in 'the reconciliation' that this is done. Hence no category is more basic to the gospel; it is essentially the message of the reconciliation (cf. 2 Cor. 5:18-20).

In this central consideration, the disharmony and disruption arising from sin, may well reside the explanation of Colossians 1:20 as it applies to the fallen angels. As already noted, it is not that they are to be restored. They are to be subjugated, brought to nought, and placed under Christ's feet. It is this finale that stands in sharp contrast with their present activity. They are now intensely active within the realm of the kingdom of God in the heavenlies (cf. Eph. 6:12) and upon earth. The church is constantly in conflict with them and they war against the saints. Since redemptive history has not reached its goal, this history is to a large extent conditioned by this conflict. It is one of warfare. The spiritual hosts of wickedness are the epitome of that enmity which constitutes the essence of sin. But redemptive history will one day be consummated and the new heavens and the new earth, the eschatological kingdom of God, will be established in righteousness. We may properly apply the words: 'The Son of Man shall send forth his angels, and they shall gather out of his kingdom all things that offend, and them which do iniquity; and shall cast them into a furnace of fire: there shall be wailing and gnashing of teeth. Then shall the righteous shine forth as the sun in the kingdom of their Father' (Matt. 13:41-43). This consummated order, however we may describe it in the various designations Scripture provides, is one from which all conflict, enmity, disharmony, warfare will be excluded; it will mean the final triumph of righteousness and peace, in a word, of reconciliation. The powers of darkness will be cast out and by the judgment executed made to 'confess that Jesus Christ is Lord to the glory of God the Father' (Phil. 2:11). Bowing the knee in compulsive submission, this will be the reconciliation as it bears upon them; it will constitute the ultimate unconditional surrender, the confessed defeat of age-long assault upon the kingdom of God. We can and must see in this grand climax of victory the fruit of the blood of Christ's cross. It was by his cross that he despoiled the principalities and powers and triumphed over them (cf. John 12:31; Col. 2:15; Heb. 2:14; 1 John 3:8). The last judgment upon them is integral to the undisturbed bliss of the new heavens and the new earth. And so we may the better understand how Paul, with this subjugation in his purview, could say that it pleased the Father through Christ 'to reconcile all things unto himself . . . through him whether they be things in the earth or things in the heavens' (Col. 1:20).

The burden of Paul's teaching on the subject of reconciliation is not, however, the cosmic implications; it is concerned with the reconciliation as it has respect to men. Thus in the same passage he proceeds: 'And you that were sometime alienated and enemies in your mind by wicked works, yet now did he reconcile in the body of his flesh through death' (Col. 1:21, 22).

(i) Here and in the close parallel from the companion epistle (Eph. 2:12, 13) we have the clearest indication of the aspect of our need arising from sin to which the reconciliation is directed. It is summed up in the term 'alienated' (Col. 1:21; Eph. 2:12; 4:18). It would not be proper to discount or suppress the hostility to God which the alienation involves. This is expressed in the coordinate description, 'enemies in your mind by wicked words' (Col. 1:21). The alienation is conditioned by our enmity and this connection is stated by Paul when he says: 'alienated from the life of God, on account of the ignorance that is in them, on account of the hardening of their heart' (Eph. 4:18; cf. also vv. 17, 18a, 19). But it is a mistake to construe the alienation as consisting in the hostility to God on the part of men. The various expressions point to the exclusion of the 'alienated' from the status, institutions, and relationships which betoken and certify God's favour. 'At that time ye were without Christ; alienated from the commonwealth of Israel and strangers from the covenants of the promise, having no hope and without God in the world' (Eph. 2:12). The thought of being 'afar off' in the succeeding verse (cf. also v. 17) is to the same effect. It is this same emphasis that must apply to the term 'alienated' in Colossians 1:21. Hence the alienation, thrust into the foreground in these passages as constituting the liability to which the reconciliation is directed, is misinterpreted when it is construed simply or even mainly in terms of man's subjective hostility. As is apparent from the various expressions used by Paul, what comes into focus is exclusion from the divine favour and blessing and, with that precise force, our alienation from God. In a word, it is to be 'without God'.[1] This determines, likewise, what the reconciliation as both action and result contemplates.

(ii) The liability to which the reconciliation is directed is the unmistakable index to that which constitutes the reconciliation both as action and result. As *action* it is the removal of the alienation characterized as exclusion from the favour of God and from the privileges which his favour insures and bestows. As *result* it means that those who were at one time far off, separated from God and his fellowship, are brought nigh to God and are at peace with him (cf. Eph. 2:13, 14, 17; Col. 1:20). Liability, action, and result all converge to establish the basic concept of alienation removed and peace constituted.

(iii) The subject of the verb 'reconcile' (Col. 1:22) and therefore of the action denoted thereby is God the Father. We must go back to verse 19 to discover who the subject is. 'It pleased the Father that in him [Christ] all the fulness should dwell.' It is apparent that the same subject is in view in verse 20 where the term 'reconcile' occurs for the first time in this passage: 'and through him to reconcile all things unto himself'.[2] This fact that God the Father is the agent requires proper recognition and emphasis. It is one of the characteristic notes of Paul's teaching on the subject of reconciliation. Perhaps it is most prominent in 2 Corinthians 5:18–21, where this appears distinctly on at least three occasions and is implicit in the coordinate expressions. 'All things are of God who reconciled us to himself through Christ' (v. 18). The distinction of persons in the titles 'God' and 'Christ' demands that 'God' refers to the Father and he is clearly the subject of the action denoted in the verb 'reconciled'. As if this were not enough there is the reiterated emphasis in verse 19: 'God was in Christ reconciling the world to himself.' And no less eloquent of God the Father's action is

---

[1] ἄθεοι in Ephesians 2:12 does not mean 'ungodly' but 'without God' or 'Godless'. This is apparent from the coordinate expressions: χωρὶς Χριστοῦ and ἐλπίδα μὴ ἔχοντες.

[2] This is one of the strongest considerations in favour of regarding 'the Father' as subject in verse 19. If 'all the fulness' were taken as the subject of εὐδόκησεν, then insuperable difficulty would arise in verse 20. How could 'all the fulness' be regarded as the subject and agent of the reconciliation? There is not only the incongruity in concept to be considered but the usage of Paul in other passages where the Father is the subject of the reconciling action.

verse 21 where Paul defines for us more specifically the kind of undertaking involved in the reconciling action: 'him who did not know
sin he [obviously God taken over from the preceding clause] made to
be sin on our behalf'. Likewise in the correlative expressions – 'and
hath given to us the ministry of the reconciliation' (v. 18); 'not reckoning to them their trespasses, and hath given to us the word of the
reconciliation' (v. 19) – the agency of the Father is unquestionable. So
the whole passage is permeated with the thought of the Father's
agency. The initiative is with the Father, the reconciling action is the
Father's, the permanent ministry is by the Father's commission.

In accord with this stress upon the Father's action or agency is the
frequency with which Christ's own action is represented in terms of
mediacy. As will be observed later, Christ is directly stated to be the
subject of the reconciling action. But it is necessary to take account
now of the way in which the action of the Father is *mediated* through
the action of Christ, in other words, to observe *how* the Father is
represented as accomplishing the reconciliation. It pleased the Father
'through him [Christ] to reconcile all things unto himself, having made
peace through the blood of his cross, through him whether they be
things in the earth or things in the heavens. And you . . . did he now
reconcile in the body of his flesh through death' (Col. 1:20–22). 'But
now in Christ Jesus ye who sometime were afar off have been brought
nigh in the blood of Christ' (Eph. 2:13). 'All things are of God who
reconciled us to himself through Christ' (2 Cor. 5:18). 'God was in
Christ reconciling the world to himself' (2 Cor. 5:19). 'God commends
his own love towards us in that while we were yet sinners Christ died
for us. How much more then, being now justified in his blood, shall we
be saved through him from the wrath. For if when we were enemies
we were reconciled to God through the death of his Son, how much
more, being reconciled, shall we be saved by his life. And not only so,
but we also joy in God through our Lord Jesus Christ through whom
now we have received the reconciliation' (Rom. 5:8–11). It is, therefore,
through Christ, by Christ, in Christ, that the Father acts in his reconciling accomplishment and the latter cannot be conceived of apart
from Christ in his person, office, and doing. In this case the reason
consists in that which the reconciliation demands and contemplates.
It has in view an exigency for which the Father by his action alone
could not provide. Paul becomes specific in enunciating the kind of
agency on Christ's part which meets this exigency and constitutes the

reconciliation. It is in the body of Christ's flesh through death that God reconciles (cf. Col. 1:22). Those afar off 'have been brought nigh in the blood of Christ' (Eph. 2:13). 'While we were yet sinners Christ died for us' (Rom. 5:8). 'We were reconciled to God through the death of his Son' (Rom. 5:10). We are pointed to that which is predicable of Christ alone – the body of his flesh, his blood, his death. All the emphasis that necessarily and properly belongs to the Father's action is not allowed to obscure the true character of reconciliation. It is not a sovereign act of clemency. It demands and is wrought by the shedding of blood and in the economy of salvation only God's own Son had such blood to shed and such life to lay down in death.

For this reason it should not surprise us that Christ is also represented as the subject and agent in the reconciling action. The most explicit statement to this effect is Ephesians 2:16. Here Paul has a particular facet of reconciliation in view, namely, the bringing together in one fellowship of Jew and Gentile so that both constitute one body and have access in one Spirit unto the Father. But it is the same reconciling action of which Paul speaks when he says of Christ specifically, as the one who is our peace (cf. v. 14), that he destroyed the enmity in order that 'he might reconcile both in one body to God through the cross'. The formula used here to signify Christ's own reconciling action, namely, 'reconcile to God', is the same in its import as that used in 2 Corinthians 5:18, 19 when the Father is represented as the reconciling agent in reconciling us to himself. Hence the efficiency predicated of Christ's own agency is not to be regarded as falling short in any respect of that of the Father. In Romans 5:10 when the same formula is used passively – 'we were reconciled to God' – we would naturally expect that, as in Ephesians 2:16, the action is to be understood as that of Christ.

We naturally raise the question: if only that which Christ could perform in the body of his flesh through death would be effective unto reconciliation, why does such emphasis fall upon the agency of the Father himself in the reconciling action? No death, no blood-shedding belongs to the Father.

Much that pertains to this question may elude us. We should not be surprised that this is so. But we may not and cannot overlook what is central to all thought respecting Christ's office and ministry. All that Christ is and does in his mediatorial offices and accomplishments is the fruit of the Father's love, design, and gift. It is with this note the most characteristic passages begin. 'God commendeth his own love toward us in that while we were yet sinners Christ died for us' (Rom. 5:8). 'And all things are of God who reconciled us to himself through Christ' (2 Cor. 5:18). 'It pleased the Father that in him all the fulness should dwell' (Col. 1:19). Our conception of the economy of redemption is deflected from the outset if we do not appreciate the primacy of the Father's counsel and action. Wherever we turn in the Bible's witness this is what confronts us. 'God so loved the world that he gave his only-begotten Son' (John 3:16). 'Herein is love, not that we loved God, but that he loved us, and sent his Son to be the propitiation for our sins' (1 John 4:10). 'He that spared not his own Son, but delivered him up for us all, how shall he not with him also freely give us all things?' (Rom. 8:32). 'All we like sheep have gone astray; we have turned every one to his own way; and the Lord hath laid on him the iniquity of us all' (Is. 53:6).

(iv) Having surveyed the data bearing on the relation of the Father's action to that of the Son, we are now in a better position to deal with the import of the expression, so much debated, 'God was in Christ' (2 Cor. 5:19). The question is whether we have in verse 19a what are virtually two propositions, namely, that 'God was in Christ' and that, as such, he was 'reconciling the world unto himself' or one proposition that 'God was reconciling the world unto himself in Christ'. In terms of punctuation the question is: are we to place a comma after 'Christ' or are we to omit the same? A formidable list of exegetes can be cited in support of either alternative.

If the former alternative were adopted, no issue of theological significance would necessarily be at stake.[1] For, in the event that this was Paul's intent, the accent would fall either upon the deity of Christ or, preferably, upon the close cooperation of the Father and the Son in the reconciling action, that it was in virtue of the indwelling of the Father in Christ that so great a work could have been wrought (cf. John 5:19, 20; 10:37, 38; 14:10).

The considerations in support of the second alternative are, however, preponderant.

(a) The formula 'God was in Christ', as a way of affirming the deity of Christ, is without parallel in Paul or in the New Testament generally. A survey of the usage will demonstrate how contrary to all

---

[1] Although no theological issue is *necessarily* at stake, this alternative interpretation can be subjected to such distortion that theological issues do become involved.

analogy it would be to reflect on Christ's deity in this manner. Hence it would be grossly arbitrary to impose such an interpretation upon the expression unless compelling reasons could be pleaded for departure from usual patterns.[1] As we shall see, no such reasons exist.

(b) The title 'God' in this instance must be taken as referring specifically to God the Father.[2] This is apparent from the preceding verse. God and Christ are distinguished and when this is done, particularly in Paul, the name 'God' is the personal title for the Father. The same is true in verse 20. It is equally patent in Romans 5:8-11. And in Colossians 1:19-22, as observed earlier, it is God the Father who is represented as the agent in the reconciliation. Thus, exegetically, there is no warrant whatsoever for the supposition that the title 'God' in the instance concerned has any reference to the deity of Christ himself. It denotes the Father and it is not the person of the Father who constitutes Jesus' deity.

(c) As commentators have observed, the 'in Christ' of verse 19 should be most reasonably interpreted as having the same force, or at least the same general import, as 'through Christ' of verse 18. The strength of this argument is enhanced when the relation of the two verses is duly noted. Verse 19 is a reiteration and expansion of verse 18 as is made clear by the introductory terms. Verse 19 is a further definition of the subject announced in verse 18. But the conclusiveness of this interpretation is established when we consider all of Paul's teaching on this topic. The thought that the Father's action in reconciliation is through the mediation of Christ is pervasive. Sometimes this is expressed simply in terms of 'through Christ' as in 2 Corinthians 5:18 (cf. Col. 1:20). But more frequently Paul is more specific and states how Christ exercised this mediation. It was 'in his blood' (Rom. 5:9), through his death (Rom. 5:10), 'in the blood of Christ' (Eph. 2:13), 'in his flesh' (Eph. 2:14), 'through the cross' (Eph. 2:16), 'through the blood of his cross' (Col. 1:20), 'in the body of his flesh through death' (Col. 1:22). Thus, when Paul says 'through Christ', there is always in view the way in which it is through him. And it should be

---

[1] It is true theologically to say with Allo: 'C'est cette présence de Dieu dans le Christ, dans l'homme Jésus, qui donne au sacrifice de la Croix son infinie valeur' (P.E.-B. Allo: *Seconde Épitre aux Corinthiens*, Paris, 1956, *ad loc.*). But this is exegetically inept.
[2] Calvin had sufficient insight to see this, even though he adopted the interpretation now being refuted. 'This is said of the Father, since it would be unnatural to say that the divine nature of Christ was in Christ' (*The Second Epistle of Paul the Apostle to the Corinthians*, E. T., Edinburgh and London, 1964, *ad loc.*).

noted that the way in which Christ accomplished this mediation is expressed by the instrumental dative, 'in his blood', 'in his flesh', 'in the body of his flesh', as well as by 'through the blood of his cross'. But perhaps most significant of all is the fact that this same truth is stated explicitly to have taken place 'in Christ Jesus'. 'But now in Christ Jesus ye who sometime were far off were brought nigh in the blood of Christ' (Eph. 2:13). The language differs and the voice is passive, when in 2 Corinthians 5:19 it is active. But surely the same act of reconciliation is in view in both instances. The situation is, therefore, that pervasively and with eloquent reiteration the reconciliation is stated to be wrought through Christ's mediation and, more specifically, through his death on the cross. This mediacy is expressed in the formula 'in Christ Jesus' as well as by such expressions as 'in the body of his flesh' and 'in his blood'. The exegetical data would indicate therefore, that when we find 'in Christ' in 2 Corinthians 5:19 no other interpretation could begin to claim for itself the support which the analogy of Paul's teaching offers to the view that here the mediacy of Christ in the reconciling action is contemplated. And so we should read: 'God was in Christ reconciling the world to himself', and 'in Christ' is to be taken along with 'was reconciling'[1] after the pattern of sustained, uniform usage in the other passages.[2]

(v) We must now turn to the question of the extent of the reconciliation as it concerns mankind. We are not now dealing with reconciliation in its more cosmic application in the sense of Colossians 1:20 but with the extent in those passages which have clearly in view lost humanity (Rom. 5:8–11; 2 Cor. 5:18–21; Eph. 2:13–20; Col. 1:21–23).

It was noted already that at Colossians 1:21 Paul becomes more restrictive and proceeds to deal with the reconciliation as it embraces men. At verse 22 the purpose of the reconciling action wrought in the body of Christ's flesh through death is stated to be the presentation of the beneficiaries as holy and without blemish and unreprovable. Our

---

[1] $\mathring{\eta}\nu$ $\kappa\alpha\tau\alpha\lambda\lambda\acute{\alpha}\sigma\sigma\omega\nu$ is a periphrastic imperfect.

[2] The argument that $\mathring{\eta}\nu$ must go with $\theta\acute{\epsilon}\mu\epsilon\nu o\varsigma$ as well as with $\kappa\alpha\tau\alpha\lambda\lambda\acute{\alpha}\sigma\sigma\omega\nu$ (cf. J. H. Bernard: *The Expositor's Greek Testament*, New York, n.d., Vol. III, *ad loc.*) is not a valid one in support of this interpretation. The aorist participle $\theta\acute{\epsilon}\mu\epsilon\nu o\varsigma$ refers to the result of the reconciling action, whether the preceding clause is taken as exepexegetical of $\mathring{\eta}\nu$ $\kappa\alpha\tau\alpha\lambda\lambda\acute{\alpha}\sigma\sigma\omega\nu$ or as the effect, and can surely stand by itself (cf. Heinrich A. W. Meyer: *Critical and Exegetical Handbook to the Epistles to the Corinthians*, E.T., New York, 1884, pp. 537 f.).

understanding of the reconciliation as action must not be dissociated from the design here stated and, to say the least, we are thus cautioned against any facile assumption that the reconciliation as action can be conceived of as embracing all mankind. Not all mankind will be presented faultless before God. In any case, there is no evidence whatsoever in this passage for universal reconciliation. Paul is writing to the saints at Colosse (Col. 1:2) and only of them does he speak when he says: 'And you who were sometime alienated . . . now did he reconcile' (vv. 21, 22).

Of equal, if not greater, relevance to the question of extent is the condition stated in verse 23: 'if ye continue in the faith, grounded and stedfast and not moved away from the hope of the gospel which ye heard'. This condition is similar to that which we find elsewhere in the New Testament (cf. Rom. 11:22; Heb. 3:6, 14) and we are reminded that the provisions and promises of salvation are not to be dissociated from the fruits appropriate to and expressive of that salvation. It might be argued that in this case the conditional sentence in verse 23 does not apply to the reconciling action (v. 22a) but only to the goal contemplated, 'to present you holy and without blemish and unreprovable in his sight' (v. 22b) and that the whole truth intended is the more obvious one, namely, that the goal is not achieved unless there is continuance in the faith. But, as noted earlier, it is impossible to think of the reconciling action apart from the design. In other words, the two elements of verse 22 are so inter-involved that the condition expressed in verse 23 cannot be attached to the second element alone. The condition belongs to verse 22 in its unity and, therefore, to the reconciling action as well as to the aim envisaged. Thus in this passage not only is it the case that there is no evidence to support the universal scope of the reconciliation; there is distinct indication that the reconciling action, as also the achievement of the designed goal, is limited in its reference to those who persevere to the end in faith and hope. We are advised that as we think of reconciliation in its objective, once-for-all accomplishment in the death of Christ upon the cross, we may never interpret the same as to its character, design, and extent apart from the actual fruitage in reconciliation received. Universalism violates the contextual data in terms of which we are to interpret the scope of the reconciling action.

It is appropriate now to turn to that other passage in connection with which the question of extent has been in dispute (2 Cor. 5:19). The question is concerned with the term 'world' in the clause 'reconciling the world to himself'.[1] It has been maintained that the thought here is that of Colossians 1:20, the reconciliation in its cosmic proportions including the subjugation of all enemies.[2] If this is the purport then the same qualifications would have to be made as in the case of Colossians 1:20. There are, however, very good reasons for rejecting this interpretation in this instance.

(a) There is no intimation in this passage of the inclusiveness characterizing the context of Colossians 1:20. Everything points to the restrictiveness which we find in Colossians 1:21, as observed above. That Paul is thinking specifically of mankind appears at the outset. 'All things are of God who reconciled us to himself through Christ' (2 Cor. 5:18). 'The ministry of reconciliation' (*id.*) is likewise one that has respect to men. It is men who are exhorted on behalf of Christ, 'Be ye reconciled to God' (v. 20). And the expiatory action (v. 21) which defines the reconciling action is one that contemplates men in its intent and effect – 'he was made sin for us that we might become the righteousness of God in him'. The universe of discourse is ruthlessly disregarded when 'world' is given cosmic denotation.

(b) It is true that on occasion Paul *may* use the word 'world' in an inclusive sense to designate what we mean by cosmos (cf. Rom. 1:20; 1 Cor. 8:4). But such instances are few and a survey of his use of the term will show that frequently he means the world of humanity viewed from various aspects (cf. Rom. 1:8; 3:19; 5:12, 13; 11:12, 15; 1 Cor. 3:19; 11:32; Phil. 2:15; 1 Tim. 1:15).[3] But of more significance is the fact that when Paul is thinking of the reconciliation in its cosmic reference he finds it necessary to use very different terms to make clear his meaning (cf. Col. 1:16–20).

(c) The explanatory clause in 2 Corinthians 5:19 points definitely to the more restrictive sense of the term 'world'. It is not so certain what the precise intent of the clause 'not imputing to them their trespasses' is. It may be taken as specifying that in which the reconciliation consisted and in that event would be closely related to the clause in verse

---

[1] It would be unwarranted to stress the anarthrous use of κόσμος and maintain that the thought is focused upon 'a world' in the sense of a saved world. The absence of the definite article cannot be made to bear this signification.
[2] Cf., most recently, Philip E. Hughes: *Paul's Second Epistle to the Corinthians*, Grand Rapids, 1962, *ad loc.*
[3] It is not necessary to discuss the various aspects in these passages. In Romans 11:12, 15, for example, the 'world' is the Gentile world as distinguished from Israel.

21, 'him who knew no sin he made to be sin for us'. In the reconciliation there was the imputation of sin to Christ and, therefore, the non-imputation of sin to the beneficiaries. Verse 19b would be epexegetical of verse 19a. However, verse 19b could also be taken as expressing the effect or fruit of the reconciling action and would be resultative. It makes no difference to the present question which of these views should be adopted. The significant feature is that verse 19b indicates the sphere within which the reconciliation (v. 19a) has relevance. What is the realm to which the non-imputation of trespasses applies? There is but one answer according to Paul and the New Testament. It is the realm of humanity. The good angels have no trespasses to be remitted. For the fallen angels there is no redemptive provision. Non-rational creation rests under the curse, subjected to vanity. But of this creation trespass is not predicable. Distinctly, therefore, only to men can verse 19b apply. Because of the close relation of the two clauses, only of men can Paul be thinking when he says, 'reconciling the world'.

If the 'world' refers to mankind, the next question is the extent of the reference within mankind. Is there any intimation in this passage and related passages of the limitation we found in Colossians 1:21–23? The interpretive clause in verse 19 – 'not reckoning to them their trespasses' – bears not only on the preceding thesis, that of restricting the 'world' to mankind, but upon our present question also. If this clause is epexegetical of the reconciling action, as it may well be, then the limited extent obviously applying to the non-imputation of trespasses must likewise apply to that of which it is interpretive, namely, the reconciling action. Since not all of mankind enjoy the remission of their trespasses, so not all come within the scope of the reconciliation. But even if 'not imputing to them their trespasses' refers to the effect of the reconciliation as that which emanates from it, the restriction is not eliminated. The two clauses of verse 19 are, in any event, so closely related that their respective scope is inter-involved. If the non-reckoning of trespasses is the effect, it is the effect that inevitably accrues from the reconciling action. The latter insures the remission of trespasses and, for that reason, cannot have broader reference than its unfailing issue. Limitation is bound up with the non-reckoning of trespasses and with the syntax of the sentence. Other considerations are confirmatory of this conclusion.

Though there is repeated emphasis upon the objective, once-for-all accomplishment in the death of Christ, it is not possible to abstract this reconciling action from its fruitage in reconciliation bestowed and enjoyed. Exegetically stated, this means that in passages where the death of Christ as a finished, historical event is clearly in view as reconciling action, those being addressed or contemplated are regarded as the beneficiaries of the reconciling action. In other words, they are conceived of as having received the reconciliation and as possessors of that insured and secured by it. In the order of the New Testament this appears first of all in Romans 5:9, 10. Here there is a parallel between 'justified now in his blood' (v. 9) and 'reconciled to God through the death of his Son'. The guarantee involved in the former is that 'we shall be saved . . . from the wrath' and of the latter that 'we shall be saved by his [Christ's] life'. This means saved from the eschatological wrath and saved in Christ's resurrection life. It may well be that 'justified' in this instance is used as the synonym of 'reconciled'. But, in any event, it is impossible to think of 'reconciled' in both instances in verse 10 (though the finished action in Christ's death is distinctly in the forefront) apart from the new status actually constituted which carries with it the guarantee of salvation by virtue of Christ's resurrection life. The thought is that if we are embraced in the scope of 'reconciled' we shall be also in that of 'saved'. And this is to say that the death of Christ as reconciling action cannot be interpreted as something broader in its scope and intent than the final outcome of reconciliation bestowed.

The same conclusions can be derived from Ephesians 2:13: 'But now in Christ Jesus ye who sometime were far off have been brought nigh in the blood of Christ.' That 'brought nigh' has the same import as reconciliation is evident from the context. The preceding verse defines the situation to which reconciliation is directed and the need it meets – 'alienated from the commonwealth of Israel and strangers to the covenants of the promise, having no hope and without God in the world'. And then in verse 16 the term 'reconcile' is used to express the same essential thought. Thus verse 13 is directly relevant to the present question.

The reference to the blood of Christ reminds us of the historic event of Jesus' cross, identified expressly in these terms in verse 16 as that through which the reconciliation had been wrought. So we cannot eliminate from this passage the thought of the reconciling action in the cross of Christ. But, when Paul says that 'now in Christ Jesus ye . . . have been brought nigh', he is certainly thinking of reconciliation in actual realization in contrast with the alienated status described in verse 12. So again the repeated reference in this passage to the cross as the reconciling action cannot be abstracted in its intent and scope from the participation of the grace which it contemplates. The same implications belong to Colossians 1:21–23. But it is not necessary to repeat what are virtually the same considerations.

It does not follow from the foregoing observations regarding the coextensiveness of objective accomplishment and subjective bestowment that the completed action wrought in Christ's death on the cross is not viewed in its distinctness as that which grounds, secures, and insures reconciliation as bestowment and possession. Men come into possession of the reconciliation as actual status in response to the gospel proclamation. This is made clear in 2 Corinthians 5:18–20. There is 'the ministry of the reconciliation' (v. 18), 'the word of the reconciliation' (v. 19), the acting of preachers as ambassadors on behalf of Christ, and the exhortation, addressed to men as of God and on behalf of Christ, 'Be ye reconciled to God' (v. 20). What constitutes this proclamation is that which God has done in the death of his Son, and the essence of the exhortation is that we should enter into this status which the once-for-all accomplishment has secured. In reality no confidence to draw nigh in the assurance of faith for the appropriation of this grace can be engendered in the hearts of men convicted of sin and of alienation from God except as there is to some extent the apprehension of what God has done in Christ once for all to meet the exigency of our sin and of its resultant separation from God. The ground of faith in answer to the exhortation is the reality of that objective accomplishment in the concreteness of the historical event of Christ's death upon the cross. So the distinctness of the once-for-all reconciling action in Jesus' blood is not only involved in the ministry and word of reconciliation; it is involved in the very act of faith by which we enter into reconciled status and enjoy peace with God.

In the light of what we have found in respect of the scope of the reconciliation as action, namely, that as accomplished action it is coextensive with reconciliation as status established, the significance of the message, of the exhortation, and of the response in faith should warn us against the distortion so prevalent that the *kerugma* consists in the announcement to all men that they have been reconciled and that faith consists in the acceptance of this as a fact.[1] It is all-important and most significant that the exhortation correspondent with the message is 'Be ye reconciled to God', an exhortation which surely implies that reconciliation as status, as one of peace with God, does not take effect until there is the response of faith. This is another reminder that we may not abstract the accomplished action from its fruitage in reconciliatoin bestowed, a bestowment always conjoined with the faith that responds to the message proclaimed.

[1] For discussion and analysis of this view of the *kerugma* and of its relations to other doctrines cf. the discriminating study by G. C. Berkouwer: *The Work of Christ*, Grand Rapids, 1965, pp. 289–294.

7

The Free Offer of the Gospel[1]

IT would appear that the real point in dispute in connection with the free offer of the gospel is whether it can properly be said that God *desires* the salvation of all men. The Committee elected by the Twelfth General Assembly in its report to the Thirteenth General Assembly said, 'God not only delights in the penitent but is also moved by the riches of his goodness and mercy to desire the repentance and salvation of the impenitent and reprobate' (*Minutes*, p. 67). It should have been apparent that the aforesaid Committee, in predicating such 'desire' of God, was not dealing with the decretive will of God; it was dealing with the free offer of the gospel to all without distinction and that surely respects, not the decretive or secret will of God, but the revealed will. There is no ground for the supposition that the expression was intended to refer to God's decretive will.

It must be admitted that if the expression were intended to apply to the decretive will of God then there would be, at least, implicit contradiction. For to say that God desires the salvation of the reprobate and also that God wills the damnation of the reprobate and apply the former to the same thing as the latter, namely, the decretive will, would be contradiction; it would amount to averring of the same thing, viewed from the same aspect, God wills and God does not will.

The question then is: what is implicit in, or lies back of, the full and free offer of the gospel to all without distinction? The word 'desire' has come to be used in the debate, not because it is *necessarily* the most

[1] The following was presented as a committee report to the Fifteenth General Assembly of the Orthodox Presbyterian Church and first printed in the *Minutes* of that Assembly (1948, Appendix, pp. 51–63). It was subsequently reprinted in booklet form under the names of John Murray and Ned. B. Stonehouse but although Dr Stonehouse, as a member of the committee, offered editorial suggestions, the material was written by Professor Murray.

accurate or felicitous word but because it serves to set forth quite sharply a certain implication of the full and free offer of the gospel to all. This implication is that in the free offer there is expressed not simply the bare preceptive will of God but the disposition of loving-kindness on the part of God pointing to the salvation to be gained through compliance with the overtures of gospel grace. In other words, the gospel is not simply an offer or invitation, but also implies that God delights that those to whom the offer comes would enjoy what is offered in all its fulness. And the word 'desire' has been used in order to express the thought epitomized in Ezekiel 33:11, which is to the effect that God has pleasure that the wicked turn from his evil way and live. It might as well have been said, 'It pleases God that the wicked repent and be saved.'

Again, the expression 'God desires', in the formula that crystallizes the crux of the question, is intended to notify not at all the 'seeming' attitude of God but a real attitude, a real disposition of lovingkindness inherent in the free offer to all; in other words, a pleasure or delight in God, contemplating the blessed result to be achieved by compliance with the overture proffered and the invitation given.

Still further, it is necessary to point out that such 'desire' on the part of God for the salvation of all must never be conceived of as desire to such an end apart from the means to that end. It is not desire of their salvation irrespective of repentance and faith. Such would be inconceivable. For it would mean, as Calvin says, 'to renounce the difference between good and evil.' If it is proper to say that God desires the salvation of the reprobate, then he desires such by their repentance. And so it amounts to the same thing to say 'God desires their salvation' as to say 'He desires their repentance.' This is the same as saying that he desires them to comply with the indispensable conditions of salvation. It would be impossible to say the one without implying the other.

SCRIPTURAL BASIS

The Committee would now respectfully submit some exegetical material bearing upon this question and with a view to the resolution of it.

Matthew 5:44–48

This passage does not indeed deal with the overtures of grace in the gospel. But it does tell us something regarding God's benevolence that has bearing upon all manifestations of divine grace. The particular aspect of God's grace reflected upon here is the common gifts of providence, the making of the sun to rise upon evil and good and the sending of rain upon just and unjust. There can be no question but all without distinction, reprobate as well as elect, are the beneficiaries of this favour, and it is that fact that is distinctly stated in verse 45.

The significant feature of this text is that this bestowal of favour by God on all alike is adduced as the reason why the disciples are to love their enemies and do them good. There is, of course, a question as to the proper text of verse 44. If we follow the Aleph-B text and omit the clauses, 'bless them who curse you, do good to them who hate you' as well as the verb 'despitefully use', the sense is not affected. And besides, these clauses, though they may not belong to the genuine text of Matthew, appear in Luke 6:27, 28 in practically the same form. Hence the teaching of our Lord undoubtedly was that the disciples were to love their enemies, do good to those who hated them, bless those who cursed them, and pray for those who despitefully used them and persecuted them. And the reason provided is that God himself bestows his favours upon his enemies. The particular reason mentioned why the disciples are to be guided and animated by the divine example is that they, the disciples, are sons of the Father. The obligation and urge to the love of their enemies and the bestowal of good upon them are here grounded in the filial relation that they sustain to God. Since they are sons of God they must be like their heavenly Father. There can be no doubt but that the main point is the necessity of imitating the divine example and this necessity is peculiarly enforced by the consideration of the filial relation they sustain to God as *their* heavenly Father.

It is just here, however, that it becomes necessary to note the implications of the similarity established and enforced as the reason for such attitude and conduct with reference to their enemies. The disciples are to love their enemies in order that they may be the sons of their Father; they must imitate their Father. Clearly implied is the thought that God, the Father, loves his enemies and that it is because he loves his enemies that he makes his sun rise upon them and sends them rain. This is just saying that the kindness bestowed in sunshine and rain is the expression of divine love, that back of the bestowal there is an attitude on the part of God, called love, which constrains him to bestow these tokens of his lovingkindness. This informs us that the gifts bestowed by God are not simply gifts which have the effect of good and blessing to those who are the recipients but that they are also a manifestation or expression of lovingkindness and goodness in the heart or will of God with reference to those who are the recipients. The enjoyment on the part of the recipients has its ground as well as its source in this lovingkindness of which the gifts enjoyed are the expression. In other words, these are gifts and are enjoyed because there is in a true and high sense benevolence in the heart of God.

These conclusions are reinforced by verse 48. There can be no question regarding the immediate relevance of verse 48 to the exhortation of verses 44–47, even though it may have a more comprehensive reference. And verse 48 means that what has been adduced by way of divine example in the preceding verses is set forth as epitomizing the divine perfection and as providing the great exemplar by which the believer's attitude and conduct are to be governed and the goal to which thought and life are to be oriented. The love and beneficence of God to the evil and unjust epitomize the norm of human perfection. It is obvious that this love and beneficence on the part of God are regarded by our Lord himself as not something incidental in God but as that which constitutes an element in the sum of divine perfection. This is made very specific in the parallel passage in Luke 6:35, 36 where we read, 'And ye shall be sons of the Most High, because he is kind towards the unthankful and evil. Ye shall be merciful, as your Father is merciful.' This word translated 'merciful' is redolent of the pity and compassion in the heart of God that overflow in the bestowments of kindness.

The sum of this study of these passages in Matthew and Luke is simply this, that presupposed in God's gifts bestowed upon the ungodly there is in God a disposition of love, kindness, mercifulness, and that the actual gifts and the blessing accruing therefrom for the ungodly must not be abstracted from the lovingkindness of which they are the expression. And, of course, we must not think of this lovingkindness as conditioned upon a penitent attitude in the recipients. The lovingkindness rather is exercised towards them in their ungodly state and is expressed in the favours they enjoy. What bearing this may have upon the grace of God manifested in the free offer of the gospel to all without distinction remains to be seen. But we are hereby given a disclosure of goodness in the heart of God and of the relation there is between gifts bestowed and the lovingkindness from which they flow. And there is indicated to us something respecting God's love or benevolence that we might not or could not entertain if we concentrated our thought simply on the divine decree of reprobation. Furthermore we must remember that there are many gifts enjoyed by the ungodly who are within the pale of the gospel administration which are not enjoyed by those outside, and we shall have to conclude that in respect of these specific favours, enjoyed by such ungodly persons in distinction from others, the same principle of divine benevolence and lovingkindness must obtain, a lovingkindness, too, which must correspond to the character of the specific gifts enjoyed.

Acts 14:17

This text does not express as much as those considered already. But it does witness to the same truth that God gave testimony to his own perfection when he did good to those whom he left to walk in their own ways. God did them good, he sent them rain from heaven and fruitful seasons, filling their hearts with food and gladness. We must infer, on the basis of what we found already, that behind this doing of good and bestowal of blessing, as well as behind the gladness of heart which followed, there was the divine goodness and lovingkindness.

Deuteronomy 5:29 (26 in Hebrew); 32:29; Psalm 81:13 ff. (81:14 ff. in Hebrew); Isaiah 48:18

The purpose of adducing these texts is to note the optative force of that which is expressed. There can be no reasonable question as to the optative force of Deuteronomy 5:29(26). It is introduced by the idiom *mi yitten* which literally means 'who will give?' but is really a strong optative expression meaning 'Oh that there were!' Consequently the text reads, 'Oh that there were such a heart in them, that they would fear me, and keep all my commandments always, that it might be well with them, and with their children for ever!' It is the Lord who is speaking and we shall have to conclude that here we have the expression of earnest desire or wish or will that the people of Israel were of a heart to fear him and keep all his commandments always. It is apparent from the book of Deuteronomy itself (cf. 31:24–29) and from the whole history of Israel that they did not have a heart to fear God and to keep all his commandments always. Since they did not fulfil that which was optatively expressed in 5:29 (26), we must conclude that God had not decreed that they should have such a heart. If God had decreed it, it would have been so. Here therefore we have an instance of desire on the part of God for the fulfilment of that which he had not decreed, in other words, a will on the part of God to that which he had not decretively willed.

In Deuteronomy 32:29 the construction is somewhat different. In our English versions it is translated, 'Oh that they were wise, that they understood this, that they would consider their latter end.' This rendering is distinctly optative and has the same effect as Deuteronomy 5:29 (26), considered above. It must be admitted that this is a perfectly legitimate rendering and interpretation. The conjunction *lu* with which the verse begins has undoubtedly this optative force. It has such force unquestionably in Genesis 17:18; Numbers 14:2; 20:3; 22:29; Joshua 7:7; Isaiah 63:19, and possibly, if not probably, in Genesis 23:13; 30:34. When *lu* has this optative force it means 'Oh that' or 'if only' and expresses strong desire. In view of what we found in Deuteronomy 5:26 there is no reason why the optative force of *lu* should not be adopted here. We may not, however, insist that *lu* must have optative force here because *lu* is also used with conditional force, as in Judges 8:19; 13:23; 2 Samuel 18:12 and elsewhere. If *lu* is understood conditionally, Deuteronomy 32:29 would be rendered as follows: 'If they were wise, they would understand this, they would consider their latter end.' This, however, is not the most natural rendering. The optative interpretation is smoother and more meaningful in the context. If this more natural construction is followed it shows the same thing as we found in Deuteronomy 5:26, that earnest desire is expressed for what is contrary to fact (cf. v. 28).

In Psalm 81:14 it may readily be detected that the conditional force of the conjunction *lu* cannot reasonably be adopted. The thought is rather distinctly optative, 'Oh that my people were hearkening unto me, that Israel would walk in my ways.'

Isaiah 48:18 could readily be rendered conditionally thus: 'If thou hadst hearkened to my commandments, thy peace had been as a river and thy righteousness as the waves of the sea.' It can also be rendered optatively as in our English versions.

It should be noted that even when the conjunction *lu* is given very distinct conditional force, the optative idea is sometimes rather noticeably in the background. This would very likely be the case in Isaiah 48:18 even if the optative rendering gives way to the conditional. The desirableness of that which is expressed in the condition and its corresponding consequence cannot be suppressed. This can be expressed in our English idiom very well when we render, 'If only thou hadst hearkened to my commandments, then had thy peace been as a river' etc. Both the conditional and optative appear here, and there is much to be said in favour of the conclusion, that whether we render Isaiah 48:18 optatively or conditionally the optative notion still persists, in the former case, of course, directly and in the latter case indirectly.

Should we make full allowance for doubts as to the exact force of the construction in the case of Deuteronomy 32:29 and Isaiah 48:18, there can be no room for question but that the Lord represents himself in some of these passages as earnestly desiring the fulfilment of something which he had not in the exercise of his sovereign will actually decreed to come to pass. This bears very directly upon the point at issue.

Matthew 23:37; Luke 13:34.

In this passage there should be no dispute that the will of Christ in the direction of a certain benign result is set in contrast with the will of those who are contemplated as the subjects of such blessing. These two stand in opposition to each other – I have willed (or wished), ye have not willed (or wished). Not only so. The will of Christ to a certain end is opposed to that which actually occurred. Jesus says he often wished the occurrence of something which did not come to pass and therefore willed (or wished) the occurrence of that which God had not secretly or decretively willed.

That which Jesus willed is stated to be the gathering together of the children of Jerusalem, as a hen gathers together her chickens under her wings. This surely means the gathering together of the people of Jerusalem under his saving and protecting grace. So we have the most emphatic declaration on the part of Christ of his having yearned for the salvation of the people of Jerusalem.

It might be said that Jesus is here giving expression simply to his human desire and that this would not indicate, therefore, the desire or will of God. In other words, it might be said that we are not justified in transferring this expression of his human desire to the *divine* desire or will, either in respect of Jesus' own divine consciousness or the divine consciousness of the other persons of the Godhead.

Christ was indeed truly human and his human mind and will operated within the limitations inseparable from human nature. His human nature was not omniscient and could not in the nature of the case be cognisant of the whole decretive will of God. In his human nature he wrought within limits that could not apply to the specifically divine knowledge, desire and will. Hence it might be argued that on this occasion he gave expression to the yearnings of his truly human will and therefore to a will that could not be aware of the whole secret purpose of God. Furthermore, it might be said that Jesus was speaking of what he willed in the past before he was aware, in his human consciousness, of the judgment that was to befall Jerusalem, stated in verses 38, 39. A great deal more might be said along this line that would lend plausibility to such an interpretation.

We are not able to regard such an interpretation of our Lord's statement as tenable. It is true our Lord was human. It is true he spoke as human. And it is true he spoke these words or gave utterance to this lament through the medium of his human nature. The will he spoke of on this occasion was certainly one that engaged the total exercise of his human desire and will. But there is much more that needs to be considered if we are properly to assess the significance of this incident and of Jesus' utterance. Jesus is speaking here in his capacity as the Messiah and Saviour. He is speaking therefore as the God-man. He is speaking of the will on his part as the Messiah and Saviour to embrace the people of Jerusalem in the arms of his saving grace and covenant love. The majesty that belongs to his person in this unique capacity shines through the whole episode and it is quite improper to abstract the divine aspect of his person from the capacity in which he gives utterance to this will and from the prerogative in virtue of which he could give expression to the utterance. What needs to be appreciated is that the embrace of which Jesus here speaks is that which he exercises in that unique office and prerogative that belong to him as the God-man Messiah and Saviour. In view of the transcendent, divine function which he says he wished to perform, it would be illegitimate for us to say that here we have simply an example of his human desire or will. It is surely, therefore, a revelation to us of the divine will as well as of the human. Our Lord in the exercise of his most specific and unique function as the God-man gives expression to a yearning will on his part that responsiveness on the part of the people of Jerusalem would have provided the necessary condition for the bestowal of his saving and protecting love, a responsiveness, nevertheless, which it was not the decretive will of God to create in their hearts.

In this connection we must not fail to keep in mind the principle borne out by Jesus' own repeated declarations, especially as recorded in the Gospel of John, namely, the perfect harmony and coalescence of will on the part of the Father and of the Son (cf. John 12:49, 50; 14:10, 24; 17:8). To aver that Jesus in the expressed will of Matthew 23:37 is not disclosing the *divine* will but simply his own human will would tend towards very grave prejudice to this principle. And, viewing the matter from the standpoint of revelation, how would it affect our conception of Jesus as the supreme revelation of the Father if in this case we were not to regard his words as a transcript of the Father's will as well as of his own? We can readily see the difficulties that face us if we do not grant the truly *revelatory* significance of our Lord's statement.

In this lament over Jerusalem, furthermore, there is surely disclosed to us something of the will of our Lord as the Son of God and divine Son of man that lies back of, and is expressed in, such an invitation as Matthew 11:28. Here we have declared, if we may use the thought of Matthew 23:37, his will to embrace the labouring and heavy laden in the arms of his saving and loving protection. And it is an invitation to all such to take advantage of that will of his. The fulness and freeness of the invitation need not now be argued. Its character as such is patent. It is important, however, to note that the basis and background of this invitation are supplied by the uniqueness of the relation that he sustains to the Father as the Son, the transcendent commission that is given to him as the Son, and the sovereignty, coordinate with that of the Father, which he exercises because of that unique relationship and in that unique capacity. We should not fail to perceive the interrelations of these two passages (Matt. 23:37; 11:28) and to recognize that the former is redolent of his divine prerogative and revelatory of his divine will. Verses 38 and 39 confirm the high prerogative in terms of which he is speaking, for there he pronounces the divine judgment. And in this connection we cannot forget John 5:26, 27, 'For as the Father hath life in himself, even so hath he given to the Son to have life in himself. And he hath given to him authority to execute judgment, because he is the Son of man.'

Ezekiel 18:23, 32; 33:11.

It does not appear to us in the least justifiable to limit the reference of these passages to any one class of wicked persons. Suffice it now to mention one or two considerations in support of this conclusion. In Ezekiel 33:4–9 the wicked who actually die in their iniquity are contemplated. It is without warrant to exclude such wicked persons from the scope of the wicked spoken of in verse 11. While it is true that a new paragraph may be regarded as introduced at verse 10, yet the new thought of verse 10 is simply the despairing argument or objection on the part of the house of Israel and does not have the effect of qualifying the denotation or connotation of the wicked mentioned in verse 11, a denotation and a connotation determined by the preceding verses. Again, the emphatic negative of the first part of verse 11 – 'I have no pleasure in the death of the wicked' – admits of no limitation or qualification; it applies to the wicked who actually die in their iniquity. Why then should there be the least disposition to limit those spoken of in the text to any class of wicked persons?

In Ezekiel 18:23 the construction is not without significance. This verse is introduced by the interrogative and then we have the emphatic construction of duplication well known in Hebrew. It might be rendered, 'Taking pleasure in, do I take pleasure in?' The question implies, of course, an emphatic negative. It should also be noted that the verb in this case takes a direct object, namely, 'the death of the wicked' (*moth rasha* without any article). In this case we do not have the preposition *be* as in Ezekiel 33:11.[1] It should be noted that the verb *chaphez* with such a construction can very properly be rendered by our English word, 'desire', as frequently elsewhere in the Old Testament. Consequently this verse may well be rendered, 'Do I at all desire the death of the wicked?' The force of this is obviously the emphatic negative, 'I do not by any means desire the death of the wicked,' or, to be very literal, 'I do not by any means desire death of a wicked person.'

The interrogative construction is continued in the latter part of the verse. Here, however, it is negative in form, implying an affirmative answer to the question, just as in the former part the affirmative form implied a negative answer. It reads, 'Is it not rather in his turning from his way (the Massoretes read 'his ways') and live?' The clear import is an emphatic asseveration to the effect that the Lord Jehovah delights rather in the turning of the wicked from his evil way that he may live.

[1] Kittel says that 20 manuscripts read *bemoth* as in verse 32. If this reading is correct, then, of course, what is said respecting the omission of the preposition *be* does not hold.

The adversative form of the sentence may well be rendered thus: 'Do I at all desire the death of the wicked, saith the Lord Jehovah, and not rather that he turn from his way and live?'

The sum of the matter may be stated in the following propositions. It is absolutely and universally true that God does not delight in or desire the death of a wicked person. It is likewise absolutely and universally true that he delights in the repentance and life of that wicked person. It would surely be quite unwarranted to apply the latter proposition less universally or more restrictively than the former. The adversative construction and the emphatic form by which the protestation is introduced are surely not compatible with any other conclusion. And if we carry over the perfectly proper rendering of the first clause, the thought can be expressed thus, 'God does not desire the death of the wicked but rather their repentance and life.'

In Ezekiel 33:11 the construction is somewhat different. The statement is introduced by the oath, 'As I live saith the Lord Jehovah.' Then we have the construction with the Hebrew *im*, which has the force of an emphatic negative and must be rendered, 'I have no delight (or pleasure) in the death of the wicked' (*bemoth harasha*; in this case the article is used). It should be noted that the preposition *be* is used in this case, as also in the second part of 18:23 as observed below.[1] This is a very frequent construction in Hebrew with reference to delight in persons or things. Interesting examples are 2 Samuel 24:3; Esther 6:6, 7, 9, 11; Psalms 147:10; Proverbs 18:2; Isaiah 65:12; Malachi 2:17. On certain occasions the Hebrew word could well be translated 'desire' in English and the word that follows the preposition taken as the direct object (e.g. 2 Sam. 24:3).

It has been argued that the preposition *be* in Ezekiel 33:11b has the force of 'when' so that the verse would run, 'As I live, saith the Lord Jehovah, I have no pleasure in the death of the wicked but when the wicked turns from his way and lives.' And so it has been claimed that all that is said in this verse is that God is pleased *when* the wicked turns and cannot be made to support the proposition that God is pleased *that* the wicked should repent, whether they repent or not. On this view it would be maintained that this verse says nothing more than

---

[1] The only instances we have been able to find in the Old Testament of *chaphez be*, followed by the infinitive construct, are Ezekiel 18:23b and 33:11b. *chaphez* without the preposition *be* is followed by the infinitive construct in other cases cf. Isaiah 53:10).

that God is pleased when a wicked man repents but says nothing respecting the pleasure of God in reference to the repentance of those who do not actually repent.

In dealing with this question a few things need be said.

(1) A study of the instances where this construction of the verb *chaphez* with the preposition *be* occurs would not suggest this interpretation of the force of the preposition *be*. The usage rather indicates that the preposition points to that upon which pleasure is placed, that to which desire gravitates, that in which delight is taken. That object of pleasure, desire, delight may be conceived of as existing, or as something not actually existent, or as something desirable, that is to say, desired to be. When the object is contemplated as desirable but not actually realized, the thought of *chaphez* does not at all appear to be simply that delight or pleasure will be derived from the object when it is realized or possessed. That thought is, of course, implied. But there is much more. There is the delight or pleasure or desire that it should come to be, even if the actual occurrence should never take place. Consequently it appears that the notion that Ezekiel 33:11b simply says that God is pleased *when* a wicked man repents robs the concept expressed by *chaphez be* of some of its most characteristic and necessary meaning. It is not in any way denied that this kind of delight is embraced in the expression. But to limit the concept to this notion is without warrant and is not borne out by the usage.

(2) The adversative construction of the verse would not by any means suggest the interpretation that verse 11b says simply that God is pleased *when* a man repents. In the same clause it is denied that God has pleasure in the death of the wicked. In accordance with 18:23 this means that it is true absolutely and universally that God does not delight in the death of the wicked. This does not mean simply that God does not delight in the death of the wicked *when* he dies. The denial is much more embracive. In like manner, it would be unnatural for us to suppose that the affirmation of that in which God does take delight is simply the turning of the wicked from his way *when* it occurs. This is just saying that it is natural to give to the preposition *be* in the second clause the same force as it has in the first. Rendered literally then the two clauses would read, 'I do not have pleasure in the death of the wicked but rather in his turning from his way and that he live.' Paraphrased the thought would be, 'It is not pleasing to me that the wicked die but that the wicked turn from his way and live.' And

the same kind of absoluteness and universality denied in the one case must be regarded as affirmed in the other.

(3) Confirmation of this interpretation may be derived from the concluding clauses of verse 11, 'Turn ye, turn ye from your evil ways, and why will ye die, oh house of Israel.' The thought of the last clause is that there is no reason why they should die. There is no reason because of the grace so emphatically declared in the earlier part of the verse and, by implication, so fully and freely proffered. There will not be any dispute regarding the universality of the exhortation and command in the clause, 'turn ye, turn ye from your evil ways.' This is a command that applies to all men without any discrimination or exception. It expresses therefore the will of God to repentance. He wills that all should repent. Nothing less than that is expressed in the universal command. To state the matter more fully, he wills that all should repent and live or be saved. When this is related to the last clause, 'why will ye die?' it means that the reason why no one need die, why there is no reason why any should die, is, that God does not will that any should die. He wills rather that they repent and live. This declaration of the will of God to the repentance and life of all, so clearly implied in the two concluding clauses, rests, however, upon the declarations of the two preceding clauses, the clauses with which we are now more particularly concerned. We should conclude, therefore, that the will to universal repentance and life, so unmistakably expressed in the concluding clauses, is also declared or, at least, implied in the words, 'I have no pleasure in the death of the wicked but that the wicked turn from his way and live.' This is just saying that the import of the hortatory and interrogative clauses at the end requires or presupposes a will of God to repentance and life, a will to which the bare notion that God is pleased *when* men repent is not by any means equal. The only adequate way of expressing the will implied in the exhortation is the will that all should repent and it is surely that truth that is declared in the oath-supported statement, 'I have no pleasure in the death of the wicked, but that the wicked turn from his way and live.'

It is not to be forgotten that when it is said that God absolutely and universally takes no pleasure in the death of the wicked, we are not here speaking of God's decretive will. In terms of his decretive will it must be said that God absolutely decrees the eternal death of some wicked and, in that sense, is absolutely pleased so to decree. But in the text it is the will of God's benevolence (*Voluntas euarestias*) that is stated, not the will of God's decree (*voluntas eudokias*). It is, in our judgment, quite unjustifiable to think that in this passage there is any reflection upon the decretive will of God in the word *chaphez*. And neither is there evidence to show that in the word *chaphez* there is here any comparative notion to the effect that God takes greater pleasure in saving men than he does in damning them.

It is indeed true that in a few passages in the Old Testament the word *chaphez* is used with reference to the decretive will of God (cf. Ps. 115:3; 135:6; the substantive *chephez*, also in Isa. 44:28; 46:10; 48:14). But in this passage everything points to the conclusion that the good pleasure or delight of God spoken of is viewed entirely from the aspect of benevolent lovingkindness. And it is in terms of that aspect of the divine will that the words 'absolutely' and 'universally' have been used above.

Isaiah 45:22

There can be no question but the salvation mentioned in this text is salvation in the highest sense. It cannot be weakened to mean temporary or temporal security. The salvation must be of the same character as that referred to in verse 17 and implied in the title appropriated by God himself in verse 21. The text is also an invitation and command to all to turn to God and to be saved. The universalism of this command should be apparent from the expression, 'all the ends of the earth.' This is a characteristic Old Testament phrase to designate all nations and peoples. The universal scope is, however, confirmed by the context. There are several intimations of this. In the preceding context the Lord asserts his Creatorhood (vv. 12, 18). This appeal to his Creatorhood has the effect of bringing to the forefront a relationship which he sustains to all men alike. Likewise the Lord protests that he is the only God, that there is none else besides him (vv. 14, 18, 21). The emphasis on this becomes more specific in the repeated assertion that he alone is the Saviour (vv. 15, 20, 21). Furthermore, that all men are contemplated is borne out by verse 23, that unto him every knee shall bow, every tongue shall swear. Finally, this note is implied in the scorn that is poured out upon the heathen in verse 20 – 'They have not knowledge that carry the wood of their graven image, and pray unto a god that cannot save.' All these considerations bear directly upon the universal reference of the appeal in verse 22. It is because God alone is God and because he alone can save that the exhortation is extended to all, 'turn ye to me and be ye saved.' We could not place any kind of limitation upon the exhortation without interfering with the universality of the prerogative claimed by God himself in the context. It is necessary to stress this because it might be thought that the universalism of the command in verse 22 is not distributive universalism but simply ethnical universalism, all nations without distinction but not all people without exception. The considerations of the context would show that there is no exception to the command any more than there is to the sole Creatorhood, sole Godhood and sole Saviourhood of the God who extends the appeal.

This text expresses then the will of God in the matter of the call, invitation, appeal, and command of the gospel, namely, the will that all should turn to him and be saved. What God wills in this sense he certainly is pleased to will. If it is his pleasure to will that all repent and be saved, it is surely his pleasure that all repent and be saved. Obviously, however, it is not his decretive will that all repent and be saved. While, on the one hand, he has not decretively willed that all be saved, yet he declares unequivocally that it is his will and, impliedly, his pleasure that all turn and be saved. We are again faced with the mystery and adorable richness of the divine will. It might seem to us that the one rules out the other. But it is not so. There is a multiformity to the divine will that is consonant with the fulness and richness of his divine character, and it is no wonder that we are constrained to bow in humble yet exultant amazement before his ineffable greatness and unsearchable judgments. To deny the reality of the divine pleasure directed to the repentance and salvation of all is to fail to accept the witness borne by such a text as this to the manifoldness of God's will and the riches of his grace.

2 Peter 3:9

In view of what we have found already there is no reason in *the analogy of Scripture* why we should not regard this passage as teaching that God in the exercise of his benevolent longsuffering and lovingkindness wills that none should perish, but that all should come to repentance. An *a priori* assumption that this text cannot teach that God wills the repentance and salvation of all is a gravely unsound assumption, for it is not an assumption derived from the analogy of Scripture. In approaching this text there should be no such prejudice. What this text does actually teach will have to be determined, however, by grammatico-historical exegesis of the text and context.

The choice of the verb 'is longsuffering' (*makrothumei*) will be considered first. In Luke 18:7, the only other instance in the New Testament where it refers to the action of God, it probably relates to the elect. But in that case it is employed in the somewhat distinctive sense of 'delay' in avenging them. The 'longsuffering' (*makrothumia*) of God, is spoken of several times, and its usage is illuminating. Romans 9:22 presents a clear instance where it has in view an attitude of God towards the reprobate; he 'endured with much longsuffering vessels of wrath.' In Romans 2:4, it is associated with the goodness and forbearance of God, and subsumed under his goodness, as that which is despised by the impenitent who treasures up for himself wrath in the day of wrath, who does not know that the goodness of God 'leadeth him to repentance' (*eis metanoian se agei*). The choice of the verb *agein* is to be noted. Since the impenitent are in view, it cannot refer to efficacious grace. Nevertheless, it is a strong verb as its use in Romans 8:14 shows: 'As many as are led by the Spirit of God, these are the sons of God' (cf. Gal. 5:18). It must be understood as a constraining influence flowing from the goodness of God which is calculated to bring men to repentance. The construction in Romans 2:4 is remarkably similar to that in 2 Peter 3:9.

On the background of these passages, the usage by Peter may be considered to advantage. In the last days, Peter says, mockers will mock because the *parousia* has not come. The day of judgment will nevertheless come. The apparent delay in its coming some count slackness. What is counted as slackness by some should, however, really be recognized as longsuffering (2 Peter 3:3–9). The long-suffering should not be counted as slackness, but as salvation (v. 15). The long-suffering is, then, a positive favour of God towards sinners which is directed to their salvation.

Up to this point, accordingly, the thought is similar to that of Romans 2:4. Men may despise God's goodness, forbearance and longsuffering towards them, not knowing that that goodness has in view their turning from their sins to God. Men may count the longsuffering as slackness on God's part, when actually they ought to account it as designed to extend salvation to them.

But this tentative judgment on the basis of the use of *makrothumia* must be related to the rest of verse 9. This aspect of the question is considerably complicated by the divergence in the textual tradition at this point. The situation is reflected in part in the divergence between

AV and ARV: 'to us-ward' and 'to you-ward.' But there is a further complication due to the fact that there is significant testimony for the preposition *dia*, resulting in the possibilities: 'on your account' or 'on our account.' The reading *dia* has come to be preferred by Mayor, Moffatt, Greijdanus, RSV mg. The difference between 'you' and 'us' or 'your' and 'our' is not especially significant, since in either case the readers of the Epistle would be primarily in view. The actual line-up of authorities does not, however, leave solid external support for the combination 'on our account', though Mayor supports it. The reading 'to us-ward' is clearly the weakest reading, judged by external evidence; and it is not commended particularly by other considerations. Hence the choice falls between 'to you-ward' and 'on your account'. While perhaps it is not possible to decide finally between these two readings, we may judge that the reading 'on your account' has a very strong claim. The external evidence for it appears to be at least as strong as for the other competing reading, and transcriptionally it may be preferred as being somewhat more unusual and difficult.

The question now arises as to the specific reference of 'you,' whether with the preposition *dia* or *eis*. Does the use of this pronoun indicate that reprobate men are out of consideration here? So it has been argued. However, if the reprobate are out of consideration here, the 'true believers' would have to be identified with the elect, and the long-suffering of God would have to be understood as the special, saving grace of God manifested to the elect alone. We do not believe that the restriction of the reference to the elect is well-established. The Epistle does not make this restriction. Moreover, since on this view, the believers addressed here are characterized as 'living lax Christian lives,' are viewed as requiring repentance, and even as about to 'perish' unless they repent, it cannot be argued plausibly that the apostle would not have allowed for the presence of some reprobate among the members of his audience. Even if the 'you' is restricted to professing Christians, one cannot exclude the possibility that reprobate men were also in view.

The 'you' of this passage can hardly be restricted to the elect. Can it even be restricted to 'believers'? Can it be restricted to believers who urgently stand in need of repentance? The determination of this question is bound up with the evaluation of the subordinate clauses. It may be acknowledged that the decision made with regard to 'you' will bear upon the meaning of the language that follows. But the reverse is also true. The language of the clauses may be such as to reflect decisively upon the persons referred to in connection with the manifestations of longsuffering. Does not, as a matter of fact, the language 'not wishing that any should perish, but that all should come to repentance' set before us a basic antithesis between the *death* or destruction that awaits impenitent sinners and, by implication, the *life* eternal which men may enter upon through repentance? God does not wish that any men should perish. His wish is rather that all should enter upon life eternal by coming to repentance. The language in this part of the verse is so absolute that it is highly unnatural to envisage Peter as meaning merely that God does not wish that any believers should perish, but that he rather wishes that all believers who live laxly should repent of their sins. If they are believers, they have already come to repentance, entered upon life, and escaped destruction, even though the struggle against sin and turning from it must continue. The language of the clauses, then, most naturally refers to mankind as a whole as men are faced with the issues of death or life before the day of judgment comes. It does not view men either as elect or as reprobate, and so allows that both elect and reprobate make up the totality in view.

The most satisfactory view of 2 Peter 3:9 is:

(1) Peter teaches that the delay of the coming of judgment should be acknowledged as a manifestation of the longsuffering or patience of God with sinners.

(2) Peter says that God is longsuffering *on your account*. It is not because of any slackness in God himself, but because of the consideration of the well-being of men. The pronoun 'you' cannot be restricted to the elect. It would certainly include the members of the Christian community as possible benefactors of the longsuffering of God, but in view of considerations adduced above may not fairly be restricted to believers.

(3) If the reading 'to you-ward' is adopted, the thrust of the passage is not essentially altered. The delay is not due to slackness in God, but is to be regarded as an expression of longsuffering towards men, including very specifically those addressed in the Epistle.

(4) The reason or ground for the longsuffering of God until the day of judgment is given in what is said concerning his 'willing.' He is longsuffering in that, or because, he does not wish that any men should perish, but rather because he wills or wishes that all should come to repentance. Repentance is the condition of life; without repentance

men must perish. But the will of God that men be saved expressed here is not conditional. It is not: I will your salvation if you repent, but: I will that you repent and thus be saved. The two clauses then go far beyond defining the longsuffering of God, for they intimate what is back of his longsuffering. This favour is grounded in God himself; it is an expression of his will with regard to sinners, his will being nothing short of their salvation.

The argument that the longsuffering of God that delays judgment could not concern the reprobate, 'for they will never repent' is to be met exactly as Calvin met similar arguments. Following his exegesis of 2 Peter 3:9, Calvin says: 'But it may be asked, If God wishes none to perish, why is it that so many perish? To this my answer is, that no mention is here made of the hidden purpose of God, according to which the reprobate are doomed to their own ruin, but only of his will as made known to us in the gospel. For God there stretches out his hand without a difference to all, but lays hold only of those, to lead them unto himself, whom he has chosen before the foundation of the world.'

CONCLUSIONS

(1) We have found that the grace of God bestowed in his ordinary providence expresses the love of God, and that this love of God is the source of the gifts bestowed upon and enjoyed by the ungodly as well as the godly. We should expect that herein is disclosed to us a principle that applies to all manifestations of divine grace, namely, that the grace bestowed expresses the lovingkindness in the heart of God and that the gifts bestowed are in their respective variety tokens of a correspondent richness or manifoldness in the divine lovingkindness of which they are the expression.

(2) We have found that God himself expresses an ardent desire for the fulfilment of certain things which he has not decreed in his inscrutable counsel to come to pass. This means that there is a will to the realization of what he has not decretively willed, a pleasure towards that which he has not been pleased to decree. This is indeed mysterious, and why he has not brought to pass, in the exercise of his omnipotent power and grace, what is his ardent pleasure lies hid in the sovereign counsel of his will. We should not entertain, however, any prejudice

against the notion that God desires or has pleasure in the accomplishment of what he does not decretively will.

(3) Our Lord himself in the exercise of his messianic prerogative provides us with an example of the foregoing as it applies to the matter of salvation. He says expressly that he willed the bestowal of his saving and protecting grace upon those whom neither the Father nor he decreed thus to save and protect.

(4) We found that God reveals himself as not taking pleasure in or desiring the death of those who die but rather as taking pleasure in or desiring the repentance and life of the wicked. This will of God to repentance and salvation is universalized and reveals to us, therefore, that there is in God a benevolent lovingkindness towards the repentance and salvation of even those whom he has not decreed to save. This pleasure, will, desire is expressed in the universal call to repentance.

(5) We must conclude, therefore, that our provisional inference on the basis of Matthew 5:44-48 is borne out by the other passages. The full and free offer of the gospel is a grace bestowed upon all. Such grace is necessarily a manifestation of love or lovingkindness in the heart of God. And this lovingkindness is revealed to be of a character or kind that is correspondent with the grace bestowed. The grace offered is nothing less than salvation in its richness and fulness. The love or lovingkindness that lies back of that offer is not anything less; it is the will to that salvation. In other words, it is Christ in all the glory of his person and in all the perfection of his finished work whom God offers in the gospel. The loving and benevolent will that is the source of that offer and that grounds its veracity and reality is the will to the possession of Christ and the enjoyment of the salvation that resides in him.

8

Paul's use of 'Nomos'

We are all only too painfully aware that the apostasy of our day within professed Christianity is not only from the basic tenets of the faith once delivered to the saints but also from the fundamental norms of the Christian ethic. It would be a formidable task to try to trace all the developments that have contributed to this revolt against Christian standards of behaviour. I am quite convinced, however, that no factor bears more of the onus than the failure on the part of well-intentioned proponents of Christian ethics to recognize and maintain the uncurtailed sanctity of law in the Christian institution, and along with this the failure to appreciate the correlativity of law and love in the life of faith. Whenever an antithesis is set up between love and law, and love is regarded as self-directive and self-instructing, then the basis is laid for all that today confronts us in what is called the 'new morality'. Hence it is, for that reason alone, appropriate to discuss Paul's use of *nomos*.

But there is another compelling reason. It is exegetical in character. In Paul's use of *nomos* it is necessary to recognize the distinct applications of the term. Grave misinterpretation of the apostle's teaching arises if we do not observe these differentiations. If, for example, we do not discern the precise import of 'under law' (ὑπὸ νόμον) in Romans 6:14, or of 'ye have been put to death to the law' in Romans 7:4, or of 'ye have been discharged from the law' in Romans 7:6, we are liable to an error that not only devastates Paul's own teaching but overthrows the whole biblical concept of law as regulative of life.

Examples of this distinction lie on the face of Paul's usage. There are those well-known passages in Paul where the expression ὑπὸ νόμον is in the sharpest contrast with the state of grace (ὑπὸ χάριν). The best known is Romans 6:14, 15. But equally obvious in the same sense is Galatians 5:18 'But if ye are being led by the Spirit, ye are not under law'. In Galatians 4:21 the ultimate effect is the same. But there is probably in ὑπὸ νόμον in this instance an additional element reflecting on the desire to remain under the bondage of the Mosaic economy. It is clear that 'under law' and 'under grace' are mutually exclusive, the former involving condemnation and bondage, the latter justification and the new life of liberty in the Holy Spirit. But in 1 Corinthians 9:20 Paul uses this same expression (ὑπὸ νόμον) to characterize his own behaviour. 'And I became to the Jews as a Jew, in order that I might win the Jews; to those under law as under law'. He cannot mean that he behaved as one 'under law' in the sense of Romans 6:14, 15 for in that event he would behave as one not under grace, an impossible supposition. Hence 'under law' in 1 Corinthians 9:20 must have another meaning. It refers to the rites and ceremonies of the Mosaic institution, and when he says he became 'to those under law as under law' he means that he accommodated himself by way of expediency to those who considered themselves still bound by these rites and ceremonies and had not yet understood the abrogation in respect of observance implicit in the redemptive events wrought by Christ.

This meaning of ὑπὸ νόμον provides the index to the force of the same expression in Galatians 3:23: 'Before faith came we were kept in ward under law, shut up unto the faith about to be revealed'. And the same import or reference applies to Galatians 4:4, 5: 'made under the law, to redeem them that were under the law' (ὑπὸ νόμον in both instances). In the preceding context Paul is dealing with the significance of the Mosaic administration. This is clear from 3:17, 19 where he specifies the law as that given 430 years after the promise given to Abraham. He then asks the pointed question: 'What then is the law?' and answers 'It was added on account of the transgressions' and 'ordained through angels in the hand of a Mediator', the Mediator being Moses. It is the pedagogy of the Mosaic institution that is in view in Galatians 3:23 (cf. 4:2, 3) and ὑπὸ νόμον cannot have the sense of the same in Romans 6:14, 15; Galatians 5:18 without the conclusion that the Mosaic economy knew no grace but the servitude, of sin and its curse. The Mosaic economy had its servitude, but it was that of nonage and pupilage, of infancy in comparison with the maturity of the fulness of time, not the servitude in total antithesis to grace with which Romans 6:14, 15 is concerned.

Another example of this use of *nomos* as referring to the Mosaic administration is Romans 5:13 ἄρχι νόμου – as is made plain from verse 14: 'But death reigned from Adam to Moses'. And this must apply also to Romans 5:20: 'And the law came in beside, that the trespass might abound' (cf. Gal. 3:19).

That 'under law' in this sense of administration is not to be construed as implying the antithesis of Romans 6:14 *et al.* is shown by such a passage as Romans 4:16: 'Therefore it is of faith in order that it might be by grace, to the end that the promise might be sure to all the seed, not only to that which is of the law (ἐκ τοῦ νόμου) but also to that which is of the faith of Abraham'. Here ἐκ τοῦ νόμου does not have any depreciatory sense. Being 'of the law' in no way militates against possession of the promise and that which is embodied in it, for the thought is that the promise is secure to those who are of the faith of Abraham as well as to those privileged by the law. The law then is the Mosaic revelation and institution and the same assessment of the Mosaic administration is in view in Galatians 3:21: 'Is the law then against the promises of God? God forbid'. This use of ἐκ τοῦ νόμου in Romans 4:16 is the more remarkable because in verse 14 ἐκ νόμου has the depreciatory sense in complete contrast to faith and to promise. 'For if those who are of the law are heirs, faith is made void and the promise of no effect'. The proximity advises us again of the flexibility of terms and the ease with which Paul can pass from one connotation to another in the use of the term *nomos*.

It is necessary now to discuss to some extent Paul's antithesis between ὑπὸ νόμον and ὑπο χάριν. The importance of the antithesis is shown by the fact that the governing thesis of both the epistle to the Romans and the epistle to the Galatians turns on this antithesis.

It should be observed at the outset that the term 'law', even in the phrase 'under law' with which we are now concerned, does not admit of any derogatory estimate or definition. It does not refer to some alien law devised or imposed or imported by men. Paul does speak of 'the law of sin' which was in his members (Rom. 7:23, 25) and of 'the law of sin and death' (Rom. 8:2). Although it would be impossible to regard 'the law' in these instances as the law of God provoking our corrupt nature to sin after the pattern of Romans 7:5, 8, 11, yet there is good reason for believing that law is used in these instances in the sense of operating principle, that the 'law of sin' is the sinful operating principle, and that the genitive is one of characterizing quality. But even if the law of God were in view, no indictment or derogation would apply to the law, but only to the sinful passions aroused to exercise by the law, and the vindications of Romans 7:12–14 would still be applicable. Throughout Paul's teaching, the law is the law of God, holy, just, good, and spiritual. (Cf. Rom. 2:17–27; Rom. 3:19.) Romans 3:19, 20 is particularly instructive in this respect. In verse 20a, 'from the works of the law' must have reference to the same law as in verse 19 and 20b. But it is apparent that there the law is that of God, convicting of sin and bringing a verdict of guilt against the whole world.

This fact that the law is the law of God makes all the more significant the derogatory force of 'under law', and the question arises: Why, since the law is the law of God, is 'under law' synonymous with bondage to sin and its curse and the antithesis of God's grace and the liberty of the Spirit?

The answer to this question resides not in any fault belonging to the law – the law is good, holy, and just, the transcript of God's own perfection, characterized by the sanctity of his character and possessing all the sanctions emanating from his holiness. The answer resides in the situation created by sin and the limitations inherent in law, as law, in reference to that situation. Two passages in Paul reflect on these limitations. They are Romans 8:3, Galatians 3:21; the former speaks of the τὸ ἀδύνατον τοῦ νόμου and the latter of its impotence to make alive. And Romans 8:3 gives the reason for this impotence: 'it was weak through the flesh'. The law as demand and command can do nothing to relieve the liability, the condemnation, the bondage of sin. It has no redemptive provision and therefore no redemptive potency or efficacy. It is here that the divinity of the law, the inviolable sanctity and sanction derived from this divinity, become significant for the implications of ὑπὸ νόμον. Sin does not suspend ὑπὸ νόμον any more than does law suspend or negate sin. Again Paul's own statement is eloquent: 'Whatever the law says it says to those who are under the law' – ἐν τῷ νόμῳ (Rom. 3:19) and that all are ἐν τῷ νόμῳ is involved in the clauses that follow: 'that every mouth may be stopped and that all the world may be guilty before God' (Rom. 3:19b). It is because the law is God's law that by divine constitution all are 'under law' and therefore under the sanctions that the law possesses, consigned to the condemnation and bondage it pronounces, and shut up to the impotence that characterizes the law. This is why in the state and condition of sin ὑπὸ νόμον is the antithesis of grace. Provisions for the condemnation and bondage to which the law consigns us must proceed from another source, the source summed up in the word 'grace'.

Since the law is the law of God and its inviolable sanctions are divine, we cannot think of sin and its consequence apart from the law. To this Paul refers in various contexts and in varying ways. Without the law there would be no sinful situation. 'Where no law is, neither is there transgression' (Rom. 4:15). 'Sin is not imputed when there is no law' (Rom. 5:13). 'Without the law sin was dead' (Rom. 7:8). 'The power of sin is the law' (1 Cor. 15:56). And the function of the law in exposing sin arises from this same consideration. 'Through the law is the knowledge of sin' (Gal. 3:20). 'I had not known sin except through the law' (Rom. 7:7). 'I was alive without the law once, but when the commandment came sin revived and I died' (Rom. 7:9). 'I through law died to law' (Gal. 2:19). Also the provoking of the flesh to exercise proceeds from the divinity of the law (cf. Rom. 7:8, 11, 13).

As indicated already, Paul's polemic in Romans and Galatians turns on the implications of ὑπὸ νόμον in the sense with which we are now concerned. It is because of the law's sanction in condemnation and its impotence in reference to deliverance from sin that the law cannot justify or release from sin's power and defilement. Hence ὑπὸ νόμον is to be equated with various other expressions with which his epistles are interspersed – ἐξ ἔργων νόμου (Rom. 3:20; Gal. 2:16) διὰ νόμου, (Rom. 4:13; Gal. 2:21), ἐκ νόμου (Rom. 4:14; Phil. 3:9), ἐν νομῳ (Gal. 3:11). And the opposite is expressed by χωρὶς νόμου (Rom. 3:21), χωρὶς ἔργων νομου (Rom. 3:28), οὐκ ἐξ ἔργων νόμου (Gal. 2:16).

Having dealt with these two distinct applications of the expression ὑπὸ νομου it is appropriate to deal with two passages in Paul that present some difficulty but at the same time are significant for our topic. They are Galatians 4:3, 9: 'Even so we, when we were babes, were in bondage under the elements of the world'. 'But now having known God, rather known of God, how turn ye again to the weak and beggarly elements, to which again ye desire to be in bondage?' (τὰ στοιχεῖα τοῦ κόσμου; τα ἀσθενῆ καὶ πτωχὰ στοιχεῖα respectively). The weak and beggarly elements of verse 9 could be interpreted as referring to the practices of pagan idolatry in view of verse 8 where Paul says that before they knew God they did service to those which by nature were not gods. But there are two reasons for questioning this interpretation.

(1) In verse 3 the τὰ στοιχεῖα refers to the rites and ceremonies of the

older economy and the proximity would suggest the same denotation in verse 9.

(2) The issue in the Galatian churches was not a lapse into crass paganism but an insistence on the part of Judaizers that observance of Mosaic rites was necessary to justification. The heresy was that of the synthesis of grace and observance of rites in order to acceptance with God, and turning again to weak and beggarly elements would have to be regarded in that light. Furthermore, the observance of days and months and seasons and years can most suitably be given this complexion.

On this premise we may proceed to the interpretation of τὰ στοιχεῖα The term is used of elements, rudiments, first principles of teaching (cf. Burton, Lightfoot, Eadie, Arndt, *ad. loc.*). This meaning is distinctly appropriate in Galatians 4:3 and τοῦ κόσμου need not be understood in a bad sense (cf. Heb. 9:1 – τὸ ἅγιον κοσμικόν). In this context the thought is the tutelage, pupilage, minority of Israel under the old covenant and the reference is to the tutelary ordinances of the Mosaic institution.

The Galatians were lapsing into pre-Christian Judaism and therefore abandoning the maturity of the fulness of the time in favour of the tutelage of the Mosaic, and the full liberty of the gospel for the relative bondage of the old economy. What folly! But, much more serious, what iniquity! It is the iniquity that is uppermost in Paul's assessment. It meant failure to understand the movement of redemptive history. It meant even the failure to understand the purpose of the Mosaic institution. In a word, it is the rejection of Christ and of the gospel, the rejection of all that is involved in Galatians 4:4–6.

And the person who stays on the level of the Mosaic or lapses back to this level is not in the position of the pre-Christian believer looking forward to the fulness of the time. He is in the position of the unbeliever, of the person ὑπὸ νόμον in the sense of Romans 6:14, 15. This is why Paul can write: 'Behold I Paul say unto you that if ye be circumcised Christ shall profit you nothing' (Gal. 5:2). 'Stand fast therefore in the liberty wherewith Christ hath made us free and be not entangled again in the yoke of bondage' (Gal. 5:1). 'Ye have been discharged from Christ as many of you as are being justified by the law, ye have fallen away from grace' (Gal. 5:4).

So in Galatians 4:8–11 Paul can address those who had been idolaters and indict them with a turning back to corresponding bondage if they adopt the propaganda of the Judaizers. This, I take it, is the force of verse 9. To espouse Judaizing legalism is as serious as to revert to pagan idolatry. We thus see that although ὑπὸ νόμον in the sense of Galatians 3:23; 4:5 is not the antithesis of grace, yet to occupy the stance of those ὑπὸ νόμον after Christ, and that for the reason of filling up a quota of works necessary to justification, has the same effect as ὑπὸ νόμον in the sense of Romans 6:14.

We must now turn to another all-important aspect of Paul's teaching, an aspect pervasive in his epistles. To say the least, one suspects that it is this reference and application of the law that he has particularly in mind when, in the heart of his polemic that by works of law no one is justified, he asks: 'Do we then make void the law through faith?' and answers, 'God forbid, yea, we establish the law' (Rom. 3:31). Although Paul does not use the expression ὑπὸ νόμον to denote this relationship to the law, he uses terms which are very similar. I am thinking of 1 Corinthians 9:21: μὴ ὢν ἄνομος θεοῦ ἀλλ' ἔννομος Χριστοῦ. He is not 'without law to God'. Therefore he is under law to God, he is bound by the law of God. As in the following clause he says he is under law to Christ, that is, 'subject to the law of Christ',[1] so he regards himself as subject to the law of God, and subject by way of obligation and obedience.

There are various other passages that lead to the same conclusion. In Romans 8:7 Paul says 'the mind of the flesh is enmity against God', and this enmity is demonstrated by the fact that 'it is not subject to the law of God'. The implication is that the opposite, 'the mind of the Spirit' (v. 6) *is* subject to the law of God and is therefore life and peace, and so the abiding relevance of the law of God within the sphere of grace is implied. This is more directly stated in Romans 8:4 because the aim of God in condemning sin in the flesh is that the ordinance of the law might be fulfilled. The context would indicate that this fulfilment is that of conformity, on the part of those who walk not after the flesh but after the Spirit, to the righteous demands of the law of God, the law being the same law characterized by impotence in Romans 8:3. This passage, therefore, is one of the clearest indexes to the effect that the same law of God, wholly impotent of itself to justify and redeem sinners and sealing their doom and servitude, is the very law whose righteous demand receives its vindication and fulfilment through the provisions of redeeming grace.

[1] W. F. Arndt and F. W. Gingrich, *Greek–English Lexicon of the New Testament*, Chicago 1957, *ad loc.*

Confirmatory of this is Romans 13:8, 10, where Paul says that 'he who loves another hath fulfilled the law' and that 'love is the fulfilment of the law'. In the intervening verse he gives examples of the law of which he speaks. If further confirmation were needed, Romans 7:16–25 furnishes the same. There he says, 'I consent to the law that it is good' (v. 16), 'I delight in the law of God after the inward man' (v. 22), and 'with the mind I myself serve the law of God' (v. 25). When he upbraids himself in this passage, the ground of self-condemnation is the failure to bring to full fruition that conformity which he approves and yearns after.

Thus, when Paul says that we 'have been put to death to the law' (Rom. 7:4) and 'have been discharged from the law' (Rom. 7:6), we are to understand these expressions as concerned with the import of ὑπὸ νόμον in Romans 6:14, 15 *et al.*, that is, as put to death to the law as the way of acceptance with God, of justification, of deliverance from the power and defilement of sin, and of fulfilment of its demands. These expressions have no reference or application to the place the law occupies and the function it performs within the relation constituted by God's justifying grace and redeeming power. It is to negate the aim and achievement of grace to conceive of the law as abrogated in its regulative claim within the sphere of redemption. And Paul's protestation in Romans 3:31 will have to be regarded as bearing most emphatically on this thesis that the law never ceases to wield its claims and demand fulfilment of its requirements. The love that fulfils the law (cf. Rom. 13:8, 10) is itself the fruit of redeeming love, it is love generated in us by the love of God in Christ Jesus (cf. John 4:19). But love is motive; it is not directive. Love is the fulfilment *of the law*.

To conclude our discussion then, we find that, according to Paul, there is no realm of human relationship in which the law as the law of God does not wield its authority, and the reason is that it is the law of God. 'Under law', in terms of Romans 6:14, 15 *et al.*, is the antithesis of grace. By being 'under law' we are consigned to hopeless doom. But this is so precisely because we are under law and the law wields its inviolable claims and executes its penal sanctions, *eternally* inviolable claims and sanctions, sanctions that extend to the judgment and its sequel (cf. Rom. 2:12–15). It is for this reason that the law itself is operative to the end of release from its curse and bondage; though it knows no grace it subserves the interests of grace. 'Whatsoever things the law says, it says to them who are under the law, that every mouth may be stopped and the whole world brought in guilty before God' (Rom. 3:19). 'Through the law is the knowledge of sin' (Rom. 3:20). 'I was alive without the law once: but when the commandment came sin revived, and I died' (Rom. 7:9; cf. v. 7). 'I through law died to law that I might live to God' (Gal. 2:19).

9

The Weak and the Strong[1]

THE term 'Christian liberty' is one that has very rich and inclusive connotation. It designates the freedom with which Christ has made his people free. The Westminster Confession of Faith provides us with an admirable statement of what is comprised in this liberty. 'The liberty which Christ hath purchased for believers under the Gospel consists in their freedom from the guilt of sin, the condemning wrath of God, the curse of the moral law; and, in their being delivered from this present evil world, bondage to Satan, and dominion of sin; from the evil of afflictions, the sting of death, the victory of the grave, and everlasting damnation; as also, in their free access to God, and their yielding obedience unto Him, not out of slavish fear, but a child-like love and willing mind. All which were common also to believers under the law. But under the new testament, the liberty of Christians is further enlarged, in their freedom from the yoke of the ceremonial law, to which the Jewish Church was subjected; and in greater boldness of access to the throne of grace, and in fuller communications of the free Spirit of God, than believers under the law did ordinarily partake of' (Chapter XX, Section I). Nothing less than this high privilege and blessing should be accorded the title 'Christian liberty'. To define Christian liberty in more restricted terms would do prejudice to the richness of the concept.

Coordinate with Christian liberty is liberty of conscience. Again the Westminster Confession provides us with a statement which is un-surpassed in its precision. 'God alone is Lord of the conscience, and hath left it free from the doctrines and commandments of men, which

[1] This chapter was first printed in *The Westminster Theological Journal*, Vol. XII, 2, 1950.

are, in any thing, contrary to His Word; or beside it, if matters of faith, or worship' (Chapter XX, Section II). A particular phase of liberty of conscience is the liberty which the believer enjoys in respect of the use of those things which are in and of themselves indifferent, that is to say, not wrong in themselves. Sometimes that liberty has been called Christian liberty. It is not without warrant from the Scripture itself that it should be called such (cf. 1 Cor. 8:9; 10:29, 30). This aspect of Christian liberty is by no means unimportant: it brings into sharp focus the lines by which Scripture defines the sphere within which the believer may exercise the liberty that belongs to him as the freeman and bondslave of Christ Jesus. Yet when this kind of liberty is designated 'Christian liberty' it should be understood that it is only a restricted aspect of Christian liberty that is in view.

It might appear that the question of the Christian's use of things not wrong in themselves is a very simple one. To assert and maintain the intrinsic rightness or goodness of things in themselves might seem to be all that is necessary. But this is not the only thing to be considered. The question is complicated by the fact that when we are thinking of the actual use of things not wrong in themselves we are thinking of use by persons. The moment we think of persons, particularly of imperfect persons, we have to take into account the subjective condition of the persons concerned. Oftentimes this practically amounts to saying that we have to take into account the conscience of the individuals in question. The problem becomes crystallized quite specifically in the consideration that Scripture itself takes into account the distinction between the weak and the strong, between those who are weak in faith and those who are strong in faith, between those whose consciences are weak and those whose consciences are strong. In a word, it is the problem of the weak and the strong.

There are in the New Testament two passages, in particular, which deal with this question. It may help to remove misunderstanding and misapplication of these passages if we examine them with a view to determining their central import. The passages concerned are Romans 14 and 1 Corinthians 8. It is with the former that we shall be chiefly concerned.

At the very outset Paul advises us that he is dealing in Romans 14 with the person who is weak in faith. And so we are required to ask the question: who is the weak person whom Paul has in mind when he says in verse 1, 'Him that is weak in the faith receive ye'?

It would be very natural for us to suppose that they were Jewish Christians who still entertained scruples regarding the use of the unclean meats of the Mosaic law. This view can be given a good deal of support by appeal to verse 5 where the distinction of days alluded to can readily be understood of the Jewish festival days. It is very easy to understand such scrupulosity on the part of Jewish Christians who had not yet arrived at a full understanding of the implications of the Christian faith in reference to Old Testament ceremonial regulations. We meet with such scruples in other parts of the New Testament.

There are, however, difficulties that encompass this interpretation. The weak referred to in this chapter abstained from all flesh-meat (v. 2) and from wine (v. 21). The Mosaic law did not condemn the use of flesh-meat but only of certain kinds of flesh, and the Mosaic law did not prohibit the use of wine except for certain persons at certain times. We are not justified then in saying that the weak at Rome were simply Jewish Christians who still adhered to the Mosaic distinctions in reference to meats.

Another view that could plausibly be pleaded is that the weak were Gentile and Jewish Christians who abstained from all meat and wine lest they should be implicated in the eating of meat and the drinking of wine that had been offered to idols, and that the situation at Rome was similar to that at Corinth, a situation with which Paul deals in 1 Corinthians 8.

But there are objections to this view also. If this were the case we should expect Paul to specify, as he does in 1 Corinthians 8, that the meat concerned was meat offered to idols. This he does not do. Again, the weak in Rome appear to have abstained from all meat and wine, an abstinence that would not be necessary if the scruple respected merely meat and wine offered to idols. In a word, if the situations at Rome and Corinth were identical we should expect Paul to deal with the situation at Rome in terms more closely similar to those found in 1 Corinthians 8.

A third view is that the weakness of certain believers at Rome took its rise from an ascetic philosophy and tendency that led to abstinence from meat and wine. Godet thinks that the party took its position on the basis of the first eight chapters of Genesis, for it was only after the flood that animal flesh was instituted for man's use. And so these Christians took their inspiration from the original ordinance of God.

It is very likely, however, that Paul would not have dealt so gently with a party which based its practice, in these respects, upon a well-defined ascetic philosophy of life. In other epistles Paul is very severe in his condemnation of such an outlook and attitude and denounces it as a doctrine of demons.

It has also been proposed that the attitudes and practices reflected in the weak at Rome were derived from the Essenes. For us there is one great difficulty in carrying out such an interpretation of the situation: it is that we know so little about the Essenes, at least in any conclusive way.

It would appear to be impossible to determine with certainty what was the source of the weakness that manifested itself at Rome. It may well be that the weakness with which Paul had to deal was derived from various considerations. The situation may have been complex and differing kinds of weakness may have contributed to the total situation with which Paul deals. It may be that not all who showed weakness were characterized by the same kind of weakness. We often find this in our own situations, and it is not difficult to understand how a situation even more accentuated in its complexity could have arisen at Rome in the first century. It may well have been the case that Jewish prejudice against certain kinds of meats may have led Jewish converts to extremes of abstinence going far beyond the prohibitions of the Mosaic law. It may well have been that fear of involvement in meat or drinks offered to idols may have led Jewish and Gentile converts to abstinence from all such kinds of meat and drink. And we can readily imagine how various streams of prejudice could converge to create in the church at Rome a very disturbing and disrupting situation.

While we cannot be dogmatic as to the origin and precise character of the weakness dealt with by the apostle there are two things of which we can be quite certain. (1) There was at Rome a scrupulosity with respect to the use of certain meats and drinks. This scrupulosity the apostle characterizes as weakness of faith. It was a scrupulosity that strength of faith and depth of knowledge with respect to the Christian faith would have removed. It needs to be stressed that this was weakness, not strength; it was due to unbelieving doubt and not to faith. (2) It was a weakness that had its basis in religious conviction. The weak abstained from certain things because they considered that these things were wrong. This is just saying that their scruples had a religious root. Their abstinences were dictated by conscience towards God, by consciousness of devotion to the Lord. Nothing could be more obvious than this. 'He who regards the day, regards it to the Lord. And he who eats, eats to the Lord, for he gives thanks to God. And he who does not eat, to the Lord he does not eat, and gives God thanks' (v. 6).

These two observations, with respect to which there can be no question, should be borne in mind. If they are not properly weighed the interpretation and application of this passage are necessarily distorted.

The difficulty of determining the source and precise nature of the weakness present in the Roman church does not confront us in the passage concerned with the church at Corinth, 1 Corinthians 8. For in this passage the following conclusions are distinctly apparent.

(1) Paul is not dealing with the eating of certain kinds of food or the drinking of certain kinds of beverage. He is dealing with the question of eating meat that had been *offered to idols*, and not at all with the same kind of meat that had not been offered to idols. There is no evidence that the weak at Corinth would have scrupled to eat certain kinds of meat, but simply meat, of whatever sort, that had been involved in the ritual of pagan idolatry. Hence the weakness of the weak in faith did not respect the use of certain kinds of meat and drink but only the use of meat and drink offered to idols.

(2) The meat and drink and the eating and drinking concerned are such as entail this technical religious involvement, meat and drink involved in the ritual of pagan worship. It is therefore unwarranted to apply the teaching of the apostle in this passage without taking into account this technical religious involvement. The sin in which the weak would be involved would not be the eating of meat against which, as such, they entertained a religious scruple, but the eating of meat offered to idols. And the reason why the weak would in such a case commit sin was not that they had eaten of a certain kind of meat against which they had scruples but that they had eaten of meat offered to idols when they were not yet able to divest themselves of some kind of religious regard for, or conscience of, the idol.

(3) The sin on the part of the strong was the inducement they offered to the weak to eat of such meat when they (the weak) had not yet attained to the knowledge and faith to understand that an idol was nothing in the world and that meat was not in the least contaminated or defiled by the mere circumstance that an idolater had devoted it to the worship of an idol.

We readily discern, therefore, that the scope of the teaching of 1

Corinthians 8 is more limited than that of Romans 14. In Romans 14 Paul is dealing with the case of those who abstained on religious grounds from certain kinds of food and drink; in 1 Corinthians 8 the question is not that of abstinence from certain kinds of food and drink, but simply that of abstinence from that which had been offered to an idol, quite irrespective of the kind of food or drink involved.

It is all-important to observe, however, that in *both cases* the weakness of the weak had respect to abstinence from certain things *on religious grounds*. The weak abstained from certain articles of food or drink because they considered that devotion to the Lord required such abstinence. In both situations, that of Rome and that of Corinth, it was true that he who did not eat, to the Lord he did not eat, and gave God thanks. These believers, though weak and not yet fully aware of the implications of the Christian faith, recognized that the guiding principle of the believer's life was to be well-pleasing to the Lord, the Lord Christ. At Rome it was because they considered that eating and drinking of certain things constituted a breach of devotion to Christ that they abstained, and their religious conviction dictated total abstinence. At Corinth they considered that eating and drinking of certain things which had been associated with idolatrous worship constituted a break of devotion to Christ, and their religious conviction dictated total abstinence from such things.

It is here that a grave distortion of the teaching of these passages must be exposed. In dealing with this distortion it is well to deal with it in relation to Romans 14 particularly. As pointed out above, Romans 14 is broader in its scope than 1 Corinthians 8 and offers, therefore, more plausibility to this widespread distortion.

In our modern context this passage is often applied to the situation that arises from excess in the use of certain kinds of food or drink. It is particularly in connection with intemperance in the matter of fermented beverages that the application is made. The argument runs along the following lines. The person addicted to excess or intemperance is called the 'weaker brother', and the temperate are urged to abstain from the use of that thing in deference to the weakness of the intemperate. This argument may be applied to a great variety of usable things but it is in connection with fermented liquors that the argument has received widest currency and has been made to appear very plausible.

It must be said quite plainly that this is a distortion and perversion of

Paul's teaching in the passage concerned. This should be apparent for the following reasons.

(1) Paul is not dealing with the question of excess in the use of certain meats and drinks. That kind of abuse does not once enter into the purview of this passage. The weak of Romans 14 are not those given to excess. They are the very opposite. They are those given to complete abstinence from certain kinds of food or drink. The 'weak' who are addicted to excess do not abstain; they take too much.

(2) The 'weakness' of those who go to excess is in an entirely different category from the weakness of those with whom Paul is dealing. In fact the 'weakness' of the former is not really weakness in the sense of Romans 14. The 'weakness' of excess is downright transgression of the law of God, it is moral iniquity. With those who are guilty of this sin Paul deals in entirely different fashion. Drunkards, for example, shall not inherit the kingdom of God (1 Cor. 6:10). And Paul enjoins upon the church that if any one called a brother is a drunkard, with such an one believers are not to keep company or even eat (1 Cor. 5:11). Drunkards are not to be regarded as brethren but as outside the kingdom of Christ and of God. How different is Paul's attitude to the weak of Romans 14! 'Him that is weak in the faith receive ye' – take him without any restraint into the bosom of love and fellowship. The weak here are indeed weak in knowledge and faith but believers in the full communion of the saints. It does havoc to the basic principles of the Christian ethic and destroys the criteria by which the purity of the church is to be guarded and maintained to confuse the weak of Romans 14 with the so-called weakness of the person given to excess in any particular. Yet this is the very havoc which is wrought, at least implicitly, by those who are the peddlers of this distortion with which we are now dealing.

(3) Even when we consider the case of those who have been converted from a life of excess in some particular we do not have a situation that is similar to that of Romans 14. It does sometimes happen that a person who had been addicted to excess in his unconverted days still possesses a tendency to overstep the bounds of sobriety. This occurs sometimes with those who had been drunkards. It may well be that in some cases the cost of sobriety is total abstinence. The words of our Lord apply. It is better to enter into life with one eye than having two eyes to go into the hell of fire. True believers afflicted with such a temptation to excess must be dealt with very tenderly and

sympathetically. Every proper measure ought to be used by their stronger brethren to support and fortify such against the weakness to which they are subjected. But again we must clearly distinguish between the weakness of those who have a tendency to overstep the bounds of sobriety and the weakness of those in Romans 14. The weakness of those plied with the temptation to excess is not the weakness of conscientious scruple. They need have no scruple against the use of these things; their case is rather that of a tendency to abuse what they have no scruple in using. There is no suggestion in Romans 14 that the weakness contemplated is the weakness of tendency to excess on the part of those who have been converted.

(4) We may envisage, however, another case that takes its origin from a past life of intemperance. It is the case of the man who has been converted from a life of excess in some particular, let us say, strong drink. It sometimes happens that such a person comes to entertain a scruple against the use of that thing because he thinks that what could have been the occasion of such debauchery is evil in itself. So on religious grounds he becomes a total abstainer. It goes without saying, of course, that he has made an erroneous judgment and has gravely failed to analyse properly the source of responsibility for his past wrongdoing. But the fact still remains that on religious grounds he regards the use of such a beverage as wrong. Such a person will have to be considered as belonging to the category of the weak in Romans 14. Consequently the exhortations of Paul would apply all along the line in such a case.

It is most important, however, to observe that the consideration of excess enters into this case only as explaining the *origin* of the scruple of the person concerned and not at all as providing the reason why the strong are urged to abstain from the use of the drink concerned. In other words, it is not the tendency to excess on the part of the weak brother concerned that is the reason for abstinence on the part of the strong – the person concerned has no tendency to excess. The reason for abstinence on the part of the strong is simply the religious scruple of this weak brother, a scruple that derives its origin, in part at least, from the revulsion he has from his past excess.

We can see, therefore, that the widespread disposition to apply the teaching of this passage without these necessary distinctions is a serious distortion. It is apparent that scruple against the use of certain things, scruple arising from religious conviction, is the principle upon which the proper interpretation turns. And to apply the teaching of the apostle to cases where there is no such religious involvement is to extend the teaching beyond its reference and intent. Paul is dealing exclusively with the scruple of weak believers, and it is with reference to such, and out of deference to such, that he gives the exhortations contained in this chapter.

There remains, however, another question of crucial importance in connection with the interpretation of Romans 14. Granting that the weakness spoken of is the weakness arising from religious scruple and not by any means the 'weakness' of being addicted to excess, the question still before us is: what is the *stumblingblock* of which Paul speaks, particularly in verse 13? 'Let us not therefore judge one another any more, but judge this rather, not to place a stumblingblock or an occasion of falling in the way of the brother.' The question is really the interpretation of verses 13–16.

It would not be entirely impossible to regard verse 13, just quoted, as directed to both weak and strong. In this event the weak would be regarded as placing a stumblingblock in the way of the strong as well as the strong in the way of the weak. The stumblingblock erected by the weak would be the argument and inducement which they would place before the strong to encourage the latter to adopt the same position and practice as the weak themselves. Such a notion is by no means pointless or meaningless. There is much need that the weak be urged to refrain from the attempt to bring down the strong to the level of the uninformed and confused state of mind in which the weak themselves are. It is the wicked thing which the weak are too prone to practise, and it is something that the apostle would very severely condemn.

But although such an interpretation as would regard verse 13 as directed to the weak as well as to the strong is not impossible and though the force of it is undoubtedly implicit in Paul's teaching in this passage as a whole, yet it is not at all likely that in verse 13 the weak are regarded as placing a stumblingblock in the way of the strong and exhorted accordingly. It would be very difficult to carry through such an interpretation in verses 14 and 15. Hence we shall proceed on the assumption that verse 13 is addressed to the strong and that they are exhorted not to place a stumblingblock before the weak. Since the strong are included in the address of verse 13 we are placed under the necessity of discovering what the stumblingblock, which the strong are conceived of as placing in the way of the weak, precisely is.

It is not necessary to enter into the discussion of the question as to the distinction between the two words Paul uses, stumblingblock and occasion of falling. Whatever differing shades of meaning there may be, they refer to an obstacle in the path that causes one to stumble and fall. The question is: what is this?

It might appear that what the strong are urged to refrain from is the annoyance which they occasion for the weak by the exercise of their liberty, the displeasure which the weak entertain when they observe the strong partake of certain things with reference to which they (the weak) have conscientious scruples. It must be admitted that the weak at Rome did engage in censorious judgment of the strong, and such censorious judgment must have been accompanied by deep displeasure that the strong were freely doing things which the weak considered they had no right to do. In a word, the conduct of the strong must have been offensive to the weak. It would be to impugn the sincerity and depth of their conviction to think otherwise. The question is: are the strong here exhorted to avoid that which gives such offence to their weak brethren?

It need not be doubted that there is some point and force in such an interpretation. It goes without saying that Christian courtesy will often dictate abstinence from certain things out of deference to the wishes of others, especially of Christian brethren whom we love in the Lord. Considerateness is a virtue much to be coveted and practised. Considerateness for what is even petty and capricious on the part of others is oftentimes a virtue.

Furthermore, this interpretation might seem to gain a good deal of support from verse 15, 'For if on account of food thy brother is grieved, no longer dost thou walk according to love.' It might seem that the grief spoken of is the grief caused in the mind of the weak when he sees the strong partake of food which he (the weak) thinks is wrong. And it might appear to gather support from 15:1-3, 'But we who are strong ought to bear the infirmities of the weak, and not to please ourselves. Let each one of us please his neighbour for good unto edification. For even Christ did not please himself.' So it might be said that the thought of Paul is, 'Avoid what is displeasing to your fellowbeliever, defer to his scruples and wishes in these matters, lest you should give occasion for these disruptive censures and suspicions which disturb harmony and peace in the body of Christ'.

There are, however, compelling reasons for rejecting this interpretation. It will not satisfy the requirements of the context.

(1) Paul in this context is condemning the censorious judgment of the strong, on the part of the weak. 'Let not him who does not eat judge him who eats, for God hath received him' (v. 3). It would be very difficult to believe that Paul would proceed to ask the strong to defer to such censorious and unjust judgment, that he would exhort the strong to indulge it by removing every occasion for the exercise of it.

(2) The interpretation proposed will not do justice to the words Paul uses in verse 13 – stumblingblock and occasion of falling. These words refer to that which occasions a fall. If what is contemplated is simply the displeasure in the minds of the weak, how could such be construed as a fall? It is true enough that the unjust judgment that underlies the displeasure is sinful and ought to be removed, but it could not properly be said that it is the exercise of liberty on the part of the strong which causes this unjust judgment to be. The unjust judgment springs from an erroneous estimate of certain things and from failure to understand the implications of the Christian faith. And though the exercise of liberty by the strong is the occasion for bringing that unjust judgment to expression, yet this registering of judgment would hardly measure up to what is implied in the notion of a fall.

(3) Verse 14 explains what is meant by the stumbling and falling envisioned in this passage. 'But to him that reckoneth anything to be unclean, to him it is unclean.' This indicates that the fall in view in verse 13 is the partaking of something which the person partaking considers to be unclean. While it is an inviolable principle that nothing is unclean of itself and while Paul propounds that principle with the strongest emphasis when he says, 'I know and am persuaded in the Lord Jesus', nevertheless it does not at all follow that everything is clean to every one. It is still true that if one reckons something to be unclean *to him* it is unclean. And so for any person to do something which he considers wrong is a grievous fault and entails a fall. We are thus pointed in the direction in which we are to seek the meaning of the stumbling and falling referred to in verse 13.

(4) Verse 15, when duly examined, makes it clear that the grief mentioned is not the mere displeasure entertained by the weak when he witnesses the use of liberty on the part of the strong. It must be, rather, the vexation of conscience that befalls the weak when he exercises a liberty which he does not yet have the faith or strength to exercise.

This is borne out particularly by the exhortation, 'Do not destroy by thy food that one on account of whom Christ died.' The word, 'destroy' here is a strong word. It means destruction and ruin of soul, and the thought is that inherent in the kind of sin contemplated – the sin committed by the weak – is a soul-destroying tendency. This sin, Paul says, leads to destruction. Of course, Paul is not here viewing the sin from the standpoint of the purpose of God with reference to the believer. He is viewing the sin from the standpoint of its inherent character and consequence, from the standpoint of human responsibility and interests. Sin tends to destruction and the strong believer must consider this consequence for the weak rather than take refuge behind the predestinating purpose of God. To take refuge in Romans 8:28–30 in order to evade the practical issues at stake and to escape from responsibility is to turn the grace of God into lasciviousness and pervert the high mystery of predestination.

It is the sin of violating conviction and conscience, therefore, which is the destructive sin of which Paul speaks, and the grief is the vexation of conscience which befalls the person guilty of this sin. It is the serious consequence for the whole body of Christ that Paul has in mind when he says, 'Destroy not by thy food that one on account of whom Christ died.' And the same thought with variation of language is expressed in verse 20, 'On account of food do not break down the work of God.'

(5) Verses 20–23 supply confirmation that the fall contemplated in this case is the fall involved in action contrary to conscience and conviction. In verse 23 the weak are undoubtedly in mind and the damnatory action is that of eating in doubt and without faith. 'But he who doubts is condemned if he eat, because it is not of faith. And everything that is not of faith is sin.' It is such sin Paul must have in mind in verse 20 and 21 where he speaks again of stumbling-block and stumbling.

We shall have to conclude, therefore, that the stumbling-block which the strong in faith are exhorted not to place in the way of the weak is the emboldenment which the use of liberty on the part of the strong affords to the weak to do what is contrary to the conviction and conscience of the latter. And the stumbling and falling implied refer to the doing on the part of the weak of what is contrary to their conviction. The weak are induced to do what they are not yet able to do in faith and with a good conscience. Thus they wound their weak conscience and sin against Christ. This is a grievous evil for the weak. But the evil also reacts upon the strong themselves. For in the body of

Christ, if one member suffers all the other members suffer with it. The plea that is urged upon the strong is, therefore: 'It is good neither to eat flesh nor to drink wine nor anything by which thy brother stumbles' (v. 21); 'If on account of food thy brother is grieved, no longer dost thou walk according to love. Destroy not by thy food that one on whose behalf Christ died' (v. 15); 'On account of food destroy not the work of God' (v. 20). The self-pleasing that is to be shunned and the pleasing of one's neighbour that is commended in verses 1 and 2 of Chapter 15 have in view the avoidance, on the part of those strong in faith, of that which will become the occasion of soul-destroying violation of conviction and of that distress of conscience attendant upon such violation which inevitably result when the weak do what is contrary to their conscientious scruples.

By way of expansion and application of what has been elicited from these passages we may set forth the following principles and observations.

(1) It is a Biblical principle that there is nothing unclean of itself. The sanction by which Paul confirms this principle is most impressive. He says, 'I know and am persuaded in the Lord Jesus that nothing is unclean of itself' (Rom. 14:14). A great deal of the so-called temperance propaganda of today and yesterday is based on the principle that there are certain things, edible, potable, or usable, that are intrinsically evil or have inherent in them some degrading or demoralizing element. It is alleged that the way of temperance is total abstinence from such things. This is directly contrary to Scripture teaching and we may be certain that any such conviction or propaganda based on such conviction is not after Christ. It is not in the Lord Jesus that such a conviction is entertained. It is by inspiration of the Spirit that Paul says, 'I know and am persuaded in the Lord Jesus that nothing is unclean of itself.' And his word to Timothy is that 'every creature of God is good, and nothing to be refused if it be received with thanksgiving, for it is sanctified through the word of God and prayer' (1 Tim. 4:4, 5). Paul warns us that it is a sign of apostasy from the faith and embrace of the doctrines of demons to command to abstain from foods which God has created to be received with thanksgiving by those who believe and know the truth. Certain types of temperance propaganda have adopted total abstinence as their motto and have urged that the witness of those who believe and know the truth is to be borne by total abstinence. The contradiction is blatant. Temperance propagandists

say certain things are to be refused and scrupulously avoided. Paul says nothing is to be refused. Temperance propagandists say the Christian witness is prejudiced when believers partake of certain things. Paul says that it is by those who believe and know the truth they are to be received with thanksgiving and that it was for that purpose God created them. Temperance propagandists imply that God's blessing cannot be invoked on the use of certain things. Paul says that it is by prayer they are sanctified. Temperance propagandists say the Word of God forbids the use of certain things. Paul says it is by the Word of God they are sanctified.

Consequently every temperance movement of whatever sort that is based upon the supposition or contention that any material thing is evil or contains within itself a tendency to evil and that therefore the use of it incites to sin is an assault upon the integrity of the Creator, and an attempt to remove the basis of responsibility for wrong from our hearts and wills to the ordinance of God. All such temperance propaganda is based upon a principle that undermines the very foundations of sobriety and of true temperance. The Biblical conception of temperance is that of moderation and self-control. Against such temperance there is no law.

(2) While it is true that there is nothing unclean of itself, it does not follow that all have the knowledge and faith and strength to use all things. In this matter of conduct we have not only to consider the intrinsic rightness of these usable things but also the subjective condition or state of mind of the person using them. There is not in every person the requisite knowledge or faith. Until understanding and faith have attained to the level of what is actually true, it is morally perilous for the person concerned to exercise the right and liberty which belong to that person in Christ Jesus. The way of edification is not that conduct should overstep the limits of knowledge and faith or to violate the dictates of conscience, but for conscience to observe the dictates of understanding and faith. 'Whatsoever is not of faith is sin.' The believer must always act out of consciousness of devotion to Christ and when he cannot do that in a certain particular he must refrain from the action concerned. We must remember that although nothing is unclean of itself, yet to him that reckoneth it to be unclean *to him* it is unclean. To use other terms, we must remember that though things are indifferent in themselves the person is never in a situation that is indifferent. Things are indifferent but persons never.

The relevance and significance of Romans 14:7 need to be appreciated in this connection. 'For no one of us lives to himself, and no one dies to himself.' As too often supposed in the easy quotation of this text this does not mean that a man is not sufficient to himself in the social and economic orders. It is not a protest against selfish or self-assertive independence in the order of society. Truly enough such selfishness and the failure to recognize the solidarity that exists in our human relationships are wrong. In this chapter as a whole such an attitude is condemned and the obligations of mutual considerateness are inculcated. But in this verse what Paul asserts is that a man lives to the Lord and dies to the Lord. That is made conclusively plain by verse 8. 'For if we live, we live to the Lord, and if we die, we die to the Lord. Whether therefore we live or die, we are the Lord's.' Verses 7 and 8 enunciate the guiding principle and aim of the believer's life – to be well-pleasing unto the Lord, the Lord Christ. The Lordship of Christ is never suspended. The believer is never in a situation that is neutral or indifferent and so he must ever live in the recognition of Christ's lordship and act in the intelligent and fully-persuaded consciousness of devotion to him.

(3) Those who, through lack of knowledge and weakness of faith, have not attained to the mature understanding that nothing is unclean of itself and that every creature of God is good and nothing to be refused must not be allowed to erect their own ignorance and weakness as the standard of morality and piety. Too frequently the weak have presumed to regard as faith what in reality is doubt. And, sadly enough, those strong in faith and mature in knowledge have succumbed to the presumptuous claims and pretensions of the weak. How tragic! Those strong in faith and mature in their understanding must not despise or set at nought the weak. But they must never allow the weak to drag them down to the lower level on which the faith and understanding of the weak operate. If the strong allow this to happen then they not only bring themselves into bondage but they also allow the truth of God to be compromised and the integrity of the Creator to be maligned.

(4) The weak must ever be reminded that their censorious judgment with respect to the exercise of liberty on the part of the strong is a sin which the Scripture condemns. 'Let not him that eateth not judge him that eateth: for God hath received him.' 'Who art thou that judgest the servant of another? To his own Lord he stands or falls. Yea, he shall be made to stand; for the Lord is able to make him stand' (Rom. 14:3,

4). The censorious judgment in which the weak are so liable to indulge is just as unequivocally condemned as is the contempt to which the strong are too prone. And with such condemnation there is the condemnation of the self-righteousness that so frequently accompanies such censoriousness.

(5) The strong must exercise all due forbearance towards the weak. 'Let not him that eats set at nought him who eats not.' The way by which advancement in understanding and faith is to secured is not by contempt or ostracism but by fellowship, esteem, forbearance, considerateness, instruction; not by provoking vexatious questionings and disputings but by edification in the bosom of Christian love and fellowship. The strong must not indulge the weak in their mistaken judgments, yet they must exercise all due considerateness for the weakness of their faith and seek to make them stand fast in the liberty wherewith Christ has made them free. Such considerateness will induce them to refrain from the use of certain rights and liberties when it appears that the exercise of such liberties would constrain the weak to do that which they are not yet able to do with a clear conscience.

(6) The progress of knowledge, of faith, of edification, and of fellowship within the body of Christ is not to be secured by legislation that prohibits the strong from the exercise of their God-given privileges and liberties, whether this legislation be civil or ecclesiastical. Legislation can never be based upon the conscience of the weak or motivated by consideration for the conscience of the weak. If we once allow such considerations to dictate law enactment or enforcement, then we have removed the ground of law from the sphere of right and wrong to the sphere of erring human judgment. God has given us a norm of right and wrong, and by that norm laws are to be made and enforced. When we in the interests of apparent expediency erect laws or barriers which God has not erected, then we presume to act the rôle of law-givers. There is one lawgiver. When we observe the hard and fast lines of distinction which God has established for us and refuse to legislate on those matters that in themselves are not wrong, then we promote the interests of Christian ethics. When we violate these lines of distinction we confuse and perplex the whole question of ethics and jeopardize the cause of truth and righteousness. We dare not attempt to be holier than God's law, and we dare not impose upon the Christian's conscience what does not have the authority of divine institution.

10

Calvin's Doctrine of Scripture[1]

THE contention that Calvin's view of the inspiration of Scripture was not the high doctrine of plenary, verbal inspiration, espoused by the Reformed dogmaticians of the 17th century, has emanated from many quarters. It is noteworthy that within the last few years this question has received from students of Calvin thorough and exacting treatment. It is gratifying that the two studies which this present decade has produced and which have brought the most painstaking research to bear on the question have reached the same conclusion, that in Calvin's esteem the original Scriptures were inerrant. In the words of E. A. Dowey: 'There is no hint anywhere in Calvin's writings that the original text contained any flaws at all.'[2] 'The important thing to realize is that according to Calvin the Scriptures were so given that – whether by "literal" or "figurative" dictation – the result was a series of documents errorless in their original form.'[3] And Kenneth S. Kantzer, even more recently, has written that the evidence in support of the view that Calvin held to the 'rigidly orthodox verbal type of inspiration . . . is so transparent that any endeavour to clarify his position seems almost to be a work of supererogation.'[4] 'The merest glance at Calvin's commentaries,' he adds, 'will demonstrate how seriously the Reformer applied his rigid doctrine of verbal inerrancy to his exegesis of Scripture' and Kantzer claims that 'attempts to discover a looser

[1] This and the following two chapters are taken from *Calvin on Scripture and Divine Sovereignty*, Grand Rapids, 1960. Reproduced by kind permission of the copyright holders, Baker Book House, Grand Rapids, Michigan, USA.
[2] Edward A. Dowey, Jr.: *The Knowledge of God in Calvin's Theology*, New York, 1952, p. 100.
[3] *Ibid.*, pp. 101 f.
[4] Ed. John F. Walvoord: *Inspiration and Interpretation*, Grand Rapids, 1957, p. 137.

view of inspiration in Calvin's teaching fall flat upon examination.'[1]

Kantzer is to be complimented on his decision not to regard the task of providing the evidence in support of the foregoing conclusions a work of supererogation. He has furnished us with what is perhaps the most complete induction of the evidence drawn from the wide range of Calvin's works. And, since it was not a superfluous undertaking for Dr Kantzer, it is perhaps not without necessity that we should devote some attention to the same question on this memorial occasion.

The present writer is not disposed to regard the question, as it pertains to Calvin's position, with any such attitude as might be described as cavalier. There are passages in Calvin that cannot be dismissed with a wave of the hand. It is significant that the passages which, in my judgment, occasion the most acute difficulty are precisely those which so able a controversialist as Charles A. Briggs has been wise enough to appeal to in support of his own contention that Calvin did not maintain biblical inerrancy.[2] It is well to place these in the forefront for two reasons. First, it is in the interest of fairness in polemics not to suppress what constitutes the strongest argument in support of an opposing position. Second, it is a principle of hermeneutics to interpret more difficult passages in the light of the more perspicuous, a principle that applies to the interpretation of theologians as well as of Scripture.

The passages in mind are Calvin's comments on Matthew 27:9; Acts 7:14–16; Hebrews 11:21. The first is concerned with the reference to Zechariah 11:13, attributed to Jeremiah and Calvin comments: 'How the name of Jeremiah crept in, I confess that I do not know, nor do I anxiously concern myself with it. The passage itself clearly shows that the name of Jeremiah was put down by mistake for that of Zechariah (11:13), for in Jeremiah we find nothing of this sort, nor any thing that even approaches to it.'[3]

---

[1] *Ibid.*, pp. 142 f.
[2] Charles Augustus Briggs: *The Bible the Church and the Reason*, New York, 1892, pp. 219 ff.; cf. pp. 110 ff.
[3] *Commentarius in Harmoniam Evangelicam, ad* Matthew 27:9. Able expositors have found in Matthew 27:9 an allusion to Jeremiah, Chapters 18 and 19: cf. E. W. Hengstenberg: *Christology of the Old Testament*, E.T., Vol. IV, Edinburgh, 1865, pp. 40 ff. Hence it need not be maintained, as Calvin alleges, that the name Jeremiah is here a textual error. As will be shown later, the mistake to which Calvin here refers is, in his esteem, one of textual corruption and not one on Matthew's part.

The second passage deals with the question of the number of souls reported by Stephen to have gone down into Egypt with Jacob and with the statement that Abraham bought a sepulchre of the sons of Hemor rather than of Ephron the Hittite, as Genesis 23:8–18 informs us. Calvin's remarks are: 'Whereas he saith that Jacob came into Egypt with seventy-five souls, it agreeth not with the words of Moses; for Moses maketh mention of seventy only. Jerome thinketh that Luke setteth not down, word for word, those things which Stephen had spoken, or that he took this number out of the Greek translation of Moses (Gen. 46:27), either because he himself, being a proselyte, had not the knowledge of the Hebrew tongue, or because he would grant the Gentiles this, who used to read it thus. Furthermore, it is uncertain whether the Greek interpreters set down this number of set purpose, or whether it crop (crept) in afterward through negligence, (mistake;) which (I mean the latter) might well be, forasmuch as the Grecians used to set down their numbers in letters. Augustine, in his 26th book of *City of God* [*De Civitate Dei*] thinketh that Joseph's nephews and kinsmen are comprehended in this number; and so he thinketh that the words *went down* doth signify all that time which Jacob lived. But that conjecture can by no means be received. For, in the mean space, the other patriarchs also had many children born to them. This seemeth to me a thing like to be true, that the Seventy Interpreters did translate that truly which was in Moses. And we cannot say that they were deceived; forasmuch as (in) Deuteronomy. 10, where this number is repeated, they agree with Moses, at least as that place was read without all doubt in the time of Jerome; for those copies which are printed at this day have it otherwise. Therefore, I think that this difference came through the error of the writers which wrote out the books (*librariorum*, copyist). And it was a matter of no such weight, for which Luke ought to have troubled the Gentiles which were accustomed with the Greek reading. And it may be that he himself did put down the true number; and that some man did correct the same amiss out of that place of Moses. For we know that those which had the New Testament in hand were ignorant of the Hebrew tongue, yet skilful in the Greek.

'Therefore, to the end (that) the words of Stephen might agree with the place of Moses, it is to be thought that that false number which was found in the Greek translation of Genesis was by them put in also in this place; concerning which, if any man contend more stubbornly, let us suffer him to be wise without measure. Let us remember that it is not without cause that Paul doth forbid us to be too curious about genealogies. . . .'[1]

In regard to verse 16 Calvin writes: 'And whereas he saith afterward, they were laid in the sepulchre which Abraham had bought of the sons of Hemor, it is manifest that there is a fault (mistake) in the word Abraham. For Abraham had bought a double cave of Ephron the Hittite (Gen. 23:9), to bury his wife Sarah in; but Joseph was buried in another place, to wit, in the field which his father Jacob had bought of the sons of Hemor for an hundred lambs. Wherefore this place must be amended.'[2]

The third passage (Heb. 11:21) is concerned with the discrepancy between the two statements that Jacob worshipped on the top of his bed and that he worshipped on the top of his staff. The difficulty in itself is by no means acute.[3] But Calvin's statement at this point is the one with which we are concerned. 'And we know,' he says, 'that the Apostles were not so scrupulous in this respect, as not to accommodate themselves to the unlearned, who had as yet need of milk; and in this there is no danger, provided readers are ever brought back to the pure and original text of Scripture. But, in reality, the difference is but little; for the main thing was, that Jacob worshipped, which was an evidence of his gratitude. He was therefore led by faith to submit himself to his son.'[4] The disturbing remark in this quotation is that 'the Apostles were not so scrupulous in this respect, as not to accommodate themselves to the unlearned, who had as yet need of milk.' For in this instance Calvin is not reflecting upon some error that might have crept in in the course of copying the text of Hebrews 11:21 but upon the practice of the inspired writers themselves to the effect that they were not concerned with precise accuracy in a detail of this kind. If this is Calvin's thought, then we might say that, in his esteem, an error of historical detail is compatible with the canons which governed the inspired writers and therefore compatible with the inspiration under

---

[1] *Commentarius in Acta Apostolorum ad* Acts 7:14; E.T. by Henry Beveridge, Grand Rapids, 1949, Vol. I, pp. 263 f.
[2] *Ibid., ad* Acts 7:16.
[3] The question turns on the difference of vowels attached to the same Hebrew consonants. If certain vowels are supplied, the term means 'bed', if others, 'staff'. There is good ground for the latter alternative, following certain versions and Hebrews 11:21.
[4] *Commentarius in Epistolam ad Hebraeos, ad* 11:21; E.T. by John Owen, Grand Rapids, 1948, p. 291.

which they wrote. As far as I am aware, this remark constitutes the most formidable difficulty in the way of the thesis that Calvin believed in biblical inerrancy. We are not, however, in a position properly to interpret and evaluate this statement and the others quoted above until we have made a broader survey of Calvin's teaching.

Calvin's greatest work *The Institutes of the Christian Religion* is interspersed with pronouncements respecting the character of Scripture and we should be overlooking some of the most relevant evidence if we did not take account of them.

'Whether God revealed himself to the fathers by oracles and visions, or, by the instrumentality and ministry of men, suggested what they were to hand down to posterity, there cannot be a doubt that the certainty of what he taught them was firmly engraven on their hearts, so that they felt assured and knew that the things which they learnt came forth from God, who invariably accompanied his word with a sure testimony, infinitely superior to mere opinion.'[1] This quotation is of interest because it is concerned with the certification accorded to men who were the recipients of revelation by other modes of revelation than that of Scripture, a certification by which certitude of the truth was engraven on their hearts. This quotation also prepares us for what Calvin regarded as providing the necessity for inscripturation. So we read in the next paragraph, 'For if we reflect how prone the human mind is to lapse into forgetfulness of God, how readily inclined to every kind of error, how bent every now and then on devising new and fictitious religions, it will be easy to understand how necessary it was to make such a depository of doctrine as would secure it from either perishing by the neglect, vanishing away amid the errors, or being corrupted by the presumptuous audacity of men' (I, vi, 3). It is the liability to error, associated with tradition, that makes inscripturation necessary, and the *documentation* of the 'heavenly doctrine' (*coelestis doctrina*) guards it against the neglect, error, and audacity of men.

We shall have occasion to give examples later on from Calvin's other works of his characteristic dictum that the Scripture speaks to us with a veracity and authority equal to that of God speaking to us

[1] In quoting from the *Institutes* and *Commentaries* in the remaining part of this lecture, I have made use of the various translations. But I have often given my own rendering when I deemed it necessary to depart from the renderings of other translators. I believe these translations of mine are more pointed and accurate in reference to the subjects being discussed.

directly from heaven. We do not read far into the *Institutes* before we come across the most explicit affirmation to this effect. 'When that which professes to be the Word of God is acknowledged to be so, no person, unless devoid of common sense and the feelings of a man, will have the desperate hardihood to refuse credit to the speaker. But since no daily oracles are given from heaven, and the Scriptures alone exist as the means by which God has been pleased to consign his truth to perpetual remembrance, the full authority which they obtain with the faithful proceeds from no other consideration than that they are persuaded that they proceeded from heaven, as if God had been heard giving utterance to them' (I, vii, 1).

It is in this same context that Calvin speaks of the Scriptures as the 'eternal and inviolable truth of God'. It is in this same brief chapter that the following propositions are plainly asserted. God is the author of the Scriptures. The Scriptures themselves manifest the plainest signs that God is the speaker (*manifesta signa loquentis Dei*). This is the proof that its doctrine is heavenly. We are never established in the faith of this doctrine until we are indubitably persuaded that God is its author (I, vii, 4 *passim*). And so he adds: 'Being illuminated therefore by him [i.e. the Spirit], we no longer believe, either on our own judgment or that of others, that Scripture is from God, but, in a way that surpasses human judgment, we are perfectly assured ... that it has come to us by the ministry of men from the very mouth of God' (I, vii, 5 – *ab ipsissimo Dei ore ad nos fluxisse*). 'We feel the firmest conviction that we hold an invincible truth' (*id.*). 'Between the apostles and their successors, however, there is, as I have stated, this difference that the apostles were the certain and authentic amanuenses of the Holy Spirit and therefore their writings are to be received as the oracles of God, but others have no other office than to teach what is revealed and deposited in the holy Scriptures' (IV, viii, 9). At this stage it is not necessary to quote further from the *Institutes*, for in these few quotations there is virtually all that can be derived from that source. It is when we turn to other sources that the implications of these statements are brought into clearer focus.

With reference to Calvin's concept of inspiration and of its effects we should expect that no passages would offer him the opportunity to express his thought more pointedly than 2 Timothy 3:16 and 2 Peter 1:20. In this expectation we are not disappointed. In reference to the former he says: 'First, he (Paul) commends the Scripture on account of its authority; and, secondly, on account of the utility that springs from it. In order to uphold the authority of the Scripture, he declares that it is divinely inspired (*Divinitus inspiratam*); for, if it be so, it is beyond all controversy that men ought to receive it with reverence. This is a principle which distinguishes our religion from all others, that we know that God hath spoken to us, and are fully convinced that the prophets did not speak at their own suggestion (*non ex suo sensu loquutos esse*) but that they were organs of the Holy Spirit to utter only those things which had been commanded from heaven. Whoever then wishes to profit in the Scriptures, let him, first of all, lay down this as a settled point, that the law and the prophecies are not a doctrine delivered by the will of men, but dictated (*dictatam*) by the Holy Spirit. ... Moses and the Prophets did not utter at random what we have from their hand, but, since they spoke by divine impulse, they confidently and fearlessly testified, as was actually the case, that it was the mouth of the Lord that spoke (*os Domini loquutum esse*).. ... This is the first clause, that we owe to the Scripture the same reverence which we owe to God, because it has proceeded from him alone, and has nothing of man mixed with it' (*nec quicquam humani habet admixtum*).

In his comments on 2 Peter 1:20 he again reminds us that the prophecies are the indubitable oracles of God and did not flow from the private suggestion of men and therefore we must be convinced that God speaks to us in the Scripture. And so he continues: 'the beginning of right knowledge is to give that credit to the holy prophets which is due to God.... He says that they were moved, not that they were bereaved of mind ... but because they dared not to announce anything of themselves (*a se ipsis*) and only obediently followed the Spirit as their leader, who ruled in their mouth as in his own sanctuary.'

Before making remarks respecting the import of these assessments of the origin, authority, and character of Scripture, it may not be amiss to cull from other places a few quotations to elucidate and confirm these statements of his. With reference to Mark as the author of the Second Gospel he says: 'Mark is generally supposed to have been the private friend and disciple of Peter. It is even believed that he wrote the Gospel as it was dictated to him by Peter, so that he merely performed the office of amanuensis or scribe. But on this subject we need not give ourselves much trouble, for it is of little importance to us, provided we hold that he is a properly qualified and divinely ordained witness who put down nothing except by the direction and dictation of the Holy Spirit.'[1] Respecting the four Evangelists he says that God 'therefore dictated to the four Evangelists what they should write, so that, while each had his own part assigned to him, the whole might be collected into one body'.[2] On Romans 15:4 Calvin paraphrases Paul's thought by saying: 'there is nothing in Scripture which is not useful for your instruction, and for the direction of your life' and then adds: 'This is an interesting passage, by which we understand there is nothing vain and unprofitable contained in the oracles of God. . . . Whatever then is delivered in Scripture we ought to strive to learn; for it would be a reproach offered to the Holy Spirit to think that he has taught us anything which it does not concern us to know; let us then know that whatever is taught us conduces to the advancement of piety.'[3]

A great deal has been written in support of the thesis that the Bible is infallible in matters that pertain to faith and life, to the doctrine of salvation and the kingdom of God, but not in other matters concerned with history or science. And the teaching of Calvin has been appealed to in support of this distinction. Perhaps you will permit a quotation from one of the ablest and most eloquent of the protagonists of this contention, Charles Augustus Briggs. He writes: 'It is well known that Calvin and Luther and other reformers recognized errors in the Scriptures. . . . But what do these errors amount to, after all? They are only in minor matters, in things which lie entirely beyond the range of faith and practice. They have nothing to do with your religion, your faith in God and His Christ, your salvation, your life and conduct. . . . The Scriptures are pure, holy, errorless, so far as their own purpose of grace is concerned, as the only infallible rule of the holy religion, the holy doctrine, and the holy life. They are altogether perfect in those divine things that come from heaven to constitute the divine kingdom on earth, which, with patient, quiet, peaceful, but irresistible might, goes forth from the holy centre through all the radii of the circle of human affairs and persists until it transforms the earth and man.'[4] It is this distinction which Briggs alleges to be implicit in Calvin's position, and his contention is to the effect that the infallibility predicated of Scripture is, therefore, for Calvin, consistent with the errors, which, he alleges, Calvin admits. But it is not only Dr Briggs who makes this

[1] 'Argumentum in Evangelium Jesu Christi secundum Matthaeum, Marcum, et Lucam.'
[2] 'Argumentum in Evangelium Ioannis.'
[3] *Comm. ad* Romans 15:4.
[4] *Op. cit.*, pp. 112, 115, 116.

kind of allegation. No one has been a more painstaking student of Calvin than Emile Doumergue. On the question of inspiration he has performed the service of exposing the fallacy of R. Seeberg's contention that Calvin taught mechanical dictation. But Doumergue also maintains that Calvin did not teach literal, verbal inspiration and that for Calvin the important thing was not the words but 'the doctrine, the spiritual doctrine, the substance'.[1]

Here we are brought to the crux of the question. Does Calvin's position on inspiration fall into line with that espoused and defended by Dr Briggs? Is it true that Calvin did not consider the words important but only the spiritual doctrine? It is this thesis that I am compelled on the basis of the evidence to controvert. In dealing with the question we shall have to take account of several considerations.

1. It is true that Calvin lays great stress, as we found in the quotations from his works, upon the heavenly doctrine of which Scripture is the depository. It is the liability to corruption on the part of men that made necessary the inscripturation of the heavenly doctrine. Thereby it is guarded against the neglect, error, and audacity of men. But that there is in Calvin the kind of alleged distinction between the heavenly doctrine and the Scripture in which that heavenly doctrine is deposited is a thesis which his own statements do not bear out. He affirms most explicitly that the Scripture is from God, that it has come to us from the very mouth of God, and that in believing the Scripture we feel the firmest conviction that we hold an invincible truth. To insinuate that this conviction has respect simply to the heavenly doctrine, as distinct from Scripture as the depository, is to interject a distinction of which there is no suggestion in the relevant passages. In other words, Calvin identifies the doctrine of which he speaks with the Scripture itself. 'The Law and the Prophecies are not a doctrine delivered by the will of men, but dictated by the Holy Spirit',[2] and this is the settled point, he insists, that must be laid down if we are to profit in the Scriptures. And the emphasis is pervasive that we owe to the Scripture the same reverence we owe to God.

2. To say the least, it would be mystifyingly strange that Calvin would have affirmed so expressly that the writers of Scripture 'did not

---

[1] E. Doumergue: *Jean Calvin: Les hommes et les choses de son temps*, Tom. IV, Lausanne, 1910, p. 78. Doumergue's discussion, referred to in these pages, is found in the tome cited above in pp. 70–82.

[2] *Comm. ad* 2 Timothy 3:16.

utter at random what we have from their hand,' that Scripture 'has nothing of man mixed with it', that the writers 'fearlessly testified that it was the mouth of the Lord that spoke' and that the Holy Spirit 'ruled in their mouth as in his own sanctuary',[1] if his conception of inspiration did not apply to the details of words and to what we might call random statements. For Calvin, there are no random statements in Scripture because the writers did not speak at random but always by divine impulse. And, furthermore, we must remember that he has warned us against the impiety of thinking that there is anything unprofitable or vain in the Scripture; the Holy Spirit has taught us everything in the Scripture it concerns us to know, and all that is taught conduces to the advancement of piety.

3. When we examine the evidence which Doumergue adduces in support of his allegations that Calvin has not taught verbal inspiration, it is nothing short of exasperating to find how destitute of relevance this supposed evidence is. Under one caption Doumergue says, 'Words have been added or suppressed'[2] and then proceeds to cite instances. He appeals to Calvin's comments on Ephesians 2:5; Hebrews 9:1; 1 Timothy 1:3; James 4:7. Let us see then what Calvin says at these points.

At Ephesians 2:5 Calvin comments, with reference to the words 'by grace ye are saved,' as follows: 'I know not whether some one else inserted this, but, as there is nothing alien to the context, I freely accept it as written by Paul.'[3] It is quite apparent that Calvin is here reflecting simply on the question as to the possibility of addition in the course of transcription. His own judgment is that these words are Pauline and proceeds to expound their import on this assumption. In short, his judgment is that they were not added. This is clearly a question of the proper text and nothing more. It has absolutely nothing to do with the question at issue.

At Hebrews 9:1 Calvin says: 'Some copies read "first tabernacle". but I think there is a mistake in the word "tabernacle", nor do I doubt but that some unlearned reader, not finding a noun for the adjective, and in his ignorance applying to the tabernacle what had been said of the covenant, unwisely added the word "tabernacle".'[4] Again, this is

---

[1] Cf. citations given above.
[2] *Op. cit.*, p. 76.
[3] *Comm. ad* Ephesians 2:5.
[4] *Comm. ad* Hebrews 9:1.

purely a matter of what Calvin regards as textual corruption by an
unlearned reader and to him alone belongs the error, not at all to the
writer of Hebrews. In fact, why does Calvin esteem this to be the
work of an unlearned reader? Precisely because he is jealous for the
accuracy of the original author. If Calvin were, as Doumergue alleges,
not concerned about words but about the spiritual doctrine, he would
not have bothered to reflect on the folly of the unlearned reader but
would have been ready to attribute what he regarded as an error to the
writer of Scripture itself.

On 1 Timothy 1:3 Calvin says: 'Either the syntax is elliptical, or the
particle *hina* is redundant; and in either case the meaning will be clear.'[1]
This is concerned solely with the question of style. An ellipsis is simply
an abbreviated manner of speech in which something plainly understood is not expressed and redundancy is simply a manner of speech by
which something is expressed which is not indispensable to the meaning.

On James 4:7 we read: 'Many copies have introduced here the
following sentence: 'Wherefore he saith, God resisteth the proud, but
giveth grace to the humble.' But in others it is not found. Erasmus
suspects that it was first a note in the margin, and afterwards crept into
the text. It may have been so, though it is not unsuitable to the passage.'[2]
Surely no comment is necessary to show the irrelevance to Doumergue's
allegation.

Another caption under which Doumergue derives support for his
thesis is that 'there are differences',[3] meaning, of course, that there are
differences between the biblical writers when dealing with the same
subjects, and cites Calvin's comments on Matthew 8:27; Matthew 9:18.
That Calvin recognizes the differences in the accounts given by the
various evangelists we should fully expect. Who with even a modicum
of understanding does not observe these differences? But that these
differences constitute any evidence of the lack of verbal inspiration or
any such judgment on Calvin's part is precisely what Calvin is most
jealous to deny. On Matthew 9:18 he says: 'Those who imagine that
the narrative, which is here given by Mark and Luke, is different from
that of Matthew, are so clearly refuted by the passage itself, that there
is no necessity for a lengthened debate. All the three agree in saying
that Christ was requested by a ruler of the Synagogue to enter his

[1] *Comm. ad* 1 Timothy 1:3.
[2] *Comm. ad* James 4:7.
[3] *Op. cit.*, p. 77.

house for the purpose of curing his daughter. The only difference is, that the name of Jairus, which is withheld by Matthew, is mentioned by Mark and Luke; and that he represents the father as saying, "My daughter is dead", while the other two say that she was in her last moments, and that, while he was bringing Christ, her death was announced to him on the road. But there is no absurdity in saying that Matthew, studying brevity, merely glances at those particulars which the other two give in minute detail. But since all the other points agree with such exactness, since so many circumstances conspire as to give it the appearance of three fingers stretched out at the same time to point out a single object, there is no argument that would justify us in dividing this history into various dates. The Evangelists agree in relating, that while Christ, at the request of a ruler of the synagogue, was coming to his house, a woman on the road was secretly cured of a bloody flux by touching his cloak; and that afterwards Christ came into the ruler's house, and raised a dead young woman to life. There is no necessity, I think, for circuitous language to prove that all the three relate the same event. Let us now come to details.'[1] Calvin's own statement on this very subject we may quote again. 'He (God) therefore dictated to the four evangelists what they should write, in such a manner that, while each had his own part assigned him, the whole might be collected into one body; and it is our duty now to blend the four by a mutual relation, so that we may permit ourselves to be taught by all of them, as by one mouth.'[2]

Again Doumergue appeals to the fact that 'the order of time is not always observed'[3] and instances Calvin's comments on Luke 4:5 and Matthew 27:51. We all know that the Evangelists do not always follow a chronological arrangement of their narratives and, of course, Calvin does also. But this is a question of literary form and not of verbal inspiration.

Finally, in connection with Doumergue's contention that for Calvin the words were not important but the 'spiritual doctrine', it is Calvin's treatment of quotations from the Old Testament in the New that Doumergue relies on chiefly in this connection.[4] He appeals to Calvin's comments on the use made by New Testament writers, particularly

[1] *Comm. in Harmoniam Evangelicam, ad* Matthew 9:18; E.T. by William Pringle, Grand Rapids, 1949, Vol. I, pp. 409 f.
[2] 'Argumentum in Evangelium Ioannis'.
[3] *Op. cit.,* p. 77.
[4] *Op. cit.,* pp. 78 f.

Paul, of Old Testament passages. In this connection a distinction must be appreciated. Calvin recognizes, of course, as every one must perceive, that the New Testament writers, in referring to the Old Testament, did not always quote the Old Testament passages verbatim. And Calvin is fully aware of the difficulty that sometimes confronts us in the use made of Old Testament passages. For example, he says with respect to Romans 10:6: 'This passage is such as may not a little disturb the reader, and for two reasons. It seems to be improperly twisted by Paul and the words themselves turned to a different meaning.'[1] And on Romans 11:8 he thinks that the words quoted from Isaiah are 'somewhat altered' and that Paul does not here 'record what we find in the prophet, but only collects from him this sentiment that they were imbued by God with the spirit of maliciousness so that they continued dull in seeing and hearing.'[2] And again on Ephesians 4:8 he says: 'To serve the purpose of his argument, Paul has departed not a little from the true sense of this quotation' (*testimonium*).[3] On the same text with reference to the clause 'and gave gifts to men', he adds: 'There is rather more difficulty in this clause; for the words of the psalm are, "thou hast received gifts for men", while the apostle changes this expression into "gave gifts" and thus appears to exhibit an opposite meaning.'

But the all-important point to be observed is that Calvin in each case goes on to justify the apostle and to show that what appears to be an unwarranted change is one perfectly compatible with the designed use of the passage in each case, a use furthermore in perfect consonance with the inspiration under which the apostle wrote. With reference to the apparently improper use of Deuteronomy 30:12 in Romans 10:6, Calvin continues: 'This knot may be thus untied' and then proceeds to give what he considers to be the necessary resolution of the difficulty. In like manner on Romans 11:8 he maintains that there is no discrepancy between what Paul elicits from the word of the prophet and what the prophet himself said, but that rather 'Paul penetrates to the very fountain.' And although on Ephesians 4:8 he admits that Paul 'deviated not a little from the true meaning' of the Old Testament passage, yet he launches immediately into a defence of the apostle against the charge of having made 'an unfair use of Scripture' and protests that 'careful examination of the Psalm will convince any reader that the words, "he ascended up on high", are

---

[1] *Comm. ad* Romans 10:6.   [2] *Comm. ad* Romans 11:8.
[3] *Comm. ad* Ephesians 4:8.

applied strictly to God alone'. Finally, with reference to the change from 'received' to 'gave' in the same text, he says: 'Still there is no absurdity here; for Paul does not always quote the exact words of Scripture, but, after referring to the passage, satisfies himself with conveying the substance of it in his own language.' In this case, however, Calvin thinks that when Paul says 'gave gifts to men' he is not intending to quote Scripture at all but uses his own expression adapted to the occasion.

We are compelled, therefore, to draw the following conclusions. (1) When Calvin recognizes that Paul, for example, does not always quote the Old Testament verbatim, he is as far as possible from insinuating that the actual words of the Old Testament were not important. And he is likewise not insinuating to the least extent that the precise and original meaning of the Old Testament passages, as indicated by their exact terms, was not important. He is not even remotely suggesting an antithesis between the 'substance' which the apostle elicits from the Old Testament text and the text of the Old Testament itself, as if the former were important and the latter not. (2) There is not the remotest suggestion that the precise terms used by the apostle in the use of the Old Testament (terms which may deviate from the precise terms of the Old Testament) are unimportant. Indeed, the opposite is the case. It is exactly because Calvin was concerned with the precise terms and words used by the apostle that he entered upon the discussion and resolution of the difference between the terms in the Old Testament and in Paul's use of the same. In reality the only inference to be drawn from these discussions on the part of Calvin, and particularly from the resolution which he offers in each case, is that in his esteem words and terms were of the greatest importance. (3) What Calvin says is that Paul, in quoting from the Old Testament in these instances, elicited from the passage what was appropriate to his purpose at the time. He does not say or imply that for Paul the exact terms and import of the Old Testament passage were unimportant, but simply that it was sufficient for the apostle to derive from the Scripture concerned the particular truth or application relevant to the subject in hand. And, for Calvin, both are important as providing us with the whole truth, the truth expressed in the Old Testament and that enunciated in Paul's interpretation and application the whole belongs to the spiritual doctrine which the Scripture conveys to us.

In these passages, therefore, there is no warrant for Doumergue's allegation that for Calvin the words were not important but only the spiritual doctrine or substance. This sets up a contrast which Calvin does not entertain and it is a contrast which Calvin's own express declarations do not tolerate.

4. A great deal of scorn has been heaped for the last seven decades upon what has been called the modern 'dogma of the inerrancy of the original autographs' and upon the 'modern scholastics who have generated this dogma'.[1] This question of the autographs and of the mistakes that have crept in in the course of transmission introduces us to a most important phase of the evidence bearing upon Calvin's view of Scripture. We have had occasion to quote several passages from Calvin in which he reflected upon these mistakes of copyists and, in one case, upon the blunder of an unlearned reader. It is not necessary to review these passages. It is sufficient to be reminded that Calvin discusses this matter of the proper text of a particular passage and registers his judgment for the very purpose of ascertaining what was the text penned by the original writer, whether it be Luke or Paul or the writer of the epistle to the Hebrews. Calvin was greatly concerned to ascertain what this text was whenever there was occasion to raise any question respecting it. Of this there is copious evidence. Now why this concern? Obviously because he was jealous to be sure of the autographic text. And is it not this jealousy that lies behind the whole science of textual criticism? Scholars differ in their judgments on particular problems. But they all have interest in getting back to the autographic text. Hence the premise of centuries of labour on this question is the importance of the autographic text.

But in the case of Calvin there was much more at stake than the abstract question of the text of the original author. We have found that his interest is also concerned with the question of veracity. He rejects a certain reading in Hebrews 9:1, for example, because that reading would not comport with the facts of the case as he construed them. He attributes the reading to an ignorant reader. Why such reflections? Surely because he is jealous not to attribute this reading to the writer of Hebrews. And that means that the assumption on which he proceeds is that the original writer could not be regarded as susceptible to such an error.

In reference to this interest on Calvin's part in the autographic text of Scripture our final observation must be that his jealousy for the

[1] C. A. Briggs: *op. cit.*, p. 97; cf. pp. 98, 114.

original text cannot be dissociated from his estimate of Scripture as the oracles of God, that Scripture has nothing human mixed with it, and that in all its parts it is as if we heard the mouth of God speaking from heaven. Errors in scribal transmission Calvin fully recognizes. In some instances he pronounces decisive judgment as to the reason and source of these errors. It is apparent that this jealousy is dictated by his conviction that the penmen of the Scriptures were the amanuenses of the Holy Spirit and could not have perpetrated such mistakes. This is tantamount to nothing less than his interest in an inerrant autograph.

We may with this in view return to the passages quoted at the beginning of this lecture and which were passed over until we should survey Calvin's teaching as a whole. These are Calvin's remarks on Matthew 27:9; Acts 7:14–16; Hebrews 11:21. On Matthew 27:9 he says that 'the name of Jeremiah was put down by mistake for that of Zechariah.' In view of what we have found, we cannot now suppose that, in Calvin's esteem, this mistake was the work of Matthew. And the term he uses earlier when he says 'How the name of Jeremiah crept in, I confess that I do not know' is precisely the term Calvin uses with reference to errors that have crept into the text. There is, therefore, not the least warrant to suppose that Calvin is thinking of an error in the work of Matthew, and there is every warrant to judge the opposite. He is thinking of scribal error.

In reference to Acts 7:16 when he says that there is a fault, that is, *erratum*, in the name Abraham and concludes by saying, 'Wherefore this place must be amended,' analogy would not allow for any other interpretation than that he is thinking of an error in the course of transcription.

In Acts 7:14 the difficulty connected with the number 75 he likewise thinks may have arisen, in the first instance, 'through the error of the copyists' of the Greek Old Testament. Here he also entertains the possibility that Luke put down the true number and that some man corrected the same out of the Greek Old Testament where the number 75 appears. Yet he thinks it also possible that Luke may have used the number 75 since it appeared in the Greek version with which readers would be familiar and that 'it was a matter of no such weight for which Luke ought to have troubled the Gentiles who were accustomed to the Greek reading.' This latter statement may be considered along with his comments on Hebrews 11:21. They both fall into the same category.

With respect, then, to these two statements that the number of the souls who went down to Egypt was not a matter for which Luke should have troubled the Gentiles who were accustomed to the Greek reading and that the writer of Hebrews was not so scrupulous but that he could accommodate himself to the unlearned who had as yet need of milk, what are we to say? Some remarks may help to place the question in proper perspective.

1. Calvin does recognize that the writers of Scripture were not always meticulously precise on certain details such as those of number and incident. And this means that the Holy Spirit, by whom, in Calvin's esteem, they wrote, was not always meticulously precise on such matters. It must be emphatically stated that the doctrine of biblical inerrancy for which the church has contended throughout history and, for which a great many of us still contend, is not based on the assumption that the criterion of meticulous precision in every detail of record or history is the indispensable canon of biblical infallibility. To erect such a canon is utterly artificial and arbitrary and is not one by which the inerrancy of Scripture is to be judged. It is easy for the opponents of inerrancy to set up such artificial criteria and then expose the Bible as full of errors. We shall have none of that, and neither will Calvin. The Bible is literature and the Holy Spirit was pleased to employ the literary forms of the original human writers in the milieu in which they wrote. If Solomon's temple took seven and a half years to build, as we can readily calculate (cf. 1 Kings 6:37, 38), are we to suppose that it is an error to say in the same context that Solomon was seven years in building it (1 Kings 6:38)? Or if a certain king is said to have reigned twenty-two years (cf. 1 Kings 14:20), we must not impose upon such a statement the necessity of his having reigned precisely twenty-two years in terms of twenty-two times three hundred and sixty-five days.[1] He may have reigned only twenty-one years in terms of actual computation and yet twenty-two years in terms of the method of reckoning in use. The Scripture abounds in illustrations of the absence of the type of meticulous and pedantic precision which we might arbitrarily seek to impose as the criterion of infallibility. Every one should recognize that in accord with accepted forms of speech and custom a statement can be perfectly authentic and yet not pedantically precise. Scripture does not make itself absurd by furnishing us with pedantry.

[1] For discussion of such questions cf. Edwin R. Thiele: *The Mysterious Numbers of the Hebrew Kings*, Chicago, 1951.

2. We need not doubt that it was this distinction between the demands of pedantic precision, on the one hand, and adequate statement, that is, statement adequate to the situation and intent, on the other, that Calvin had in mind when he said that 'the apostles were not so punctilious as not to accommodate themselves to the unlearned'. We are not necessarily granting that Calvin's remarks are the best suited to the solution of the questions that arise in connection with Acts 7:14 and Hebrews 11:21. We may even grant that the language used by Calvin in these connections is ill-advised and not in accord with Calvin's usual caution when reflecting on the divine origin and character of Scripture. But, if so, we should not be surprised if such a prolific writer as Calvin should on occasion drop remarks or even express positions inconsistent with the pervasive and governing tenor of his thinking and teaching. In Calvin we have a mass of perspicuous statement and of lengthened argument to the effect that Scripture is impregnable and inviolable, and it would be the resort of desperation to take a few random comments, wrench them from the total effect of Calvin's teaching, and build upon them a thesis which would run counter to his own repeated assertions respecting the inviolable character of Scripture as the oracles of God and as having nothing human mixed with it.

11

Calvin and the Authority of Scripture

In the preceding lecture we have dealt with Calvin's doctrine of Scripture and have controverted the allegation that Calvin did not espouse a view of Scripture which would imply its inerrancy and verbal inspiration. In the situation in which we are placed today and more particularly in view of a good deal that has been written in comparatively recent years on Calvin's position in reference to Scripture, there would be a serious lacuna in our discussion if we did not reflect on other topics which are bound up with Calvin's teaching on the character of Scripture as the Word of God and with the interpretations of Calvin which have been advanced in reference to these topics.

One of these topics is that of the relation of Scripture to Christ as the Word incarnate. And this is pointedly stated as the relation of the written Word to the incarnate Word. Calvin leaves us in no doubt whatsoever that in his esteem the incarnate Son is the focal point of divine revelation. In the *Institutes* and the *Commentaries* the centrality of Christ is in the foreground. 'The saints in former ages, therefore, had no other knowledge of God than what they obtained by beholding him in the Son as in a mirror. What I mean by this is that God never manifested himself to men except through his Son as his unique wisdom, light, and truth. From this fountain Adam, Noah, Abraham, Isaac, Jacob, and others drew all the knowledge they possessed of heavenly doctrine. From the same fountain all the prophets likewise drew whatever they taught of the celestial oracles.'[1] Again, to quote another example, he says: 'For this reason Christ commands his disciples to believe in him, in order that they may distinctly and perfectly believe in God. . . . For although, properly speaking, faith ascends from Christ

[1] *Inst.*, IV, viii, 5.

176

to the Father, nevertheless he indicates that, even though it were fixed on God, it would soon disappear unless he interposed to give it stability. . . . Wherefore although I accept that common saying that God is the object of faith yet it needs some correction; because it is not without reason that Christ is called the image of the invisible God (Col. 1:15). By this appellation we are advised that, unless God meets us in Christ, it is not possible for us to have the knowledge that is unto salvation.'[1] This line of thought Calvin brings to a climax when he says that the Turks in modern times 'though they boast of having the Creator of heaven and earth as their God, yet substitute an idol in the place of the true God as long as they reject Christ'.[2] In view of this indispensable interposition and mediation of Christ we should not be in the least surprised to read early in the *Institutes*, in reference to Scripture itself: 'The letter, therefore, is dead and the law of the Lord slays its readers wherever it is divorced from the grace of Christ and only sounds in the ears without touching the heart.'[3] 'As soon as we have gone out of Christ, we shall have nothing else than the idols which we have formed, but in Christ there is nothing but what is divine and what keeps us in God.'[4]

It is perfectly true, therefore, as Wilhelm Niesel says, that Calvin 'considers the word of the Bible as a dead and ineffectual thing for us if it is not divinely vivified . . . and so soon as it is separated from Him [Christ] it becomes a dead body of letters without soul. Christ the soul of the law alone can make it live.'[5] 'Jesus Christ is the soul of the law, the focal point of the whole of Holy Scripture.'[6] But is this position regarding the centrality of the incarnate Word as the focal point of revelation in any way incompatible with the doctrine of verbal inspiration? This is what Niesel asserts. 'When we hear Calvin assert so much we realize how misleading it is to regard him as the exponent of a literal theory of inspiration',[7] and he affirms bluntly that Calvin for these reasons did not believe in the 'inspired literal inerrancy' of Scripture. 'Although he may incidentally speak of the divine inspiration of Holy Scripture, such remarks must in no case be interpreted to mean

[1] *Ibid.*, II, vi, 4.
[2] *Idem.*
[3] *Ibid.*, I, ix, 3.
[4] *Comm. ad* John 14:10.
[5] *The Theology of Calvin*, E.T. by Harold Knight, Philadelphia, 1956, p. 32.
[6] *Ibid.*, p. 33.
[7] *Idem.*

that Scripture as such is identical with the truth of God. No; the truth of God is Jesus Christ. . . . The teaching about literal inspiration leads to Bibliolatry and overlooks the fact that there is only one incarnation of the divine word, of which Holy Scripture is the witness.'[1]

There are in particular two things to be said respecting this contention, a contention which is representative of the argument advanced by the dialectical theology respecting the relation of the incarnation to the doctrine of Scripture.

First of all, we find in Calvin himself no sense of incongruity between Scripture as being itself the truth of God and Christ as truth incarnate, nor even between an inerrant Scripture and Christ as the focal point of revelation. It is in this same context, in which he insists that Christ is the fountain from which the saints in all ages must have drawn whatever they knew of celestial doctrine, that Calvin delineates for us the process of revelation and particularly the process by which the truth of God became inscripturated. But what is of special interest for us in terms of the present discussion is his estimate of Scripture itself as the inscripturated Word of God. We must not fail to note what Calvin says, that 'when it pleased God to raise up a more visible form of the church, it was his will that his Word be committed to writing'.[2] It is the Word of God that is committed to writing and so Scripture is the Word inscripturated. So he sums up the case for the whole Old Testament by saying: 'That whole body of Scripture, therefore, consisting of the law, the prophets, the psalms, and the histories was the Word of the Lord to the ancient people (*verbum Domini fuit veteri populo*), and to this rule the priests and teachers, to the coming of Christ, were bound to conform their doctrine; nor was it lawful for them to deviate to the right hand or to the left, because their office was wholly confined within these limits, that they would answer the people from the mouth of God.'[3] The implication is clear that Scripture, because it is the Word of God written, is the mouth of God and therefore, as we have found repeatedly, is as if we heard the voice of God from heaven.

At this point Calvin does not suppress in the least degree the stupendous import of Christ's advent in the flesh. Christ is the sun of righteousness and, since he has shone upon us, 'we have the full splendour of divine truth' and this is 'the last and eternal testimony

[1] *Ibid.*, p. 36.
[2] *Inst.*, IV, viii, 6.
[3] *Id.*

that we shall have' from God.[1] But the significant fact is also that, when Calvin has thus unfolded the splendour, the uniqueness, and finality of the revelation in Christ as the incarnate Son, there is not even the suggestion that Scripture is bereft of any of the finality and authority that belongs to it as the Word or oracle of God written. And not only that there is no retreat; there is the emphatic reaffirmation of this assessment of Scripture. It is just after having asserted that in the Son incarnate God has given 'the last and eternal testimony that we shall have from him' that we read: 'Let this, therefore, be a fixed axiom that nothing should be admitted in the church as the Word of God (*Dei verbum*) but what is contained first in the law and the prophets and then in the writings of the apostles (*scriptis apostolicis*), and that there is no other method of teaching aright in the church than according to the prescription and norm of this Word.'[2] What the apostles did they did from the Lord and 'under the direction and dictation of the Spirit of Christ.'[3] 'The apostles,' he says, 'were the certain and authentic amanuenses of the Holy Spirit and therefore their writings are to be received as the oracles of God.'[4]

It should be recognized, therefore, as beyond dispute that for Calvin there is no incompatibility between Christ as being himself the incarnate Word of God, the full splendour of divine truth, the last and eternal testimony of God to us, on the one hand, and Scripture as the Word of God, invested with the oracular quality of God's mouth, on the other. And so, far from there being any necessity to tone down Calvin's estimate of the nature and effect of inspiration, as set forth in other places, the case is that, in these very contexts where the finality and centrality of Christ are most plainly and eloquently expressed, there also the same concept of inspiration is introduced in order to support the thesis that Scripture is the Word of God written.

But, secondly, not only is it true that in Calvin there is no sense of incongruity between the finality that belongs to Christ as the incarnate Word and the finality of Scripture as the Word of God written, but we may also ask the question: Why should we look for any sense of incongruity? Calvin was a profound thinker and an eminently consistent thinker. I submit that the reason why these two theses lie side

[1] *Ibid.*, IV, viii, 7.
[2] *Ibid.*, IV, viii, 8.
[3] *Id.*
[4] *Ibid.*, IV, viii, 9.

by side in Calvin without any suggestion of contradiction is precisely because Calvin was faithful to the testimony of Jesus as God's last and eternal testimony to us and understood the implications of this same testimony. And I further submit that it is because Wilhelm Niesel and others like him have failed to appreciate the implications of the axiom that Jesus is the focal point of revelation that they institute an antithesis between Scripture as the veritable Word of God written and Christ as the incarnate Word.

It is to be confessed without any reserve that Christ as the Son of God incarnate is the supreme revelation of God. He is the hypostatic Word, the effulgence of God's glory and the very transcript of his being. When we are confronted with him, we are not only confronted with a revelatory word of God but with God himself manifested in the flesh, and God, be it remembered, in his unabridged identity and majesty. We behold his glory as that of the only-begotten from the Father, full of grace and truth. In him dwells the totality of Godhead bodily. And it must be confessed with Calvin and the whole host of Christian confessors that apart from Christ there is no knowledge unto salvation. Yes, all of this and much more must be said of the transcendent uniqueness and finality of Christ's person and of the revelation that came with him. Here is the incomparable fact of God's revelatory and redemptive accomplishment.

But are we to suppose that all that is involved in this fact, that Jesus Christ is the hypostatic Word, impinges in any way upon the possibility or actuality of an inspired and infallible inscripturated Word? This question lies close to the question that is the most urgent and practical question with which all that has been said of the uniqueness, finality, and centrality of Christ confronts us. For the question is: how do we come into relevant encounter with Jesus as the incarnate Word? It was indeed a great privilege bestowed on those who encountered Jesus in the days of his flesh and heard the gracious words that proceeded from his lips. We have abundant evidence of this sense of privilege on the part of the disciples. But Jesus is not here. And how do *we* come to enjoy this encounter with God manifest in the flesh? It is that question exactly that can be answered only in terms of a Scripture produced by the agency and invested with the property of which Calvin wrote.

It is a fact that Christ as the incarnate Word is never brought into contact with us apart from Scripture. This men like Wilhelm Niesel freely admit. And so there need be no debate on the necessity of the

Bible for encounter with the personal Word. But, if so, why should an infallible Scripture in any respect militate against the encounter which, it is admitted, the Bible must minister? In other words, why should the quality of inerrancy prejudice this encounter with the incarnate Lord? Is there some liability inherent in inerrancy as such? To ask these questions is to recognize the fallacy of the premise on which this contention is based. There is nothing belonging to inerrancy as such that is inimical to the interests of encounter with the incarnate and exalted Lord. The obvious fact is that inerrancy is rejected on other grounds, and the argument that encounter with the incarnate Word partakes of a strictly personal character is lugged in to give plausible support to the rejection of biblical infallibility – plausible because it seems to do honour to the centrality and finality of Christ as the incarnate Word when, in reality, the doctrine of biblical inerrancy does not impinge in the least degree upon the glory that belongs to, or the faith exercised in, or the worship rendered to the incarnate Lord.

And not only is it true that there is nothing attaching to biblical inerrancy inconsistent with the uniqueness of the revelation embodied in and given by Christ, but it can also be shown how consonant with each other these two tenets are.

The revelation that Christ is and gave to us men cannot be divorced from the witness which he bore to himself in the days of his flesh or from the witness borne to him from the Father in verbal utterance. To think of the revelation Jesus gave apart from the words he spoke and apart from the words spoken from heaven in witness borne to him as the beloved Son of the Father is a pure abstraction. The words Jesus spoke were inspired and infallible. On any other assumption we must abandon the infallibility of Jesus as the incarnate Word as well as the centrality and finality of the revelation he was and bore. This infallibility of his spoken word did not in the least degree interfere with the fact that he was the incarnate Word. Rather, it is correlative with his being the incarnate Word; the former flows necessarily from the latter. The fact that he was *the* truth guaranteed the infallibility of his utterances. The inference is, therefore, patent. Inspired and inerrant words are not in the least inconsistent with the fact that Christ himself is the focal point of revelation but, instead, are indispensable to it. It is the infallible spoken word that certified to the disciples the reality and significance of his own self as the hypostatic

Word. Revelatory word was the medium of contact and encounter with him in his identity as the Word incarnate.

We today do not have contact with the Son of God as he was manifested in the days of his flesh; we do not hear him speak as the disciples heard him. But revelatory word is just as indispensable for us as it was for the disciples, if we are to have saving encounter with him as the Word made flesh. Hence there must be some other way by which this indispensable medium of contact is supplied. The only medium is that of Scripture.

It is a striking fact that, however great was the sense of privilege on the part of the disciples who saw and heard and handled and touched the Word of life, these same disciples do not represent those others of us who do not enjoy that privilege as in any way bereft of encounter and fellowship with him in the full reality and benefit of Jesus as the Word made flesh. No, they reiterate in their own way the truth Jesus spoke to Thomas, 'Because thou hast seen me, thou hast believed: blessed are they that have not seen, and yet have believed' (John 20:29).

To say the least, it would be strange if believers, who are shut off from the special kind of privilege enjoyed by the disciples and, more particularly, shut off from what was for the disciples the indispensable medium of believing encounter with the incarnate Word, namely, his infallible verbal communication to them, should be placed at the disadvantage of having no infallible verbal revelation. For this would mean a radical difference in respect of a factor which is cardinal in the situation of encounter with the incarnate Word. There is not the slightest hint in the New Testament of this radical differentiation and of the corresponding disadvantage for us.

We must go one step further. There is the clearest evidence that no such disadvantage exists. Our Lord and his apostles appealed to Scripture as a finality. They appealed to it as the Scripture that could not be broken. The evidence supporting this view of Scripture on the part of Christ and the apostles has been repeatedly presented and need not be argued now. This means that an inscripturated Word of God is a mode of verbal revelation that meets the requirements of the type of infallible word which is perfectly suited to the demands of our situation, the situation of which we have been speaking. The witness of our Lord and his apostles is to the effect that no mode of verbal revelation can be more authoritative than that of inscripturation and that no mode of revelation that God has been pleased to furnish to us men is as stable and secure as that of inscripturation.

Hence the sum of the matter is this. Infallible verbal revelation is not inimical to the interests which belong to the centrality and finality of Christ as the incarnate Word. The fact is that infallible words were the indispensable medium of confrontation with him in that capacity. *Inscripturated* verbal revelation is the only mode of such revelation available to us. The quality of infallibility does not in the least degree militate against the purpose to be served by that mode of verbal revelation; it enhances that purpose. The witness of our Lord and his apostles is to a Scripture imbued with that quality. An infallible word revelation does no prejudice to the uniqueness of Christ as the incarnate Word but rather continues to insure for us that which the disciples undoubtedly enjoyed. The absence of any tension in Calvin's thought between what he rightly claimed for Christ as God's ultimate and eternal testimony, on the one hand, and the Scriptures of both Testaments as the Word of God written, on the other, witnesses to his fidelity to the testimony of Jesus himself and to his perception that the Scriptures as God's inscripturated Word, invested with the infallibility of God's own sacred mouth, are correlative with the centrality of Christ as the image of the invisible God and indispensable to the situation in which we are placed in this last era of what is the consummation of the ages.

We come now to the next subdivision of our present study, the relation of Scripture to the internal testimony of the Holy Spirit. We shall deal with this question from the angle of the relation of the internal testimony to the authority of Scripture. This is the direction in which the debate respecting Calvin's position has been turned. It is natural that it should be so; Calvin himself pays a good deal of attention to the question as it is thus oriented.

It is in *Institutes*, I, vii, that Calvin deals specifically with the internal testimony of the Holy Spirit, and the summary at the head of the chapter indicates the extent to which this subject is related to the question of the authority of Scripture. 'By what testimony ought the Scripture to be established, namely, of the Spirit, in order that its authority may remain certain; and that it is a wicked invention to say that the faith of Scripture depends upon the judgment of the church.' And the first sentence in this chapter indicates the same. 'Before I proceed any further, it is proper to introduce some observations on the authority of Scripture, not only to prepare our minds to receive it with reverence but also to remove every doubt.'[1]

When we speak of the authority of Scripture, we must distinguish between the authority that is intrinsic to Scripture and our persuasion or conviction that it is authoritative. This is the distinction between that which *imparts* authority to Scripture and that which is the *source* of our conviction that it is authoritative, between that in which the authority resides and that from which our assurance proceeds. It is the distinction between objectivity and subjectivity as it pertains to this question.

It may have to be conceded that this distinction is not as clearly formulated in Calvin as we might desire. At least, as far as the term 'authority' is concerned, there appears to be some ambiguity. In the 1539 edition of the *Institutes*[2] he says that the authority of Scripture is to be sought from the internal testimony of the Holy Spirit. And there are statements in the definitive edition which are similar. If Calvin means that the authority of Scripture rests upon or is derived from the internal testimony, then it does not rest upon that which is intrinsic to Scripture by reason of the activity by which it was produced. On the other hand, there is so much evidence in Calvin to the effect that the authority resides in the divine speaker and, therefore, in that which Scripture inherently is, that, in respect of *authority*, we are pointed in a different direction.

Hence we should not be surprised that some of Calvin's interpreters allege that he bases the authority of Scripture to some extent upon the internal testimony. When R. Seeberg says that Calvin grounds the authority of the Scriptures partly upon their divine dictation and partly upon the testimony of the Holy Spirit,[3] we must understand how easily this interpretation could be inferred from Calvin's own remarks. E. A. Dowey, notwithstanding the excellence of his treatment of Calvin's doctrine of Scripture, can write as follows: 'True enough, the Bible has intrinsic validity. But this does not constitute its authority or even one source of its authority. The authority derives solely from the inner witness of God himself through which the intrinsic validity or inherent truth of the sacred oracles is recognized and confirmed.'[4]

---

[1] *Ibid.*, I, vii, 1.
[2] In this edition cf. I, 24.
[3] Reinhold Seeberg: *Lehrbuch der Dogmengeschichte*, IV, 2, Erlangen, 1920, p. 569; cf. E.T. by Charles E. Hay, Philadelphia, 1905, II, pp. 395 f.
[4] *Op. cit.*, p. 108.

And Dowey adds that the internal testimony of the Holy Spirit 'is meant to take the weight of the authority of Scripture off of unstable supports and rest it solely upon the "author", God'.[1] It is to be admitted that these statements of Dowey scarcely cohere with other statements which reflect a more accurate perception of the distinction between intrinsic authority and the accreditation of that authority, between the authority as such and authority with us.[2]

If, as Seeberg maintains, Calvin grounds the authority of Scripture upon the inspiration of Scripture and the internal testimony of the Spirit, the most reasonable view would be that the term 'authority' is not used in precisely the same sense in both cases; that when authority is grounded in divine authorship Calvin is thinking of the authority intrinsic to Scripture and therefore objective to us, whereas, when authority is conceived of as established by the internal testimony, he is thinking of the authority as registered or, for that matter, established in our minds. It is quite apparent that these two senses should not be confused. And if this inference as to Calvin's twofold use of the term 'authority' is correct, it would be altogether incorrect and confusing to say that authority in the first sense is grounded in the internal testimony, just as it would be equally confusing to say that authority in the second sense is derived from inspiration. If Calvin at any time grounds the authority of Scripture in the internal testimony, our only conclusion must be that he must be thinking in such a case of authority *with us*, that is, of authority as registered in our hearts, and not at all of the authority intrinsic to Scripture by reason of its inspiration. We are driven to this conclusion by a series of considerations derived particularly from the chapters in the *Institutes*, directly devoted to the question.

1. It is instructive to observe the precise connections in which the term 'authority' occurs in Calvin's exposition of this topic. With reference to the Scriptures as the only extant oracles of God he says that 'they obtain complete authority with believers only when they are persuaded that they proceeded from heaven.'[3] Now it is plain that here Calvin is dealing with the *persuasion* which he proceeds to show is derived from the internal testimony. But he is not in the least suggesting that the authority itself is derived from this source. It is the 'authority with believers' (*apud fideles autoritatem*). In other words, he is dealing

---

[1] *Ibid.*, p. 109.
[2] Cf. *ibid.*, p. 111.
[3] *Inst.*, I, vii, 1.

with the authority as registered in the hearts of believers. Furthermore, this authority is obtained when they are assured that the Scriptures proceeded from heaven. It is, therefore, the *recognition* of heavenly origin that induces the conviction. But it is the heavenly origin itself that invests the Scripture with the authority recognized. Again we read: 'It must be maintained, as I have already asserted, that the faith of this doctrine is not established until we are indubitably persuaded that God is its author. Hence the highest proof of Scripture is always taken from the character of God the speaker.'[1] That 'God is its author' is that of which we are persuaded. Divine authorship is the antecedent fact and is not created by our persuasion nor by that which induces this recognition on our part. It is divine authorship, therefore, that invests Scripture with authority and it is not by the internal testimony that this authorship is effected.

In another place Calvin says: 'Without this certainty, better and stronger than any human judgment, in vain will the authority of Scripture be defended by arguments, or established by the consent of the church, or confirmed by other supports.'[2] The certainty referred to is that produced by the internal testimony of the Spirit. But the authority is the authority of the Scripture, that which belongs to it as Scripture by divine inspiration, and not that which is created by the internal testimony. It is that which may be made the subject of demonstration and argument because the Scripture exhibits the plainest evidence that it is God who speaks in it. It is not, however, the internal testimony that invests Scripture with that quality but the agency of the Spirit by which it was produced. And Calvin's point here is simply that assured faith in Scripture will never be induced by argument but proceeds only from the work of the Spirit in our hearts. So in this passage again the *authority* is something quite distinct from the internal testimony and is conceived of as that which exists antecedently to the effectual work of the Spirit in us.

2. When Calvin deals with the internal testimony of the Holy Spirit, it is always related in one way or another to our persuasion and to the agency by which this *persuasion* is secured. In other words, the internal testimony has efficiency and relevance in respect of assurance in our minds. Let us listen to a catena of quotations. The question in his own words is: 'Who will assure us that they [the Scriptures] came forth

[1] *Ibid.*, I, vii, 4.
[2] *Ibid.*, I, viii, 1.

from God?'[1] 'If we wish to consult most effectually with our consciences . . . this persuasion must be sought from the secret testimony of the Spirit.' 'Though any one vindicates the sacred word of God from the aspersions of men, yet it will not fix in the heart the certitude which is necessary to piety.' 'For as God alone is a sufficient witness to himself in his own word, so also the word will never gain credit in the hearts of men until it is sealed by the internal testimony of the Spirit. It is necessary, therefore, that the same Spirit who spoke by the mouth of the prophets penetrate into our hearts in order that he might persuade us that they faithfully delivered what had been divinely entrusted to them.' 'The Spirit,' he continues, 'is denominated a seal and an earnest for the confirmation of the faith of the godly, because, until he illuminates their minds, they always fluctuate amidst a multitude of doubts.'[2] 'Let it remain then a fixed truth that those whom the Spirit inwardly teaches firmly acquiesce in the Scripture, and that the same is self-authenticating (*autopiston*) and that it ought not to be made the subject of demonstration and arguments but obtains the certitude which it deserves with us from the testimony of the Spirit. For although it conciliates our reverence by its own majesty, nevertheless it seriously affects us only when it is sealed on our hearts by the Spirit. Therefore being illuminated by his virtue we now believe that the Scripture is from God, not by our own judgment or that of others, but, in a way that transcends human judgment, we are indubitably convinced (*certo certius constituimus*) . . . that it has flowed to us from the very mouth of God by the ministry of men. . . . Only let it be known that that alone is true faith which the Spirit of God seals in our hearts.'[3] Finally, in his comments on 1 John 2:27, he says: 'The Spirit is like a seal, by which the truth of God is testified to us. When he adds, 'and is no lie,' by this particular he designates another office of the Spirit, namely, that he endues us with judgment and discernment, lest we should be deceived by a lie, lest we should hesitate or be perplexed, lest we should vacillate in doubtful things.'[4] It should, therefore, be clear that the function of the internal testimony is, after all, what the term 'internal' implies, namely, an operation in our minds directed to the persuasion, assurance, conviction appropriate to that which Scripture intrinsically is.

[1] *Ibid.*, I, vii, 1.
[2] *Ibid.*, I, vii, 4.
[3] *Ibid.*, I, vii, 5.
[4] *Comm. ad* 1 John 2:27.

3. There is the sustained insistence on Calvin's part upon the intrinsic character of Scripture and of the evidence which Scripture contains of its intrinsic divinity. 'The Scripture exhibits as clear evidence of its truth as white and black things do of their colour, or sweet and bitter things of their taste.'[1] 'It is true that, if we were to argue the point, many things might be adduced which easily prove that, if there is a God in heaven, the law, and the prophecies, and the gospel have proceeded from him. . . . The Scripture exhibits the clearest evidences of God speaking in it, which manifests its doctrine to be divine. . . . If we bring to it pure eyes and sound minds, the majesty of God will immediately confront us, which will subdue our presumption and compel us to obedience.'[2] And when Calvin speaks of 'the majesty of the Spirit,' he is not referring to the internal testimony but to the quality belonging to Scripture by reason of divine inspiration. Referring to the prophets, he says, that, wherever we read, 'that majesty of the Spirit, of which I have spoken, is everywhere conspicuous.'[3] 'The same thing is true of Paul and Peter in whose writings, although most are blind to it, that same heavenly majesty attracts and rivets the attention of all.'[4] 'There are other reasons neither few nor invalid by which the Scripture's own dignity and majesty are not only maintained in the minds of the godly but also completely vindicated against the cavils of slanderers.'[5]

The sum of this is clear. God speaks in Scripture. In it he opens his sacred mouth. In Scripture the majesty of God confronts us. This divinity inheres in the Scripture and it therefore exhibits the plainest evidence that it is God's Word. When we bring sound minds it compels our submission and obedience. And our conclusion must be that this is but another way of saying that Scripture is by its nature divinely authoritative. These quotations also illumine for us what Calvin means when he says that Scripture is 'self-authenticating.' The predicate itself should advice us that he is not referring here to the internal testimony. For of *Scripture* he says 'it is self-authenticating' (*autopistos*). He must be referring to that evidence which the Scripture inherently contains of its divine origin, character, and authority, the evidence which demonstrates that it is God himself who speaks in it. It is only those who are inwardly taught by the Spirit who perceive this evidence and

[1] *Inst.*, I, vii, 2.
[2] *Ibid.*, I, vii, 4.
[3] *Ibid.*, I, viii, 2.
[4] *Ibid.*, I, viii, 11.
[5] *Ibid.*, I, viii, 13.

only from them does it receive the credit it deserves. But it should be equally clear that the evidence by which Scripture authenticates itself is the evidence it contains and not the internal testimony.

4. There is a fourth consideration that supports this same conclusion. It is that Calvin speaks of the internal testimony as confirmation and seal. 'For as God alone is a sufficient witness to himself in his own word, so also the word will never gain credit in the hearts of men until it is sealed by the internal testimony of the Spirit.'[1] 'For although it conciliates our reverence by its own majesty, then only does it seriously affect us when it is sealed on our hearts by the Spirit.'[2] 'Only let it be known that that alone is true faith which the Spirit seals on our hearts.'[3] 'The office of the Spirit, therefore, who is promised to us . . . is to seal to our hearts that same doctrine which is commended to us through the gospel.'[4] It should be apparent that the function of a seal is simply to confirm and authenticate what is intrinsically and antecedently true. The seal adds nothing by way of content. If it is by the Spirit that the authority is sealed, the authority is presupposed and is no more created by the seal than is the truth of a promise created by its confirmation. So the simple notion of seal is, of itself, evidence that in Calvin's conception the internal testimony does not impart authority to Scripture but merely confirms to us the authority which is antecedent and extrinsic to the internal testimony itself.

Suffice it to conclude by appeal to one passage which, if any doubt should still persist, places beyond all question the thesis that for Calvin the authority of Scripture does not reside in the internal testimony but in that which Scripture is by reason of divine inspiration. It is that passage dealt with already which, as much as, if not more than, any other statement in the whole range of his works enunciates his concept of Scripture as to its origin, character, and authority, namely, his comments on 2 Timothy 3:16. We read: 'First he [Paul] commends the Scripture from its authority, and then on account of the utility that springs therefrom. In order that he may uphold the authority of Scripture he declares that it is divinely inspired. For if it be so it is beyond all controversy that men ought to receive it with reverence.' Two facts are incontestable. (1) Here Calvin says nothing of the internal

[1] *Ibid.*, I, vii, 4.
[2] *Ibid.*, I, vii, 5.
[3] *Id.*
[4] *Ibid.*, I, ix, 1.

testimony. He deals with that in the succeeding paragraph where he speaks of it as the witness which is borne to our hearts. (2) It is divine inspiration that is the authority-imparting factor and that for which it ought to be received with reverence. And so there is no room for question that it is to the fact of inspiration that Calvin would appeal in support of the proposition that Scripture is authoritative. And this is but to confirm what we have found repeatedly, that the authority *resides* in its authorship and not in that by which divine authorship is confirmed.

12

Calvin on the Sovereignty of God

No treatment of the subject of God's sovereignty has surpassed in depth of thought, in reverence of approach, and in eloquence of expression that which we find in the last three chapters of Book I of the *Institutes*. It is sufficient to be reminded of one or two of the classic statements which we find in these chapters to appreciate anew the intensity of Calvin's faith in the all-pervasive and over-ruling providence of God. 'So it must be concluded,' he says, 'that while the turbulent state of the world deprives us of judgment, God, by the pure light of his own righteousness and wisdom, regulates these very commotions in the most exact order and directs them to their proper end.'[1] Or, again, it is Calvin who has given us the formula which has become in many Reformed circles a household word for thankfulness, resignation, and hope. The necessary consequences of the knowledge that God governs all creatures, including the devil himself, for the benefit and safety of his people, are 'gratitude in prosperity, patience in adversity, and a wonderful security respecting the future'.[2]

What then for Calvin does the sovereignty of God mean? I suppose that no Christian in the catholic tradition, not to speak of the evangelical and Reformed traditions, will formally deny the sovereignty of God. For to say that God is sovereign is but to affirm that God is one and that God is God. But we may not be misled by the formal use of vocables. It is possible for us to profess the sovereignty of God and deny it in the particulars in which this sovereignty is expressed, to assert a universal but evade the particularities. It is precisely in this respect that Calvin's doctrine of the sovereignty of God is to be assessed and appreciated.

[1] *Inst.*, I, xvii, 1.   [2] *Ibid.*, I, xvii, 7.

THE SOVEREIGNTY OF GOD IN DECREE

That Calvin regards everything that occurs as embraced in the eternal decree of God lies on the face of his teaching at every point where he finds occasion to reflect on this subject. While repudiating the Stoic doctrine of necessity, arising from a perpetual intertwining and confused series of causes contained in nature, he is insistent that God is the arbiter and governor of all things 'who, of his own wisdom, from the remotest eternity, decreed what he would do, and now by his own power executes what he has decreed. Whence we assert, that, not only the heaven and the earth and inanimate creatures, but also the deliberations and volitions of men are so governed by his providence that they are directed exactly to their destined end'[1] and thus nothing happens fortuitously or contingently. 'The will of God is the supreme and first cause of all things, because nothing happens but by his command or permission.'[2] And in his extensive tract on *The Eternal Predestination of God*, dedicated on January 1, 1552, he says to the same effect that 'the hand of God no less rules the internal affections than it precedes the external acts, and that God does not perform by the hand of men those things which he has decreed without first working in their hearts the very will which precedes their acts'.[3]

It is of greater relevance to us in the theological situation in which we are placed today to understand and assess the position which Calvin espoused and defended on the question which brings to focal and acute expression his doctrine of the eternal decree. It is that concerned with the question of election and reprobation. It is of interest that in his earliest commentary, that on the Epistle to the Romans, dedicated at Strassburg on October 18, 1539, he provides us with his thought on this question at a comparatively early age. It is well for us to take heed to Calvin's own advice that 'the predestination of God is indeed a labyrinth from which the mind of man can by no means extricate itself'. But we are not for that reason to avoid every thought of it. For 'the Holy Spirit,' he says, 'has taught us nothing but what it behooves us to know. . . . Let this then be our sacred rule, to seek to know nothing concerning it, except what Scripture teaches us; when the

[1] *Ibid.*, I, xvi, 8.
[2] *Id.*, John Allen's translation.
[3] *De Aeterna Dei Praedestinatione*, in *Opera* (Brunswick, 1870), VIII, col. 358; cf. E.T. by Henry Cole: *Calvin's Calvinism*, London, 1927, p. 243. It is regrettable that Cole unnecessarily embellishes his translation. I have often given my own renderings.

Lord closes his holy mouth, let us also stop the way, that we may go no further.'[1]

While Calvin thus properly cautions us to be silent when God closes his own sacred mouth and to seek to know nothing but what God teaches us in Scripture, he at the same time upbraids that false modesty that suppresses the doctrine of Scripture and pleads caution as an excuse to refrain from subscribing to its witness. This kind of caution he brands as preposterous; the honour of God is not to be protected by the pretended modesty which refuses to listen to what God has revealed. When God has spoken we cannot remain ignorant without loss and harm.[2] What Calvin is maintaining in these contexts is the free and absolute sovereignty of God in the discrimination that exists among men in respect of election, on the one hand, and reprobation, on the other. In the matter of election he insists that 'the salvation of believers depends on the eternal election of God, for which no cause or reason can be rendered but his own gratuitous good pleasure'.[3] 'Inasmuch as God elects some and reprobates others, the cause is not to be found in anything else but in his own purpose.'[4] It would be unnecessary and unduly burdensome at this time to show how Calvin rejects the subterfuge of appeal to foreknowledge in order to evade the force of the emphasis which Scripture places upon the pure sovereignty of God's election of some and rejection of others. Suffice it to quote one word of his in this connection. 'The foreknowledge of God, which Paul mentions, is not a bare prescience, as some unwise persons absurdly imagine, but the adoption by which he had always distinguished his children from the reprobate.'[5]

In connection with election Calvin fully recognizes that this election was in Christ. Nothing, however, could be more remote from Calvin's thought than to suppose that this fact in the least interferes with the pure sovereignty and particularism of the election itself. On the contrary, he says expressly that this is the confirmation that 'the election is free; for if we were chosen *in* Christ, it is not of ourselves'.[6] And the practical import for us of this truth is that no one should seek confidence in his own election anywhere else than in Christ. 'Christ,

---

[1] *Comm. ad* Romans 9:14; cf. E.T. by John Owen.
[2] Cf. *De Aeterna Dei Praedestinatione*, as cited, coll. 263 f.; E.T., pp. 34 f.
[3] *Ibid.*, col. 270; E.T., p. 44.
[4] *Comm. ad* Romans 9:14.
[5] *Comm. ad* Romans 8:29; E.T. by John Owen.
[6] *Comm. ad* Ephesians 1:4.

therefore, is both the clear glass in which we are called upon to behold the eternal and hidden election of God, and also the earnest and pledge.'[1] Referring to John 17:6, he says, 'We see here that God begins with himself (*a se ipso*), when he condescends to elect us: but he will have us to begin with Christ in order that we may know that we are reckoned among that peculiar people.'[2] 'Election, indeed, is prior to faith, but it is learned by faith.'[3]

As respects reprobation we are required to ask, in the main, two questions. The first question concerns what has been called its ultimacy. In the esteem of Calvin, is the passing over or rejection of the non-elect as eternal and as sovereign, in that sense as ultimate, as the choosing of the elect to eternal salvation? It appears to me that the frequency and the clarity with which Calvin deals with this question leave no doubt that the answer must be affirmative. It needs to be appreciated that his long dissertation on *The Eternal Predestination of God* was directed chiefly against the thesis of Pighius that the origin of reprobation was God's foreknowledge that some would remain to the last in contempt of divine grace and so the wicked deprive themselves of the benefit of universal election. Pighius denied that certain persons were absolutely appointed to destruction.[4] It is on this background that we must understand Calvin's repeated assertions to the contrary. He appeals to Augustine who, 'tracing the beginning of election to the gratuitous will of God, places reprobation in his mere will likewise'.[5] 'There is,' he continues, 'most certainly an inseparable connection between the elect and the reprobate, so that the election, of which the apostle speaks, cannot consist unless we confess that God separated from others certain persons whom it pleased him thus to separate.'[6] 'It is indeed true that the reprobate bring upon themselves the wrath of God by their own depravity, and that they daily hasten on to the falling of its weight upon their own heads. But it must be confessed that the apostle is here treating of that difference which proceeds from the secret judgment of God.'[7]

In his commentary on Romans 9 Calvin likewise says: 'That our

---

[1] *De Aeterna Dei Praedestinatione*, as cited, col. 318; cf. E.T., p. 132.
[2] *Ibid.*, col. 319; cf. E.T., p. 133.
[3] *Ibid.*, col. 318; cf. E.T., p. 133.
[4] Cf. *Ibid.*, coll. 259 f.; E.T., pp. 27 f.
[5] *Ibid.*, col. 267; cf. E.T., p. 41.
[6] *Ibid.*, col. 270; cf. E.T., p. 45.
[7] *Ibid.*, col. 288; cf. E.T., pp. 76 f.

mind may be satisfied with the difference which exists between the elect and the reprobate, and may not inquire for any cause higher than the divine will, his [Paul's] purpose was to convince us of this – that it seems good to God to illuminate some that they may be saved, and to blind others that they may perish: for we ought particularly to notice these words, *to* whom he wills, and, *whom he wills*: beyond this he allows us not to proceed.'[1] 'It is indeed evident that no cause is adduced higher than the will of God. Since there was a ready answer, that the difference depends on just reasons, why did not Paul adopt such a brief reply? But he placed the will of God in the highest rank for this reason – that it alone may suffice us for all other causes. No doubt, if the objection had been false ... a refutation would not have been rejected by Paul. The ungodly object and say, that men are exempted from blame, if the will of God holds the first place in their salvation, or in their perdition. Does Paul deny this? Nay, by his answer he confirms it, that God determines concerning men, as it seems good to him ... for he assigns, by his own right, whatever lot he pleases to what he forms.'[2]

These quotations are sufficient to show that no doubt can be entertained respecting Calvin's position that the differentiation that exists among men finds its explanation in the sovereign discrimination which God in his eternal counsel was pleased to make and that the passing by and rejection of the reprobate, in respect of differentiation and the diverse destiny entailed, are correlative with the election of those appointed to salvation. The sovereign will of God as the highest and ultimate cause is just as rigorously posited in reprobation as it is in election. And if the formula, 'the equal ultimacy of election and reprobation' is intended to denote this precise consideration, then there can be no room for hesitation in asserting that Calvin would have subscribed to that formula.

On the other hand, in respect of ultimacy, if the question is that of consequent destiny, there likewise needs to be no doubt but that, for Calvin, ultimate and irreversible perdition is coextensive with the decree of reprobation. It is scarcely necessary to adduce evidence in support of this conclusion. The way in which Calvin discusses the whole question of reprobation would be nullified as to its relevance and necessity if reprobation did not have as its implication eternal destruction, or election eternal salvation. But one or two quotations may be

[1] *Comm. ad* Romans 9:18; E.T. by John Owen.
[2] *Comm. ad* Romans 9:20; E.T. by John Owen.

offered to confirm this conclusion. 'As the blessing of the covenant separates the Israelitic nation from all other people, so the election of God makes a distinction between men in that nation, while he predestinates some to salvation, and others to eternal condemnation.'[1] 'Paul teaches us, that the ruin of the wicked is not only foreseen by the Lord, but also ordained by his counsel and his will; and Solomon teaches us the same thing – that not only the destruction of the wicked is foreknown, but that the wicked themselves have been created for this very end – that they may perish (Prov. 16:4).'[2]

The second question that arises in connection with reprobation is one that must never be overlooked. If we do not take account of this consideration we fail to appreciate the radical distinction that obtains between the predestination to life, which belongs to election, and the foreordination to death, which inheres in reprobation. Calvin insisted, as we have found, and insisted rightly, that in the differentiation between election and reprobation we must seek for no higher or more ultimate cause than the sovereign will of God, and that the pure sovereignty of God's good pleasure is the origin and explanation of reprobation no less than of election. But there is a factor in reprobation that does not enter into the salvation which is the fruit of election. This factor is that reprobation cannot be conceived of apart from the everlasting condemnation which it involves and condemnation always presupposes guilt and ill-desert. Guilt and ill-desert attach themselves to us. And, therefore, reprobation must never be conceived of apart from the ground or basis which resides in us for the condemnation that reprobation entails. In a word, the ground of condemnation is sin and sin alone. And sin is ours and ours alone. So reprobation always finds in men themselves a basis which never can be applied to the salvation which is the issue of election. To reiterate, the ground of the discrimination that exists among men is, as Calvin has maintained, the sovereign will of God and that alone. But the ground of the damnation to which the reprobate are consigned is sin and sin alone.

Calvin has not failed to recognize this distinction. We have an intimation of this in his statement: 'In the salvation of the godly nothing higher must be sought than the goodness of God, and nothing higher in the perdition of the reprobate than his just severity.'[3] It is

---

[1] *Comm. ad* Romans 9:11; E.T. by John Owen.
[2] *Comm. ad* Romans 9:18; E.T. by John Owen.
[3] *Comm. ad* Romans 9:11; E.T. by John Owen.

that term 'just severity' (*justa severitas*) that points to the exercise of judicial infliction in the matter of reprobation, that is, the execution of just judgment. It indicates that the judicial enters into the concept of reprobation. And he does not permit us to be in any doubt as to what he means by 'just severity'. He has his own way of enunciating this truth, and the import is clear. 'It is indeed true,' he says, 'that here is the proximate cause of reprobation, because we are all cursed in Adam.'[1] And when he inveighs against the clamour of the ungodly he says: 'being not content with defending themselves, they make God guilty instead of themselves; and then, after having devolved upon him the blame of their own condemnation, they become indignant against his great power.'[2] Again he says that although the secret predestination of God is the first cause and 'superior to all other causes, *so* the corruption and wickedness of the ungodly afford a reason and an occasion for the judgments of God' (*locum materiamque praebet Dei judiciis*).[3] 'The ungodly are indeed, on account of their evil deeds, visited by God's judgment with blindness; but if we seek for the source (*fontem*) of their ruin, we must come to this, that being accursed by God, they cannot by all their deeds, sayings, and purposes, get and obtain anything but a curse.'[4]

So it is quite apparent that Calvin does not think of reprobation as taking effect apart from the curse that rests upon sin. Sin is the proximate cause of damnation, and no man can justly plead that punishment executed is the consequence of aught but that for which he is to be blamed. It is therefore 'just severity'.

So Calvin is fully cognizant of the judicial aspect of reprobation. We should not be doing justice to Calvin, however, were we to overlook the contexts in which these references to sin as 'the proximate cause of reprobation' occur. The term 'proximate cause', of itself, advises us that there is a more ultimate cause and this is stated in the same sentence to be 'the bare and simple good pleasure of God' in electing and reprobating by his own will. When he speaks of 'the blame of their own damnation', which men seek to load upon God, it is in a context in which the accent falls upon the fact that 'those who perish have been destined by the will of God to destruction' and that the

[1] *Id.*
[2] *Comm. ad* Romans 9:19; E.T. by John Owen.
[3] *Comm. ad* Romans 9:30.
[4] *Comm. ad* Romans 11:7.

will of God holds the first place in salvation and perdition. And when he admits that the pravity and wickedness of the ungodly provide the material for God's judgments, yet he protests that it is to invert all order to set up causes 'above the secret predestination of God'.[1] What may we infer as to the reason for this jealousy with respect to the sovereign will and good pleasure of God? There can be but one answer.

When Calvin establishes the judicial factor in reprobation, he is bound to reckon with the fact that the *reason* why some are consigned to the curse, which we all inherit from Adam, and others are pre-destined to salvation is simply and solely the sovereign will of God. After all, ill-desert is not the reason for the discrimination, though it is the ground for the condemnation executed. And it is the note of secret predestination that is uppermost in Calvin's thought at these points, because this is the only explanation why the reprobate are left to reap the curse which their evil deeds deserve and for which they have no answer before God. This is why we are compelled to take account of the ultimacy, even in the matter of the judicial or penal aspect of reprobation, of the sovereignty of God's will, a sovereignty which is not one whit less sovereignly differentiating at the point of reprobation than it is at the point of election to life.

The formula, 'the equal ultimacy of election and reprobation', is not one that, in my judgment, is most felicitous because it is liable, by reason of its brevity, to obscure the penal, judicial, and hell-deserving ingredient which must enter into the concept of reprobation. But we must not affirm less than the equal ultimacy of the pure sovereignty of God's good pleasure in election and reprobation and that the sovereign discrimination that is exemplified in election is brought to bear upon reprobation at the point of its judicial execution as well as at the point of preterition. This, I believe, is the precipitate of Calvin's thinking on this topic, and I am not able to regard it as other than the precipitate of biblical teaching.

We should not, however, be giving a fair transcript of Calvin's teaching on this subject if we omitted to make mention of his warning. 'Proud men clamour, because Paul, admitting that men are rejected or chosen by the secret counsel of God, alleges no cause; as though the Spirit of God were silent for want of reason, and not rather, that by his silence he reminds us, that a mystery which our minds cannot

[1] *Comm. ad* Romans 9:30.

comprehend ought to be reverently adored, and that he thus checks the wantonness of human curiosity. Let us then know, that God does for no other reason refrain from speaking, but that he sees that we cannot contain his immense wisdom in our small measure; and thus regarding our weakness, he leads us to moderation and sobriety.'[1] 'And far be it from any one of the faithful to be ashamed to confess his ignorance of that which the Lord God has enveloped in the blaze of his own inaccessible light.'[2]

THE SOVEREIGNTY OF GOD IN HIS PROVIDENCE

The providence of God embraces all events, past, present, and future, and applies to the evil as much as to the good, to sinful acts as much as to the holy acts of men and angels. Unsanctified sense is liable to conceive of providence as consisting simply in the unfolding of potencies and virtues implanted in the world at its creation, and so the utmost of its adoration is to perceive the wisdom, power, and goodness of God in the work of creation. It conceives of God as a mere spectator. For the believer the presence of God appears no less in the perpetual government of the world than in its origin. Perhaps the most distinctive emphasis in this connection is Calvin's insistence that providence does not consist in a general motion or superintendence, but that all events whatsoever are governed by the secret counsel and directed by the present hand of God (*occulto Dei consilio gubernari . . . praesenti Dei manu diriguntur*). Calvin does not deny but rather asserts that created things are endowed with properties and laws which operate according to their nature. Yet they are only instruments into which God infuses as much efficacy as he wills and according to his own will turns to this or that action. The sun, for example, 'the godly man does not regard as the principal or necessary cause of those things which existed before the creation of the sun but only as an instrument which God uses, because he so wills, since he could dispense with it and act directly without any more difficulty'.[3] God made the sun to stand still (Josh. 10:13) to testify that 'the sun does not daily rise and set by a secret instinct of nature but that he himself governs its course to renew the memory of his fatherly favour towards us'.[4] God's omnipotence is not a vain, idle,

[1] *Comm. ad* Romans 9:20; E.T. by John Owen.
[2] *De Aeterna Dei Praedestinatione*, as cited, col. 316; E.T., p. 128.
[3] *Inst.*, I, xvi, 2.
[4] *Id.*

and, as it were, slumbering potency but a vigilant, efficacious, and operative agency constantly exerted on every distinct and particular movement (*ad singulas et particulares motus*). Not a drop of rain falls and no wind ever blows but at the special command of God (*speciali Dei jussu*).[1] Every year, month, and day is governed by a new and special providence of God (*nova et speciali Dei providentia temperari*).[2] Chance and fortune do not belong to a Christian man's vocabulary. Events are often fortuitous to us because their order, reason, end, and necessity are hid in the counsel of God and are not apprehended by the mind of man. But they are not fortuitous for God – they proceed from his will.

This insistence upon the ever-present and ever-active will of God in each particular movement obviously rules out the notion of bare permission. But Calvin takes pains to reflect on this subterfuge. It is particularly in connection with the sinful acts of Satan and of wicked men that the postulate of bare permission appears to offer escape from the allegation that the presence of the will and agency of God would be inconsistent with the responsibility and guilt which devolve upon the perpetrators of iniquity. In Calvin's esteem, this resort to the idea of permission is only to evade the difficulty. For 'that men can effect nothing but by the secret will of God, nor can they be exercised in deliberating anything but what he has previously with himself decreed and determines by his secret direction, is proved by innumerable and express testimonies'.[3] 'Whatever is attempted by men, or by Satan himself, God still holds the helm in order to turn all their attempts to the execution of his judgments.'[3] So it is nugatory and insipid to substitute for the providence of God a bare permission. The very 'conceptions we form in our minds are directed by the secret inspiration of God to the end which he has designed' (*arcana Dei inspiratione ad suum finem dirigi*).[4]

It is obvious what questions arise in connection with this doctrine. And Calvin was well aware of the objections and faced up squarely to their apparent validity. There is, first of all, the question of authorship. Is not God, therefore, the author of the crimes which the instruments of iniquity conceive and perpetrate? At certain points Calvin does speak

[1] *Ibid.*, I, xvi, 7.
[2] *Id.*
[3] *Ibid.*, I, xviii, 1.
[4] *Ibid.*, I, xviii, 2.

of God as author and cause. According to Scripture God 'himself is said to give men over to a reprobate mind and cast them into vile lusts, because he is the principal author (*praecipuus autor*) of his own righteous vengeance, and Satan is only the minister of it'.[1] 'Again he says: And I have already sufficiently shown that God is called the author (*autor*) of all these things which these censors wish to happen merely by his idle permission.'[2]

There are, however, certain qualifications which must be appreciated if we are to assess these statements correctly. Calvin is equally emphatic to the effect that God is not the *author* of sin. With respect to Adam's fall he says expressly, that although God ordained the fall of Adam, 'I so assert it as by no means to concede that God was the author.'[3] 'But *how* it was that God, by his foreknowledge and decree, ordained what should take place respecting man, and yet so ordained it without his being himself in the least a participator of the fault, or being at all the author (*autor*) or the approver of the transgression; *how* this was, I repeat, is a secret manifestly far too deep to be penetrated by the human mind, nor am I ashamed to confess our ignorance. And far be it from any of the faithful to be ashamed to confess his ignorance of that which the Lord envelops in the blaze of his own inaccessible light.'[4]

Furthermore, Calvin will allow for no equivocation on the principle that in those operations which are common to God and men God is free from all fault and contracts no defilement from men's vices. No one has expended more care than Calvin in developing the distinction in respect of the motive, reason, and end by which men are actuated in the commission of sin and the motive, reason, and end by which God makes the vices of men to fulfil his holy purposes. 'So great is the difference,' he says in quoting from Augustine, 'between what belongs to the human will, and what to the divine, and between the ends to which the will of every one is to be referred, for approbation or censure. For God fulfils his righteous will by the wicked wills of wicked men.'[5] There is a complete disparity between the wills of wicked men and the will of God which is operative in the same event. When men sin they do not perform evil actions with the motive or design of

[1] *Id.*
[2] *Ibid.*, I, xviii, 3.
[3] *De Aeterna Dei Praedestinatione*, as cited, col. 315; cf. E.T., p. 126.
[4] *Ibid.*, col. 316; cf. E.T., p. 128.
[5] *Inst.*, I, xviii, 3.

promoting the will of God but because they are inflamed with the violence of their own passions and deliberately strive to oppose him. 'God only requires of us conformity to his precepts. If we do anything contrary to them, it is not obedience, but contumacy and transgression . . . they [men] can lay no blame upon God, for they find in themselves nothing but evil, and in him only a legitimate use of their wickedness.'[1] There is thus a coincidence of the wicked wills of wicked men and the holy will of God. Both are operative in and converge upon the same event, and yet God contracts no defilement from the perversity which is the instrument of his holy designs. The difficulty this may pose for our understanding arises from the fact that 'because of the weakness of our mind we do not comprehend how in different respects (*diverso modo*) he does not will and wills the same thing' (*nolit fieri et velit*).[2]

It is not only, however, the disparity that exists between the wicked wills of men and the holy will of God, as both converge upon the same event, but also the disparity that exists within the will of God. There is a twofold aspect to the will of God. And there is the *disparity* between the decretive will and the preceptive will, between the determinations of his secret counsel that certain events will come to pass and the prescriptions of his revealed will to us that we do not bring these events to pass. It cannot be gainsaid that God decretively wills what he preceptively forbids and decretively forbids what he preceptively commands. It is precisely in this consideration that the doctrine of God's sovereignty is focused most acutely with its demands for our faith and reverence. If I am not mistaken it is at this point that the sovereignty of God makes the human mind reel as it does nowhere else in connection with this topic. It should be so. It is the sanctified understanding that reels. And it is not the mark of intelligence to allege or claim a ready resolution of the apparent contradiction with which it confronts us. How can God say: This comes to pass by my infallible foreordination and providence, and also say to us: This thou shalt not bring to pass?

Calvin was well aware of this question and he did not tone down the mystery with which it confronts us. He is constantly refuting, by appeal to Scripture, the objections which unbelief registers against this doctrine. Much of the argumentation in the last three chapters of

---

[1] *Ibid.*, I, xvii, 5; E.T. by John Allen.
[2] *Ibid.*, I, xviii, 3.

Book I of the *Institutes* is concerned with it. It is of interest that the last work in which Calvin was engaged before his work was arrested by the hand of death was his exposition of the prophecy of Ezekiel. His work ended with Ezekiel 20:44. He did not even complete his exposition of the chapter. At Ezekiel 18:23, in dealing with the discrepancy between God's will to the salvation of all and the election of God by which he predestinates only a fixed number to salvation, he says: 'If any one again objects, This is making God act with duplicity, the answer is ready, that God always wishes the same thing, though by different ways, and in a manner inscrutable to us. Although, therefore, God's will is simple, yet great variety is involved in it, as far as our senses are concerned. Besides, it is not surprising that our eyes should be blinded by intense light, so that we cannot certainly judge how God wishes all to be saved, and yet has devoted all the reprobate to eternal destruction, and wishes them to perish. While we look now through a glass darkly, we should be content with the measure of our own intelligence.'[1]

I said previously that in this discrepancy the doctrine of God's sovereignty comes to its most pointed expression. It is so, I submit, because the sovereignty of God bears upon us at no point more relevantly and with more irresistible sanction than in his command. Nothing underlines God's sovereignty over us and his propriety in us, as creatures made in his image, as does his sovereign command. In his command his sovereignty is addressed to our responsibility and our responsibility defines our creaturehood as made in his image. And the command of God registers his supremacy and our complete subjection to him. The providence of God, as also his decretive will, is at no point exemplified and vindicated as to its all-inclusiveness more effectively than at the point where our responsible agency is exercised in violation of his command. There is, after all, the contradiction that we by sin offer to God's sovereignty. It is the contradiction of the claim

---

[1] *Comm. ad* Ezekiel 18:23; E.T. by Thomas Myers. It is more probable that the Latin verb *velle*, translated on three occasions above by the English term 'wishes', should rather be rendered 'wills'.

The present writer is not persuaded that we may speak of God's will as 'simple', after the pattern of Calvin's statement. There is the undeniable fact that, in regard to sin, God *decretively* wills what he *preceptively* does not will. There is the contradiction. We must maintain that it is perfectly consistent with God's perfection that this contradiction should obtain. But it does not appear to be any resolution to say that God's will is 'simple', even in the sense of the Latin term *simplex*.

which his sovereignty demands of us and the contradiction of what is God's good pleasure. But if the providence of God did not embrace that very contradiction, then there would be a sphere outside the realm of God's providence and, therefore, outside the sphere of his sovereign control and direction. The simple upshot of that alternative would be that God would not be sovereign, and man in his sin would be able to command a realm impervious to God's providence.

What a dismal perspective and prospect that alternative would offer to us! We must boldly maintain and profess the only alternative which Calvin so insistently asserted. In the realm of sin we do have the contradiction of God's revealed and prescriptive good pleasure. But that very contradiction is embraced in the determinate counsel and foreknowledge of God. And it is just because this is the case, it is just because the contradiction which sin offers to his sovereignty in command is embraced in the sovereignty of both decree and providence and does not create a realm impervious to his efficient foreordination and operation, that the sovereign provisions of his grace invade that same realm and emancipate men from the contradiction itself and therefore from the curse, condemnation, thraldom, and misery which the contradiction entails. It is this doctrine of God's sovereignty in the realm of sin that is the precondition of sovereignty in redemptive grace.

13

Calvin, Dordt, and Westminster on Predestination – A Comparative Study[1]

ON December 4, 1646, the Confession of Faith, prepared by the Assembly of Divines meeting at Westminster, was completed. The date is more than a century later than that of the earlier editions of Calvin's masterpiece, *The Institutes of the Christian Religion* and also of the first edition of what is one of his most notable commentaries, the *Commentary on the Epistle to the Romans*. The century that intervened was one of prodigious theological output and intense controversy. Within the Reformed Churches the gravest issue was that focused in the Arminian Remonstrance of 1610 and it was this issue that gave occasion for the Synod of Dordt in 1618 and 1619. It would be unhistorical and theologically unscientific to overlook or discount the developments in the formulation of Reformed doctrine that a century of thought and particularly of controversy produced. Study even of Calvin's later works, including his definitive edition of the *Institutes* (1559), readily discloses that his polemics and formulations were not oriented to the exigencies of debates that were subsequent to the time of his writing. It is appropriate and necessary, therefore, that in dealing with Calvin, Dordt, and Westminster we should be alert to the differing situations existing in the respective dates and to the ways in which thought and language were affected by diverse contexts. In applying this principle, however, caution must be observed. This is particularly necessary in the case of Calvin. Too frequently he is enlisted in support of positions that diverge from those of his successors

[1] First published in *Crisis in the Reformed Churches*, Essays in Commemoration of the great Synod of Dordt, 1618–19, ed. P. Y. de Jong, Grand Rapids, 1968.

in the Reformed tradition. It is true that Calvin's method differs considerably from that of the classic Reformed systematizers of the 17th century. But this difference of method does not of itself afford any warrant for a construction of Calvin that places him in sharp contrast with the more analytically developed formulations of Reformed theology in the century that followed.

It would be expected that the vantage point occupied by the Assembly of Divines at Westminster, the unsurpassed care exercised in the composition of the documents that were the products of its labours, and the lengthy debates that characterized the Assembly would impart a precision scarcely equalled by earlier creedal formulations. This is conspicuously true in its Confession of Faith and Catechisms. In this essay we are concerned with the subject of predestination. No chapter in the Westminster Confession exhibits more of the qualities we might expect than Chapter III, 'Of God's Eternal Decree'. The chapter has eight sections. Sections I and II deal with the decree in its cosmic, all-inclusive reference, Sections III and IV with the decree as it has respect to men and angels in common, and Sections V–VIII with the decree as it applies to men distinctively. This order and the proportions of emphasis evince the competence which marks the Confession throughout.

The divines thought it meet to use the terms 'predestinate' and 'predestination' with reference to those appointed to everlasting life and the term 'foreordain' for those appointed to everlasting death. 'By the decree of God, for the manifestation of His glory, some men and angels are predestinated unto everlasting life; and others foreordained to everlasting death' (Sect. III). This variation is maintained in subsequent sections (cf. Sects. IV, V, and VIII). It cannot be said that any difference is intrinsic to the terms such as would require this restriction and it cannot be that greater or less efficacy was intended to be expressed by the one term in distinction from the other. What consideration dictated the usage concerned it may not be possible to say. But it cannot be denied that in the structure of the chapter as a whole the interest of differentiating between the elect and non-elect is thereby promoted and the felicity of the expression 'predestinated unto life' is made more apparent.

The doctrine of the Confession on predestination and foreordination is unequivocal. The differentiation involved and the diversity of destiny arising therefrom are clearly asserted. 'These angels and men, thus predestinated, and foreordained, are particularly and unchangeably designed, and their number so certain and definite, that it cannot be either increased or diminished' (Sec. IV). It is worthy of note that this statement of the Confession includes both angels and men and is so framed that in respect of the doctrine set forth it has equal relevance to men and angels. This feature goes beyond what we find in the Canons of Dordt. The Canons are concerned solely with the election and 'reprobation' of men. The reason for this is obvious. The Remonstrant tenets against which the Canons were directed dealt with the decree of God with reference to mankind and the issue would have been unnecessarily perplexed by introducing the subject of angels. But Dordt enunciates the same position in respect of mankind. 'And as God himself is most wise, unchangeable, omniscient, and omnipotent, so the election made by him can neither be interrupted nor changed, recalled nor annulled; neither can the elect be cast away, nor their number diminished' (Cap. I, Art. XI; cf. Art. VI). In the Rejection of Errors, Articles II, III, and V, the reason for this emphasis upon definiteness is given. The opposing position is stated to be that 'God's election to eternal life is manifold, the one general and indefinite, the other particular and definite . . . the one election to faith, the other to salvation . . . that the good pleasure and purpose of God, of which Scripture makes mention in the doctrine of election, does not consist in this, that God elected certain men above others, but in this, that God from all possible conditions . . . elected faith, in itself unworthy, and the imperfect obedience of faith as the condition of salvation', a position pronounced to be pernicious error, prejudicial to the good pleasure of God and the merit of Christ. The Westminster Confession is oriented against the same error but the reference to angels in the same section is a reminder that the scope of its interest in Chapter III is more embracive than that of the Canons.

The parallelisms of Sections V–VIII of the Confession with the First Head of Doctrine in the Canons is conspicuous and comparison at various points will disclose not only the agreement of the two documents on what is germane to the doctrine of predestination, but also the debt the Assembly of Divines owed to the deliberations and conclusions of Dordt. There is, of course, the marked contrast in proportions. Compact brevity is a distinguishing feature of the Confession. The four sections of the Confession comprise not more than one eighth of the space occupied by the eighteen affirmative and nine negative articles of the Canons. But the Canons are not to be accused of redundancy, and it should be kept in mind that there is in the text of the Canons copious quotation of Scripture in support of the doctrine asserted and in refutation of the errors rejected, a practice not adhered to in the Confession.

In contrast with the Remonstrant teaching, predestination to life and salvation is in both documents construed as unconditional, that is, as constrained by the sovereign good pleasure of God and not by any difference belonging to men themselves. This is expressed in the Confession in these terms: 'Those of mankind that are predestinated unto life, God, before the foundation of the world was laid, according to His eternal and immutable purpose, and the secret counsel and good pleasure of His will, hath chosen in Christ, unto everlasting glory, out of his mere free grace and love' (Sect. V). The terms of the Canons are: 'Election is the unchangeable purpose of God, whereby, before the foundation of the world, he hath, out of mere grace, according to the sovereign good pleasure of his own will, chosen, from the whole human race . . . a certain number of persons to redemption in Christ' (Art. VII); 'The good pleasure of God is the sole cause of this gracious election' (Art. X; cf. also Arts. XV and XVIII). So there is not only an identity of doctrine but also to a large extent of language.[1]

The negative counterpart of the emphasis upon mere free grace and the sovereign pleasure of God is, in contrast likewise with Remonstrant teaching, that election is not determined by any foresight of faith or of perseverance. 'Without any foresight of faith, or good works, or perseverance in either of them, or any other thing in the creature, as conditions, or causes moving Him thereunto' (Sect. V) says the Confession. 'This election was not founded upon foreseen faith, and the obedience of faith, holiness, or any other good quality or disposition in man, as the prerequisite, cause, or condition on which it depended' (Art. IX) say the Canons (cf. also Rejection of Errors, Art. V).

That redemption by Christ and all the grace necessary to the fruition of God's electing purpose should flow from election rather than be the determinants of it is a correlate of the positive and negative declarations just noted. Both documents are careful to state this expressly. 'The

[1] Space will not permit us to adduce the teaching of Calvin on this subject. A cursory reading of the *Institutes*, Book III, Chapters XXI–XXIII and of his *Commentary on the Epistle to the Romans*, Chapter 9 will show that this same insistence is sustained and pervasive. Cf. my *Calvin on Scripture and Divine Sovereignty* (Grand Rapids, 1960).

elect God hath decreed to give to Christ to be saved by him, and effectually to call and draw them to his communion by his word and Spirit; to bestow upon them true faith, justification, and sanctification; and having powerfully preserved them in the fellowship of his Son, finally to glorify them for the demonstration of his mercy, and for the praise of the riches of his glorious grace' (Canons, Art. VII; cf. Art. IX). It can scarcely be denied, however, that the formulation of Westminster excels in not only tying up the fruits with election but also in stating the certainty of effectuation in both redemption and application. 'As God hath appointed the elect unto glory, so hath He, by the eternal and most free purpose of His will, foreordained all the means thereunto. Wherefore, they who are elected, being fallen in Adam, are redeemed by Christ, are effectually called unto faith in Christ by His Spirit working in due season, are justified, adopted, sanctified, and kept by His power, through faith, unto salvation' (Sect. VI).[1]

The section just quoted from the Confession requires comment from another angle. On the question of the order of the divine decrees the Canons of Dordt are infralapsarian. This would appear to be the purport of Article VII when it says that election is that whereby God hath 'chosen in Christ unto salvation a certain number of men from the whole human race, which had fallen by their own fault from their original integrity into sin and destruction, neither better nor more worthy than others but with them involved in common misery'. But it is clearly set forth in Article X when it is said that God was pleased 'out of the common mass of sinners to adopt some certain persons as a peculiar treasure to himself'. The Confession might seem to have the same intent. 'Wherefore, they who are elected, being fallen in Adam, are redeemed by Christ.' This would not be correct. The words, 'being fallen in Adam', do not imply that the elect when elected were contemplated as fallen in Adam. The words simply state an historical fact which explains the *necessity* of redemption by Christ and the other phases of salvation. The Confession is non-committal on the debate between the Supralapsarians and Infralapsarians and intentionally so, as both the terms of the section and the debate in the Assembly clearly show. Surely this is proper reserve in a creedal document.

No paragraph in the whole compass of confessional literature excels for precision of thought, compactness of formulation, and jealousy for the various elements of truth in the doctrine concerned than Section

[1] Cf. Calvin: *Institutes*, III, xxiv, 1–4.

VII of the Confession. 'The rest of mankind, God was pleased, according to the unsearchable counsel of His own will, whereby He extendeth or withholdeth mercy, as He pleaseth, for the glory of His sovereign power over His creatures, to pass by; and to ordain them to dishonour and wrath for their sin, to the praise of His glorious justice.' Several observations should be noted.

The section deals with what has often been called the decree of reprobation. In distinction from Dordt (cf. Arts. VI, XV, and XVI)[1] the Confession does not use this term. This restraint must be commended. Although the Scripture uses the term that is properly rendered 'reprobate' (cf. Rom. 1:28; 1 Cor. 9:27; 2 Cor. 13:5, 6, 7; 2 Tim. 3:8; Tit. 1:16), yet its use is such that the elements entering into the decree of God respecting the non-elect could not legitimately be injected into it. The presumption is that the Westminster divines hesitated to employ it for this reason. *Biblical* terms should not be loosely applied.

The precision of the formulation is evident in the distinction drawn between the two expressions 'to pass by' and 'to ordain them'. The former is not modified, the latter is. No reason is given for the passing by except the sovereign will of God. If sin had been mentioned as the reason, then all would have been passed by. The differentiation finds its explanation wholly in God's sovereign will and in respect of this ingredient the only reason is that 'God was pleased ... to pass by'. But when ordination to dishonour and wrath is contemplated, then the proper ground of *dishonour* and *wrath* demands mention. And this is sin. Hence the addition in this case, 'to ordain them to dishonour and wrath for their sin'.

A third observation, however, is all-important. It might be alleged that the Confession represents judicial infliction and ill-desert as the only factor relevant to the ordaining to dishonour and wrath, that what has been called 'reprobation' as distinct from preterition is purely judicial. The Confession is eloquent in its avoidance of this construction and only superficial reading of its terms could yield such an interpretation. The earlier clauses – 'God was pleased, according to the unsearchable counsel of His own will, whereby He extendeth or withholdeth mercy, as He pleaseth, for the glory of His sovereign power over His creatures' – govern 'to ordain them to dishonour and wrath' as well as 'to pass by'. So the sovereign will of God is operative in ordaining to dishonour and wrath as well as in passing by. And careful

[1] Calvin frequently uses the term 'reprobation'. Cf. citations given above.

analysis will demonstrate the necessity for this construction. Why are some ordained to dishonour and wrath when others equally deserving are not? The only explanation is the sovereign will of God. The *ground* of dishonour and wrath is sin alone. But the reason why the non-elect are ordained to this dishonour and wrath when others, the elect, are not, is sovereign differentiation on God's part and there is no other answer to the question.

The genius of the fathers of Dordt did not lie in the direction of such compact and yet adequate definition. And the situation confronting them required more expanded treatment. But Dordt was likewise alert to the need for these same distinctions and to the diverse factors entering into what it called the decree of reprobation (*decretum repro- bationis*). 'What peculiarly tends to illustrate and recommend to us the eternal and unmerited grace of election is the express testimony of sacred Scripture, that not all men are elect but certain non-elect are passed by in God's eternal election, and these God out of his most free, most just, irreprehensible, and immutable good pleasure decreed to leave in the common misery into which they by their own fault have plunged themselves, and not to bestow upon them saving faith and the grace of conversion, but, left to their own ways and under just judgment, at length, not only on account of unbelief but also for all other sins, for the declaration of his justice to condemn and punish for ever' (Art. XV; cf. also Art. VI).

The Canons are at this point careful to guard against the inference that the decree of reprobation makes God the author of sin. 'And this is the decree of reprobation which by no means makes God the author of sin (the very thought of which is blasphemy), but declares him to be an awful, irreprehensible, and righteous judge and avenger' (Art. XV). The Confession reiterates the same caution. Although God ordains 'whatsoever comes to pass: yet so, as thereby neither is God the author of sin, nor is violence offered to the will of the creatures' (Sect. I).

On the distinction between the sovereign and judicial elements in foreordination to death Calvin likewise is cognizant. He draws the distinction in terms of the difference between 'the highest cause' (*suprema causa*) and the 'the proximate cause' (*propinqua causa*).[1] The highest cause is 'the secret predestination of God' and the proximate cause is that 'we are all cursed in Adam'. 'But as the secret predestination

---

[1] *Comm. ad* Romans 9:30 and 9:11 respectively.

is above every other cause, so the corruption and wickedness of the ungodly affords a ground and provides the occasion for the judgments of God.'[1] Thus for Calvin, as for Dordt and Westminster, the *reason* for discriminating is 'the bare and simple good pleasure of God' (*ad* Rom. 9:11) and the *ground* of damnation is the sin of the reprobate, a damnation to which they have been destined by the will of God (cf. *ad* Rom. 9:20).[2]

It will be admitted that in 'the decree of reprobation' the doctrine of God's absolute predestination comes to sharpest focus and expression. On this crucial issue, therefore, Calvin, Dordt, and Westminster are at one. The terms of expression differ, as we might expect, and the Westminster Confession with inimitable finesse and brevity has given to it the most classic formulation. But the doctrine is the same and this fact demonstrates the undissenting unity of thought on a tenet of faith that is a distinguishing mark of our Reformed heritage and without which the witness to the sovereignty of God and to his revealed counsel suffers eclipse at the point where it must jealously be maintained. For the glory of God is the issue at stake.

The abuses of the doctrine of predestination and the alleged conflict thereby instituted with other doctrines of Scripture are matters with which Calvin, Dordt, and Westminster were compelled to deal. The Westminster Confession with characteristic felicity reads: 'The doctrine of this high mystery of predestination is to be handled with special prudence and care, that men, attending the will of God revealed in His Word, and yielding obedience thereunto, may, from the certainty of their effectual vocation, be assured of their eternal election. So shall this doctrine afford matter of praise, reverence, and admiration of God; and of humility, diligence, and abundant consolation to all that sincerely obey the Gospel' (Sect. VIII). The situation Dordt encountered demanded much more expansion of these same caveats, exhortations, and assurances pertaining to the doctrine. The first article of the Arminian Remonstrance required that Dordt should give prominence to the universal sin and condemnation of mankind, to the love of God manifest in the giving of Christ, to the proclamation of the gospel, to the summons of men without distinction to repentance and faith, to the guilt and consequence of unbelief as well as to the saving effect of faith, and to the responsibility of men in the rejection of the gospel.

[1] *Ibid. ad* 9:30 (E.T., 1960), p. 216.
[2] Cf. also *Inst.*, III, xxiii, 3, 8, 9 and 10.

It was necessary to show that these truths were not curtailed or negated by the doctrine of predestination and the latter had to be set in proper focus in relation to them. Hence the first five articles of the Canons are devoted to such aspects of the gospel. But, after the pattern followed by the Westminster Confession and in greater fulness, Dordt deals with the proper uses of the doctrine and warns against the distortions to which it is liable to be subjected. The way of attaining to the assurance of election is set forth in Article XII. The elect may attain to this assurance, 'though in various degrees and in different measure . . . not by inquisitively prying into the secret and deep things of God but by observing in themselves with spiritual joy and holy pleasure the infallible fruits of election designated in the Word of God'. The consolations of the sense and certainty of election and the corresponding responses in humiliation, adoration, and gratitude are reflected on in Article XIII and the danger of carnal security, rash presumption, remissness in observing the commandments of God receives proportionate emphasis. Of particular and distinctive interest are Articles XIV and XVI, the *former* in setting forth the obligation to proclaim constantly, in due time and place to the glory of God's most holy name, the doctrine of election and the *latter* for the concern that the proper response should be offered to the doctrine of reprobation. Those who do not yet experience living faith in Christ and its accompanying confidences ought not to be alarmed or terrified by the doctrine of reprobation or rank themselves among the reprobate, provided they persevere in the use of the means of grace and earnestly desire to be turned to God. But it is a terror to those who are forgetful of the claims of Christ and indulge the lusts of the flesh.[1]

In dealing with abuses of the doctrine of foreordination one objection that both Dordt and Westminster found it necessary to controvert is that it makes God the author of sin and exculpates the human agent. No one has exposed the fallacies underlying this objection with greater effect than Calvin. A great deal of his argumentation in *Institutes*, Book I, Chapters XVI–XVIII is devoted to a refutation. With eloquent reiteration he develops the distinction between the motive, reason, and end by which men are actuated in the commission of sin, on the one hand, and the motive, reason, and end entertained by God, on the other. In Calvin there is no toning down of the fact that the will of God is the first and ultimate cause of all that comes to pass. But there

[1] Cf. Calvin: *Inst.*, III, xxi, 1 and 2; xxiii, 5, 12, 13 and 14.

is total disparity between the will of God and the will of man as these two wills are operative in the same event. When men sin they are not actuated by the design of fulfilling God's purpose but by evil passions in contravention of his revealed good pleasure. Here is the same principle asserted by both Dordt and Westminster that foreordination is not the *rule* of our action but the will or commandments of God revealed in his Word. 'From what source do we learn but from his Word? In such fashion we must in our deeds search out God's will which he declares through his Word. God requires of us only what he commands. If we contrive anything against his commandment, it is not obedience but obstinacy and transgression.'[1]

In reference to election there is one other aspect that may not be overlooked. It is that election was in Christ. Calvin repeatedly stresses this. There are three lessons derived from it. First, it certifies that 'the election is free; for if we were chosen in Christ, it is therefore not of ourselves'.[2] Second, we cannot find assurance of our own election anywhere else than in Christ. Election is prior to faith but it is learned only by faith. Third, we learn thereby that election is discriminating; not all are members of Christ. It is noteworthy that both Dordt and Westminster introduce this aspect in contexts where the sovereignty and freeness of election are set in the forefront (Confession, Sect. V; Canons, Art. VII). They are thus in accord with the position emphasized by Calvin. But in neither document is there reflection upon the more practical lessons mentioned by Calvin. We could scarcely expect the limits of creedal formulation to permit this. Both Dordt and Westminster also speak of God's decree to give the elect to Christ to be saved by him (Confession, Chap. VIII, Sect. I; Canons, Art. VII). This decree from eternity must have been conceived of as distinct from and logically subsequent to election in Christ. No index is given, however, in either document as to how the framers conceived of this election in Christ. This is to their credit. The revelatory data do not warrant dogmatism as to the precise *character* of the 'in Christ' although the Scripture makes apparent its manifold consequences.

The conclusion constrained by this comparative study is that although Calvin, Dordt, and Westminster exhibit distinguishing features appropriate to their respective contexts and to the demands these

[1] *Inst.* I, xvii, 5 (E.T., 1960), p. 217.
[2] *Comm. ad* Ephesians 1:4. Cf. *Inst.*, III, xxii, 1 and 2; *De Aeterna Dei Praedestinatione*, in *Opera* (Brunswick, 1870), VIII, coll. 318 f.

contexts exacted, yet on the subject of predestination there is one voice on all essential elements of the doctrine. This is but one example of what is true in respect of the system of doctrine espoused by the Reformed Churches. There is what must be called the consensus of Reformed theology. Our debt is unmeasured. It is also one to humble us. In no doctrine is the *soli Deo gloria* more demanded of us than in our thought of predestination. Nowhere in the compass of theological formulation is the praise of God's glory more central than in the work of Calvin, Dordt, and Westminster.

14

Covenant Theology[1]

COVENANT theology denotes a development of theological thought and construction within the Reformed or Calvinistic tradition. This does not mean that the idea of God's covenantal relations with men has been ignored in other theological traditions. The term *covenant* is a Biblical term, and any theology which regards the Scripture as the rule of faith is compelled to recognize the frequency with which the relationship that God established with men is set forth in covenantal terms. Hence, within Protestant churches both Lutheran and Arminian theologians have taken account of the covenant form in which God has revealed himself to men.[2]

Covenant theology is, however, a distinguishing feature of the Reformed tradition because the idea of covenant came to be an organizing principle in terms of which the relations of God to men were construed.

I. DEFINITION

From the beginning and throughout the development of covenant theology, covenant has been defined as a contract, or compact, or agreement between parties. From the earliest Reformed treatise on the

[1] First published in *The Encyclopaedia of Christianity*, vol. III, ed. P. E. Hughes, Delaware, 1972.
[2] Cf. J. A. Quenstedt, *Theologia Didactico-Polemica*, Leipzig, 1715, II, 1298 f.; D. Hollazius, *Examen Theologicum Acromanticum*, Leipzig, 1763, 1045 ff.; M. Chemnitz, *Examen Concilii Tridentini*, Frankfort, 1609, 242b; P. Limborch, *Theologia Christiana*, The Hague, 1736, 195 ff., 203 f., 603 f.; S. Episcopius, *Opera Theologica*, London, 1678, 31 f., 45 f., 155 f.; S. Curcellaeus, *Opera Theologica*, Amsterdam, 1675, 188–196, 347 ff.; R. Watson, *Theological Institutes*, London, 1846, II, 337 f., 611; III, 472–493; W. B. Pope, *A Compendium of Christian Theology*, London, 1880, II, 13, 60, 93–96; III, 100 ff.

subject, that of Henry Bullinger (*De Testamento seu Foedere Dei Unico et Aeterno Brevis Expositio*, 1534), through the classic period of formulation, and continuing to recent times this concept has exercised a great influence upon the exposition of God's covenant relations with men. Hence, in the words of Zachary Ursinus, God's covenant is 'a mutual promise and agreement, between God and men, in which God gives assurance to men that he will be merciful to them. . . . And, on the other side, men bind themselves to God in this covenant that they will exercise repentance and faith . . . and render such obedience as will be acceptable to him' (Eng. tr., G. W. Williard, *The Commentary on the Heidelberg Catechism*, Grand Rapids, 1954, 97). And Charles Hodge, three centuries later, insisted that since covenant 'when used of transactions between man and man means a mutual compact' we must give it the same sense 'when used of transactions between God and man' (*Systematic Theology*, II, 354). The formulation of a covenant, therefore, took the form of a fourfold division – contracting parties, conditions, promises, threatenings. It was also defined in terms of *stipulation*, denoting the demand of God placed upon man, of *promise* on the part of God to man, of *astipulation*, referring to the acceptance on man's part of the conditions prescribed by God, and, finally, of *restipulation*, whereby man could claim the promise on his fulfilment of the prescribed demands.

This formulation became the occasion of ardent dispute when it was applied to the Covenant of Grace. This dispute concerned particularly the matter of condition, the question being: Is the Covenant of Grace to be construed as conditional or unconditional? The controversy continues up to the present time, and it is not apparent that a solution can be obtained without a reorientation in terms of a revised definition of the Biblical concept of covenant.

2. THE COVENANT OF WORKS

Towards the end of the 16th century the administration dispensed to Adam in Eden, focused in the prohibition to eat of the tree of the knowledge of good and evil, had come to be interpreted as a covenant, frequently called the Covenant of Works, sometimes a covenant of life or the Legal Covenant. It is, however, significant that the early covenant theologians did not construe this Adamic administration as a covenant, far less as a covenant of works. Reformed creeds of the 16th century such as the French Confession (1559), the Scottish Confession

(1560), the Belgic Confession (1561), the Thirty-Nine Articles (1562), the Heidelberg Catechism (1563), and the Second Helvetic (1566) do not exhibit any such construction of the Edenic institution. After the pattern of the theological thought prevailing at the time of their preparation, the term 'covenant,' insofar as it pertained to God's relations with men, was interpreted as designating the relation constituted by redemptive provisions and as belonging, therefore, to the sphere of saving grace.

It might appear from certain expressions that John Calvin enunciated the doctrine of what came later to be known as the Covenant of Works. He uses such terms as 'the covenant of the law' and 'the legal covenant' (*foedus legis, pactum legis, foedus legale*; cf. *Inst.*, II, xi, 4; *Comm. ad* Jer. 32:4). In these references, however, it is clear that it is the Mosaic covenant, in distinction from the new covenant of the Gospel age, that he calls the covenant of the law and the legal covenant. There is no allusion to the Adamic administration, nor can there be any suggestion to the effect that the Mosaic covenant was legal or one of works in contrast with grace; Calvin is insistent that the covenant of all the fathers is identical with the new in substance and differs only in the mode of administration (*Inst.*, II, x, 2 and 8; II, xi, 1). This use of terms to designate the Mosaic covenant or, more inclusively, the Old Testament should guard us against the assumption that they have any affinity with or give any support to what, later on, had come to be called the Covenant of Works.

There is, however, another sense in which Calvin uses the expression 'covenant of the law.' The law of God as commandment does prescribe the rule of a devout and perfect life, and promises the reward of life to perfect fulfilment of its demands (*Comm. ad* Gen. 15:6; *Inst.*, II, ix, 4). It must be noted, however, that this kind of righteousness or the merit accruing therefrom is for Calvin purely hypothetical. For in this connection he says that such observance of the law is never found in any man. Nevertheless, in view of Calvin's use of the expression 'covenant of the law' with this import, and since he believed that Adam had been created in righteousness and holiness, there would appear to be good ground for applying the term 'covenant' to that administration which had been constituted with Adam in the state of innocence. It is noteworthy that he does not make this application and evinces great restraint in this regard. The interpretation of Hosea 6:7 in which allusion might be found to an Adamic covenant he vigorously rejects, and he is insistent that there was no *covenant* answering to the requirements of justification and acceptance with God prior to the covenant with Abraham (*Comm. ad* Gal. 3:17).

This restraint on Calvin's part does not mean that the doctrine of Adam's representative headship, which later on came to be formulated in terms of the Covenant of Works, is absent from his teaching. He maintains that all men were created in the first man, that what God designated for all he conferred on Adam, that the condition of mankind was settled in Adam's person, and that Adam by his fall ruined himself and drew all mankind into the same ruin (*Comm. ad* 1 Cor. 15:45; Rom. 5:12 ff.). But he did not construe this Adamic constitution as a *covenant* of works or of law.

It is difficult to discover the genealogy of the doctrine of the Covenant of Works which appeared in fully developed form in the last decade of the 16th century. It may be that the earliest suggestion is found in Caspar Olevianus. After the pattern of what we find in Calvin, Olevianus speaks of the legal covenant as the eternal rule of righteousness to which man is obligated and to which is annexed the promise of life on the fulfilment of perfect obedience and the threat of death in the event of transgression. This is a principle always recognized in covenant theology. But in Olevianus we find what goes beyond this application of the term 'covenant.' He applies the term to the administration under which Adam fell by the temptation of Satan: 'For we see that Satan, in order to destroy that first covenant or relationship which existed between God and man created in the image of God, set before man the hope of equality with God' (*De Substantia Foederis Gratuiti inter Deum et Electis*, Geneva, 1585, 9 f.). He then speaks of the 'impious covenant' by which man sold himself to the devil. It is more likely that he construed the 'first covenant' as a special administration to Adam rather than as merely the legal covenant insofar as it applied to Adam (cf. also F. Junius in *Theses Theologicae*, XXV, 3, *Opuscula Theologica Selecta*, Amsterdam, 1882, 184).

But by whatever processes in the course of covenant thinking the doctrine of the Covenant of Works came to occupy a place in the formulation of covenant theology, we find it clearly enunciated in all its essential features in Robert Rollock, first in his treatise *Quaestiones et Responsiones Aliquot de Foedere Dei* (Edinburgh, 1596) and then in his *Tractatus De Vocatione Efficaci* (1597; Eng. tr. by Henry Holland, London, 1603). It is significant that the premise of Rollock's thought is that all of God's Word pertains to some covenant; God speaks nothing to man without covenant.

The Covenant of Works, also called the Covenant of Nature, Rollock defines as the covenant in which God promises to man eternal life on the condition of good works performed in the strength of nature, a condition which man in turn accepts. The *foundation* of this covenant was the holy and perfect nature with which man was endowed at creation and is thus to be sharply distinguished from the foundation of the Covenant of Grace, which is in Christ and the grace of God in Christ. The *condition* was good works performed in virtue of the holy nature with which man was created and not faith in Christ or the works of grace. The heads of this condition are the commands of the Decalogue written first of all upon man's heart. The *promise* is eternal life accruing to man, not on the basis of his original righteousness or integrity, but on the basis of the good works performed in the strength of this integrity. As regards *repetition*, the covenant is repeated again and again from the creation and fall of man to the coming of Christ but particularly in the promulgation from Mount Sinai by the hand of Moses (Ex. 19:5–8). The end of this repetition, however, was not that men might be justified and live by this covenant, but that, being convicted of sin and of the impossibility of good works in the strength of nature, they might take refuge in the Covenant of Grace. The *threat* of the covenant was the curse epitomized in the twofold death which followed upon the breach, death corporal and spiritual (see W. M. Gunn, ed., *The Select Works of Robert Rollock*, Edinburgh, 1849, I, 33–38).

The concept of legal covenant, found in Calvin but not applied by him to the Adamic administration, is here in Rollock clearly utilized in the interpretation and construction of the Adamic institution. From this time on the rubric of the Covenant of Works is part of the staple of covenant theology. M. Maternus Heyder, in theses presented to Grynaeus, Stuckius, and Pareus, dated November 25, 1602, and titled *De Foedere Dei et Conjunctis Aliquot Capitibus*, says that there is a twofold covenant, of works and of grace. The Covenant of Works he defines as that in which God promises to man immortality and eternal life on the performance of the most absolute and perfect obedience to the law of works, a covenant entered into between God and men immediately upon the first creation. Heyder also propounds the notion of repetition and the purposes fulfilled thereby in a way similar to that of Rollock. Amandus Polanus in his *Syntagma Theologiae Christianae* (Hanover, 1609) follows the same pattern in respect of definition, repetition, and the purposes promoted by repetition. But he also becomes more explicit respecting the time and persons involved when he says that God made this covenant from the beginning with our first parents, Adam and Eve, in the state of primitive integrity (*Lib.* VI, *Cap.* XXXIII, 2904 ff.).

It is not certain that William Perkins, though he plainly speaks of the Covenant of Works as God's covenant made on the condition of perfect obedience and expressed in the moral law (*A Golden Chaine*, London, 1612, 32), conceived of the special administration to Adam in these terms. There is no mention of a covenant with Adam at an earlier point in his treatise where he deals with Adam and the consequences of his sin (*ibid.*, 19 ff.). The Covenant of Works may have been for Perkins another way of describing what in Calvin, for example, was a hypothetical legal covenant. In John Preston, however, Perkins' younger contemporary, the Covenant of Works is expressly stated to have been made with Adam and expressed by Moses in the moral law, but which now by reason of sin is no more than the ministration of naked commandment, of servile fear, and of death (*The New Covenant or the Saints Portion*, London, 1639, 314 ff.).

This interpretation of the Adamic administration in terms of covenant found expression in creedal formulation for the first time in The Irish Articles of Religion (1615). Article 21 reads: 'Man being at the beginning created according to the image of God . . . had the covenant of the law ingrafted in his heart, whereby God did promise unto him everlasting life upon condition that he performed entire and perfect obedience unto his Commandments, according to that measure of strength wherewith he was endued in his creation, and threatened death unto him if he did not perform the same.' In more explicit form it is set forth in the Westminster Confession of Faith and Catechisms. In Chapter VII, Sections I and II, the Confession says:

The distance between God and the creature is so great, that although reasonable creatures do owe obedience unto Him as their Creator, yet they could never have any fruition of Him as their blessedness and reward, but by some voluntary condescension on God's part which He hath been pleased to express by way of covenant.

II. The first covenant made with man was a covenant of works, wherein life was promised to Adam; and in him to his posterity, upon condition of perfect and personal obedience.

In Chapter XIX, Section I, we read:

God gave to Adam a law, as a covenant of works, by which He bound him and all his posterity to personal, entire, exact, and perpetual obedience, promised life upon the fulfilling, and threatened death upon the breach of it, and endued him with power and ability to keep it (cf. The Larger Catechism, 20–22; The Shorter Catechism, 12).

The doctrine of the Covenant of Works was more extensively unfolded in the classic Reformed theologians of the 17th century. New aspects or at least emphases appear. Francis Turretine may be mentioned as representative of the more detailed expositions (*Institutio Theologiae Elencticae, Loc.* VIII). A few features are worthy of special attention.

Adam, as a *contracting party*, is to be regarded in the bond of union that existed between him and the whole human race descending naturally from him. This bond of union is twofold, *natural* because he is the common father of all and *forensic* because he was a public person and constituted the representative prince and head of the human race. The *obligation* of the covenant was partly general and partly special, general in respect of the moral law and special in respect of abstinence from the forbidden tree. The *promise* was that of the greatest felicity in heaven. The obligation which God assumed in this promise was wholly gratuitous; God had no debt, strictly speaking, from which a right could belong to man. The only debt was that of his own faithfulness to the promise. And as for man, he could not, strictly and properly, obtain merit from his obedience and could not seek the reward as a right. The worthiness of works could bear no proportion to the reward of life eternal.

In these features we can see that the conception entertained moved away from that of a *legal covenant*, and the gracious character of what was still called the Covenant of Works came to be recognized and accented. This is the emphasis which appears in the Westminster documents when covenant is construed as 'voluntary condescension' and 'special act of providence.' And the designation 'covenant of life' in both Catechisms is much more in accord with the grace which conditions the administration than is the term 'covenant of works.'

3. THE COVENANT OF GRACE

It is with the Covenant of Grace that the covenant theologians of the 16th century were concerned almost exclusively. And even in later developments of covenant theology it was not the Covenant of Works that claimed the chief interest; the latter was but the preface to the unfolding of the Covenant of Grace, which is constitutive of the history of redemption.

The Covenant of Grace from the earliest period of the Reformation was conceived of in terms of the administration of grace to men and belonging, therefore, to the sphere of historical revelation. It was regarded as having begun to be dispensed to men in the first promise given to Adam after the fall, but as taking concrete form in the promise to Abraham and progressively disclosed until it reached its fullest realization in the New Covenant.

Henry Bullinger in his tractate of 1534 mapped out the lines along which the thinking of covenant theologians proceeded. He found the essence and characterizing features of what he calls 'the one and everlasting testament' or covenant, in 'the covenant made with Abraham' (Gen. 17).

Here God, of His ineffable mercy and grace and moved by nothing else than mere goodness, entered into covenant with the seed of Abraham, promising to be a God to them and requiring of them that they walk perfectly before Him, a covenant that is perpetual in its reference and confirmed by a bloody ceremony. Here he says is the mystery that surpasses human comprehension, that the eternal God, the Creator and Preserver of all, should join Himself in covenant with miserable mortals corrupted by sin, to the end that He should not deal with them after their sins nor execute His wrath upon them. It was this covenant that Christ confirmed. It is confirmed by the fact that He is God-with-us, that we are complete in Him in whom dwells all the fulness of the Godhead, and that out of His fulness we all receive grace for grace. The condition, likewise, is confirmed by Christ; there is no retraction of the demand that we walk before Him and be perfect. He that says he abides in Christ ought to walk even as He walked. Hence the covenant of God with men is one and it is perpetual, as was indicated to Abraham when God said 'and between thy seed after thee in their generations for an everlasting covenant' (*op. cit.*, 155–161).

It was noted above that Calvin regarded the covenant made with Abraham as the first *covenantal* administration answering to justification and acceptance with God. Calvin, like Bullinger, finds in the Abrahamic covenant substantial features of all that is involved in God's covenant relationship with men. It is the promise of the covenant with Abraham that Christ fulfils, and fulfilment constitutes the New Covenant. But of particular interest in connection with unity and continuity is Calvin's insistence that the Mosaic covenant was not of a different character or governed by a different principle but was a confirmation of the Abrahamic. 'It then follows,' he says, 'that the first covenant was inviolable; besides, he had already made his covenant with Abraham, and the Law was a confirmation of that covenant. As then the Law depended on that covenant which God made with his Servant Abraham, it follows that God could never have made a new, that is, a contrary or a different covenant. From whence do we derive our hope of salvation, except from that blessed seed promised to Abraham? . . . These things no doubt sufficiently show that God has never made any other covenant than that which he made formerly with Abraham, and at length confirmed by the hand of Moses' (*Comm. ad* Jer. 31:31, 32, Eng. tr. by John Owen, Grand Rapids, 1950; cf. *ad* Gal. 3:17, 18, 19, 23; Heb. 8:6, 10; Ex. 24:5). Even the New Covenant is not so called because it is contrary to the first covenant but because there is a clearer and fuller manifestation of the gratuitous adoption which the Abrahamic covenant revealed and the Mosaic confirmed (*id.*).

It is necessary to observe the extent to which Calvin recognized the principle of historical progression in the disclosure of covenant grace. The recognition of progressive revelation long antedates Cocceius. Nothing surpasses the following excerpt from Calvin's greatest work:

For this is the order and economy which God observed in dispensing the covenant of his mercy, that as the course of time accelerated the time of its full exhibition, he illustrated it from day to day with additional revelations. Therefore, in the beginning, when the first promise was given to Adam, it was like the kindling of some feeble sparks. Subsequent accessions caused a considerable enlargement of the light, which continued to increase more and more, and diffused its splendour through a wide extent, till at length, every cloud being dissipated, Christ, the Sun of righteousness, completely illuminated the whole world (*Inst.*, II, x, 20, Eng. tr. by John Allen).

Calvin devotes two chapters to the subject of the similarities and differences between the two Testaments (*Inst.* II, x and xi), and subsequent discussions follow the pattern delineated in these chapters. The formula adopted to express the three features of unity, continuity, and consummation in Christ was oneness in substance but difference in mode of administration (*Inst.*, II, xi, 1).

This tradition received its most succinct formulation in the Westminster Confession of Faith in Chapter VII, Sections V and VI:

V. This covenant was differently administered in the time of the law, and in the time of the gospel: under the law, it was administered by promises, prophecies, sacrifices, circumcision, the paschal lamb, and other types and ordinances delivered to the people of the Jews, all fore-signifying Christ to come; which were, for that time, sufficient and efficacious, through the operation of the Spirit, to instruct and build up the elect in faith in the promised Messiah, by whom they had full remission of sins, and eternal salvation; and is called the Old Testament.

VI. Under the gospel, when Christ, the substance, was exhibited, the ordinances in which this covenant is dispensed are the preaching of the Word, and the administration of the sacraments of Baptism and the Lord's Supper: which, though fewer in number, and administered with more simplicity, and less outward glory, yet, in them, it is held forth in more fulness, evidence, and spiritual efficacy, to all nations, both Jews and Gentiles; and is called the New Testament. There are not therefore two covenants of grace, differing in substance, but one and the same, under various dispensations.

The covenant theologians who followed Calvin, such as Jerome Zanchius, Zachary Ursinus, and Caspar Olevianus, adhere to a rather uniform pattern in expounding the doctrine of the Covenant of Grace. First of all, it is noteworthy that they do not orient their exposition to a comparison and contrast with the Covenant of Works, as later theologians were wont to do. The following summary, in terms largely of Olevianus' exposition, will serve to illustrate the pattern pursued.

The covenant is that by which God reconciles us to himself in Christ and bestows upon us the twofold benefit of gratuitous righteousness in the remission of sins and renovation after God's image. The emphasis falls to a large extent upon the gratuitous character.

It is gratuitous in three respects: in respect of the Mediator, in respect of us, and in respect of the ends contemplated. (1) It is gratuitous in respect of the Mediator because he was given freely for us, the Father accepts from him the price of reconciliation, the merit of the Mediator is freely imputed to us, and the promise of grace in Christ is gratuitous. (2) It is gratuitous in respect of us because the faith by which we embrace the gift of reconciliation is given to us freely by the Holy Spirit.

(3) It is gratuitous in respect of the ends contemplated – God willed reconciliation that all the glory might redound to himself, and the peace of conscience we enjoy can be gained only by God's free favour and provision.

The foregoing emphasis upon the gratuitous character is correlative with unconditional character. Since the covenant as to substance consists in the remission of sin and the renovation of our hearts (Jer. 31:31 ff.), this twofold promise belongs to the elect and to them alone. And the faith itself by which we are ingrafted into the seed of Abraham is the gift of God freely bestowed by the Holy Spirit. Even in the administration of the covenant, as distinct from its substance, the Holy Spirit prepares the hearts of the elect in due time and by his internal efficacy imparts the gift of faith and repentance. The whole covenant, therefore, is merely of grace.

Christ is the Mediator. Since he was constituted such by the Father, he came with the *mandate* of the Father, ordained as high priest to make sacrifice and intercession, received the *promise* from the Father that the sacrifice and intercession would be accepted and the Holy Spirit given, and became, in turn, *sponsor* to make satisfaction for the sins of all whom the Father gave him and to insure for them peace of conscience and renewal in the image of God.

The gratuitous and unconditional character of the covenant is not construed in any way as prejudicing the demand for faith. Zanchius, for example, is equally insistent that as the covenant pertains to God's promise it is altogether gratuitous, absolute, and without any condition, that God fulfils the promise out of mere mercy and goodness. But he also recognizes that from the side of man there are the stipulations imposed by God. These are twofold: (1) faith by which man believes that God for Christ's sake is a Father to him and that his sins have been pardoned, and (2) obedience in conformity of life to the good pleasure of God (*Opera Theologica*, Geneva, 1613, Tom. V, 43b).

In this early period there had not emerged the tension which developed in the 17th century on the question whether the covenant was to be conceived of as conditional or unconditional. It is apparent, however, that the question which was the occasion for so much debate later on had already been posed in the insistence of these 16th-century theologians upon the unconditional nature of the covenant and at the same time upon the stipulations arising for the beneficiaries of covenant grace.

In Robert Rollock, who, as noted above, formulated the doctrine of the Covenant of Works, we find that the formulation of the Covenant of Grace is from the outset oriented to the contrast between the two covenants. To give but one example, the ground of the Covenant of Grace is, first, the Mediator Jesus Christ and, second, the grace and mercy of God in contrast with the strength of nature, which was the ground of the Covenant of Works. It is of particular interest to observe how Rollock answers the question of *condition* as it pertains to the Covenant of Grace. 'The very name of the Covenant of Grace,' he says, 'might seem to require no condition, for it is called a free covenant, because God freely, and, as it might seem, without all condition, doth promise herein both righteousness and life. . . . But we are to understand that grace here, or the particle freely, doth not exclude all condition, but that only which is in the Covenant of Works, which is the condition of the strength of nature, and of works naturally just and good . . . which can in no wise stand with God's free grace in Christ Jesus' (*Select Works*, Edinburgh, 1849, I, 39). This condition is none other than faith as that which comports with Christ and with God's free grace. And faith itself is also of grace and is the free gift of God. So we are to remember 'that whereas God offereth righteousness and life under condition of faith, yet doth he not so respect faith in us, which is also his own gift, as he doth the object of faith, which is Christ, and his own free mercy in Christ, which must be apprehended by faith. . . . Wherefore the condition of the Covenant of Grace is not faith only, nor the object of faith only, which is Christ, but faith with Christ, that is, the faith that shall apprehend Christ, or Christ with faith, that is, Christ which is to be apprehended by faith' (*ibid.*, 40). The viewpoint here set forth is essentially the same as that of Rollock's predecessors mentioned above, but faith as the condition is brought into clearer focus and its relation to the covenant carefully defined so as in no way to prejudice free mercy and grace.

In the confessions of the 16th century, as was noted, the Edenic institution is not construed in terms of covenant. But there is also a marked paucity of the use of the term 'covenant' in reference to the provisions of redemptive grace. When the term is used, it occurs most frequently in connection with the sacraments, particularly with reference to the baptism of infants (cf. Heidelberg Catechism, 74; Belgic Confession XXXIV; Second Helvetic Confession, XX, 2 and 6). On occasion the term 'testament' is used with covenantal signification. It is surprising, however, that the term 'covenant' should be used with such infrequency, especially when we remember that the confessions were framed in terms of the truths which covenant grace represents and that both the concept and the term occupied so important a place in the thinking of those whose influence was paramount in the preparation of them. The Westminster Confession of Faith and Catechisms evince a marked change in this respect. The scheme of salvation is in these documents expressly set forth as the provision of the Covenant of Grace (Confession, VII, iii–vi; XIV, ii; XXVIII, i; L. C., 30–36, 166; S. C., 20, 94).

In the theology so far delineated the Covenant of Grace had been conceived of and formulated as the covenantal relation established on God's part with *men* and the grace dispensed to them. This continued to be the definition throughout the classic period of covenant theology, and the doctrine was unfolded in these precise terms. It is stated expressly thus in the Westminster Confession: 'Man, by his fall, having made himself uncapable of life by that covenant, the Lord was pleased to make a second, commonly called the covenant of grace' (VII, iii). That the words 'make a second' are to be understood in the sense of 'make a second with man' is plain from the title of the chapter, 'Of God's Covenant with Man', and also from the terms of the preceding section, where we read, 'The first covenant made with man,' which implies that the second was also made with man. In theologians such as Amandus Polanus, John Ball, Johannes Cocceius, Francis Turretine, Edward Leigh, Samuel Rutherford, and John Owen this designation is maintained and, with qualifications to be noted later, this may be said to have been the prevailing view. Turretine's formulation, herewith summarized, is representative.

'The Covenant of Grace is a gratuitous pact between God the offended one and man the offender, entered into in Christ, in which God freely on account of Christ promises to man the remission of sins and salvation, and man in dependence upon the same grace promises faith and obedience' (*op. cit.*, *Loc.* XI, Q, II, v). With respect to the nature of this covenant there are four things to be observed: (1) The *author* is God, of his goodness and free good pleasure, so that it is always called God's covenant and never man's. It is common to the whole Trinity but with the distinction that each person, in a way suited to this economy, has his own peculiar way of working. God the Father instituted the covenant and sends the Son and Holy Spirit. God the

Son is the cause and foundation. The Holy Spirit is the witness and earnest of the heavenly inheritance. The instruments of God's administration are the Word and sacraments and the ministers of both. (2) The *contracting parties* are God as the offended one, man as the offender, and Christ as the Mediator – God, not as Creator, Lord, and Lawgiver but as merciful Father and Redeemer; man, not as creature but as sinner; and Christ, as reconciling man the offender to God the offended one. (3) The *things covenanted* are, on the part of God, the promised benefits and, on the part of men, the duties prescribed. The promised benefits are principally: reconciliation and communion with God, the communication of all good gifts of grace and glory of this life and of the life to come, conformity to God's likeness so that as far as can apply to finite creatures we are made partakers of the Divine nature, and, finally, the eternal possession and fruition of the blessings bestowed. (4) The duties prescribed are faith and repentance, worship and obedience, separation from the world and consecration to God, all of which may be summed up in the obligation to be God's people and live as his redeemed.

The question which aroused the most ardent dispute in the 17th century, especially in the British Isles, was whether the covenant is to be conceived of as conditional or unconditional. Lest the nature of the dispute be misunderstood, there are certain considerations that must be kept in mind. (1) No theologian within the Reformed camp took the position that, in the saving provisions of which the Covenant of Grace is the administration, the thought of condition is to be completely eliminated. Those who were most jealous for the unconditional character of the covenant as an administration of grace to men were insistent that for Christ as the Mediator of the covenant there were conditions which had to be fulfilled. It was customary for those holding this position to appeal to Christ's fulfilment of the conditions as a reason, if not the main reason, why the covenant, as it respects men, is without condition. (2) Those who maintained the conditional nature of the covenant were jealous at the same time to maintain that the fulfilment of the conditions on the part of men was wholly of God's grace. There was no thought of the covenant as contingent upon human autonomy or as deriving any of its ingredients from a contribution which man in the exercise of his own free will supplied. In the words of John Ball, 'the covenant of grace doth not exclude all conditions, but such as will not stand with grace' (*A Treatise of the Covenant of Grace*, London, 1645, 17). (3) The dispute was to a large extent focused upon the relation which faith, repentance, obedience, and perseverance sustained to the covenant. None held that the covenant relation obtained or that its grace could be enjoyed apart from those responses on the part of the person in covenant fellowship with God. However, in this connection, there was no disposition to exclude infants and others uncapable of being outwardly called by the ministry of the Word from the embrace of the covenant blessing.

One of the most outspoken exponents of the covenant as unconditional was John Saltmarsh. He expresses the viewpoint thus:

God makes no Covenant properly under the Gospel as he did at first. . . . Man is not restored in such a way of Covenant and Condition as he was lost, but more freely; and more by Grace and Mercy; and yet God Covenants too; but it is not with Man only, but with him that was God and Man, even Jesus Christ; he is both the Covenant and the Messenger or Mediator of the Covenant. God agreed to save Man, but this Agreement was with Christ, and all the Conditions were on his part; he stood for us, and performed the Conditions for Life and Glory. . . . God takes us into Covenant, not upon any Condition in us before; he brings with him Christ, and in him all the Conditions, and makes us as he would have us; not for the Covenant, but in it, or under it. . . . A Soul is then properly, actually, or expressly in Covenant with God, when God hath come to it in the Promise; and then when it feels itself under the Power of the Promise, it begins only to know it is in Covenant . . . so as they that believe, do rather feel themselves in that Covenant which God hath made with them, without any thing in themselves, either Faith or Repentance (*Free Grace: or, The Flowings of Christ's Blood Freely to Sinners*, London, 1700, 101–103).

Saltmarsh had deviated in several respects from Reformed patterns of thought. But the viewpoint reflected in these quotations was one espoused by others who could not be classified with Saltmarsh in other respects. Tobias Crisp is equally emphatic in maintaining the unconditional character of the Covenant of Grace and, in this respect, the total difference between this covenant and all other covenants in which there is 'mutual agreement between parties upon certain articles, or propositions, propounded on both sides; so that each party is bound and tied to fulfil his own conditions' (*Christ Alone Exalted, Complete Works*, London, 1832, I, 83). 'But in this covenant of grace, to wit, the new covenant, it is far otherwise; there is not any condition in this covenant . . . the new covenant is without any conditions whatsoever on man's part' (*ibid.*, 86). Crisp will not allow that faith, though in-dispensable to a state of salvation, can be regarded as the condition of the covenant. Christ alone justifies, he insists, and therefore a man is justified before he believes (*ibid.*, 90 ff.). In answer to the objection that this doctrine encourages licence Crisp replies: 'You must make a difference between doing anything in reference to the covenant, as the condition thereof, and doing something in reference to service and duty, to that God who enters into covenant with you' (*ibid.*, 89).

Thomas Blake was one of Crisp's chief opponents on this issue. He devotes much space and argument to the thesis that the Covenant of Grace is conditional. He does not question the covenant between God and Christ in respect of which there are no conditions fulfilled by men. But the Covenant of Grace is between God and man, and astipulation on the part of man is integral to such a covenant relationship. The conditions he specifies are chiefly faith and repentance (*Vindiciae Foederis, or, A Treatise of the Covenant of God Entered with Mankind*, London, 1653, 74, 93 ff., 105 ff.). Blake stresses the place occupied by the command of God's law in the Covenant of Grace and the corres-ponding sincerity in the way and work of God which the covenant requires and accepts (*ibid.*, 112). He inveighs against the severance of promise and duty 'so that Christ is heard only in a promise, not at all in a precept, when they hear that Christ will save; but are never told that they must repent. These are but delusions; promise-Preachers, and no duty-Preachers; grace-Preachers and not repentance-Preachers' (*ibid.*, 144).

One of the most polemic opponents of the position adopted by Crisp was Daniel Williams. In his *Gospel-Truth Stated and Vindicated* (1692) a chapter is devoted to the conditionality of the Covenant of Grace in which he maintains that faith and repentance are acts of ours which, though performed by the grace of Christ freely given to sinners, are nevertheless required of us in order to the blessings of the covenant consequent thereupon and are required in accordance with the cove-nant constitution. In a later work, *A Defence of Gospel-Truth* (1693), Williams is largely concerned with a reply to Isaac Chauncy and de-velops his thesis with still greater vigour and fulness. He distinguishes between the Covenant of Redemption, which allows for no conditions to be fulfilled by men, and the Covenant of Grace, which requires our believing consent as a condition of pardon and glory. In terms of the former, God absolutely promised and covenanted with Christ that the elect will believe and persevere in faith and holiness to eternal life. But in terms of the latter, it is God's will that duty and benefit are so connected that the enjoyment of the benefit is conditioned upon the fulfilment of the duty, not because any merit attaches to the duty nor because the benefit is less of grace, but because the duties required comport with grace and avail for the bestowment of grace by the promise of God. He is also careful to distinguish between 'the promise of grace, which is absolute, and the promises to grace, which are conditional' (*ibid.*, 313).

Herman Witsius, the noted continental theologian, agrees with those who take the position that the Covenant of Grace has no conditions, properly so called. Witsius is aware that none come to salvation except in the way of faith and holiness, that it is impossible to please God without faith, and that many have for these reasons called faith and a new life the conditions of the covenant. But, he continues, 'they are not so much conditions *of the covenant*, as *of the assurance* that we shall continue in God's covenant, and that he shall be our God' and thus, 'to speak accurately, and according to the nature of this covenant, they are, on the part of God, the execution of previous promises, and the earnest of future happiness, and, on the part of man, the performance of those duties, which cannot but precede the consummate perfection of a soul delighting in God' (*The Economy of the Covenants between God and Man*, Eng. tr., Edinburgh, 1771, I, 389 f.). He appeals to the testamentary nature of the covenant as consisting in God's immutable purpose, founded on the unchangeable counsel of God, and ratified by the death of the testator. Thus it is not possible for it to be made void by the unbelief of the elect or made stable by their faith. 'The Covenant of Grace is *testamentary*, and to be distinguished from a covenant founded on a compact, agreement, or law' (*ibid.*, 386 f.). This unilateral character of the covenant does not, however, remove the obligations descending upon him who accepts the promises of the covenant. He binds himself to the duties, and only thus can he assure himself of the fulfilment of the promises. In this respect the covenant is mutual (*ibid.*, 391 f.). And Witsius does not regard the unilateral character as interfering with the free overtures of grace in the Gospel nor as toning down the threatenings pronounced upon unbelief (*ibid.*, 393 ff.).

In the more recent development of covenant theology, Herman Bavinck represents this same position that the Covenant of Grace is unconditional. He does not tone down the responsibilities devolving upon those embraced in the covenant; it comes to us with the demand for faith and repentance. But 'taken by itself the covenant of grace is pure grace, and nothing else, and excludes all works. It gives what it demands, and fulfils what it prescribes. The Gospel is sheer good tidings, not demand but promise, not duty but gift' (*Magnalia Dei*, Kampen, 1931, 261; Eng. tr., *Our Reasonable Faith*, Grand Rapids, 1956, 278). 'We have to note particularly therefore that this promise is not conditional. . . . God does not say that He will be our God if we do this or that thing. . . . People can become unfaithful, but God does not forget His promise. He cannot and may not break His covenant; He has committed Himself to maintaining it with a freely given and precious oath: His name, His honor, His reputation depends on it' (*ibid.*, Eng. tr., 274 f.; cf. *Gereformeerde Dogmatiek*, Kampen, 1918, III, 210 f.).

Francis Turretine resolves the question by his characteristic method of distinguishing the different respects in which the term *condition* may be understood. If condition is understood in the sense of meritorious cause, then the Covenant of Grace is not conditioned: it is wholly gratuitous and depends solely upon God's good pleasure. But if understood as instrumental cause, receptive of the promises of the covenant, then it cannot be denied that the Covenant of Grace is conditioned. The covenant is set forth with an express condition (John 3:16, 36; Rom. 10:7): there would otherwise be no place in the Gospel for threatenings, and it would follow that God would be bound to man but not man to God, which is absurd and contrary to the nature of all covenants. Furthermore, there is the distinction between the promises respecting the *end* and those respecting the *means*, namely, salvation in the former case and faith and repentance in the latter. The promises respecting salvation are on the condition of faith and repentance, and no one can deny that these promises are conditional. But when the promises respect the means (faith, regeneration, repentance), then they are not conditional but simple and absolute: otherwise the process would be infinite, which again would be absurd.

When it is said that faith is the condition of the covenant, this is not to be understood *absolutely* but *relatively and instrumentally* as embracing Christ and through his righteousness obtaining the title to everlasting life. Only thus would it comport with the grace of God, with the condition of the sinner, with the righteousness of the Mediator, with life eternal as the gift of God, and with the promises which set life before man not as something to be acquired but as something already acquired (*op. cit., Loc.* XII, Q. III).

The construction exemplified in Turretine, whereby the covenant is conceived of as conditioned upon faith and repentance, is in accord with the classic formulation in terms of *stipulation, promise, astipulation,* and *restipulation* (cf. Francis Burmann: *Synopsis Theologiae,* 1687, I, 476; J. H. Heidegger: *Medulla Theologiae Christianae,* 1696, I, 238 ff.). This same viewpoint is reflected in the *Synopsis Purioris Theologiae* of 1624 (see *Disp.* XXIII, xxix). It is clearly stated in the Westminster Larger Catechism (Q. 32) and is implied in the Confession of Faith (VII, iii). It should be understood that the insistence upon this conditional feature of the Covenant of Grace, within the frame of thought espoused by these theologians, impinged in no way upon the sovereignty of God's grace nor upon the covenant as a disposition of grace, and they were unanimous in maintaining that the fulfilment of the conditions proceeded from operations of grace which were not themselves conditional.

4. THE COVENANT OF REDEMPTION

The covenant theologians of the 16th century and early 17th conceived of covenant, as it applied to the provisions of God's saving grace, in terms of administration to men. By the middle of the 17th century, however, the relations of the persons of the Godhead to one another in the economy of redemption came to be formulated under the rubric of covenant. The eternal counsel of God as well as the relations of the persons to one another in the temporal execution of that counsel were construed in covenantal terms. This signalized a distinct development in the formulation of covenant theology. At the end of the 16th century the Adamic administration came to be construed in covenant terms, and so there was an extension of the covenant idea in that direction. Now we find expansion in a different direction; the covenant concept was applied to the Trinitarian counsel and economy of salvation.

The term 'Covenant of Redemption' was not, however, a uniform designation. It cannot be said to be sufficiently descriptive to serve the purpose of distinguishing the aspects of God's counsel denoted by it. For this reason the use of other terms by some of the most representative covenant theologians is easily understood. Furthermore, in some cases, the avoidance of the term 'covenant' to identify the intertrinitarian arrangements no doubt reflects hesitation as to the legitimacy of this use of the term.

Johannes Cocceius, though he on occasion uses the word 'covenant' in reference to this convention between the persons of the Godhead, more characteristically speaks of it as a pact. He takes over the language of Zechariah 6:13 and calls it 'the counsel of peace.' It is construed as 'the ineffable economy' in terms of which the Father requires obedience unto death on the part of the Son and promises to him in return a kingdom and spiritual seed. The Son gives himself to do the will of the Father and in turn demands from the Father the salvation of the people given to him from the foundation of the world. In this mystery of our salvation the Father sustains the character of both Legislator and Governor – Legislator in demanding the demonstration of justice and punishing sin in his own Son, and Governor in giving his Son as Sponsor for the exercise of mercy towards his creatures. The Son represents the mercy of God by assuming flesh and condemning sin in it. He is the Testator by whose death we receive the inheritance. The Holy Spirit exercises the power of God in the regenerate, and through him the Father and Son dwell in those whom he seals for the heavenly inheritance.

In this pact of salvation the will of the Father and Son is the same. But since the Father and Son are distinct, this one will must be viewed distinctly, on the one hand as giving and sending, and on the other as given and sent. Thus in this mystery, God is the one who judges and is judged, who satisfies justice and accepts that satisfaction – God himself satisfies himself by his own blood. The Son, being one with the Father, satisfies the justice of the Father and at the same time satisfies his own justice (*Summa Doctrinae de Foedere et Testamento Dei, Cap.* V, *Summa Theologiae*, Amsterdam, 1701, Tom. VII, 60 ff.).

Francis Turretine calls this aspect of the counsel of redemption the pact between the Father and the Son. He thinks that it is superfluous to dispute whether the covenant was made with Christ, and in him with all his seed, or whether it was made in Christ with all the seed. These alternatives amount to the same thing. But that there is a twofold pact, the one between the Father and the Son to execute the work of redemption, the other with the elect in Christ on the condition of faith and repentance, is not to be disputed.

For Turretine, the pact between the Father and the Son consists in the will of the Father in giving the Son as Redeemer of his mystical body and the will of the Son in giving himself as Sponsor for the redemption of the members of his body. In this 'economy of salvation' the Father is represented in Scripture as demanding obedience unto death and promising the reward, the Son as presenting himself to do the Father's will, as promising faithful execution, and at length demanding in return the kingdom and glory promised. This formulation follows the pattern found already in Cocceius.

Of peculiar interest is what Turretine calls the three periods of this covenant. The first concerns *destination* when, from eternity in the counsel of the holy Trinity, Christ was given to the church (Prov. 8:23; 1 Pet. 1:20; Ps. 2:8); the second has respect to the *promise* when, immediately after the Fall, Christ offered himself for the actual performance of what he had promised from eternity and, in his actual appointment as Mediator, began to do many things pertaining to this office; and the third respects *execution* when, in the incarnate state, Christ accomplished the work of salvation. Thus, Christ perfectly fulfilled all that was necessary to the consummation of the Covenant of Grace (*op. cit. Loc.* XII, Q. II, xi–xvi).

Peter van Mastricht uses the terms 'eternal' and 'temporal' to express the distinction. The former was made in eternity between the Father and the Son, the latter is made in time between God and the elect sinner, the former being the prototype, the latter the ectype. He construes the eternal covenant after the usual pattern as a transaction between the Father and the Son, comprehending the mutual demands and promises as they pertain to the eternal salvation of the elect, and insists upon the distinctness of the capacity in which each Person of the Trinity acts in this economy (*Theoretico-Practica Theologia*, 1698, *Lib.* V, *Cap.* I, vii–xi; cf. J. H. Heidegger, *op. cit.*, 234 ff.).

Herman Witsius develops this phase of covenant theology in great detail and with characteristic clarity. He calls it the compact (*pactum*) between the Father and the Son, and distinguishes it from the testamentary disposition by which God bestows upon the elect eternal salvation and all things relative thereto. This compact he regards as the foundation of our salvation, and it consists in the will of the Father in giving the Son to be the Head and Redeemer of the elect and the will of the Son in presenting himself as Sponsor for them (*op. cit.*, 222–381).

In Samuel Rutherford the designation 'Covenant of Redemption' is the characteristic one. It is to be considered in two ways, he says: as transacted in time by the actual discharge on Christ's part of his offices as King, Priest, and Prophet, and as an eternal transaction in the compact between Father and Son. In respect of the latter there are three eternal acts – designation, ordination, and delectation. Rutherford is jealous to maintain the distinction that the Covenant of Redemption is eternal as one of *designation* but temporal as one of *actual* redemption. And he likewise develops the differences between the covenant of suretyship and redemption made with Christ and the Covenant of Grace and Reconciliation made with sinners. The latter is no more eternal than is the creation itself; it was made in paradise. Though decreed from everlasting, it had no existence as a covenant until revealed to Adam after the Fall (*The Covenant of Life Opened: or, A Treatise of the Covenant of Grace*, Edinburgh, 1655, 282 ff.).

Edward Leigh is another representative. 'The whole business of man's salvation was transacted between the Father and the Son long before it was revealed in Scripture, there was a covenant of redemption between God the Father and the Son for the salvation of the Elect' (*A Systeme or Body of Divinity*, London, 1662, 546; cf. also T. Goodwin, *Works*, Edinburgh, 1863, V, 3 ff.; T. Jacomb, *Sermons on the Eighth Chapter of the Epistle to the Romans*, Edinburgh, 1868, 187; A. Hamilton, *A Short Catechism Concerning the Three Special Divine Covenants*, Edinburgh, 1714, 8).

As noted, in the earliest formulations of covenant theology, the Covenant of Grace was conceived of historically as God's administration to men. Later on, when the inter-Trinitarian counsel of salvation came to be construed in terms of covenant, the term 'Covenant of Grace' continued to be used to denote the covenant made with men and thus distinguished from the Covenant of Redemption. But there is a further development, exemplified in Thomas Boston, whereby the Covenant of Grace itself is conceived of in terms of the inter-Trinitarian counsel and economy. In Boston's words, 'The Covenant of Redemption and the Covenant of Grace are not two distinct covenants, but one and the same covenant. . . . Only, in respect of Christ, it is called *the Covenant of Redemption*, forasmuch as in it he engaged to pay the price of our redemption; but in respect of us *the Covenant of Grace*, forasmuch as the whole of it is of free grace to us' (*The Complete Works*, London, 1853, I, 333 f.). Since Boston constructs the Covenant of Grace in terms of purpose, appointment, commitment, and fulfilment on the part of the persons of the Godhead, he is insistent that 'the Covenant of Grace is absolute and not conditional to us' (*ibid.*,

334). All the conditions were laid upon Christ, and he has fulfilled the same. Boston is careful to distinguish between conditions of connection or order in the covenant and conditions of the covenant (*idem*). Here again we meet the same kind of insistence found earlier in Crisp, Witsius, and others. In this case, however, the demand that the Covenant of Grace be regarded as unconditional *for us* is relieved of the objection which it readily encounters in the context of the earlier debates. Once the Covenant of Grace is interpreted in terms of the 'eternal compact' between the Father and the Son (*ibid.*, 317), it is obvious that requirements devolving upon men cannot be construed as conditions of its execution.

Herman Bavinck uses 'Counsel of Redemption' and 'Covenant of Grace' as terms to designate the distinction. But he also maintains that 'the Counsel of Redemption is itself a covenant – a covenant in which each of the three persons, so to speak, receives His own work and achieves His own task. The Covenant of Grace which is raised up in time and is continued from generation to generation is nothing other than the working out and the impression or imprint of the covenant that is fixed in the Eternal Being. . . . The Counsel of Redemption and the Covenant of Grace cannot and may not be separated, but they differ from each other in this respect, that the second is the actualization of the first. The plan of redemption is not enough in itself. It needs to be carried out' (*Magnalia Dei*, 256; Eng. tr., 273). The inter-relationship between the eternal and the temporal is thus established, and it is readily seen how, as noted earlier, Bavinck can maintain the monopleuric and unconditional character of the Covenant of Grace. The Covenant of Grace must be viewed in its organic relation to the whole counsel of Redemption.

5. THE EXTERNAL DISPENSATION OF THE COVENANT OF GRACE

Covenant theologians, though maintaining the particularity of the Covenant of Grace, nevertheless distinguished between the internal essence and the external dispensation, the former corresponding to the effectual call and the latter to the external in promulgation and presentation. In this external administration it is extended even to the reprobate who are within the visible church and includes the external benefits which accrue from the promulgation of the Gospel and obtain within the sphere of profession (cf. Turretine, *op cit.*, Loc. XII, Q. VI, v, vi). In the words of Witsius, 'Moreover, as we restrict this covenant to the elect, it is evident we are speaking of the *internal*, mystical, and spiritual *communion* of the covenant. For salvation itself, and every thing belonging to it, or inseparably connected with it, are promised in this covenant, all which none but the elect can attain to. If, in other respects, we consider the *external* œconomy of the covenant, in the communion of the word and sacraments, in the profession of the true faith, in the participation of many gifts, which, though excellent and illustrious, are yet none of the effects of the sanctifying Spirit, nor any earnest of future happiness; it cannot be denied, that, in this respect, many are in the covenant, whose names, notwithstanding, are not in the testament of God' (*op. cit.*, Eng. tr., 384 f.; cf. M. Leydecker, *Synopsis Theologiae Christianae, Lib.* V, *Cap.* I, ix, x; P. Mastricht, *op. cit., Lib.* V, *Cap.* I, xxviii, xxix). Herman Bavinck, recognizing that not all were Israel who were of Israel and that there are evil branches in the vine, expresses this distinction by saying that there are persons 'who are taken up into the Covenant of Grace as it manifests itself to our eyes and who nevertheless on account of their unbelieving and unrepentant heart are devoid of all the spiritual benefits of the covenant.' Thus there are 'two sides to the one covenant of grace,' the one visible to us but the other visible perfectly to God alone. Bavinck, however, rejects the distinction between an internal and external covenant (*Magnalia Dei*, 261 f.; Eng. tr., 278 f.; cf. Louis Berkhof, *Systematic Theology*, Grand Rapids, 1941, 284 ff.).

6. THE SACRAMENTS OF THE COVENANT OF GRACE

In covenant theology the sacraments were always construed as holy signs and seals of the Covenant of Grace. Since the covenant was conceived of as one in substance under both dispensations, circumcision and the passover under the Old Testament were regarded as having essentially the same significance as baptism and the Lord's supper under the New Testament. As signs and seals they possessed no virtue in themselves but derived all their efficacy from the spiritual realities signified by them. As seals of the covenant they were confirmations of God's faithfulness to the promises which the covenant enshrined.

The most distinctive feature of covenant theology in connection with the sacraments is the inference drawn from the nature of the covenant in support of paedobaptism. The argument, reduced to its simplest terms, is that the seals of the covenant pertain to those to whom the covenant itself pertains. But that the covenant pertains to infants is clear from Genesis 17:7 and Acts 2:39. From God's ordinance his grace extends from parents to children. Since the things signified in baptism, namely, remission of sins, regeneration, and the kingdom of heaven, belong to infants, there is no reason why the sign should not also be added (cf. F. Turretine, *op. cit.*, Loc. XIX, Q. XX, v).

Of particular importance is the emphasis placed on the unity and continuity of the covenant. In covenant theology the argument for infant baptism falls into its place in the schematism which the organic unity and continuity of covenant revelation provided. In the words of Calvin: 'For it is most evident that the covenant which the Lord once made with Abraham continues as much in force with Christians in the present day, as it did formerly with the Jews; and consequently that that word is no less applicable to Christians than it was to the Jews. . . . Now, as the Lord, immediately after having made the covenant with Abraham, commanded it to be sealed in infants by an external sacrament, what cause will Christians assign why they should not also at this day testify and seal the same in their children? . . . Since the abrogation of circumcision, there always remains the same reason for confirming it, which we have in common with the Jews. . . . The covenant is common, the reason for confirming it is common. Only the mode of confirming it is different; for to them it was confirmed by circumcision, which among us has been succeeded by baptism. Otherwise, if the testimony by which the Jews were assured of the salvation of their seed be taken away from us, the effect of the advent of Christ has been to render the grace of God more obscure and less attested to us than it was to the Jews' (*Inst.*, IV, xvi, 6; Eng. tr. by John Allen). 'But if the covenant remains firm and unmoved, it belongs to the children of Christians now, as much as it did to the infants of the Jews under the Old Testament. But if they are partakers of the thing signified, why shall they be excluded from the sign? If they obtain the truth, why shall they be debarred from the figure?' (*ibid.*, IV, xvi, 5).

15

The Theology of the Westminster Confession of Faith[1]

THE Westminster Confession of Faith was prepared by the assembly of divines meeting at Westminster, England, and was completed on December 4, 1646.[2] It has been the profession of faith and the creedal bond of fellowship for churches of Reformed persuasion for more than three centuries. The first church to adopt the Confession was the Church of Scotland. On August 27, 1647, the General Assembly 'found' the Confession 'to be most agreeable to the Word of God, and in nothing contrary to the received doctrine, worship, discipline, and government of this Kirk' and declared: 'The General Assembly doth, therefore, after mature deliberation, Agree unto and Approve the said Confession, as to the truth of the matter, (judging it to be most orthodox and grounded upon the Word of God;) and also as to the point of uniformity, agreeing, for our part, that it be a common Confession of Faith for the three kingdoms.'[3]

[1] Published originally in *Scripture and Confession*, edited by John H. Skilton, Presbyterian & Reformed Publishing Co., 1973.
[2] The Assembly was reluctant to append proof texts for the Confession on the ground that this would have required a volume, and that when texts were debated in the Assembly they were never put to a vote. On the insistence of the House of Commons, however, proof texts were annexed and this work was completed by the end of April, 1647. Cf. A. F. Mitchell and J. Struthers, eds., *Minutes of the Sessions of the Westminster Assembly of Divines* (Edinburgh, 1874), pp. 294 f.; A. F. Mitchell, *The Westminster Assembly* (London, 1883), pp. 367 f.; S. W. Carruthers, *The Westminster Confession of Faith* (Manchester, 1937), p. 13.
[3] *Acts of the General Assembly of the Church of Scotland, 1638–1842* (Edinburgh, 1843), pp. 158 f. The reservation respecting Chapter XXXI, Section II, that the Assembly understood some parts 'only of Kirks not settled or constituted in point of government' (*ibid.*, p. 159) is interesting, and shows the care with which the Confession had been examined and approbation guarded.

The question cannot be dismissed: Is a document drawn up more than three centuries ago an adequate Confession for the church today? There are various considerations that give weight to the necessity and relevance of this question.

First of all, it should be borne in mind that the creeds of the church have been framed in a particular historical situation to meet the need of the church in that context, and have been oriented to a considerable extent in both their negative and positive declarations to the refutation of the errors confronting the church at that time. The creeds are, therefore, historically complexioned in language and content and do not reflect the particular and distinguishing needs of subsequent generations. If we think of error as a factor determining to a large extent the form of creedal confession, we cannot ignore the diversity of form unbelief assumes, and the demand resting upon the church to meet error with the directness and precision of confessional declaration after the example of the church throughout its history. Unless we maintain that the tradition established in the church from the early 4th century until the 17th was a mistake, there can be no gainsaying of the demand that creedal confession must keep pace with the challenge of heresy. And not only so; there is much to support the suspicion, if not the indictment, that the incursions of error have often undermined the witness of the church because the church has failed to enunciate and guard its faith in creedal expression directed against those deviations that pervert the purity of the faith once delivered to the saints.

Again, there is the progressive understanding of the faith delivered to the saints. There is in the church the ceaseless activity of the Holy Spirit so that the church organically and corporately increases in knowledge unto the measure of the stature of the fulness of Christ. The progressive correction and enrichment that the promise and presence of the Holy Spirit insure should find embodiment in a confession that is the precipitate of the church's faith. No Confession in the history of the church exemplifies this more patently than the Westminster Confession. It is the epitome of the most mature thought to which the church of Christ had been led up to the year 1646. But are we to suppose that this progression ceased with that date? To ask the question is to answer it. An affirmative is to impugn the continued grace of which the Westminster Confession is itself an example at the time of its writing. There is more light to break forth from the living and abiding Word of God.

Finally, it must be borne in mind that all human composition is fallible and is, therefore, subject to correction and improvement.

How do these considerations bear upon the question of the adequacy for the present day of the Westminster Confession as the creedal symbol of a Reformed church? However valid these considerations are, the question cannot be answered without assessing the Confession in the light of what, by way of witness, is required of the church in the context in which the church is now placed. We must, then, turn to the topic that is the theme of this chapter.

When the chapter 'Of the Holy Scripture' was placed first in the Westminster Confession it was not because Protestant or Reformed tradition had determined this priority. Most of the Protestant creeds had not adopted this order.[1] So the choice was deliberate and, no doubt, for reasons that to the framers appeared paramount. But if wisdom and good judgment dictated this choice for the assembly of divines in 1646, the need for this priority in our day is compelling. For it is apparent that variant conceptions of what Scripture is are at the basis of those divergences that are of greatest concern to the church.

Whatever may be one's estimate of the doctrine of Scripture set forth in the Confession, the appraisal of B. B. Warfield will have to be acceded to, that 'there is certainly in the whole mass of confessional literature no more nobly conceived or ably wrought-out statement of doctrine than the chapter "Of the Holy Scripture", which the Westminster Divines placed at the head of their Confession and laid at the foundation of their system of doctrine. It has commanded the hearty admiration of all competent readers.'[2]

The up-to-date relevance of certain features are of particular interest.

If there is any phase of doctrine of fundamental importance in the thinking of the church at the present time, it is the relation of Scripture to revelation. Is Scripture itself revelatory or is it but the witness to revelation? There can be no equivocation on this issue. If Scripture is itself revelatory, the church has never been in greater need of saying so in its confessional manifesto. If it is not revelatory, the church must not err in saying so. The Confession is unequivocal on this issue at the

---

[1] The First Helvetic Confession (1536), the Second Helvetic Confession (1566), the Irish Articles of Religion (1615), and the Formula of Concord (1576) began with the article on Scripture.

[2] *The Westminster Assembly and Its Work* (New York, 1931), p. 155.

very outset. It was not because the divines had anticipated the dialectic that makes this issue so crucial now. But the confessional formulation does evince the perpetual relevance of what is the transcript of Scripture's teaching. This formulation is found in the second sentence in Section I. The words 'to commit the same wholly unto writing' obviously refer to Scripture, as the words that immediately follow, 'which maketh the Scripture to be most necessary', also show. The antecedent, fixing the denotation of what is committed wholly to writing, is not the sum-total of revelations given at sundry times and divers manners, as might be too readily assumed, but that which is implied in the words, 'it pleased the Lord . . . to reveal Himself and, to declare that His will unto His Church', namely, God's self-revelation and declaration of his will. It is this that is now committed wholly to writing, and the purport is clearly that the only extant saving and special revelation is the inscripturated Word. If confirmation were needed it is supplied by what concludes the sentence: 'those former ways of God's revealing His will unto His people being now ceased'. Holy Scripture is now the sole mode of revelation for us and is, therefore, not merely the vehicle of revelation but also itself revelatory as truly as were the revelations formerly given 'at sundry times and in divers manners'.

This position is not only in conflict with the current view of Scripture as the witness to revelation; it is also the corrective to what, mistakenly, is sometimes said, that Scripture is to a large extent the *record* of revelation and not directly revelation. It is true that Scripture provides us with the history of revelation. But even when it records for us the revelatory data given in past ages, it is the inscripturated record and, because inscripturated, takes on the character that inscripturation as a distinct mode of revelation and the final mode of revelation imparts to it.

In accordance with what has been said in Section I, the Confession in the next section proceeds to characterize Scripture as 'the Word of God written'. No predication could more pointedly express the catholic doctrine of Scripture in distinction from the deceptive claims of current theology. The issue is focused in the word 'written'. Many are not only willing to say, 'The Bible is the Word of God' but insist upon this proposition as basic to all that is conceived to be Christian faith. But with vehemence it is also maintained that the Word of God must not be identified with what is *written*. This, it is alleged, would petrify and incarcerate the Word of God. So, again, to confess the historic, orthodox faith that Holy Scripture is the Word of God, no expression is better suited to the demands of our situation than that furnished by the Westminster Confession. Indeed, it is the development of thought in the last few decades that has demonstrated as never before the relevance of the emphasis that the Scriptures are the Word of God *written*.[1]

Another feature of the teaching in Chapter I that not only exemplifies the precision of thought characteristic of the Confession but also its remarkable relevance to the present is that concerned with the authority of Scripture in Sections IV and V. It has been said that the Confession represents the authority of Scripture to be derived from the internal testimony of the Holy Spirit, that Scripture is authoritative only as it is borne home to the man of faith by this inner witness of the Spirit.

This conception of the authority belonging to Scripture is the way by which its authority may appear to be maintained when the Scripture is not identified with God's revelatory Word but construed as the witness to revelation, and when revelation is regarded as something distinct from Scripture and virtually equated with the continuing and ever-recurrent activity of the Holy Spirit. The formulation in the Confession distinctly and eloquently guards against this construction. If it were being drawn up today, it could scarcely be more articulate in controverting the interpretation placed upon it and referred to above.

Section IV deals with the authority of Scripture and the ground upon which the authority rests. It rests upon the fact that God is its author, that it is the Word of God. In the terms of Section II, it is because the Scriptures 'are given by inspiration of God' and are 'the Word of God written' that they are authoritative and are to be received as such. No

---

[1] 'The Confession of 1967' as adopted by the 179th General Assembly of the United Presbyterian Church in the U.S.A. does declare that the Holy Scriptures 'are received and obeyed as the word of God written' (*Minutes of the General Assembly of the Presbyterian Church in the United States of America*, Part I [Philadelphia, August, 1967], p. 735). But in view of the conception of Scripture set forth in this 'Confession', and in the light of the question relevant to Scripture put to those who are to be ordained to office, one cannot maintain that the intent of this characterization is the same as that of the Westminster Confession. The question reads: 'Do you accept the Scriptures of the Old and New Testaments to be the unique and authoritative witness to Jesus Christ in the Church catholic, and by the Holy Spirit God's word to you?' (*ibid.*, pp. 130, 132).

word is said in Section IV or the preceding sections about the internal testimony of the Spirit, and the teaching of the Confession is to be seen from that conspicuous omission as well as from the positive assertions anent divine authorship. The place and function of the internal testimony are set forth in Section V.

The authority of Scripture resides in its character as the Word of God; it is, therefore, inherent in Scripture and objective to us. But how do we become persuaded of this authority? It is with this question that Section V deals, and of particular relevance are the concluding words: 'yet notwithstanding, our full persuasion and assurance of the infallible truth and divine authority thereof, is from the inward work of the Holy Spirit bearing witness by and with the Word in our hearts'. The distinction is patent. It is persuasion and assurance on our part that are constrained by the inward work of the Holy Spirit. The authority is antecedent and rests upon its own ground, divine authorship by inspiration of God. Any confusion is fatal to a proper doctrine of Scripture, and confusion the confessional formulation could not more clearly obviate.

Another statement in this chapter, pertinent to the subject of authority, calls for comment. It is that in Section X. 'The supreme judge by which all controversies of religion are to be determined . . . can be no other but the Holy Spirit speaking in the Scripture.' The concluding clause is particularly significant. It does not refer to the internal testimony of the Spirit. The latter has already been defined in Section V as 'bearing witness by and with the Word in our hearts'. The Confession is now dealing with Scripture itself as the final court of appeal in all controversies of religion and by which 'all decrees of councils, opinions of ancient writers, doctrines of men, and private spirits, are to be examined'. Thus the Spirit's bearing witness *in our hearts* and 'the Holy Spirit speaking in the Scripture' are obviously not to be equated.

What is especially noteworthy is the way in which Scripture is characterized, 'the Holy Spirit speaking in the Scripture'. In the 17th century it was necessary to stress this feature of Scripture in order to counteract Rome's insistence on the necessity of a *living* voice in addition to Scripture, namely, the voice of the church, and also to guard against the claims of enthusiasts to special revelation coordinate with Scripture. The same need applies to the 20th century. The divines of Westminster were jealous to maintain in their appeal to the finality of Scripture that the church was not deprived of a living voice. And the living voice is that of the Holy Spirit. The Spirit continues to speak in Scripture for the simple reason that the Word of God is living; it never becomes a dead word bereft of its relevance and power.

Our century, however, has given new relevance to all that is involved in this denotation, 'the Holy Spirit speaking in the Scripture'. It is the charge repeatedly made that to identify the Word of God with Scripture is to petrify the Word of God and to mortify faith. The Word of God, it is claimed, must be personal; it must create living encounter with God. The answer to this charge is twofold. First, who has ever maintained that the Word of God is anything other than personal? The Word of God is always *God's* speech directed to *us*. And, second, why should the permanence imparted by inscripturation interfere with its personal character? 'The word of the Lord abides for ever' (1 Pet. 1:25). Terms could not have been more relevantly or felicitously chosen than those adopted by the framers of the Confession to express the doctrine of Scripture as the living and abiding Word of God – 'the Holy Spirit speaking in the Scripture'.

Many other aspects of this chapter could be instanced to show its competence and relevance as a creedal statement on the subject that is cardinal to the witness of the church of Christ. The features dealt with suffice to illustrate how in respect to those very questions that are foremost in present-day discussion, the confessional statements are not only pointedly relevant but unsurpassed in their condensed precision. What is perhaps more significant is that the formulation, though dated as respects composition, is undated in its adequacy. No phase of the doctrine of Scripture that we could reasonably expect to be incorporated in creedal confession is neglected. And the paramount virtue is that all these qualities are brought to bear upon fidelity to the witness of Scripture itself respecting its divine origin, character, and authority.

One of the characteristics that must impress every careful reader of the Confession is that of conciseness – so much in so little. The divines had a profound sense of the speciality of their task, and the economy of words was their concern. This appears in every section and chapter. Chapter II is an outstanding example. So inclusive and yet so compressed are the two sections dealing with the being, attributes, and counsel of God that it is difficult if not impossible to discover the order of thought followed. Section III deals with the doctrine of the Trinity. It can scarcely be passed over without a word of comment. Its brevity is striking and its simplicity is matched only by its brevity. Both surprise and gratification are evoked by the restraint in defining the distinguishing properties of the persons of the Godhead. It had been Nicene tradition to embellish the doctrine, especially that of Christ's Sonship, with formulae beyond the warrant of Scripture. The Confession does not indulge in such attempts at definition. Later generations lie under a great debt to Westminster for the studied reserve that saved the Confession from being burdened with such speculative notions as commended themselves to theologians for much more than a thousand years, but to which Scripture did not lend support. Hence all we find on this subject is the brief statement: 'the Father is of none, neither begotten, nor proceeding; the Son is eternally begotten of the Father; the Spirit eternally proceeding from the Father and the Son'.

Perhaps no chapter has been more distasteful to those out of sympathy with the system of doctrine set forth in the Confession than the third, 'Of God's Eternal Decree'. It teaches double predestination, not in the form acceptable to modern dialectic that all are elect and all are reprobate, but in the sense of determinate differentiation on the part of God so that 'by the most wise and holy counsel of His own will' he did 'freely, and unchangeably ordain' that 'for the manifestation of His glory, some men and angels are predestinated unto everlasting life; and others foreordained to everlasting death'. And the number in each category is 'so certain and definite, that it cannot be either increased or diminished'. In the esteem of many, here is a rigid, scholastic determinism that makes of God's counsel a monstrosity and entertains a conception of God irreconcilable with his infinite love and goodness.

It is true that in no creedal statement has the doctrine of God's sovereign and immutable decrees been stated in more forthright terms. There can be no question as to meaning and intent. Equivocal dialectic has no place. It is well to understand that the orientation expressed in this formulation conditions the teaching of the Confession throughout, and that removal or radical modification would only mean a hiatus that the teaching of later chapters would require to supply.

It is not our task now to prove from Scripture the doctrine set forth in the Confession. The proof texts adduced by the Assembly suffice as an index to the biblical data in support of the thesis of the Confession, that God ordains whatsoever comes to pass and that, therefore, the ultimate destinies of men and angels are immutably foreordained. It is the foreordination of sin and evil that constitutes for so many the stumblingblock to acceptance of the doctrine. If Scripture is the norm of faith, how are we to escape the explicit import of Acts 2:23 (cf. Acts 4:27, 28)? It refers to the crucifixion of Christ and is charged against the men of Israel (cf. v. 22) as perpetrated through the hand of lawless men. It is the arch-crime of human history. But stronger language could not be used to express the determinate foreordination of God in the event: 'him being delivered by the determinate counsel and fore-knowledge of God, through the hand of lawless men ye have crucified and slain'. There is no suspension of human responsibility arising from God's counsel, nor does any impugning of God's counsel proceed from the crime perpetrated by human agency. Thus we have exemplified in the clearest terms the doctrine formulated in the Confession and set forth in Scripture throughout.

The sequence followed in Chapter III should not be overlooked. Sections I and II deal with the decree of God in its cosmic, all-embracing reference, Sections III and IV with the decree as it respects men and angels, and Sections V–VIII with the decree as it applies to men. Both order and proportion show the competence that a creedal statement would require. It is in the sections concerned with men that the care and finesse of thought and expression are particularly manifest. Three observations will illustrate.

(1) In Section VI the statement: 'Wherefore, they who are elected, being fallen in Adam, are redeemed by Christ . . .' is so drawn as to be non-committal on the supralapsarian and infralapsarian debate. This is shown not only from the Minutes of the Assembly[1] but also from the actual terms. The words 'being fallen in Adam' do not imply that the elect when elected were contemplated as fallen in Adam. This would be expressly infralapsarian. These words simply state a historical fact on which both schools were equally agreed and which explains the *necessity* for redemption by Christ and the other phases of salvation mentioned. And election *insures* that those embraced in it will be redeemed and saved.

(2) While the Confession was carefully drawn so as to leave the supralapsarian and infralapsarian constructions of election an open question, there is no such tolerance of the view that denies the pure

[1] Cf. Mitchell and Struthers, *Minutes of the Sessions*, pp. 150 ff.

sovereignty of God in his electing grace. The doctrine set forth in the Confession is that of unconditional election. 'Those of mankind that are predestinated unto life, God ... hath chosen, in Christ, unto everlasting glory, out of His mere free grace and love, without any foresight of faith, or good works, or perseverance in either of them, or any other thing in the creature, as conditions, or causes moving Him thereunto: and all to the praise of His glorious grace' (Section V).

(3) In the whole of confessional literature there is no formulation that surpasses in precision of thought and expression that which we find in Section VII. 'The rest of mankind, God was pleased, according to the unsearchable counsel of His own will, whereby He extendeth or withholdeth mercy, as He pleaseth, for the glory of His sovereign power over His creatures, to pass by; and to ordain them to dishonour and wrath for their sin, to the praise of His glorious justice.' This is an analysis of the clause in Section III, 'and others foreordained to everlasting death', in so far as this clause has reference to mankind. It is an all-important elucidation of the elements comprised in the foreordination to death of the non-elect of men. This is often spoken of as the decree of reprobation, a designation from which the Confession properly refrains.

The distinction of chief interest is focused in the two expressions, 'to pass by' and 'to ordain them'. The former is not modified in any way; the latter is. Once the word 'ordain' is used, then that to which the persons are ordained must be specified. But of greatest importance is the reason given for the appointment to dishonour and wrath, namely, 'for their sin'.

No ground or reason is assigned for the passing by the non-elect except the sovereign will of God – 'God was pleased, according to the unsearchable counsel of His own will, whereby He extendeth or withholdeth mercy, as He pleaseth ... to pass by.' If sin were introduced as the reason for passing by, then all would be passed by and all mankind would be in this category. But it is otherwise when the thought of ordination to dishonour and wrath is introduced. The only ground upon which dishonour and wrath may be inflicted is sin. These are the judgment of God upon sin; therefore, sin must be posited wherever they are in exercise. The distinction is thus obvious, and if we once accede to the pure sovereignty of God in the differentiation between elect and non-elect, the distinction will be seen to be necessary. We must go one step farther, however, if we are to discover the finesse of formulation contained in this section.

It might be thought that the sovereign will of God applies to the passing by alone and that the ordaining to dishonour and wrath is a purely judicial act in the execution of retributive justice. The terms of the Confession do not support this simplified analysis. It must be noted that the earlier clauses govern the words 'to ordain them to dishonour and wrath' as well as the words 'to pass by'. Thus even the sovereign good pleasure of God, 'whereby He extendeth or withholdeth mercy, as He pleaseth', is expressed in the ordaining to dishonour and wrath as well as in the passing by. A little reflection will show the propriety of this construction, and the divines were not superficial or remiss so as to overlook the necessity of formulating the doctrine accordingly. We must ask the question: Why are some of mankind ordained to dishonour and wrath when others equally deserving of dishonour and wrath are not ordained to this end? The only answer is sovereign differentiation on God's part. Thus to regard the ordaining to dishonour and wrath as simply and solely due to judicial processes would completely fail to take account of the factors that enter into the foreordination to death. Of this failure the Confession is not guilty. The ground of dishonour and wrath is sin and sin *alone*. But the reason why the non-elect are ordained to this dishonour and wrath when others, the elect, are not, is *solely* due to the sovereign will of God. These two considerations the Confession has included when it says: 'The rest of mankind God was pleased, according to the unsearchable counsel of his own will . . . to ordain . . . to dishonour and wrath for their sin.'

The Confession is jealous to warn against the abuse of the doctrine formulated in this chapter. 'The doctrine of this high mystery of predestination is to be handled with special prudence and care' (Section VIII). And we are reminded that there is no direct or esoteric way of discovering God's secret counsel. It is only as men attend to 'the will of God revealed in His Word' and yield obedience thereto that they 'may, from the certainty of their effectual vocation, be assured of their eternal election'. Human thought must go upstream. Only then will the comfort of God's predestinating love be enjoyed, 'praise, reverence, and admiration' be accorded to God, and the proper fruits of humility and diligence induced in us.

The Confession commendably avoids expressions that might appear to relieve God's decree of its immutable and predetermining efficiency. It does not speak of permissive decree nor is its teaching compatible with such an idea. If decree refers to what God has decreed to come to pass, the interjection of the term 'permissive' at best confuses and in reality contradicts the thought of decree. Decree is essentially efficient; there are no degrees of decretive determination. It is perhaps more significant that the Confession does not use or endorse the idea of permissive providence. The terms in which providence is defined do not allow for such a qualification. If God by his providence 'doth uphold, direct, dispose, and govern all creatures, actions, and things, from the greatest even to the least' (Chap. V, Sect. I), then it extends 'itself even to the first fall, and all other sins of angels and men; and that not by a bare permission' (Sect. IV). This does not mean that the Confession will not speak of events as being permitted by God. With respect to the first sin it says: 'This their sin, God was pleased, according to His wise and holy counsel, to permit, having purposed to order it to His own glory' (Chap. VI, Sect. I). Nor is the Confession unmindful of the reality of subordinate agency in the execution of the divine decrees and in the fulfilling of providence. So in reference to the decree we read: 'yet so, as thereby neither is God the author of sin, nor is violence offered to the will of the creatures; nor is the liberty or contingency of second causes taken away, but rather established' (Chap. III, Sect. I). And in reference to providence we have a similar reservation: 'yet so, as the sinfulness thereof proceedeth only from the creature, and not from God, who, being most holy and righteous, neither is nor can be the author or approver of sin' (Chap. V, Sect. IV). Thus when the Confession says that God was pleased to *permit* sin it is not for the purpose of toning down the decree or providence of God to the notion of mere permission, but to conserve the responsibility of the human agents and to maintain that the decree and providence of God, though all-inclusive and immutably certain, do not operate so as to deprive moral agents of their liberty[1] and responsibility. Furthermore, the Confession, like all Reformed theology, is jealous to assert that the efficiency of both decree and providence and the certainty of occurrence arising therefrom do not make God the author or approver of sin. This is jealousy for the pervasive witness of Scripture that the agency and responsibility for sin as sinfulness are to be referred to the perpetrator – 'the sinfulness thereof proceedeth only from the creature, and not from God' (Chap. V, Sect. IV).

[1] 'Liberty' is used in the sense of free agency.

Creedal confession is confession of faith and must have at its centre the articles that pertain to salvation. A doctrine of salvation that is not oriented to God's election of grace is not the biblical doctrine. The whole process of salvation emanates from election in Christ before the foundation of the world, and moves to everlasting glory. The fidelity of the Confession to this biblical orientation is shown in Chapter III: 'Those of mankind that are predestinated unto life, God, before the foundation of the world was laid, according to His eternal and immutable purpose, and the secret counsel and good pleasure of His will, hath chosen in Christ, unto everlasting glory' (Sect. V). Salvation, however, is basically salvation from sin, and our concept of salvation is, therefore, conditioned by our view of the gravity of that to which salvation is directed.

There are two aspects of sin that must be in the forefront if our confession respecting salvation is to be biblically conditioned. They are sin as guilt and sin as depravity. These are central in the Westminster Confession. 'Every sin, both original and actual, being a transgression of the righteous law of God, and contrary thereunto, doth, in its own nature, bring guilt upon the sinner, whereby he is bound over to the wrath of God, and curse of the law, and so made subject to death, with all miseries spiritual, temporal, and eternal' (Chap. VI, Sect. VI). The stress upon the wrath of God is worthy of particular attention. The liability of sin finds its epitome in God's wrath and any confession that overlooks or suppresses the reality and implications of God's wrath stands condemned, not only as failing to assess the gravity of sin and of our relation to God because of sin but also as failing to construe aright the salvation which faith appropriates and which is central in the Christian confession. How eloquent of this complex of thought and conviction is the apostle's word in his exposition of the reconciliation! – 'How much more then, having been justified now in his [Jesus'] blood, shall we be saved from the wrath through him' (Rom. 5:9).

When we think of sin as depravity, here again the Confession does not fail in its emphasis. 'From this original corruption, whereby we are utterly indisposed, disabled, and made opposite to all good, and wholly inclined to all evil, do proceed all actual transgressions' (Chap. VI, Sect. IV). The severity of this indictment is not a hairbreadth greater than that of Scripture itself. Recoil from the terms of the Confession means either an avowed rejection of the biblical testimony or failure to reckon with it. For the Confession goes no further than the verdicts: 'And God saw that the wickedness of man was great in the earth, and that every imagination of the thoughts of his heart was only evil continually' (Gen. 6:5); 'There is none righteous, no, not one: there is none that understandeth, there is none that seeketh after God' (Rom. 3:10, 11); 'There is no fear of God before their eyes' (Rom. 3:18); 'The carnal mind is enmity against God: for it is not subject to the law of God, neither indeed can be' (Rom. 8:7). This is the doctrine of total depravity, and a salvation that is not conceived of as the outreach and downreach of redeeming grace to meet a situation thus characterized is not the salvation of which the Bible speaks.

A confessional statement respecting salvation must be oriented to God's sovereign election. This, as we found, the Confession does. But the purpose of grace originating in election comes to realization in history in covenantal administration. Biblical theology demonstrates that redemptive revelation and accomplishment are covenantal. Covenant in Scripture denotes administration to men in the sphere of history. This concept of covenant is clearly enunciated in the Confession, and it is to its credit that the extensions and refinements to which the idea of covenant was being subject did not find expression in the Confession itself. Covenant refers to something made with man. And so we read: 'Man, by his fall, having made himself uncapable of life by that covenant [the covenant of works], the Lord was pleased to make a second, commonly called the covenant of grace' (Chap. VII, Sect. III). Subsequent sections deal with the historical unfolding of covenant grace and the diverse modes of administration in the two testaments. The significance of the perspective provided by this formulation cannot be overestimated; it guards the unity of redemptive history, relates this history to the consummating time and event, the coming of Christ, and accords to soteriology the covenantal structure that is indispensable if it is scripturally conceived.

It is again symptomatic of theological competence that the chapter 'Of Christ the Mediator' should occur in this sequence. However much we may be constrained to prize the virtue of compressed formulation in earlier chapters, it is this one that excels in that distinction. No chapter in the Confession contains as much pertinent to what is central in Christian confession as does Chapter VIII. The first section is enough to evince this evaluation. 'It pleased God, in His eternal purpose, to choose and ordain the Lord Jesus, His only begotten Son, to be the

Mediator between God and man, the Prophet, Priest, and King, the Head and Saviour of His Church, the Heir of all things, and Judge of the world: unto whom He did from all eternity give a people, to be His seed, and to be by Him in time redeemed, called, justified, sanctified, and glorified.'

One hesitates to select certain features for comment, in light of the unity, coherence, and richness of the chapter. But with this warning a few observations may be of interest.

The longer formula of Chalcedon is condensed without any sacrifice of what is essential to the Christology concerned. 'So that two whole, perfect, and distinct natures, the Godhead and the manhood, were inseparably joined together in one person, without conversion, composition, or confusion. Which person is very God, and very man, yet one Christ, the only Mediator between God and man' (Section II). For succinctness and adequacy this is surely unsurpassed. And shall we not say unimprovable?

It is in this chapter more than in any other that the doctrine of the atonement is set forth. This is as it should be; the atonement belongs to the mediatorial work of Christ. It is remarkable that so many of the categories in terms of which the Scriptures unfold for us the facets from which the one atoning work is to be viewed, are comprised in so brief a formulation. Obedience, sacrifice, satisfaction of justice, reconciliation, and redemption are all present, and with these are co-ordinated fulfilment of the law, the endurance of suffering, the Lamb slain, and bruising the serpent's head. To use a figure, these are all woven into the texture at the appropriate points.

The atonement occupies a central place in the Christian faith. But centrality is misconceived if it is not related to the whole of which it is the centre. Treatments of the atonement are liable to lose sight of the organic connections with other aspects of revelation. This charge cannot be brought against the Confession. The chapter in which the atonement finds its fullest expression is an index to the avoidance of any such abstraction, and examination proves that the framers were jealous to give the doctrine its proper locus. The atonement is carefully related to Christ's own election to office, to the election of his people in him, to the various offices he executes as Mediator, and to his person as the God-man. The interdependence is set forth in such a way that disjunction is not only avoided but is perceived to be impossible.

It has been maintained that the Assembly formulated at least one section so as to allow for an Amyraldian doctrine of the atonement.[1] The *Minutes* of the Assembly give no support to this contention.[2] There are three principles enunciated in the Confession that exclude the Amyraldian view. The first is that redemption has been purchased for the elect. 'The Lord Jesus, by His perfect obedience, and sacrifice of Himself . . . purchased, not only reconciliation, but an everlasting inheritance in the kingdom of heaven, for all those whom the Father hath given unto Him' (Chapter VIII, Section V). The second is that impetration and application are coextensive. 'To all those for whom Christ hath purchased redemption, He doth certainly and effectually apply and communicate the same' (Chapter VIII, Section VIII). This excludes any form of universal atonement. The redemption purchased includes, as the preceding quotation implies, the purchase of an everlasting inheritance, and this is therefore said to be communicated to all for whom redemption was purchased. If all were included then all would be the partakers of the everlasting inheritance in the kingdom of heaven, a position clearly denied in the Confession elsewhere. The third principle is the exclusiveness of redemption. 'Neither are any other redeemed by Christ, effectually called, justified, adopted, sanctified, and saved, but the elect only' (Chapter III, Section VI). In the preceding sentence the elect are said to have been 'redeemed by Christ'; now it is said that they alone are redeemed. Other lines of argument could be elicited from the Confession to show that it allowed for no form of universal atonement, not even the hypothetical universalism propounded on the floor of the Assembly.[3] But the foregoing principles are sufficient to show that the particularism in terms of which the whole doctrine of salvation is constructed is not sacrificed at the point of the atonement.

There is one other statement in this chapter that may be selected for comment. It occurs in Section III and refers to the Lord Jesus as the one 'in whom it pleased the Father that all fulness should dwell'. This is, of course, virtual quotation from Colossians 1:19. What is of particular interest is the context in which the reference is made. The whole sentence deals with the grace bestowed upon and the equipment furnished to the Lord Jesus as the God-man, in his capacity as mediator and surety and unto the successful execution of these offices. Thus the text in question is interpreted in terms of economical investiture and

[1] Cf. A. F. Mitchell in *Minutes of the Sessions,* pp. lvi ff.; see also *ibid.,* p. xx.
[2] Cf. *ibid.,* pp. 152 ff.   [3] *Ibid.*

not ontologically. This betrays fine exegetical insight as well as theological alertness. The context of Colossians 1:19, when duly examined, establishes the propriety of this interpretation, and it is easy to see how the analogy of Scripture renders untenable the ontological application.

Disproportionate emphasis is too often the vice of theology. This appears, for example, in the controversy that has been waged over free will. On the one hand, there are those so insistent upon human autonomy that they fail to assess aright man's depravity. On the other hand, the doctrine of total depravity has been construed in such a way that the foundation for human responsibility has been eliminated and the logical result must be the denial of depravity itself. The Confession, as noted, enunciates in unambiguous terms the doctrine of total depravity. But theology and creedal formulation will be searched in vain to find any definition that equals Chapter IX, Section I, in respect to the 'liberty' indispensable to moral agency and responsibility. 'God hath endued the will of man with that natural liberty, that it is neither forced, nor by any absolute necessity of nature, determined to good or evil.' It is apparent that coercion would be inconsistent with liberty and responsibility. This needs no comment. It is the second part of the negation that is most significant.

It might seem that 'necessity of nature' denotes the natural order in which man is placed, and that it is not to be regarded as determining man to good or evil. It would not be irrelevant to make such a negation. Good or evil in man does not proceed from his environment. But the terms themselves as well as the usage of contemporary theology exclude this reference. What is denied is something intrinsic to the will of man as endowed with 'natural liberty'. 'Absolute necessity of nature' refers to an intrinsic quality by which deliberate, unconstrained, spontaneous choice is eliminated. Just as 'forced' refers to external compulsion, so the other refers to inward necessity. There is nothing in the will of man that makes one kind of moral action inherently necessary. And not only so; to eliminate spontaneous choice would be to violate the nature of will. It is this kind of necessity the Confession excludes. Consequently this 'natural liberty' is inalienable; it belongs to the definition of man and is applied in the subsequent sections of the chapter to the four states in which man is found – innocency, the fall, grace, and glory.

In the state of sin, the Confession proceeds, man 'hath wholly lost all ability of will to any spiritual good accompanying salvation' (Sect. III). By depravity man is under an unholy necessity of sinning (cf. Chap. VI, Sects. II and IV; Chap. XVI, Sect. VII). This, however, is a necessity arising from moral perversity and must be distinguished from 'absolute necessity of nature'. The spontaneity is uncurtailed, but the sphere within which it is exercised is that of sin; man has lost all *ability* of will to what is good and well pleasing to God. These distinctions are indispensable to the doctrines of man and of sin, and we lie under permanent debt to the Confession for the succinct and precise way in which they are set forth.

In Chapters X–XVIII the Confession deals with the various elements of the application of redemption. Respecting order there are two observations of interest and importance. The order of treatment indicates that the actions or processes in which God is the agent are unfolded first – effectual calling, justification, adoption, and sanctification. Then we find the chapters concerned with the responses on the part of the persons savingly acted upon by God – saving faith, repentance, good works, perseverance, assurance. The order is not, therefore, to be interpreted as providing us with the conception entertained concerning the *ordo salutis*. This would have to be derived from other considerations, and on the crucial questions it becomes apparent what the position of the Confession is. The second observation concerns the priority of effectual calling. It is clear from the place it occupies and from the way it is defined in relation to other aspects of the application that calling is regarded as that action of God with which the application of redemption begins. In this the Confession shows the exegetical competence of its framers. The biblical evidence should be regarded as conclusive to this effect.

The Shorter Catechism is the finest document produced by the Westminster Assembly, and it is the most perfect document of its kind in the history of the church. Its definition of effectual calling, however, is distinctly defective, and not in accord with scriptural teaching. It represents calling as specifically and by way of eminence the work of the Holy Spirit. Scripture represents calling as specifically the action of God the Father. The Catechism defines calling very largely in terms of subjective response, whereas the emphasis in Scripture falls upon the divine *action*. Calling is not strictly a *work* in terms of the Catechism's own usage. It is an *act*, as justification and adoption are said to be. In these respects the Confession goes a long way to remedy these short-comings. God the Father is surely the person in view when we read: 'All those whom God hath predestinated unto life, and those only, He is pleased . . . effectually to call, by His Word and Spirit . . . to grace and salvation, by Jesus Christ' (Section I). Then again God's monergism is emphasized: 'This effectual call is of God's free and special grace alone, not from anything at all foreseen in man. who is altogether passive therein' (Sect. II). The Confession also distinguishes between the call and the answer: 'until, being quickened and renewed by the Holy Spirit, he is thereby enabled to answer this call' (*ibid.*). These are the lines along which the doctrine of the call should be developed if the scriptural emphases are to be followed. It is only in this way that the specific character of calling, its richness, and the place it occupies in the application of redemption can be appreciated.

Chapter XI on justification provides another example of fulness and brevity. The positive aspects of the doctrine are combined with the refutation of contrary views, and those acquainted with the history of doctrine will readily detect the relevance, especially in the polemics of the Reformation period, of the various negations that occur repeatedly. The framers of the Confession were aware that they would have abdicated their responsibility if they did not set forth the truth in opposition to the denials and distortions by which the truth of the gospel was being perverted and the liberty of the gospel undermined. Hence Section I reads: 'Those whom God effectually calleth, He also freely justifieth: not by infusing righteousness into them, but by pardoning their sins, and by accounting and accepting their persons as righteous; not for anything wrought in them, or done by them, but for Christ's sake alone; nor by imputing faith itself, the act of believing, or any other evangelical obedience to them, as their righteousness; but by imputing the obedience and satisfaction of Christ unto them, they receiving and resting on Him and His righteousness, by faith; which faith they have not of themselves, it is the gift of God.'

The chapter on adoption is the briefest in the Confession. But two observations are in order. First, adoption is not subsumed under justification as if it were a phase or corollary of the latter. The doctrine of adoption has sometimes suffered eclipse by failure to recognize the distinctness of the privilege it connotes as the apex of redemptive grace. Second, there is no aspect of the doctrine that is not mentioned or implied in the one brief section devoted to it.

In the treatment of sanctification there are two features particularly germane because they are so often overlooked. The first concerns the statement that those called and regenerated are further sanctified 'through the virtue of Christ's death and resurrection'. This must be regarded as the virtue constantly emanating from the death and resurrection of Christ, and so these events are brought into direct relation to the *process* of sanctification. This evinces a grand insight into Paul's teaching in particular and points to the consideration that the dynamic in sanctification is the virtue proceeding from the glorified Christ, a virtue residing in him by reason of his death and resurrection. The second feature is the assertion that 'the dominion of the whole body of sin is destroyed'. This again reflects New Testament teaching, and properly accents the definitive aspect of sanctification by which every one united to Christ has been released from and has broken with the power of sin.

The space allotted will not permit further delineation of the confessional teaching. The samples given suffice to demonstrate that in respect to fidelity to Scripture, precision of thought and formulation, fulness of statement, balanced proportion of emphasis, studied economy of words, and effective exposure of error, no creedal confession attains to the same level of excellence characterizing that of Westminster. This evaluation is not to depreciate other creeds or catechisms of the Reformation period. It is simply to recognize that no other is its peer when all the qualities mentioned are taken into account. That it should occupy this unique place is explained by the advantage arising from the time in which the Confession was written, by the painstaking labour expended on its composition, and by the devotion to the cause of truth and godliness characterizing those engaged in the work. Nor does the foregoing evaluation mean that the Confession is a perfect document. Some of its defects will be mentioned presently. To appraise it as perfect and not susceptible to improvement or correction would be to accord it an estimate and veneration that belong only to the Word of God. This would be idolatry, and would amount to the denial of that progressive understanding which the presence of the Holy Spirit in the church guarantees. What the evaluation does mean is that for the church of Christ to fail in bringing its confession of faith to the level exemplified in the Westminster Confession is to discount the grace of God in the movements of history and of his providence which reached a climax in the framing of the Confession. It means that to discard the Confession as a medium of understanding and witness is to depreciate the ripe fruit of a progressive understanding and talent for formulation which have been the gifts of the Spirit of truth. The Confession has thus garnered the past and has incorporated the permanent values of the ancient creeds, but it has done so in more succinct, precise, and felicitous terms. As we have found, however, it is also singularly relevant and up to date on the great issues of the faith in contemporary life. Creedal expression when faithful to the revealed counsel of God never becomes obsolete. It never 'comes to resemble a monument marking the past',[1] and it is misleading to say that the Confession is not 'ancient enough to represent the past'.[2]

What of the considerations mentioned at the beginning of this chapter, that every creed is historically complexioned in language and content, that the progressive understanding of the truth of which the Confession is a conspicuous example did not terminate with 1646, and that the Confession is fallible and shows the marks of human infirmity? When the Confession is examined carefully in the light of Scripture and in relation to the demands of confessional witness in the church today, the amazing fact is that there is so little need for emendation, revision, or supplementation. And of greater importance is the fact that justifiable or necessary amendments do not affect the system of truth set forth in the Confession. In other words, the *doctrine* of the Confession is the doctrine which the church needs to confess and hold aloft today as much as in the 17th century.

A few instances of the way in which the Confession reflects the terminology of the period in which it was written may be of interest. When in Chapter II it says that God is 'without body, parts, or passions', it is most likely that the word 'passions' is used in a sense not current today. The word could refer to sufferings or to violent emotions in the sense of bad temper. But when associated with body and parts it more likely designates passive qualities or properties applicable to physical objects, a sense obsolete in present-day usage. In the same chapter the expression 'one substance' applied to the three persons of the Godhead is misleading because of its physical associations. The word 'essence' would be more felicitous. The term 'covenant of works' to designate

---

[1] *Report of the Special Committee on a Brief Contemporary Statement of Faith* (Philadelphia, 1965), p. 21.
[2] *Ibid.*, p. 22.

the Adamic administration (Chap. VII, Sect. II) is not an accurate designation. If the term 'covenant' is used, the designation in the Shorter Catechism, 'covenant of life', is preferable. In the same chapter it is said that the 'covenant of grace is frequently set forth in Scripture by the name of a testament'. The term 'frequently' reflects the position taken by the divines in interpreting the terms for covenant. But it is very questionable if more than Hebrews 9:16, 17 could be cited in support of the proposition concerned, and so 'frequently' is scarcely warranted. When, in reference to progressive sanctification, it is said that 'the regenerate part doth overcome' (Chap. XIII, Sect. III), this is not a satisfactory way of representing the relation of regeneration to the sanctifying process, nor is it in line with earlier statements in the chapter concerned. The distinction between the invisible church and the visible was current in the theology of the Reformation and has continued to be so in certain circles. The Confession states its doctrine of the church in terms of this distinction (Chap. XXV, Sects. I–III). While the distinction between visibility and invisibility will have to be maintained, yet the distinction is that of the aspect from which the church is to be viewed. For that reason as well as others, biblical study will scarcely warrant the definition: 'The visible Church ... consists of all those throughout the world that profess the true religion' (Sect. II). The *church* as visible may not be *defined* in terms of mere profession.

As respects content,[1] there are examples of oversight and of inadequate statement. Providence is properly stated to be all-inclusive. But when we read that 'by the same providence, He ordereth them [all things] to fall out, according to the nature of second causes, either necessarily, freely, or contingently' (Chap. V, Sect. II), there is

---

[1] It would take us too far afield to discuss the merits or demerits of the revisions of the Westminster Confession adopted by the Presbyterian Church in the U.S.A. throughout its history. The process of revision began in 1788. Besides, it is not necessary to reflect on these revisions and additions. There is no longer a formula of subscription requiring adoption of the Confession of Faith and Catechisms as containing the system of doctrine taught in the Holy Scripture. The *Church* now simply declares that it, 'under the authority of the Scriptures, and in the tradition of the one catholic and apostolic Church, is guided especially' by the nine creeds, confessions, and catechisms contained in the new *Book of Confessions*, among which are included the Westminster Confession and the Shorter Catechism, and the candidate for office is now required to pledge no more than the following in respect to these creedal confessions: 'Will you perform the duties of a minister of the gospel [or ruling elder or deacon, as the case may be] in obedience to Jesus Christ, under the authority of the Scriptures, and under the continuing instruction and guidance of the confessions of this Church?' (*Minutes of the General Assembly*, pp. 131, 132).

surely a slip here. Not all things come to pass by the operation of second causes. And this is clearly stated in the next section, where we read that God is free to work without means, at his pleasure. An important omission occurs when, with reference to our first parents and their sin, the Confession says: 'They being the root of all mankind, the guilt of this sin was imputed.' Something else is needed to ground the imputation of Adam's sin to posterity, namely, the representative headship of Adam. This is an oversight. The divines were not unaware of the headship of Adam and of its relation to the imputation of his sin. One could wish that the expression 'conceived by the power of the Holy Ghost, in the womb of the virgin Mary' (Chap. VIII, Sect. II) had been more accurately stated. Jesus was *begotten* by the Holy Spirit and *conceived* by the virgin. But it is an improvement on the so-called Apostles' Creed, for it says 'conceived . . . of her substance'.

It is with something of an apology that attention is drawn to these blemishes. But they serve to point up and confirm the observation made earlier that any amendment necessary does not affect the system of truth set forth in the Confession, and they remind us of the imperfection that must attach itself to human composition so that we may never place human documents or pronouncements on a par with the one supreme standard of faith. Of this latter the Confession has admirably advised us. 'All synods or councils, since the Apostles' times, whether general or particular, may err; and many have erred. Therefore they are not to be made the rule of faith, or practice; but to be used as a help in both' (Chap. XXXI, Sect. IV).

In the matter of supplementation opinions would differ among those loyally adhering to the faith of which the Confession is the exponent. But it may not be presumptuous to suggest that chapters on regeneration, union with Christ, the preaching of the gospel, and Christian supernaturalism would be fruitful addenda in their appropriate locations. It is not that the doctrine pertaining to these topics is absent from the Confession. On regeneration, for example, practically everything germane is stated in one place or another. But the exigencies of witness in our day could be met and the faith embodied in the Confession brought to clearer focus and fuller expression by chapters on such topics as these. Would that the genius for confessional formulation possessed by the divines at Westminster were present in the church today!

16

Tradition: Romish and Protestant[1]

The Romish View

THE position of the Romish church with reference to tradition has been officially declared by the Council of Trent. It is found in the 'Decree concerning the Canonical Scriptures' of April 8, 1546. The Council declares that the Gospel 'of old promised through the Prophets in the Holy Scriptures, our Lord Jesus Christ, the Son of God, promulgated first with His own mouth, and then commanded it to be preached by all His Apostles to every creature as the source at once of all saving truth and rules of conduct. It also clearly perceives that these truths and rules are contained in the written books and in the unwritten traditions which, received by the Apostles from the mouth of Christ Himself, or from the Apostles themselves, the Holy Ghost dictating, have come down to us, transmitted as it were from hand to hand. Following, then, the examples of the orthodox Fathers, it receives and venerates with a feeling of piety and reverence all the books both of the Old and New Testaments, since one God is the author of both; also the traditions, whether they relate to faith or to morals, as having been dictated either orally by Christ or by the Holy Ghost, and preserved in the Catholic Church in unbroken succession' (cf. H. J. Schroeder: *Canons and Decrees of the Council of Trent*, pp. 17, 296).

I SUMMARY OF ROMISH VIEW

It is apparent that the premise of this official pronouncement is that the source of all Christian truth, by which the faith and morals of the church are to be determined, is the Lord Jesus Christ, the Son of God.

[1] From *The Presbyterian Guardian*, 1947, May 10 and 25.

The question with which the Council is particularly concerned is the way in which this Christian truth, pertaining both to faith and morals, is conveyed to us. The Council's emphatic declaration is that it has come to us by two streams, Scripture and unwritten traditions. The latter have an authority in this matter equal to that of Scripture; they are to be received and venerated with a feeling of piety and reverence similar to that with which the Scriptures are received and venerated. For these traditions were dictated either orally by Christ or by the Holy Spirit and have been preserved in the Catholic Church in continuous succession. The outlines of the Romish doctrine of tradition, therefore, should be rather obvious. The summary statement of Sylvester J. Hunter may help to elucidate what has just been set forth. 'Christian truth', he says, 'was delivered to the Apostles by the spoken word of Christ or by the inspiration of the Holy Ghost, and . . . it has come from them to us, partly committed to written books and partly by unwritten tradition' (*Outlines of Dogmatic Theology*, Vol. I, p. 107).

Though this summary is in some respects simple enough, we are not to suppose that the Romish doctrine is as simple and intelligible as might appear from this formal statement. There are two things that need to be said.

II SIGNIFICANT FEATURES OF ROMISH VIEW

First, it is not to be supposed that nothing of what is implied in unwritten tradition has ever been committed to writing. The Romish Church does not mean that the whole content of authoritative tradition must be jealously guarded from ever finding its way into either script or print. In other words, it is not claimed that this teaching is such an esoteric secret that no one may presume to give any indication of its character or purport by committing it to writing. It is fair to conclude that the word 'unwritten' is first of all intended to distinguish the mode of its transmission from the mode by which the revelation of Scripture has come, namely, inscripturation. The authoritative teaching embodied in tradition is not conveyed to us by *inspired* writings. It does not follow, however, that other writings have not played a part in the conveyance and even in the exposition of what this tradition embraces. For example, the Church of Rome in its defence of tradition as an authoritative rule and in the support of certain traditions makes frequent appeal to the *writings* of the church fathers. Again the symbols of faith and the definitions of the ecumenical councils are important elements of tradition. But these, of course, are committed to writing and all may have access to them as documents of tradition.

But, secondly, the Church of Rome does place great stress upon the fact that tradition is oral and unwritten. In terms of this emphasis we shall look in vain for any summary or codification of what is involved in tradition. As one Protestant writer has said, 'so far as we are aware, there is no publication which contains a summary of what the Church believes under the head of tradition' (Charles Elliott: *Delineation of Roman Catholicism*, p. 40). Indeed, if there could be a codification or summation of the 'unwritten traditions', this would destroy the very principle that underlies the whole superstructure of tradition, namely, the Romish conception of the church. For Rome, the church as a visible, palpable organization and living organism, subject particularly to the papal see, is the depository of tradition. If writings were the depositories of tradition, this would radically interfere with the function ascribed to the church. The organs of this tradition are the official ministers of the church, the successors of the apostles. Christ and the Holy Spirit dictated these unwritten instructions to the apostles, the apostles committed them to their successors, and of these there has been an unbroken succession in the Romish hierarchy. So, while Rome does not aver that tradition receives no expression in writing, yet she is very jealous to maintain that the church is the medium through which tradition is transmitted, and not written documents.

III THE VOICE OF THE CHURCH

As indicated already, the church for Rome, is that visible, palpable organization professing subjection to the hierarchy which finds its head in the bishop of Rome. It is in this Church, called, presumptuously enough, 'the Catholic Church', that these traditions are preserved in continuous succession. These traditions, therefore, do not exist outside the communion of the Romish Church; she is their sole possessor and custodian. And this claim of Rome is to be understood, not in the sense in which she claims to be the custodian and infallible interpreter of Scripture, but rather in the sense that tradition does not exist except as an oral transmission passed on from hand to hand by Rome's official ministers.

Furthermore, tradition is not to be regarded as a verbatim transmission of sayings and directions given by Christ orally or by dictation of the Holy Spirit. Tradition is not a static corpus of oracles handed down from generation to generation. Tradition is rather that which the Church propounds in each successive generation; it is the living voice of the Church. Hence new decrees and dogmas may be officially declared from time to time which are invested with all the authority claimed for tradition. Rome, indeed, does not claim that such official pronouncements regarding faith and morals are new inventions of the Church. It is claimed rather that they are concrete expressions and formulations of what was implicit from the beginning in the tradition of the Church. By the authority vested in the Church they are declared to be infallible dogmas which are implicit in and grow out of tradition.

We can readily see how fluid and flexible this concept of tradition really is, and how difficult it is to determine what exactly is included in it. Indeed, there is something banefully elusive about it all. We get good examples of what the doctrines of tradition and of the Church can produce in the hands of the Roman hierarchy when we think of the dogmas of the immaculate conception (1854) and of papal infallibility (1870). Blasphemous pretensions can emanate from so elusive, but for Rome so convenient, a doctrine!

Protestants should be alive to the consequences of the Romish position, particularly in two respects. First, in the name of tradition there can be foisted upon the church what is the antithesis of the truth of the Gospel. We see this in the impious claims of the papacy. Secondly, Protestants should understand that the claim of Rome implies that the protestant church is excluded from access to one of the indispensable media of divine revelation, with the result that it cannot possibly be the church of Christ.

IV EXAMINATION OF ROMISH VIEW

In examining the Romish position, a thorough discussion would take us far beyond the limits of such an article as this. But a few considerations may be briefly adduced.

(1) It is true that the Gospel was at first orally communicated and transmitted. We have no evidence that Christ Himself gave to the apostles or to the church written documents. Even the first of our New Testament books was not written for several years after the ascension of Christ. The Gospel by this method of oral transmission was indeed the same Gospel and was the power of God unto salvation.

(2) All that Christ revealed and spoke was infallible and normative for faith and morals. If we today possessed any actual instructions of

Christ which have not been committed to Scripture and if these instructions could be authenticated to us by some infallible criterion, then these unwritten sayings of our Lord would be on a plane of authority equal to that of Holy Scripture. The same would hold of instructions or revelations given to the apostles by dictation or inspiration of the Holy Spirit, provided they were also authenticated by an infallible criterion.

(3) It is a remarkable providence that notwithstanding the many sayings and deeds of our Lord not included in the canonical Scriptures, alluded to, for example, in John 20:30; 21:25, the number of sayings or of deeds, not incorporated in the canonical books, which have come down to us are very few indeed and are of such doubtful authenticity that we cannot rely upon them or make use of them in any determinative way in matters of faith or morals. When we bear in mind the mass of material that existed in the instructions and deeds both of our Lord and of His apostles, not included in Scripture, and then ask the question: how much of that material has been conveyed to us by a really authentic tradition? we are really confronted with an amazing phenomenon. There is scarcely anything. We are constrained to ask: is this not a fact of God's providence intended to confine the church to the canonical Scriptures as the only infallible rule of faith and morals?

(4) The very doctrine of tradition as propounded by the Romish Church is indicative and indeed corroborative of the foregoing providential facts. The 'unwritten traditions' of Rome do not purport to be simply sayings of our Lord or inspired utterances of the apostles that have come down to us by authentic transmission. Tradition is not by any means conceived of as a collection or corpus of such instructions. Tradition, for Rome, is something quite different. But the only tradition that we would concede would be equally authoritative with Scripture would be the tradition of instructions given or deeds done by our Lord and inspired utterances and deeds of the apostles, communicated to us by infallibly authentic testimony. The only tradition then which we Protestants could place on a par with Scripture is that kind of tradition which does not exist, and which, indeed, Rome does not aver.

(5) Protestants, particularly Reformed Protestants, do not deny that there is such a thing as tradition to which all due deference must be paid. At the outset the word 'deference' should be noted. We have not used the word 'reverence'. In this resides a very important distinction.

V PROTESTANTS AND TRADITION

There is truly a *catholic* tradition to which all due respect is to be paid and for which we should thank God. The Romish Church has attempted to monopolize the word 'Catholic' by trying to fix upon itself the denominational name, 'the Catholic Church'. Protestants should not be the dupes of Rome in this respect and should resist every attempt on the part of Rome to appropriate that denomination. The Church of Rome is not the catholic church. It is presumption for her to claim to be. We should understand that all who profess the true religion belong to the catholic church and in the catholic tradition we glory. The catholic tradition is enshrined particularly in the ecumenical creeds, and is found also in the line of orthodox interpreters and theologians throughout the centuries:

There is also a Protestant tradition. It is the viewpoint of the Protestant church as over against the perversions and apostasies of the Romish communion. This tradition is enshrined in the great Protestant creeds and in the theology of the Protestant reformers. It is also embodied in the worship and practice that prevailed in the Protestant churches of the 16th and 17th centuries.

There is in like manner a reformed tradition. It is enshrined in the reformed creeds, theology, worship and practice. It is in this latter tradition that we specially glory. And we glory in it because we believe that it is the purest repristination and expression of apostolic Christianity. It is in this tradition that we move; it is the stream along which we are borne; it is the viewpoint we cherish, foster and promote. We cannot abstract ourselves from it; it gives direction and orientation to our thought and practice.

The Protestant View

There is then a catholic, a protestant and a reformed tradition. It would be false to disavow them. It would be presumptuous and even absurd to try to extricate ourselves from these traditions. We cannot do it and we should not attempt to. And we must bear in mind that these traditions of which we speak are not transmitted and carried on simply in the documents that enshrine and exemplify these traditions. In a highly real and important sense each tradition is established and perpetuated from generation to generation within the community and communion of those embracing and cherishing it. The family, the visible church, the school, to a certain extent even state institutions and various other organizations are instruments whereby these traditions are fostered and communicated. For example, a reformed community breathes in a certain atmosphere, is animated by a certain spirit, embraces a certain viewpoint, is characterized by a certain type of life and practice, maintains and promotes certain types of institutions. We call this the reformed tradition; it permeates the whole life of that community. When we pass on to another community of a different tradition, we immediately notice the difference. In these respects the fact of tradition and of its all-permeating influence on thought and life is undeniable. Where it is a good tradition, it should be welcomed, embraced, cherished, promoted. It is the way whereby God in His providence and grace establishes and furthers His kingdom in the world.

We must ask then: what is the difference between this view of tradition and that of the Romish Church? The difference is not to be sought in the denial that there is such a thing as tradition. Undoubtedly there is a reformed tradition, and Romish tradition, and Lutheran tradition and Methodist tradition. Neither is the difference to be sought in the badness of tradition as such. We would not condemn Romish tradition simply because it is tradition in the sense of our immediately foregoing discussion. If it stood a fair test of the criteria of Christianity, it would be good. But our present discussion is not concerned with an analysis of Romish tradition in the sense in which we also properly speak of reformed or Lutheran tradition. What we are concerned with is the Romish claim to the 'unwritten traditions' which Rome says are to be received and venerated with a feeling of piety and reverence equal to that with which Scripture is received and venerated. We can immediately perceive that we are here dealing with something that is distinctive of Rome and finds no analogy in any protestant avowal. The difference between Romanists and Protestants is not that Rome claims one set of 'unwritten traditions' which are to be received with piety and reverence, and Protestants claim another set of 'unwritten traditions' which stand in opposition to those of Rome, but which are also to be received and venerated with piety and reverence. No, not at all. The difference is that Rome claims such 'unwritten traditions' and Protestants deny that there are any such. For Protestants there are not two streams by which Christian revelation has come to us; there is but one – Holy Scripture. For Protestants there are not two norms of faith and morals, both equally authoritative; there is but one – Holy Scripture. It is precisely here the issue is joined, not at all in the denial of a protestant tradition and of its potent and beneficent influence.

It is, of course, quite true that the Romish view of the 'unwritten traditions', which are regarded as on a par with Scripture in the matter of authority, has deeply affected the Roman Catholic tradition in thought and life. And any evaluation of the Romish tradition would have to take into account the influence exerted upon that tradition by Rome's view of the 'unwritten traditions'. But our concern now is simply Rome's claim to the 'unwritten traditions'.

Protestants unequivocally deny that there are 'unwritten traditions' which provide any of the content of divine revelation or any of the instructions that are of divine authority. What then, we must ask, is the place or function of tradition in the protestant heritage?

Tradition, in the true sense of the word as delineated above, has the greatest potency and, if of the proper kind, the greatest value. But one thing must be appreciated, namely, that tradition, even when it is the best, has no *intrinsic* authority. Tradition is always subject to the scrutiny and test of Scripture. Its rightness or value is always determined by its conformity to Scripture. This is just saying that it is never proper to appeal to tradition as having intrinsically an authority in matters of faith or morals. Tradition when true and right and good always flows from the Scripture and is simply God's will as revealed in Scripture coming to expression in thought and life. Tradition, when right, is always derived; it is never original or primary. And this is invariably true from whatever aspect tradition is viewed.

Perhaps the best example that can be provided is that of a creed. In the reformed tradition, particularly, creeds or confessions of faith have held a highly honoured place and have exerted a powerful influence for good. A creed is a formulation of the truth believed, a confession of the faith of that branch of the visible church which adopts it. It should not be disputed that the church has a right and duty to declare what it believes to be the system of truth contained in Scripture as well as to declare what it believes to be the sense or meaning of any particular part or teaching of Scripture. In such cases the creed is the bond of fellowship, a bulwark against the incursions of errors, a testimony to the faith once delivered unto the saints, and an instrument for the preservation of both purity and peace. The persons subscribing to that creed are bound to adhere to its teachings as long as they enjoy the privileges accruing from that subscription and from the fellowship it entails. They must relinquish these privileges whenever they are no longer able to avow the tenets expressed in the creed. In this sense a creed may be said to be normative within the communion adopting it. For the Church concerned officially declares in the creed what it believes the teaching of Scripture to be. And so the person who has come to renounce the tenets of the creed to which he once subscribed has no right to continue to exercise the privileges contingent upon subscription. He may not in such a case protest his right to these privileges by appeal to Scripture as the supreme authority. It is entirely conceivable that the creed may be in error and his renunciation of it warranted and required by Scripture. But his resort in such a case must be to renounce subscription and with such renunciation the privileges incident to it. Then he may proceed to expose the falsity of the creedal position in the light of Scripture. In a true sense, therefore, the creed, even in a reformed Church has regulative authority. But while full recognition must be given to this fact, there are certain positions that must be very jealously guarded lest we fall into the Romish conception of ecclesiastical authority.

(i) A creed never possesses by reason of the Church's action or adoption an authority that is intrinsic to itself. The action of the Church in framing the creed or the action of the Church in adopting it in no way guarantees the truth or correctness of the interpretation the creed embodies or of the formulation it presents. No creed or other official declaration of the Church is by the action of the Church invested with divine authority. A creed by reason of its being a creed is never *per se* authoritative so as to bind the conscience in matters either of faith or of morals.

(ii) A creed or any other ecclesiastical pronouncement derives its whole authority from its consonance with Scripture. It is only as it reproduces and insofar as it reproduces the teaching of Scripture that it possesses authority over the faith and lives of men. As it is the transcript or reproduction of the teaching of Scripture, it has binding authority for the simple reason that what is scriptural rests upon the authority of Scripture itself and carries with it the mandate of Scripture.

(iii) The person who adopts a creed and subscribes to it is never justified in doing so merely on the authority of the Church or simply because it is the creed of the Church to which he belongs. Creedal adoption or subscription must always proceed from the conviction that the creed is in accord with Scripture and declares its truth. The person adopting can never pass on the responsibility for such personal and individual conviction to the Church and its official action. The moment acceptance is conceded on the basis that it is the interpretation and formulation of the Church rather than on the basis of consonance with Scripture, in that moment the Church is accorded the place of God and the authority of the Church is substituted for the authority of God's Word. The gravity of such a spiritual catastrophe cannot be measured. For in principle the idolatry perpetrated by Rome has been conceded and the basis has been laid for the gross impieties and tyrannies that have followed the career of the Romish Church. We need to guard jealously the position so eloquently expressed in the Westminster Confession: 'God alone is Lord of the conscience, and hath left it free from the doctrines and commandments of men, which are in anything contrary to His Word; or beside it, if matters of faith or worship. So that, to believe such doctrines, or to obey such commands, out of conscience, is to betray true liberty of conscience; and the requiring of an implicit faith, and an absolute and blind obedience is to destroy liberty of conscience, and reason also' (Chap. XX, Sect. II); 'The whole counsel of God concerning all things necessary for His own glory, man's salvation, faith, and life, is either expressly set down in Scripture, or by good and necessary consequence may be deduced from Scripture: unto which nothing at any time is to be added, whether by new revelations of the Spirit, or traditions of men' (Chap. I, Sect. VI).

II

Reviews
1954–1967

1

IN THIS NAME. THE DOCTRINE OF THE TRINITY IN CONTEMPORARY THEOLOGY.
By Claude Welch. New York: Charles Scribner's Sons. 1952. xiii, 313.

From the standpoint of historical theology and from that of theological
discussion this volume is an exceedingly valuable and scholarly contribution
to the subject with which it deals. The course of thought from Schleiermacher to the present is traced and evaluated with discrimination and highly
gratifying lucidity. In the historical survey Welch is never forgetful of the
main questions: what place does the doctrine of the Trinity occupy in
the affirmations of Christian faith? what is the Christian doctrine of the
Trinity? In the main these are the two questions with which the book is
concerned.

For Schleiermacher Christian theology consisted in the explication of the
contents of the Christian religious self-consciousness. Hence, according to
Schleiermacher, 'the doctrine of the Trinity is not a primary affirmation of
faith, but secondary and dependent ... a "combination of utterances"
rather than a direct utterance of the Christian consciousness' (pp. 75 f., cf.
p. 159 and *passim*). At the other end and in marked antithesis is the conception
that 'the doctrine is an *immediate* implication of the fact, form and content of
revelation' and is therefore a 'primary witness' of Christian faith, not 'the
result of an attempt to put together or synthesize various elements of the
primitive revelation' (p. 156). Barth is, for Welch, the leading representative
and exponent of this latter conception. A great deal of the trinitarian theology of the 19th and 20th centuries may be said to turn on the pivots of these
two opposing conceptions. In Welch's judgment the view that the doctrine
of the Trinity is 'a combination or synthesis of elements of faith clearly
dominates contemporary thought' (*id.*). He illustrates by appeal to J. S.
Whale, C. W. Lowry, W. R. Matthews and, in a modified way, to L. S.
Thornton and L. Hodgson (cf. pp. 157 ff.). Welch's sympathies are decidedly
with Barth on this basic issue. He maintains that the elaborations which
proceed on the assumption that the doctrine is a synthesis have not been able
'to meet the charge that the doctrine is in a measure secondary to other
primary affirmations of faith', whereas Barth 'escapes that difficulty because
he understands the process of "interpretation" ... as "analytical" rather
than "synthetic" ' (p. 168).

As regards the content of the doctrine the crux of the debate is epitomized
in the word 'person' or 'personality'. May we speak of three personalities in
the Godhead or must we restrict 'personality' to the oneness of God, that is,
to the one single essence? In Welch's esteem the formula *tres personae in una*

substantia was quite acceptable as long as the psychological analogy for the Trinity was the pattern of thought. *Persona* did not then mean what is meant by the modern term 'personality' and 'three persons in one God', he thinks, could not be equated with three 'personalities *in* God' (cf. p. 270). But 'since the time of Descartes and Locke, self-consciousness has come to be viewed as of the essence of personality' and once 'a person, or personality, came to be defined as a self-conscious centre of individuality or activity, or a distinct centre of consciousness, the term became a source of profound embarrassment to trinitarian theology' (pp. 270 f.). Welch appears again to be decidedly on the side of Barth, whose contention is that 'the "personality" of God is to be associated with his one single essence, rather than with the three "Persons" ' (p. 187) and that to speak of three personalities in God would be the worst expression of tritheism.

Welch is quite insistent that there is a 'threefoldness in the very being or essence of the God who has revealed himself in Christ Jesus' and that 'God is one God . . . who distinguishes himself eternally and in this way' (p. 252). He affirms 'the absolute "immanence" in God of the trinitarian distinctions and relations' (p. 184), that 'the terms Father, Son and Holy Spirit refer to eternal and co-equal "distinctions" in the One Being or Essence of God' (pp. 218 f.). But Welch's position, as also that of Barth, calls for some comment in this connection.

We must jealously avoid the danger of attaching the formulation of the doctrine of the Trinity to certain terms of merely human device if these terms are shown to be inadequate or misleading, and we must not allow the doctrine of the Trinity to be prejudiced by the fluctuations of meaning to which words are subjected in different periods of thought. For this reason we cannot but subscribe to the sentiment of Calvin: 'I could wish them (exotic words), indeed, to be buried in oblivion, provided this faith were universally received, that the Father, Son, and Holy Spirit, are the one God; and that nevertheless the Son is not the Father, nor the Spirit the Son, but that they are distinguished from each other by some peculiar property' (*Inst.* I, xiii, 5). But, as Calvin at the same time reminds us, we may not reject words which have not been rashly invented. With reference to the word 'person' or 'personality', it does not appear to the present reviewer that the alleged change since the time of Descartes and Locke has ruled out the propriety of the use of the word 'person' or even 'personality' with reference to the distinctions and differentiations that are immanent and eternal in God. In Welch's own terms, why should we have any hesitation in thinking of 'self-consciousness' as predicable of each of the persons of the Godhead? Why should we have difficulty in viewing each person as 'a distinct centre of consciousness'? One cannot but suspect that there is more than the fear of tritheism behind the insistence that 'personality' must be restricted to the one single essence, that there is failure to take into account what is implicit in the catholic doctrine of the Trinity and, of even more consequence, what is implied in the Scripture itself. This becomes rather patent when Welch, in expounding Barth, says, 'The lordship of God is not tripled, it is "triply one", "God is the one God in a threefold repetition". In other words, God meets us, according to Scripture, as *one* "Thou" (in threefold repetition), therefore unquestionably as *one person*' (pp. 187 f.). 'The modern concept of the personality of God . . . can never mean three "Thou's" or three "I's" if we are to hold to the biblical witness to the unity of the lordship of Christ with the lordship of the Father' (p. 188). Does not the Scripture represent the Father as addressing the Son as 'Thou' and the Son the Father as 'Thou'? It is surely to eviscerate the import of such explicit witness not to recognize the distinctiveness of the 'Thou's' involved. And the same must hold true of the Holy Spirit if trinitarian distinction applies to him as well as to the Father and the Son. And does not the Scripture teach us to address the persons of the Trinity in their distinctiveness as well as their in unity? If we are to address the Father in his distinctiveness as the Father in heaven, his 'Thou' must be distinct from the 'Thou' of the Son and of the Spirit. It undermines the biblical witness to the elements of the doctrine of the Trinity to plead the unity of lordship or the unity of essence as in any way impingeing upon or inconsistent with the reality of the distinctive self-consciousness of the persons in reference to one another and the recognition of this distinctness of self-consciousness in our faith and in all the approaches and devotions of faith. One can hardly avoid the suspicion of a unitarian bias in the failure to appreciate distinguishing self-consciousness in the three persons of the Godhead.

It is fully admitted that this constitutes a great mystery. How can there be the distinction of threefold self-consciousness and yet unity of essense? That is the mystery, and it is precisely in these terms that it is the mystery that it is. We must not evaporate the mystery by eliminating any of its elements. If we are to bow to the witness of Scripture these are surely the elements. Welch and Barth have prejudiced the mystery by interfering with one of its essential polarities. It is just as necessary that we guard against the unitarian bias as that we should avoid tritheism.

Barth maintains that 'the *doctrine* of the Trinity is not to be found in the Scripture. The Bible presents us only with the *possibility* of the doctrine' (p. 166). Adequate analysis of this statement would take us too far afield. It is to be borne in mind that for Barth the Bible is not itself revelation but the witness to revelation. And that conception must radically affect his handling of the witness which Scripture embodies. It is no wonder then that he should fail to assess the import of the Scripture teaching and readily discount some of the most relevant evidence.

Furthermore, Welch, in apparent endorsement of Barth's position, says
that 'we must make the doctrine of immanent Trinity conform exactly in
content to the economic Trinity' (p. 184). God's 'whole essence is revealed
to us in his operation. His operation is his essence' (p. 185). There are, of
course, important distinctions made in this context which should not be
overlooked. Barth insists on distinguishing God's essence as such from his
operation (cf. *id.*) and he maintains perhaps more insistently that both the
Father and the Son are *antecedently* what they reveal themselves to be and
they *are* what they reveal themselves to be (cf. pp. 183, 186). The terms
Father, Son, and Spirit do not designate simply distinctions of manifestation
but 'eternal distinctions . . . which refer to the very existence of God' (p. 226).
Yet critical comment is necessary.

First, it is not strictly proper to speak of the 'economic Trinity'. Orthodox
theologians use the term indeed, but in our modern context it is more
necessary to dispute its strict propriety. The persons of the Trinity do sustain
economic relations to one another in the economics of creation and redemption. These are relations which they come to sustain to one another; they
have relevance only to what is *ad extra*, as distinct from what is *ad intra*. It is
scarcely accurate to speak of the economic *Trinity* unless we are using the
word 'Trinity' in the sense merely of threefold relationship. And that is
somewhat confusing; it does not accord with the strict meaning of the term.

Second, the economic relations are certainly consonant with the immanent
and eternal relations; in that sense they 'conform' to the eternal relations.
They are not inherently necessary expressions of the immanent relations, but,
positing the sovereign good pleasure of God in the decrees of creation and
redemption, the economic relations are congruous with and appropriate
expressions of the immanent relations.

Third, it is in the economies of creation and redemption, specifically in the
redemptive, that the revelation of the immanent trinitarian relations is given
to us. It could not be otherwise, for it is in the economy of creation we exist
as creatures and it is in terms of the economy of redemption that we exist as
believers.

But, finally, it is an entirely different proposition to aver that the doctrine
of the immanent Trinity must 'conform exactly in content to the economic
Trinity' and that God's 'whole essence is revealed to us in his operation'
(pp. 184 f.). It is symptomatic of what is one of the most perplexing features
of the Barthian theology. While, on the one hand, there is the insistence on
the distinction between the immanent Trinity and the 'economic Trinity' and
on the eternal antecedence of the former, yet, on the other hand, there are
also the terms which are tantamount to identification and equation. The
Trinity, in other words, is set forth to such an extent in terms of economic
manifestation and operation that one is never sure whether it is *the doctrine*

of the Trinity. While, of course, the knowledge we have of the triune God and therefore of his Triunity comes through economic revelation, manifestation and operation, yet our *doctrine* of the Trinity is not a doctrine of the *Trinity* at all if it is construed in terms of economic manifestation and operation. Our doctrine of the Trinity must be that of what God is, in and of himself, immanently and eternally, irrespective of creation and redemption. If our doctrine of the Trinity is not that, then the God whom we conceive of is not the eternal, self-existent, and self-sufficient God, but a God of whom temporality is an attribute. The implications are far-reaching. And that is why we must sharply contest such statements as these: 'we must make the doctrine of immanent Trinity conform exactly in content to the economic Trinity'; God's 'whole essence is revealed to us in his operation' (*id.*). In this reviewer's judgment the direction of thought is one devastating to the doctrine of the Trinity and therefore of the one true and living God.

2

SO GREAT SALVATION. THE HISTORY AND MESSAGE OF THE KESWICK CONVENTION. *By Steven Barabas.* Westwood, N.J.: Fleming H. Revell Company. n.d. [*c.* 1952]. xiv, 193.

In the foreword to this volume Fred Mitchell, chairman of the Keswick Convention Council from 1948 to 1951, says: 'It is a book which is faithful and accurate; it is well annotated with sources of his (Dr Barabas') information; it is saturated with an appreciative spirit, for he himself has been so much helped by Keswick. The book will form a text-book and a reference book on this unique movement which has been reproduced with more or less similarity in every continent.' (p. x). This endorsement by one so closely associated with Keswick is borne out by perusal of the book. Dr Barabas has utilized the most representative spokesmen of Keswick and, without being tedious, has quoted freely on practically every phase of Keswick's witness.

This book is very well written. Oftentimes there is repetition, but this is obviously intentional and is dictated by the necessity of driving home the message of Keswick and of showing the large measure of agreement that prevails among Keswick leaders on those subjects with which the Keswick movement concerns itself.

There is a useful survey of the history of the movement, dealing with the antecedents of Keswick in the Higher Life Movement and with the Broad-lands Conference, the Oxford Union meeting, and the Brighton Convention, leading up to the first convention at Keswick in June 1875. At the end of the book there are biographical sketches of nine Keswick leaders.

The Keswick movement in England must be assessed with both appreciation and discrimination. Any one who is sensitive to the high demands of the Christian vocation and who is aware of the low level on which Christian life and testimony are so frequently conducted must find himself in deep agreement with the earnest contrition which has characterized so many of the Keswick leaders and with their insistent plea for the appropriation and application of the resources of God's cleansing and sanctifying grace. Keswick is intended to be a spiritual clinic for the cure of the lethargy and coldness, the self-complacency and indifference which are so prevalent in protestant churches. Certain emphases which Keswick propounds call for special commendatory mention.

1. Keswick has evinced a renewed appreciation of the implications for *sanctification* of the union of the believer with Christ. In this respect Romans 6 may be said to be the key passage, and Keswick has focussed attention on the once-for-allness of the victory over sin secured for the believer in virtue of his union with Christ in the efficacy of his death and the power of his resurrection. 2. Keswick recognizes that sanctification is a process in connection with which the believer's responsibility is to be fully exercised. J. Elder Cumming's statement of the case (pp. 67 ff.) is representative of the stress which Keswick placed upon the necessity of diligence, watchfulness, and prayer. In Evan Hopkins' words, ' "Sanctification in the sense of conformity to the life and character of Christ is a process, a gradual process, a continuous process, an endless process" ' (p. 114). 3. There is the recognition of, indeed constant stress upon, the work and presence of the Holy Spirit in the heart and life of the believer; the 'Spirit-filled life' is the 'central, dominating theme of the Convention' (p. 146). We need only elementary appreciation of the claims of Christ upon his disciples to understand how significant was the rehabilitation of such truths as these in an age when evangelical fervour had fallen to a very low ebb. Furthermore, when we think of the honoured names which have been associated with Keswick, like those of Handley Moule, Webb-Peploe, Andrew Murray, A. T. Pierson, we have to reckon with a movement which enlisted the support of cultured and devoted servants of Christ and one hesitates to embark upon criticism. But the cause neither of truth nor of love is promoted by suppressing warranted criticism. A few examples will be given of points at which adverse judgment seems to be demanded.

1. Keswick has not been successful in delivering itself from one of the greatest liabilities of its predecessor, the Higher Life Movement. While

Keswick stresses the gravity of sin, there is still an underestimation of the consequence for the believer of remaining indwelling sin, of what Keswick itself calls the tendency to sin. Going hand in hand with this failure is a corresponding preoccupation with what it calls known sin, apparent in its definition that ' "the *normal* Christian life is one of uniform sustained victory over known sin" ' (p. 84; cf. p. 99). If sin still dwells in the believer, if there is still the tendency to sin, if corruption has not been eradicated, all of which Keswick admits, then we ought to be always conscious of that sin. It is not by any means a virtue to say, as Evan Hopkins says, that we need not be ' "*conscious* of that tendency" ' (p. 50). Keswick insists upon counteraction as opposed to suppression and eradication. But it is just here that what we are compelled to censure as the superficiality of Keswick's conception of the consequence of remaining indwelling sin appears. Indwelling sin is still sin and the believer ought *always* to be conscious of it as such. To fail to be conscious of it amounts either to hypocrisy or self-deception. To have sin in us and not to be conscious of it is itself grave sin; it is culpable ignorance or culpable ignoring. As long as sin remains there cannot be freedom from conscious sin, for the simple reason that in the person who is sensitive to the gravity of sin and to the demands of holiness this sin that remains is always reflected in consciousness. Again, indwelling sin is defiling and it defiles the holiest of the believer's thoughts, words, and actions. The specifically deliberate and volitional is never immune to the defilement which proceeds from the corrupt nature and that is why the most sanctified of saints are oftentimes most acutely aware of their sinfulness just when by the power of Christ and the grace of the Holy Spirit they are engaged in the holiest of their undertakings.

If we are to use any of the terms mentioned above with reference to the grace of God as it is brought to bear upon the corrupt nature, namely, suppression, counteraction, eradication, the last is the only proper one. It is by progressive renewal of heart and mind that we are progressively sanctified. And that is just saying that it is by progressive eradication of inward corruption that we are progressively conformed to the image of Christ; a progressive conformation which comes to expression in the life of conscious understanding, feeling, and will. It is only as we are sanctified within that we can be sanctified in what is more overt and voluntary. B. B. Warfield comes in for criticism at Barabas' hands in this connection. But the criticism exposes the fallacy and even inconsistency of the Keswick position. What Warfield said was that the Holy Spirit ' "cures our sinning precisely by curing our sinful nature; He makes the tree good that the fruit may be good" ' (p. 71). This Barabas regards as 'unscriptural and dangerous' (p. 72). But on any scriptural view of human nature and of sanctification how could progressive conformation to divine holiness be by any other process than by that of cleansing the heart of its inherent corruption? And this is nothing if it is not eradication of that corruption, an eradication, of course, which will not be complete until sanctification is complete. Besides, Warfield means in principle what is formally expressed by Barabas himself when he speaks of 'a gradual transformation by the Holy Spirit who works within' (p. 85). And Warfield would be the first to say of this process that it can 'never be said to be complete in this life' (*id.*). Barabas' averment to the effect that on Warfield's position 'it should be practically, if not entirely, impossible to sin' (p. 73) toward the end of the believer's life evinces again failure to assess the gravity and liability of any remaining corruption, a gravity of which Warfield took full account.

2. While Keswick maintains in commendable fashion the implications for sanctification of union with Christ in his death and resurrection and places a much-needed emphasis upon Paul's teaching in Romans 6, there is at the same time shortcoming in the interpretation and application of this passage and of others of like import. The freedom from the dominion of sin of which Paul speaks is the *actual* possession of every one who is united to Christ. It is not merely *positional* victory which every believer has secured (cf. pp. 84 ff.). When Paul says in Romans 6:14, 'Sin shall not have dominion over you', he is making an affirmation of certainty with respect to every person who is under the reigning power of grace and therefore with respect to every one who is united to Christ. This victory is received by faith in Christ and in effectual calling. It is not achieved by process or by prolonged effort directed to that end. It is the once-for-all gift of God's grace in uniting us to Christ in the virtue of his death and resurrection. But it is not simply positional, far less is it potential; it is actual. And because it is actual it is experimental. To speak of freedom from the dominion of sin in terms other than the actual as, if we will, experimental is to indulge in an abstraction which has no relevance to the question at issue. It is true that there are differing degrees in which the implications of this freedom from the dominion of sin are realized in experience. In other words, there are differing degrees in which the 'reckoning' to which Paul exhorts in Romans 6 is applied and brought to expression in the life and experience of believers. But the victory over sin is not secured by the 'reckoning'; it is secured by virtue of union with Christ in that initial faith comprised in effectual calling and is therefore the possession of every believer, however tardy may be his advance in the path of progressive sanctification. Reckoning ourselves to be dead indeed unto sin but alive to God is not the act of faith whereby victory is achieved; this reckoning is the reflex act and presupposes the deliverance of which Paul speaks in Romans 6:14. If we fail to take account of this basic and decisive breach with sin, specifically with the rule and power of sin, which occurs when a person is united to Christ in the initial saving response to

the gospel, it is an impoverished and distorted view of salvation in Christ that we entertain and our doctrine of sanctification is correspondingly impaired.

3. It is to be appreciated that the Keswick leaders, as a rule, interpret Romans 7:14–25 as depicting the experience of one who is a believer. But when they maintain that 'the experience of struggle and defeat here described is not the God-intended normal experience of Christians, but shows what happens when any person, regenerate or unregenerate, tries to conquer the old nature by self-effort' (p. 77), then we must dissent on several grounds. It is a bold assertion to describe the struggle of Romans 7:14 ff. as one of defeat and that categorically and without qualification. And where is the evidence to support the inference that this depicts the struggle which ensues when a person 'tries to conquer the old nature by self-effort' or that it 'is descriptive of a Christian *regarded in himself*, apart from active faith in Christ' (p. 78)? Are such protestations as 'I delight in the law of God after the inward man' (v. 22) and 'Consequently then I myself with the mind serve the law of God' (v. 25), the language of a Christian 'apart from active faith in Christ'? Finally, if, even on Keswick assumptions, we properly estimate the implications of the sin which still dwells in the believer, then the conflict, indeed the contradiction, delineated in Romans 7:14 ff. is inevitable. Granting the presence of sin in any form or to any degree and granting that the person is regenerate, it is futile to argue that this conflict is not normal. Anyone imbued with sensitivity to the demands of holiness and who yearns to be holy as the Father in heaven is holy must experience the contradiction which Romans 7:14 ff. portrays. A believer without this tension would be abnormal. The more sanctified the believer is, the more conformed he is to the image of his Saviour, the more he must recoil against every lack of conformity to the holiness of God. If we take seriously the contradiction which resides in the believer between the flesh and the Spirit, between sin and righteousness, between unholiness and holiness, how could it be otherwise? As long as sin remains there is contradiction within the saint, and it is contradiction without reservation. It is only by ignoring the reality of the contradiction that we can get away from the *necessity* of this inward conflict. The holier a regenerate person is the more conscious will he be of the gravity of the sin that remains and the more poignant will be his detestation of it. There is no need or place for a contrast between the exultant confidence of Romans 8 and the struggle of Romans 7:14 ff. The more intense the conflict of Romans 7, the more the apostle gloried in the triumphing grace and hope of Romans 8 and of Romans 7 itself. And the more he gloried in the certitudes of Romans 8 and 7, the more he would be conscious of the contradiction which rested in his own bosom. It is only by evading the realities of sin and grace that we can escape from the stern realism of the conflict of

Romans 7. There is a grand candour in this passage, the candour of inspired utterance.

4. The representatives of Keswick have a passionate concern for deliverance from the oppressing consciousness of sin and the dissatisfaction arising from this consciousness. Every person who has his eye upon the goal of redemption must be aware of the oppression which sin involves and must long for deliverance from it. But we must beware of the tendency to complacency which is the snare of perfectionism. As long as sin remains we must have the consciousness of it and the ensuing dissatisfaction. The more sanctified the believer becomes the more acute becomes his conviction of the sinfulness that is his, the more he loathes it and reproaches himself for it. Here again one feels that the passion for freedom from the oppressing consciousness of sin, so characteristic of Keswick leaders, betrays a lack of appreciation of what the presence of sin ought to mean in the consciousness of the believer.

5. Keswick insists upon the distinction between the gradual and continuous process by which we are conformed to the image and character of Christ and the definite decision for holiness, the whole-hearted dedication to God, which is a point or crisis (cf. pp. 86, 114 f.). But must we not bear in mind that decision for holiness or dedication to God is itself something to which progressive sanctification must be applied? We may not assume that dedication is as whole-hearted as it needs to become and as it will become for the believer who grows in the knowledge of Christ and of the demands of his Lordship.

To the present reviewer Keswick appears to be still encumbered by liabilities which impair its effectiveness as a convention 'for the promotion of *scriptural* holiness' (p. 30). These liabilities might be assessed in various ways. But, in a word, they are related to or stem from failure to take adequate account of the implications of the presence of sin in the believer and of the effects which must follow in his consciousness. This reflects a defective view of holiness and of its demands, which, in turn, gravely prejudices what is the central message of Keswick, '*scriptural* holiness'.

3

THE ROOT OF THE VINE. ESSAYS IN BIBLICAL THEOLOGY. *By Anton Fridrichsen* et al. New York: Philosophical Library. 1953. vii, 160.

This volume consists of seven essays by members of Uppsala University and a brief introduction by A. G. Hebert. The book is of distinct value because it reflects a certain type of biblico-theological interest which is widespread at the present time in Scandinavian countries. There are two essays which have particularly impressed the present reviewer. They are 'The New Exodus of Salvation according to St. Paul' by Harald Sahlin and 'The Ministry in the New Testament' by Harald Riesenfeld. They are contributions of merit and are eloquently written.

Sahlin shows that 'the typological parallel between the historical Exodus and the Messianic deliverance' (p. 82) is fundamental for the New Testament and, specifically, of fundamental importance in the theology of the apostle Paul. By examination of relevant passages he demonstrates how Paul's view of both baptism and the Lord's supper must be related to this typological background. Sahlin's thesis is a refreshing reminder that the Exodus from Egypt is the Old Testament redemption and his discussion throws a flood of light not only on the Pauline allusions to it but also on such a significant text as Luke 9:30, 31.

Riesenfeld's essay is one that challenges to careful study of the implications for the official ministry, as now exercised in the church, of those passages in which Jesus institutes a comparison between his own mission by the Father and the mission upon which he himself sent the disciples as his envoys. We are introduced here to one of the most crucial questions relevant to New Testament polity: what is the relation of the ministers of the church now to the apostles whom Christ appointed and to whom he committed such unique authority?

As an example of the kind of inference which Riesenfeld draws from his study, it is worth while quoting what he says regarding the different functions of the two sexes: 'Thus it is no mere chance that we find in the New Testament unanimous pronouncements as to the different functions of the two sexes, and can establish that the ministers of the Church were invariably men, namely, the apostles sent forth with full authority by Christ, the missionaries who founded churches, and the heads of the local congregations. It is unlikely that the absence of female ministers should be due to any consideration paid by Christ and the early Church to the socially inferior position of the woman at that time' (p. 127).

There is much of great value in these essays. But we must not suppose that the 'Biblical Theology' which this series of essays represents is Biblical Theology in the historically accepted sense of the term nor that it meets the canons prescribed by orthodox theology. This can be seen, for example, quite plainly in G. A. Danell's essay 'The Idea of God's People in the Bible'. The critical reconstructions of biblical history are not necessarily rejected. And so Danell can say: 'Even if it is possible in the Old Testament Scriptures to trace a development or a progressive revelation from a relatively unreflecting monolatry to a more theologically elaborated monotheism, it is quite clear that the Old Testament as a whole, in its present condition, represents a monotheistic position' (p. 24). Biblical Theology properly conceived and developed must proceed on the assumption that the representation given in the Scriptures is the delineation of what history, specifically the history of revelation and redemption, really was. It is a precarious theology which builds upon the unity of the Bible as a whole (cf. p. vi) if it fails to build also upon the organic unity of the process of divine revelation of which Holy Scripture is the depository.

4

STUDIES IN DOGMATICS. FAITH AND JUSTIFICATION. *By G. C. Berkouwer.* Grand Rapids: Wm. B. Eerdmans Publishing Co. 1954. 207.

Professor Berkouwer is a theologian in the tradition of Reformed theology. If, for that reason, we expect this monograph to be little more than a stereotyped reproduction of the Reformation polemic we have made a great mistake and we have done Professor Berkouwer grave injustice. If anything is true of this volume, as of Berkouwer's other works, it is that our author speaks with the most direct relevance to our own present situation. He does this for three reasons – he is fully abreast of the movements of thought in the field of theological debate, he is keenly sensitive to the demands made upon the preacher of the gospel in our present day, and, above all, is he aware that theology 'is relative to the Word of God' and is therefore 'occupied in continuous attentive and obedient listening to the Word of God' (p. 9). This is perhaps the most gratifying feature of Berkouwer's work as a whole. Here is no arid traditionalism – we are always confronted anew with the Word of God and there is always the voice of the humble and devout exegete. To express the thought in Berkouwer's words: 'There must be no contrast between theological reflection and the personal word of Scripture. Dogmatics can do no more than reflect upon the nature and the implications of this correlation; it can never construct a system for the exclusive enjoyment of professional theologians. Theology is not an excursion into the stratosphere that lies beyond scriptural speech in time; it may not travel beyond the borders of faith's perspective' (p. 160).

In this volume the pivot of the study is the 'correlation between human faith and divine justification' (p. 18). In dealing with the subject of justification the whole question of the protestant Reformation is thrust into the foreground. It is here that Berkouwer is particularly at home and to the analysis and assessment of Rome's position he devotes a great deal of attention. He is fully cognizant of and alert to the contentions of more recent Roman Catholic apologists to the effect 'that the religious motive of the Reformation is fully honoured by the Roman Church' (p. 40). Two chapters are specifically devoted to the consideration of the Reformation doctrine. Special attention is given to the question of the forensic character of justification in opposition to the Romish concept of infused grace. Obviously this is at the heart of the question. With the notion of infused grace is bound up the question of merit, whether it be the merit of faith or of the works done in faith. Whenever merit in any shape or degree finds a place in the doctrine of justification then the *sola gratia* of justification is eliminated. 'The Reformed confession', Berkouwer says, 'offers the strongest possible resistance against every entanglement of our salvation with a concept of faith watered down with a mixture of merit' (p. 91).

The contention of Schneckenburger that the Lutheran doctrine was in sharper antithesis to that of Rome than was the Calvinistic, that the Lutheran doctrine was more 'synthetic' and the Reformed more 'analytic', is rejected. Berkouwer shows that in the crucial points there is profound correspondence between the Reformed and Lutheran confessions (pp. 48 ff.). It is also noteworthy that he does not give any quarter to the generalization that the Lutheran confessions are anthropocentric and soteriological while the Calvinistic are theocentric and theological. These are false antitheses, he says, and have bothered us too long (p. 55).

The last three chapters of the book are of particular merit. Berkouwer's treatment of such subjects as judgment according to works (pp. 103 ff.), the idea of reward in Scripture (pp. 112 ff.), the alleged conflict between Paul and James in reference to justification (pp. 129 ff.) is an eminent contribution to the resolution of these controversial issues. A few sample quotations will illustrate the effectiveness of his conclusions. In reference to the works of faith he says: 'We do not read in Scripture a series of isolated utterances on faith-righteousness and then again another series, equally isolated, on judgment according to works' (p. 107). In reference to Romans 12:1, Paul 'is not thinking in an ethical channel isolated from the main arteries of the gospel. Nor does he try to graft a moralism to the main trunk of grace' (*id.*). Faith 'does not create a field alongside of itself for moral exercise. It *defines* life, not merely as a dynamic force with a discrete causality, but as trust in God's mercy and as a "therefore stand" in freedom' (p. 109). In reference to the question of reward, there is a finesse of analysis which clearly defines and vindicates the distinction between reward according to merit and reward according to grace. Berkouwer also lays bare the fallacy of what he calls 'an atheistic ethic' which maintains that 'good is done only for the sake of the good, with no consideration of reward for the doing of it' (p. 117). He shows that Scripture 'takes quite another attitude than such "pure-ethical" views. . . . The morality of the Bible is in this sense an offence to the teachers of the "purely moral" ' (p. 118).

In dealing with the question of the relation of eternal life to the reward of works, Berkouwer appears to regard as unsatisfactory Abraham Kuyper's distinction between eternal life as such and special honour as the reward of works. The evidence from Scripture, which Berkouwer presents, would indicate that this distinction can hardly be maintained with consistency. Yet this reviewer has not been able to find in Berkouwer any satisfactory statement of the relationship.

It is gratifying to find the question of justification from eternity placed in its proper focus. The controversy between Brakel and Comrie and the difference between Kuyper and Bavinck are clearly set forth. Berkouwer's own position could have been anticipated. The correlation of faith and justification is the pivot of this study. 'The correlation is in time, it can be nowhere else. . . . There is no place for an eternal justification side by side with a justification in time. Naturally we do not mean to confine God's love within time's horizon. We are moved by the fact that the eternity of divine mercy comes to us in the historical revelation and that this is understood and adored only in faith' (p. 160).

It is too readily assumed that the insistence upon justification by faith alone in the Reformed confession finds its explanation in the fact that faith is itself the gift of God. But this is not the precise point of the congruity of justification by grace alone through faith alone. It is not the point of Paul's emphasis that it is of faith that it might be by grace. Berkouwer has his own way of placing this question in its proper light. It is not in the mere fact that faith is the gift of God that 'the lustre of the *sola fide*' is to be found (p. 179). 'The marvellous fact is this, that *the way of salvation is the way of faith just because it is only in faith that the exclusiveness of divine grace is recognized and honoured*. . . . As penitence excludes all merit, so too faith, directed only to divine mercy, excludes all worthiness. Paradoxical though it may be, it is in this exclusion of worthiness that the worth of true faith is brought out' (pp. 188 f.). It might be added that the propriety of faith as the sole instrument of justification consists in the fact that the specific quality of faith is the abandonment of all self-confidence and commitment to the grace of God in Christ. It is because faith is trust, entrustment of oneself to the free mercy of God, that justification is both *sola fide* and *sola gratia*. To use our author's words, 'faith is completely directed to the power and blessing of God' (p. 189).

It is easy for a reviewer to criticize an author for his omissions; it can be very picayune. A writer has to be selective and he rightly selects those aspects of a theme which are most germane to his central thesis as well as those on which he feels he can make the greatest contribution. Obviously Berkouwer has been guided by that principle of selection. There are, however, two subjects in particular that could properly be regarded as calling for fuller treatment – they are directly relevant to the thesis and to the particular phases discussed. I have in mind the unfolding of the concept of 'the righteousness of God' and the exposition of the constitutive aspect of God's justifying act. The former is represented by Romans 1:17 and the latter by Romans 5:19.

Berkouwer, of course, does not overlook the subject of the righteousness of God as referred to, for example, in Romans 1:17. He recognizes that this 'is a text of unusual importance in the history of theology' (p. 92). But he does not direct his discussion to an analysis of this specific concept as the justifying righteousness of the believer. It would have greatly enriched the development of this theme from the standpoint both of dogmatics and of polemics. Nothing exposes the perversity of Rome and the grandeur of the gospel more than the fact that justifying righteousness is a God-righteousness and therefore contrasted not only with human unrighteousness but with human righteousness.

In connection with the nature of justification there remains a hiatus in our presentation of the doctrine unless we take account of the constitutive aspect of the divine action. When we recognize this constitutive ingredient and formulate the doctrine accordingly there is no infringement upon the strictly forensic and declarative character. It seems to the present writer that when this aspect is given its proper accent a new orientation is given to the debate respecting the distinction between an analytic and synthetic judgment, a debate precipitated anew in this century by the contentions of Karl Holl (cf. pp. 15 ff.). It is always true that God's judgment is according to truth. When God declares a sinner to be righteous, this declaration must be conceived to presuppose the constitutive act or be conceived as in itself declaratively con-stitutive. Since the constitutive act is the imputation of righteousness, the reckoning of the sinner *as* righteous is not properly understood unless it is construed as the reckoning of righteousness *to* his account. This sets the whole question of the 'as though' in a new perspective. No doubt all of this is implied in Berkouwer's discussion, but it would have promoted the interest of greater clarity and fulness if the matter had been developed along this line.

It would appear that Berkouwer in dealing with the *ordo salutis* tends to underestimate the importance of the logical arrangement of the steps. We can endorse without reserve his statement to the effect that the paramount concern is that 'sovereign divine grace is properly respected' (p. 30). But exegesis demands that *order* be appreciated also and that to a greater extent than Berkouwer is willing to concede. For example, he is not prepared to allow that an *ordo* may be read from Romans 8:30. The reasons he gives are that sanctification is conspicuously absent in Paul's list here when systematic arrangement would require its presence (p. 31), and that in 1 Corinthians 6:11 sanctification is placed before justification (p. 32). Hence, he thinks, a simple biblicism would bring us into trouble. These considerations, however, are not cogent or conclusive. The question is not at all that the exact *ordo* is followed by the New Testament writers at all times. If that were maintained then we should certainly be in trouble. In connection with Romans 8:30 there are so many considerations drawn from the context and from the verse in question to indicate that Paul is thinking in terms of order that we are warranted to infer that a broad outline of the *ordo* is intended. The fact that sanctification is omitted has really no relevance. It would not be hard to find a good reason for its omission here if the point were to be pressed. Furthermore, the context of 1 Corinthians 6:11 does not evince jealousy for order as is evidenced in the case of Romans 8:28–30. It should also be borne in mind in reference to the *ordo salutis* that the sequence is not always one of causal factors. There is logical sequence when the thought of causal sequence must be vigorously resisted.

This volume has its omissions and its blemishes. But it is a great manifesto in our existential situation from a scholar of eminent erudition, a preacher of passionate concern for the relevance of the gospel of sovereign grace, and a Christian of humble faith.

We owe a debt of gratitude to the translator, Lewis B. Smedes, for the literary quality of the translation as well as for the translation itself. It is regrettable that the publishers should continue to allow the splendid work they are undertaking to be marred by so many inexcusable typographical errors.

5

INTRODUCTION TO THEOLOGY: AN INTERPRETATION OF THE DOCTRINAL CONTENT OF SCRIPTURE, WRITTEN TO STRENGTHEN A CHILDLIKE FAITH IN CHRIST. *By John Christian Wenger*. Scottdale, Pennsylvania: Herald Press. 1954. xii, 418.

It is a pleasure to introduce readers of this *Journal* to another member of the faculty of Goshen College Biblical Seminary. His distinguished senior colleague, Harold S. Bender, was accorded something of the appreciation and honour due to him in the issue for November 1950. The volume now before us by John Christian Wenger is a *Systematic Theology* written by a scholar of

Mennonite persuasion. In that sense it could be called a Mennonite *Systematic Theology*. Herein resides a great deal of the value of the book. If by reason of a distorted perspective we expect to find a good deal of fanaticism here, we shall soon be disillusioned. Dr Wenger writes, as he thinks and acts, with signal sobriety. For example, regarding the subject of baptism with the Holy Spirit and being filled with the Spirit, what could be more wholesome than the following? 'The New Testament knows nothing of converts to Christ receiving salvation and still standing in need of Holy Spirit baptism. Nowhere in the epistles does one read of Christians who are such without possessing the Holy Spirit' (p. 262). 'To be filled with the Holy Spirit therefore means to receive the person of the Holy Spirit for one's sanctification and guidance, making Christ the Lord of one's life' (p. 214). 'There is hardly an area of Christian doctrine on which it is more unfortunate for earnest believers to be misled than that connected with the various unscriptural and fanatical doctrines associated with so-called Holy Spirit baptisms' (p. 216).

The book is written in a style that makes it readable to the layman. We are not to think that Wenger's knowledge and scholarship are thereby impugned. It is quite apparent that the author has the tools and equipment of a scholar, but he has refrained from burdening this volume with such weight of theological discussion and allusion that the purpose of intelligible presentation to and instruction of the people would be defeated.

Dr Wenger is an evangelical believer in the historic sense of these terms. He bases his theology squarely on the Bible which he accepts as the Word of God. It would be hard, if not impossible, to find another book of this character permeated to such an extent by quotation from Scripture. This virtue, however, becomes sometimes its weakness. For example, in dealing with the second coming of Christ (pp. 334–60) we have little more than a catena of Scripture quotations, useful without question, but scarcely what we expect in a theological treatise.

It is refreshing to find such an unambiguous disavowal of the modern dispensational construction of divine revelation (cf., e.g., pp. 364–6). Wenger is not premillennial either; his predilection appears to be the amillennial position. Dr Wenger's discussion of the question, especially some of his remarks pertaining to the postmillennial and amillennial viewpoints, serves to underline the need of placing the views entertained in the course of Christian history, particularly those of protestant writers of the 16th and 17th centuries, in proper perspective.

This book is Anabaptist-Mennonite. We should expect, therefore, that characteristically Mennonite positions would be maintained. Infant baptism is rejected (pp. 235 ff.). It is gratifying to find that Wenger does not insist on any particular mode as of the essence of valid baptism. 'The Bible does not indicate what the mode of baptism shall be' (p. 237). There is also the most emphatic rejection of baptismal regeneration. The two distinctive points of ethics in the Anabaptist-Mennonite tradition are eloquently and feelingly argued, namely, nonresistance and separation from the world (pp. 313 ff.). Lest the latter should be misunderstood, we must bear in mind that it does not involve any such thing as aloofness to the well-being of society. 'The Christian does not withdraw from society and live on a pillar or on an island, physical or cultural. It is the responsibility of the Christian to enter actively into the life of his community' (p. 317). 'If this central responsibility (evangelization) is being faithfully attended to, then it would seem to follow that individual Christians . . . can enter generally into the life of their communities, *in so far as the activities involved in community service do not call for the violation of any Christian principle*' (p. 318).

The Mennonite tradition appears also in affinity with what may be characterized in broad terms as the Arminian position. This comes to expression on such topics as free agency, election, atonement, the character of saving grace, and perseverance. It is disappointing to read such a statement as this: 'The Arminians believe in total depravity but stress human responsibility more than do the Reformed' (p. 70). Or again: 'In the final analysis the controversy between the Reformed and the Arminians is due largely to dissimilar emphases. The differences are relative, not absolute' (pp. 71 f.). In like manner, when dealing with the differences between the Romish, Lutheran, and Reformed views of the divine image, it does not promote the interests of the issues to say that 'these differences are largely matters of words' (p. 84). Apparently Wenger's failure to assess the issues at stake in the Romanist view of man's primitive condition lies close to his own view of man's condition as created: 'God created man holy in the sense that he was sinless and yet he was merely innocent, not positively holy' (p. 88). This is distinctly Arminian and not as good even as the Wesleyan Arminianism of Richard Watson.

In reference to the imputation of Adam's first sin to posterity, Wenger rejects immediate imputation. He does not think Romans 5:12–19 teaches it. But the view he holds cannot be equated, as he thinks, with mediate imputation. Mediate imputation does not deny the imputation of Adam's sin to posterity; it maintains that the first sin of Adam *is* imputed to posterity, but mediately, not immediately, that is, it is imputed through the mediation of inherited depravity. But Wenger himself holds that 'the race is not guilty of Adam's sin; each man is guilty for his own sin, yet he is a sinner because of Adam's transgression' (p. 95). It is pursuant to his exegesis of Romans 5 as it bears upon both sin and grace that we read: 'One concludes from reading Romans 5 that so far as the curse had gone through the sin of Adam, so far does the atonement of Jesus Christ extend' (p. 276). And then the inference is drawn: 'All children prior to the age of accountability are therefore saved' (*id.*), an astonishing statement.

Wenger is probably correct when he says that the early Anabaptists 'tended to be more paradoxical than either the Calvinists or the Arminians' (p. 70). This tendency appears rather patently in Wenger himself, especially when he deals with election and the nature of saving grace. Election to eternal salvation, he believes, rests upon God's foreknowledge of faith (cf. pp. 72, 270). And yet Wenger can say in the same context: 'The doctrine of election therefore becomes a means of ascribing to God the glory for the salvation of each Christian in that the believer's choice of Christ is grounded eternally in the love and goodness of God' (p. 268). And, perhaps more pointedly, he says of the believer as he matures in Christian life and understanding that 'there will come to him a growing awareness that the decision which he made to accept Christ, although genuinely his, was ultimately due to the electing love and mercy of God' (p. 269). If this is so, as verily it is, then surely the faith which God foresees is the faith to which he elects and hence the foresight of faith presupposes election. We cannot have it both ways – election to faith and election because of faith. Yes, indeed, in Wenger's words, the New Testament attributes 'the surrender of faith on the part of believers to the electing love and mercy of a gracious God' (p. 270).

It may not be amiss to point out a few mishaps which may well be remedied in any future edition. The infralapsarian position is not correctly stated (p. 72). This is rather the Amyraldian view of the order of the divine decrees. A common misunderstanding of the distinction between active and passive obedience is reproduced (p. 208). The distinction is not that between the life of Christ and his death on the cross. If the Reformed doctrine of the perseverance of the saints is in view on page 308, it is not properly described as that of 'unconditional eternal security'. While we properly speak of 'unconditional election', it is quite misleading and indeed incorrect to speak of 'unconditional security'. Security or perseverance is always conditioned upon the fulfilment of the means.

In what is perhaps a different category, and of more moment, are a few observations which might promote better understanding, if not correction. The inclusion of God's 'eternity' under the transitive attributes may show how inadequate is a *classification* of attributes (cf. p. 49). It is surely indispensable to clarity of thought and to soundness of exposition to distinguish between the will of decree and the will of good pleasure in God, in other words, between the decretive and preceptive will (cf. pp. 52, 71). Does elementary exegesis bear out the thesis that the *decree* of God is simply permissive in respect to sin (p. 71)? Is it not contrary to Scripture to say with Menno Simons that 'only one sin can damn a man, namely, unbelief' (p. 92)? It is true that no sin will condemn if a man repents and believes. But surely any and every sin can and does damn. It is a false antithesis to say that sin should be defined as a lack of love rather than as transgression of law (pp.

92 f.). How can free will involve 'the power of contrary choice' if 'men are depraved and hopelessly lost in sin, totally unable to deliver themselves' (p. 103)? Has Dr Wenger not slipped into a kenosis doctrine of the incarnation, perhaps unintentionally, when he says that Jesus 'divested Himself of the full prerogatives of deity to undergo the experience of being truly human' (p. 200)? It should be distinctly understood that the doctrine of universal atonement is not indispensable to nor an inference to be drawn from the free and full offer of the gospel to all (pp. 265 f.). The Reformed doctrine of limited atonement stresses emphatically the universal offer of the gospel and the will of God to the salvation of all referred to in such a passage as Ezekiel 33:11. The will of God expressed in the free offer must be distinguished from his decretive will.

The present reviewer cannot refrain from expressing regret that Wenger has generally quoted from the Revised Standard Version of the English Bible. This version has its virtues, without question. But it offends against exegetical and theological sensitivity to be confronted with the unreliable and indefensible translations of this version.

It may be arbitrary to select any one feature of this book for appreciative evaluation. But the reviewer has been impressed most of all perhaps by the sustained emphasis upon the love of God and the reciprocal response on the part of the believer in the simplicity of love and trust. One quotation will illustrate: 'Christian faith ventures obedience, ignoring consequences, desiring only to step forward at the command of Christ. In other words, he who has Christian faith does not live on the basis of prudence; he does not reckon with selfish outcomes. He serves God out of sheer love for Him, asking only for grace to perform whatever God asks' (p. 275). And much else might be quoted from Wenger and from the sources he quotes to evince zeal for the fervour of evangelical simplicity in the faith of God's love and in the love which is the fruit of the Spirit.

6

ETERNAL HOPE. *By Emil Brunner*. Philadelphia: The Westminster Press. 1954. ii, 232.

In the postscript Brunner informs us that the present volume was written upon the occasion of the choice of theme which provided the principal subject of debate at the meeting of the World Council of Churches at Evanston in August 1954 (p. 211). Brunner was one of the group chosen to prepare a message on the theme, 'Christ – the Hope of the World'. It is Brunner's judgment that the document aimed at in this appointment was 'unable to penetrate sufficiently deeply into the questions which cause a tension between the modern man and the message of hope in Christ as to succeed in proclaiming convincingly the Biblical word to our modern age' (p. 212). And the reason he gives is that the question as to the substance of the Christian hope has remained for so long outside the scope of debate and therefore the church is not in a position to speak decisively and relevantly on this article of faith (p. 213). He acknowledges the contribution made by Karl Barth and his co-operators but, as far as achievement is concerned, he has to 'confess with shame and astonishment that at this point a great lacuna is visible' (*id.*).

It was not, however, the present theological situation that provided the primary reason for this eschatological study; it was 'the conviction that a church which has nothing to teach concerning the future and the life of the world to come is bankrupt' (p. 219). Deeply sensitive to the exigencies of the present ecclesiastical and theological situation and to the tensions which arise for the modern man, Brunner attempts to do something to fill up the lacuna and to present the message of the Christian faith regarding the hope of the future. Brunner is insistent that the hope of eternal life belongs to the total structure of the Christian faith. 'The hope of eternal life is not just a part of the faith, the final section, called eschatology; it is rather the point at issue in the faith as a whole, without which therefore it would not simply be minus something, but without which it would utterly cease to exist' (p. 90). 'A Christian faith without expectation of the Parousia is like a ladder which leads nowhere but ends in the void' (pp. 138 f.). In our present situation Brunner's polemic waxes most urgent and emphatic against that demythologization of the New Testament which eliminates 'the dimension of the future'. Brunner is no fundamentalist; he is far removed from what he regards as its 'naïve Biblicism'. 'But still further . . . are we removed', he himself informs us, 'from a theology of de-mythologizing which expects us to recognize an interpretation of New Testament faith which eliminates from it the whole dimension of the future' (p. 119).

With this emphasis upon the hope of the future we should expect, and we actually find, much that is of great value. At numerous points Brunner not only stimulates thought but contributes to our understanding of the significance, character, and implications of the Christian message of hope. And sometimes we come across the finest of insights. For example, his chapter on 'Belief in the Progress of Humanity' places in sharp focus the radical antithesis between the idea of eternal recurrence, which characterizes pagan eschatology, and the linear conception of history which we find in Christianity, as the same chapter also exposes the nihilism in which 'the self-confidence and self-security of man' (p. 17), which characterized 19th-century humanism, ends. And, again, what could be more effective in laying bare the totally unchristian character of the doctrine of the immortality of the soul as it comes to expression, for example, in Platonism than what Brunner says in two pages (pp. 100 f.) in his chapter on 'The Mystery of Death'. 'The effect of this Platonic dualism', he says, 'is not merely to make death innocuous but also to rob evil of its sting' (p. 101).

In terms of our present-day ecclesiastical and theological situation, what is Brunner's *locus*? In terms of the biblical witness, how are we to assess his position? Brunner will not have the eschatology of traditional orthodoxy – it literalizes, he thinks, the apocalyptic symbolism of Scripture. This apocalyptic symbolism cannot be adjusted to the cosmology or world-view with which science has provided the modern man. On the other hand, he will not have that de-mythologizing that eliminates the dimension of the future. He wants to 'avoid an undue literalism or a false spiritualization' (p. 118). In the judgment of this reviewer, it is the de-mythologizing motif that is paramount in Brunner's construction of the Christian hope and it is in what we may call his de-mythologization that his deviation from biblical eschatology appears. This can be illustrated in his construction of the three pivotal events, the parousia, the resurrection, and the judgment.

Brunner is quite convinced that there is a basic discrepancy between the world-picture and the time-picture portrayed in the Scripture and the world-picture and time-picture which the modern man can accept. Consequently in connection with the *form* in which the parousia will take place the pronouncements of the New Testament are unacceptable to us. They are unacceptable because they are mythical and reflect the world-picture of the apostles and not that of man today (p. 139). 'We no longer live in a world in which the stars can fall from Heaven' (p. 119). In connection with 1 Thessalonians 4:16, 17, 'we feel immediately', he says, 'that just here the world-picture of the Bible clashes with our own' (p. 139).

To say the least, there is something very unsatisfactory in Brunner's discussion at this point. He is convinced that here, for example, there is a clash between our world-view and that of the Bible and that the latter we cannot accept – we must de-mythologize. But what is there in 1 Thessalonians 4:16, 17 that clashes with our world-picture? Is it the fact that God is represented as blowing a trumpet? But Brunner says that Paul could 'hardly have imagined God as blowing a trumpet' (*id.*). Well, if Paul did not imagine it that way he did not mean us to understand it that way, and, hence, Paul does not teach here that God will blow a literal trumpet. And, if so, then a world-view which envisions God as literally blowing a trumpet is not present in this text. How then could this detail be in any way construed as creating a world-picture contrary to that which we are compelled to accept? One can only say that there is a looseness in this type of discussion that is not worthy of the sober and careful interpretation which Scripture deserves. What, we ask, is there in our world-view that makes it impossible for us to think of Jesus as coming visibly and in glory and of the saints resurrected and changed as snatched up into the air to meet him? We need much more than Brunner has adduced to make evident the alleged discrepancy. And is it not either naïve or presumptuous for us to say that we no longer live in a world in which the stars can fall from heaven? The language of Scripture is oftentimes, as with all language, the language of the phenomenal and is to be understood accordingly. Does our cosmology, the cosmology furnished, for example, by the science of astronomy, make it impossible for us to conceive of such commotions in the visible cosmos that to this world's perspective they would be the falling of the stars from heaven? It is only de-mythologization of the Bultmann type that can tolerate the elimination of that cataclysmic regeneration which the parousia of the day of God will bring (cf. 2 Pet. 3:12) and by which the creation itself also will be delivered from the bondage of corruption into the liberty of the glory of the children of God (cf. Rom. 8:21). If we have this perspective – and we must have it if our eschatology is faithful to the *essence* of the New Testament witness – then the phenomenon of the stars falling from heaven is but one incident of such a cosmic upheaval.

In this same connection one further example may be given of the way in which faulty exegesis can be used to perplex what should not be perplexed. Brunner says, 'On the one hand Jesus spoke very concretely about a coming of the Son of Man on the clouds of heaven. But another time He expresses the same idea in the language of abstract symbolism when He says it will be like "lightning which flashes from the east to the west". . . . The lightning flash is probably of all the possibilities of expression to us the one symbol which expresses most effectively this transcendence of space and time' (p. 140). But why should we find any contrast between the concrete and the abstract in such passages as these? What Jesus is emphasizing when he uses the similitude of lightning is the public, visible character of his parousia (cf. Matt. 24:25-7; Luke 17:23, 24). He is warning against deceivers who will say, he is here or he is there. Don't be deceived, Jesus is saying in effect: When I shall come every one will know about it. No one will have to tell another; it will be as public and visible and universal as the lightning. In the similitude of the lightning there is nothing to interfere in the least degree with the concreteness of Christ's coming on the clouds of heaven. In fact the emphasis upon the public and visible and recognizable only serves to accentuate the concreteness.

It is this same bent of thought that comes to expression in Brunner's view of the resurrection, an underestimation of the concrete. It is verily true that the resurrection is incomprehensible – there is mystery that far surpasses our understanding. But the language Brunner uses is such as would place the resurrection outside the realm of intelligent and intelligible understanding and statement. 'The resurrection of Jesus', he says, 'is as an event utterly incomprehensible and transcendent, the beginning of the Parousia, of which the – one might say – obvious characteristic is its incomprehensibility, its non-co-ordinability, the utter impossibility of expressing it in the terms of our thought and ideas' (p. 144). And he speaks of the 'utter otherness' of Jesus' resurrection being and mode of presence (p. 145).

Our limits will not permit an adequate analysis of the superlatives of such statements. But we may focus attention on a particular phase of Brunner's thought which will help to explain the dialectic which his terms express. Brunner is explicit to the effect that there is no resurrection of the flesh. He says emphatically, 'But the flesh will not rise again. The resurrection of the flesh stands of course in the creed but is excluded by what Paul says in 1 Cor. 15:35–53. The resurrection has nothing to do with that drama of the grave-yard pictured by mediaeval fantasy. . . . Every man will rise again in his own likeness, his own unchangeable individuality, but not in his flesh' (p. 149). It is to be admitted that Brunner's meaning is not perfectly perspicuous. If he is using the word 'flesh' of corruptible flesh, as obviously Paul is in 1 Cor. 15:50, and thinking expressly of the resurrection to life, then indeed there will be no resurrection of the 'flesh'. However much we might wish to place that specific connotation upon his use of the word 'flesh', the evidence will scarcely warrant it. For, with reference to the resurrection of Jesus, Brunner says, 'Jesus is not awakened again to physical life (Bultmann) according to the Resurrection narratives, but to a spiritual corporeality' (*id.*). That Jesus was 'free from the conditions of material corporeality' lies, he says, at the basis of Paul's 'idea of the *soma pneumatikon*' (*id.*). Now, unless Brunner indulges in very faulty use of terms (an assumption which we may not enter-tain), here is a view of the resurrection that must be emphatically challenged. It is not the biblical and therefore not the Christian concept of the resurrec-tion. In the case of Jesus there was the resuscitation of that material body that was laid in the tomb. And without this there was no resurrection of Jesus. This is not the whole truth of the resurrection of Jesus but without this factor there is no truth at all of the resurrection from the dead. And what is Brunner going to do with the word of Jesus to his disciples: 'See my hands and my feet, that it is I myself: handle me and see, because (or that) a spirit has not flesh and bones as ye see me having' (Luke 24:39)? Jesus had 'flesh' after his resurrection because he rose in the body with which he suffered. And this is just to say that there was the resurrection of his flesh. Jesus' own witness knows nothing less. And neither does the witness of the apostles.

Furthermore, Paul's idea of the *soma pneumatikon* is not one that rules out 'material corporeality'. It is to misunderstand not merely the general New

Testament concept of resurrection but Paul's doctrine in particular to understand the term *pneumatikon* as reflecting upon the non-material composition
of the body (*soma*). The latter would not be a body if it were not material.
The resurrection body of Jesus and that of believers is undoubtedly endowed
with new qualities but to rule out its materiality is to eviscerate the resurrection. Paul said, 'This corruptible will put on incorruption and this mortal
will put on immortality' (1 Cor. 15:54). And whatever may be said of
'mediaeval fantasy' we must not spurn 'the drama of the graveyard'. It was
Jesus who said, 'All who are in the graves will hear his voice and will come
forth; those who have done good unto the resurrection of life, those who
have done evil unto the resurrection of judgment' (John 5:28, 29). There is
much we do not know, but the *consistent* witness of Scripture respecting the
resurrection is characterized by a concreteness which brings the doctrine
within the realm of articulate thought and concretely formulated conception.

It might appear that Brunner recognizes the final discriminating issues of
the last judgment. 'But judgment', he says, 'not only implies a manifestation
of what is hidden in man; it is also a matter of crisis and separation. Nowhere
is this division of the ones from the others so vividly and graphically represented as in Jesus' parable of the Last Judgment, where there takes place a
visible separation of the sheep from the goats, the blessed from the accursed,
and an allocation of the former to eternal life, of the latter to eternal perdition' (p. 177). There is a good deal more in this context that might be
quoted with approval, especially on the subject of the correlation of freedom
and determinacy, of responsibility and the fact of the last judgment (cf. pp.
178 f.). But, as we read on, we find that Brunner will not affirm the future
reality of such a final and irrevocable separation of just and unjust. The 'static
symmetry picturing the two opposites' is a symmetry which Brunner recognizes as present in the 'picture-symbol' of Jesus' judgment discourse (Matt.
25:31–46), nevertheless he insists that 'the intention of the words of Jesus is
quite different' (p. 180). It is not to teach the salvation of the blessed and the
damnation of the accursed; the Word of Jesus is rather 'a summons calling
for decision' (*id.*). 'God's Word . . . is a Word of challenge, not of doctrine'
(p. 183).

It is undoubtedly true that Jesus' teaching respecting the judgment (as in
Matt. 25:31–46) is for us now living in this world a word of challenge calling
for decision, a word of solemn warning that should arouse all to whom it
comes to repentance and faith. How frequently has it been instrumental to
that gracious purpose! To the fullest extent we must recognize the existential
demand of this revelatory word. But this fact that Jesus' words are to us *now*
words pregnant with grace to the end that we may escape the judgment of
the wicked does not eliminate, nor in the least degree attenuate, the factuality
of that judgment and its issue in the everlasting separation of just and unjust;

it does not eliminate the grim reality of the 'static' when the day of judgment arrives. For Jesus speaks here not simply in terms of what is calculated to arouse us *now* to decision and faith but in terms of the coming factuality of the final blessedness of the righteous and the irrevocable damnation of the impenitent. He reveals to us here not merely God's will to the salvation of men but he unveils to us what *will be true* in the final issues of the last judgment.

To say the least, there is equivocation in Brunner's treatment of the last judgment and the unequivocal declarations of Scripture regarding the irrevocable issues of that judgment for eternal bliss and eternal damnation are subjected, we know not how, to what he himself calls a 'process of exegetical chemistry' which deprives them of 'the definiteness of their ulti-mate character'. And 'we have here evasion rather than exegesis' (*id.*). We must remember that God in his Word reveals to us not only his will to our salvation but also the will of his discriminating foreordination. Our con-clusion can only be that Brunner's view of incompatibility and contradiction in the word of Scripture compels him to adopt a dialectic which has its affinities not with the biblical revelation but with the de-mythologization which, he himself contends, demolishes the total structure of the Christian faith.

7

CALVIN'S DOCTRINE OF THE WORK OF CHRIST. *By John Frederick Jansen.* London: James Clarke & Co., Ltd. 1956. 120.

This is not a large book. But it represents a great deal of research on a subject that called for the study which the author has devoted to it. The general theme is that of the three offices of Christ and, as the title indicates, particular attention is given to the three offices in the theology of Calvin. The first part of the volume provides an instructive survey of the history of thought on the question of Christ's offices both before and after Calvin. The author shows that prior to the time of Calvin there were 'two traditional readings of the messianic name' (p. 38), one in terms of three offices, the other in terms of a two-fold office, and that 'in Calvin's immediate reformation background, the messianic office of the Redeemer is usually understood as the two-fold work of king and priest' (p. 36).

In the first edition of the *Institutes* (1536) Calvin spoke only of a two-fold unction but in the second edition (1539) the prophetic office begins to appear and in the edition of 1545 there is a clear statement of the three offices of

Christ (pp. 39 ff.). Every student of Calvin knows that in the definitive edition (1559) a separate chapter (II, xv) is devoted to the three offices, the prophetical, the regal, and the sacerdotal. Jansen maintains that this development on Calvin's part was not dictated by exegetical considerations but by dogmatic (cf. p. 45). And Jansen's main thesis is that the change from a two-fold structure to a three-fold was 'peripheral rather than essential'. He continues: 'I would go further. While Calvin suggests the formula as a theological category in his later dogmatics, he himself does no more with it – for the very good reason that he cannot make use of it. The essential structure of his doctrine of Christ's work remains two-fold' (p. 51). Jansen does not indulge in overstatement in seeking to establish this thesis. He does not make much of the fact that Calvin devotes 'only one short chapter to the three offices in his last edition of the *Institutes*' (p. 52). Nor does he under-estimate the place which the 'revelatory aspect of Christ's mission' (p. 58) occupies in Calvin's thought. He adduces copious evidence from Calvin's works and particularly from his commentaries and sermons to show that Calvin in his interpretation of Scripture as a whole does not utilize the formula of the triple office as he does that of the two-fold. Jansen is aware that there are numerous passages in the commentaries and sermons which speak of Christ as prophet and teacher, but his contention is that 'nowhere does Calvin make this teaching a separate messianic dignity alongside with the messianic offices of king and priest' (p. 61; cf. p. 99).

The present reviewer does not dispute the relevance of the evidence to which Jansen appeals in support of his thesis, nor is he prepared to challenge the contention that Calvin in his commentaries and sermons accords to the two-fold office the emphasis which the witness of Scripture and faithful exegesis demand. It is to be fully appreciated that Calvin was too sober and faithful an exegete to allow any formula which might be required in the systematization of the teaching of Scripture as a whole to impose itself upon the interpretation of particular passages. Hence, however much Calvin might be persuaded of Christ's prophetic office he will not artificially drag in that office and distort the teaching of particular texts by subjecting them to the mould of the triple formula. Every careful reader of Calvin's more dogmatic treatises as well as of his commentaries must recognize how essentially biblical and exegetical his method is. That he should not have imported the prophetic office of Christ where the text does not warrant it is symptomatic of what we find repeatedly in Calvin. He is conspicuously free of dogmatic constructions and inferences which are not drawn from biblical data and in this respect does not indulge in the dogmatic refinements and elaborations characteristic of many of his successors. The space devoted to the prophetic office in the *Institutes* reflects, it would appear, what, in Calvin's esteem, is the proportion of emphasis which the total witness of Scripture warrants and demands. We must not underestimate this proportion when we are assessing the place which the prophetic office occupied in the structure of his thought, and I am not able to subscribe to Jansen's thesis that 'the three-fold office is for Calvin a dogmatic, not an exegetical category' (p. 45).

When Jansen deals with the question of the place to be given to the prophetic office in systematic theology, he believes that 'the doctrine of the three offices is an embarrassment rather than help, while the double office illustrates and interprets the meaning of revelation' (p. 108). While it is true, as Jansen says, that when 'God discloses Himself, He claims us, and He condescends to us' and so the New Testament rules out 'a detached knowledge of God' (*id.*), yet why should the prophetic office of Christ be any embarrassment to this vital interest? The distinctiveness belonging to the prophetic function of Christ must always be appreciated, as Calvin himself was careful to observe (cf. *Inst.* II, xv, 1). Jesus was never a prophet who taught merely about redemption (cf. p. 109). In his prophetic capacity he always confronts us as the one who is himself the truth as well as the way and the life. Again, how could the prophetic office lend itself to 'a concept that makes revelation a precept rather than a person' (p. 119)? It is only when an unreal and truncated conception of Christ's prophetic office is entertained that any such liabilities should be contemplated.

Besides, the existential nature of revelation as deposited for us in the Scripture does not in the least eliminate or interfere with the necessity of teaching *about* redemption any more than does the revelation that comes to us in the person of Christ obviate revelation as precept also. We may be grateful indeed that Calvin the reformer did not give way to false antitheses. The truth surely is that our existential encounter with God in his revelation cannot be divorced from our knowledge of the truth about God. When we place our alleged encounter with God outside the context of the truth respecting him, we confuse a nebulous experience with existential encounter.

8

THE DOCTRINE OF ETERNAL PUNISHMENT. *By Harry Buis.* Philadelphia: Presbyterian and Reformed Publishing Company. 1957. xi, 148.

In view of the widespread scepticism respecting the doctrine of everlasting punishment it is with some misgiving that one takes up a volume with the above title. Within protestant circles we almost expect the sinister influence of a dialectic that vitiates the canons of biblical exegesis. The outstanding virtue of this study by Mr Buis is that it completely disappoints these fears. It is a candid forthright witness to the reality of hell. In the words of the author's preface, 'the thought of hell terrifies. It ought to make us all shudder. But it is a fact taught in God's Word' (p. ix). Buis adduces in considerable detail the evidence derived from the Scripture itself in support of the doctrine with which the book is concerned. This is not by any means superfluous. It is by such a method that we are apprised of the cumulative force of the evidence. He takes particular pains to show that the Saviour himself 'has more to say about hell than any other individual in the Bible' (p. 33).

Buis's survey of the history of thought on the subject is distinctly valuable, and he shows wide acquaintance with the literature. A large part of the volume is devoted to this survey (pp. 53–111). The treatment of universalism and conditional immortality (pp. 112–26), though brief, brings to bear upon these denials of the doctrine the most relevant considerations which expose their fallacy. In setting forth the teaching of Scripture Buis is insistent that the essence of the woe which constitutes eternal punishment is not the literalizing of the symbols which Scripture uses to portray the torments of hell but separation from God and the unmitigated execution of the wrath of God (cf. p. 130). It may be, however, that Buis has overstated the case when he suggests that the grotesque imagery used by many to portray the agonies of the lost has been responsible in so many cases for reaction against the doctrine. It is true that unbelief has taken occasion from such excesses to deny the truth which the exponents of the doctrine have sought to convey by graphic sensuous descriptions. But antipathy to the doctrine stems from something more deep-seated than recoil from certain fanciful attempts at portrayal, a fact of which Buis is fully aware. Sensuous torment and even grotesque descriptions of it fall far short of the misery of spirit which the infliction with God's wrath creates. The opposition to the doctrine of hell springs, in the last analysis, from rejection of the reality of this infliction. Furthermore, we must not underestimate the physical aspect of damnation. It is in the integrity of personal life that hell will be endured and the torment must therefore have its physical aspects. The Scripture always stresses the phenomenal as well as what we call the 'spiritual'.

The concept of *Sheol* in the Old Testament calls for a more discriminating treatment than has been given in Buis's volume. Suffice it to suggest that the meaning 'the grave', not in the sense of 'a grave' but in the semi-abstract or more general sense in which the expression is used in Scripture and in our modern usage, deserves more consideration. This sense suits numberless instances in the Old Testament and when applied to the interpretation of these passages provides a different perspective from that frequently espoused by even conservative scholars. There are very good reasons for contending that this is the meaning in Psalm 16:10 (cf. Acts 2:27, 31).

The church lies under profound debt to Mr Buis for this defence of a much neglected theme. May this volume be instrumental in arousing the church to the gravity of the issues with which this book confronts us. And may Mr Buis's pen not be idle in the days to come.

9

A COMMENTARY ON THE EPISTLE TO THE ROMANS (Harper's New Testament Commentaries). *By C. K. Barrett.* New York: Harper and Brothers, 1957. viii, 294.

This is not a commentary in which we shall find detailed exegesis of each phrase, clause, and verse in the epistle to the Romans. Neither is it one that the layman may be expected to use. In fact it is not a commentary that could be recommended to the layman. For one thing, the translation which Barrett provides takes considerable liberty with Paul's text and a layman not conversant with the Greek would be unable readily to subject Barrett's interpretive translations to the scrutiny that is necessary.

Barrett's work, however, is a scholarly contribution to the exegesis of Romans. At numerous points there are manifest the insights of an accomplished exegete and many of the conclusions on difficult points of interpretation are supported by scholarly research and discrimination.

It is gratifying to the present reviewer that Barrett is quite decisive in taking ὁρισθέντος in Rom. 1:4 in the sense 'appointed'. Recognizing that the rendering 'declared' has the advantage of avoiding the charge of adoptionism that can be brought against 'appointed', yet he concludes that 'there is little else to be said for it. Hellenistic evidence and New Testament usage both favour "appointed" (e.g. Acts 10:42; 17:31)' (p. 19). In this same connection the words 'in power' may 'most plausibly' be understood adjectivally as qualifying 'Son of God' and 'would not exclude his having previously been Son of God, though without the manifestation of power which took place in the resurrection' (p. 20).

With reference to the wrath of God (Rom. 1:18), Barrett's conclusion is surely correct that 'wrath is God's personal (though never malicious or, in a bad sense, emotional) reaction against sin' (p. 33), and he could well have been more decisive in rejecting the view that 'Paul thought of the divine wrath in impersonal terms' (*id.*) as he might also have reflected on the inadequacy of construing God's wrath in terms simply of his will to punish.

On the difficult question of the import of προεχόμεθα (Rom. 3:9) the view that Barrett considers most in harmony with Paul's thought is as follows: 'Well, then, since there is advantage in being a Jew (vv. 1 f.), do we Jews excel? Not at all, for we have charged both Jews and Greeks. . . .' (p. 68).

On the question of δικαιόω the forensic force is maintained. 'The verb means to "count, or treat as, righteous". Justification means that God treats sinful men as if they were of complete and unstained virtue'. While admitting that the verb means 'to make righteous', yet the word 'righteous' 'does not mean "virtuous", but "right", "clear", "acquitted" in God's court'. And so he concludes that justification 'far from being a legal fiction . . . is a creative act in the field of divine-human relations' (pp. 75 f., cf. pp. 50, 89).

On the question of the correct reading in Rom. 5:1 Barrett shows sane judgment. He admits that 'the textual support for "let us have" is so strong that a measure of doubt will always remain'. But he properly pleads in favour of the reading 'we have' that 'the context is not hortatory, but indicative', that Paul 'is not urging his readers to do and be what as Christians they ought to do and be, but reminding them of the facts on which all their doing and being rest', and that the indicative is therefore theologically more appropriate (p. 102).

Again Barrett's good judgment appears when in Rom. 5:18 he renders δικαίωμα as 'act of righteousness' rather than as 'justification', and he admirably sums up the reasons for this conclusion (p. 116).

The difficulty which commentators have encountered in the application which Paul makes in Rom. 7:4 of the analogy of marriage and the death of the husband (Rom. 7:1-3) is resolved very briefly and, in this reviewer's judgment, correctly when Barrett says: 'In Christian life, the law does not die (as analogy would require); Christ dies, and by faith Christians die with him. All Paul needs for his purpose is a death' (p. 136). This is in agreement with the correct rendering and interpretation of verse 6 that 'we died to that by which we were held fast'.

The difficulties inherent in the questions of Rom. 10:6, 7 – 'Who shall ascend into heaven?' and 'Who shall descend into the abyss?' – are taken as tantamount to a denial of the incarnation and resurrection respectively. And surely this is the view which the context would suggest and has the most to commend it.

With respect to the hardening of Rom. 11:7, he says that 'it is incorrect to stress the use of the passive voice . . . as if Paul were unwilling to commit himself to the view that God himself had hardened men . . . there is no doubt who is the subject of the active verb in the next verse' (p. 210). Yet he rightly notes that the hardening must not be dissociated from the disobedience – they are concurrent processes. This is but a reminder that hardening as a judicial infliction must always presuppose desert. Only we must also remember that all deserve this hardening, and differentiation in the remnant is altogether of grace.

These are examples of Barrett's exegetical competence and they are sufficient to show that any one who henceforth undertakes the exegesis of Romans can ill afford to neglect this contribution to its interpretation. Much more could have been adduced to support this evaluation of Barrett's work. It is to be regretted, therefore, that this evaluation cannot remain unqualified. For there are also the debits, and some of these are on pivotal questions.

It is irritating, to say the least, that Barrett can so readily indulge in such strictures as the following with respect to Paul's terms and constructions. He speaks of Paul's words as 'very awkwardly co-ordinated' (p. 46), of 'the clumsiness of the second part' of Rom. 5:17 (p. 115), and of 'the string of genitives' in Rom. 8:21 as 'inelegant' (p. 166). Paul's expressions often cause difficulty for us. But to call them awkward, or clumsy, or inelegant betrays a strange insensitivity to their eloquence. The strings of genitives which we find in Paul are magnificent examples of compact utterance expressive of the richness and strength of his thought and Rom. 8:21 is no exception. Besides, Barrett's interpretation of $\kappa\alpha\theta'$ $\dot{\upsilon}\pi o\mu o\nu\dot{\eta}\nu$ $\check{\epsilon}\rho\gamma o\upsilon\dot{\alpha}\gamma\alpha\theta o\hat{\upsilon}$ in Rom. 2:7 is surely far off the mark. He renders it 'with patient endurance look beyond their own well-doing'. One cannot see how this rendering 'is confirmed both by the words that follow, and by the parallel sentence in the next verse' (p. 46). The emphasis in the context upon works as the criterion of God's judgment (cf. v. 6) indicates that the phrase in question points to constancy or perseverance in well-doing as a characteristic of those whose aspirations are toward glory, honour, and incorruption.

With reference to $\dot{\epsilon}\rho\iota\theta\epsilon\dot{\iota}\alpha$ in Rom. 2:8, Barrett is dogmatic that it is derived from $\check{\epsilon}\rho\iota\theta o s$, a hireling, and $\dot{\epsilon}\rho\iota\theta\epsilon\dot{\upsilon}\omega$, to act as a hireling, and therefore means 'the activity, or characteristics, or mind, of a hireling' (p. 47). He appeals to the other Pauline passages (2 Cor. 12:20; Gal. 5:20; Phil. 1:17; 2:3) and makes much of the argument that in two of these passages 'the word occurs in lists along with $\check{\epsilon}\rho\iota s$, and if the familiar translation "faction" is employed, Paul is made to repeat himself' (*id.*). Several scholars have maintained this view and it is true that the sense of 'selfish ambition' is an appropriate characterization of the persons concerned. But the case for this meaning is not conclusive. In Phil. 1:17 the sense is surely close to that of $\check{\epsilon}\rho\iota s$ in verse 15. And the fact that in lists of vices both terms occur is not a decisive argument for sharp differentiation of meaning. In Paul's lists of vices terms appear which show only a slight shade of difference. And the difference between $\check{\epsilon}\rho\iota s$ and $\dot{\epsilon}\rho\iota\theta\epsilon\dot{\iota}\alpha$ may be that between 'strife' and 'faction'.

Barrett's interpretation of the term 'propitiation' in Rom. 3:25 illustrates the tenacity with which exegetes and theologians hold on to a notion that is the heritage of the liberal tradition, namely, that propitiation is to be equated with expiation and thus the idea of propitiation, strictly understood as the propitiation of the wrath of God, is eliminated from the doctrine of the atonement. Orthodox theology has always detected the fallacy of this contention. But, in view of the thorough and exacting studies of Leon Morris and Roger Nicole in more recent times, scholars should recognize that the contention has been effectively exploded. Barrett's argument is singularly lacking in relevance when he says: 'The common Greek meaning "to propitiate" becomes practically impossible when, as sometimes happens, God is the subject of the verb. God cannot be said to propitiate man' (p. 77). Who would maintain that in Rom. 3:25 (cf. Heb. 2:17; 1 John 2:2; 4:10) the propitiation has man as its object?

No passage in Paul's epistle places the exegete under greater demands than 5:12–19. And pivotal in the interpretation of the passage is the appreciation of the place which the one trespass of Adam occupies in the universality of sin, condemnation, and death and also of the relation which this one trespass sustains to the whole race. After the pattern of so many present-day exegetes, Barrett here completely fails. In dealing with what, on all accounts, is the crucial clause (Rom. 5:12b), he says: 'That is, all men sin (cf. iii. 23), and all men die because they sin' (p. 111). Whatever we may think of Paul's teaching, exegesis requires that 'all sinned' of verse 12 be identified with the one trespass of Adam (vv. 15, 16, 17, 18) and the only resolution is that the sin of Adam was also the sin of all. Barrett's exposition makes clear that this is not what 'all sinned' in verse 12 is taken to mean.

There is nothing more surprising in Barrett's book than his remarks on the expression 'the likeness of sinful flesh' in Rom. 8:3. His translation is clearly defective and misleading – 'in the form of flesh which had passed under sin's rule'. After stating what is good exegesis of Paul's formula that 'the incarnation was perfectly real, but only *in the likeness* of "flesh of sin"', so that he remained sinless', he proceeds: 'It is doubtful, however, whether this is what Paul means. . . . We are probably justified . . . in deducing that Christ took precisely the same fallen nature that we ourselves have, and that he remained sinless because he constantly overcame a proclivity to sin' (p. 156). Both the completely unwarranted suggestion that our Lord's human nature was sinful and the failure to discern the force of Paul's carefully chosen terms betray a lack of sensitivity that is exegetically unpardonable.

No commentary of the proportions that Barrett's represents could be expected to deal with every verse in detail. Brevity is frequently a virtue. Barrett shows much of that virtue. But when 'whom he foreknew, he also foreordained' (Rom. 8:29) is disposed of with only a brief paragraph and one in which little is said pertinent to the far-reaching questions involved, disappointment befalls the reader. In this same connection to say, in reference to Rom. 9:21, that 'the doctrine of apparent double predestination implies

not a crude numerical division within the human race but a profound definition of God and of his purpose for men in terms of mercy' (p. 188) is to evade
the implications of Paul's teaching in this context. Certainly we have here in
Paul 'profound' reflection on God's sovereignty but it is sovereignty related
to the destinies of *men* distributively considered and Barrett's quotation from
Barth (p. 171) does not remedy the vacuity at this point. Romans 8:29a provides us with what Paul conceives to be the ultimate source of the whole
process of salvation and a construction of soteriology which is not oriented
to the differentiation which this verse supplies is not Pauline.

10

CHRIST IN OUR PLACE. THE SUBSTITUTIONARY CHARACTER OF CALVIN'S DOCTRINE
OF RECONCILIATION. *By Paul van Buren.* Grand Rapids: Wm. B. Eerdmans
Publishing Company. 1957. xiii, 152.

Since this year marks the four hundred and fiftieth anniversary of Calvin's
birth and the four hundredth of the publication of the definitive edition of
the *Institutes,* much attention is being given to Calvin's theology as well as
to other phases of his life and work. Though van Buren's work was first
published in 1957, it is a worthy contribution to the library of studies associated with this anniversary occasion. No topic in Calvin's theology is more
central than that dealt with in *Christ in Our Place.* Van Buren has focused
our thought on what is basic in Calvin's treatment of this cardinal theme and
he has compelled us to examine anew not only Calvin's exposition but also
the questions of paramount concern in our understanding of the mystery of
godliness.

Van Buren has taken pains to provide us all along the line with a well-
documented transcript of Calvin's own thought. The book is not burdened
with the discussion of the views of others respecting Calvin. He interjects
questions at various points and suggests lines of thought whereby Calvin's
formulations might, in certain particulars, be corrected or expanded. The
work is characterized by commendable modesty and caution and betrays a
concern to let Calvin speak for himself. There is also evident a deep sympathy
with the theology the author seeks to expound.

Every aspect with which van Buren deals is important in assessing Calvin's
teaching on the substitutionary character of reconciliation. There are four
chapters, however, which, in the esteem of the present writer, deserve
special mention. They are those on 'The Obedience of Christ' (pp. 27–39),

'Sustained our Punishment' (pp. 51–80), 'The Means of Incorporation' (pp. 95–106), and 'The Consequence of Incorporation' (pp. 107–24). In these chapters are brought to the forefront the three features of Calvin's soteriology which must, on all accounts, be regarded as pivotal – the voluntary high priestly activity of Christ, the substitutionary character of his sacrifice, and union with Christ as that which binds us to all the virtue that resides in him as redeemer. In reference to union with Christ it is well to be reminded, as Calvin and van Buren remind us, that Christ in his redemptive offices, work, and ministry may never be conceived of apart from his people nor his people apart from him (cf. pp. 95 f.). Since all saving blessing is enjoyed in union with Christ, we may never dissociate any gift of salvation from all the others. This is well illustrated in the indissoluble connection between justification and sanctification. ' "We cannot be justified freely through faith alone without at the same time living holily. For these free gifts are connected, as if by an indissoluble bond, so that he who attempts to sever them does in a manner tear Christ in pieces" ' (p. 108).

There are several points at which this reviewer is compelled to dissent from van Buren's findings. One of these is closely related to that which he has commendably emphasized, namely, union with Christ. It is not altogether surprising that van Buren should have interpreted Calvin as giving to the atonement a universal reference. Calvin frequently uses universalistic expressions when referring to the sufferings and death of Christ, as, for example, that Christ 'suffered for the sins of the whole world' (*Comm. ad* Rom. 5:18) and that 'many' sometimes denotes 'all' (cf. *Comm. ad* Isa. 53:12; Mark 14:24). Van Buren has quoted and cited copious evidence of this type of expression. Hence Calvin is interpreted as teaching universal atonement. 'The work of Christ', van Buren says, 'is for all men, therefore, and if some will not accept it, that is their fault, and in no way due to any inadequacy in what Christ has done' (pp. 77 f.). 'Christ died for all in the place of all and is offered to all. On that there is no compromise' (p. 103). And so he insists that Calvin did not resolve the tension between the universal offer of salvation and the fact that faith is not common to all 'by retreating to a position of limited atonement' (*id.*; cf. p. 50).

This contention on van Buren's part calls for a few observations.

First of all, it cannot be contested that Calvin taught the free and full offer of salvation to all without distinction and that, if many to whom the gospel is offered do not accept it, this is not due to any inadequacy in the work of Christ. They perish by their own fault. But the universal offer is not tantamount to universal atonement – Calvin's teaching respecting the offer of salvation must not be loaded with that inference.

Secondly, Calvin does not suppress the hard and fast line of distinction between the elect and the reprobate. Although it is true, as van Buren says, there is 'for Calvin a complete suspension of judgment' (p. 103), as far as we are concerned, respecting those embraced in the decree of reprobation, yet he never leaves out of account the distinction as it pertains to God's counsel and judgment. It is sufficient to be reminded of his tract *The Eternal Predestination of God* and his commentary on Romans 9 in this connection.

Thirdly, Calvin does expressly reflect on the limited reference of the atonement. In his comments on 1 John 2:2, in reference to the clause 'and not for ours only', he says: 'He added this for the sake of amplifying, in order that the faithful might certainly be assured, that the expiation made by Christ extends to all the faithful who embrace the gospel by faith. Here a question may be raised how the sins of the whole world have been expiated. I pass by the dotages of the fanatics who, under this pretext, admit all the reprobate and therefore Satan himself to salvation. Such an extravagance is not worthy of refutation. Those who wished to avoid this absurdity have said that Christ suffered sufficiently for the whole world but efficiently for the elect only. This solution has commonly obtained in the schools. Though I confess that what has been said is true, yet I deny that it suits this passage. For the design of John was no other than to make this benefit common to the whole church (*toti ecclesiae*). Therefore it does not include all the reprobate but designates those who would believe as well as those who were scattered through various parts of the world. For then the grace of Christ is truly made evident, as is meet, when it is proclaimed to be the only salvation of the world.' This is an explicit statement to the effect that the reprobate are not included in the propitiation and that 'the whole world' refers to all throughout the world who are the partakers of salvation without distinction of race, or clime, or time. Confirmation is derived from Calvin's comments on 'who wills all men to be saved' and 'a ransom for all' in 1 Timothy 2:4, 6. He says: 'Hence we see the childish folly of those who represent this passage to be opposed to predestination. "If God," say they, "wishes all men indiscriminately to be saved, it is false that some are predestinated by his eternal counsel to salvation, and others to perdition." They might have had some ground for saying this, if Paul were speaking here about individual men (*singulis hominibus*); although even then a solution would not have been wanting; for, although the will of God ought not to be judged from his secret decrees, when he reveals it to us by outward signs, yet it does not therefore follow that he has not secretly determined what he wills to do to each individual man. But I pass over that subject because it has nothing to do with this passage. For the apostle simply means that there is no people or rank in the world that is excluded from salvation, because God wills that the gospel should be proclaimed to all without exception' (*ad* 1 Tim. 2:4). 'The universal term ought always to be referred to races of men, not to persons; as if he had said, not only Jews, but Gentiles also, not only common people, but princes also, were redeemed by the death of Christ' (*ad* I Tim. 2:5; cf. also *ad* I Tim. 2:6 and *The Eternal Predestination of God*, E. T., London, 1927, pp. 105 f.). Calvin is not 'holding back from the consequences of his own exegesis' at this point, as van Buren alleges (p. 19). He is simply recognizing what every exegete must reckon with, that a universal term does not always imply distributive universalism. It is surely significant that if there are any texts which offered Calvin the opportunity to set forth the doctrine of universal atonement they are I John 2:2; I Timothy 2:4, 6. But it is in connection with these passages that he is careful to distinguish between distributive universalism and ethnic universalism.

Fourthly, since Calvin is explicit at these points on the distinction between individuals distributively considered and individuals without distinction of race or class, we are not only justified but required to reckon with that distinction in numerous other passages where, in connection with the vicarious sacrifice of Christ, he uses universal terms. We must also bear in mind that Calvin's jealousy for the proclamation of the gospel of reconciliation to all without exception is not in the least incompatible with his exclusion of the reprobate from the scope of the expiation wrought by Christ. Calvin is indeed aware of the tension that arises for us when we consider that the gospel is to be proclaimed to all without exception and yet that God has secretly predestinated the reprobate to death. But this tension is not that between universal atonement and the decree of reprobation. It is the tension between the secret will of purpose and the proclaimed will for us, a tension with which Calvin deals at great length at various places.

Hence we must submit that in dealing with Calvin's view of the extent of the atonement van Buren has not taken into account some of the most relevant evidence and that all-important considerations have been overlooked. If union with Christ plays so important a rôle in Calvin's soteriology, we may not forget that this means election in Christ before the foundation of the world. Election is fundamental in Calvin's thinking, and election implies differentiation at the fountain of the whole process of salvation. The evidence indicates that Calvin did not discount this differentiation at the point of Christ's expiatory offering. And the upshot appears to be that, if we do not appreciate the orientation afforded by predestination to life, we are not in a position to interpret correctly Calvin's view of substitutionary sacrifice. When the orbit defined by election is perceived, then there can be no place for making Christ in his redemptive work 'only the *possibility* of reconciliation' (p. 19) or of his 'having gained only the possibility of our salvation' (p. 33). In this connection one cannot but suspect the influence of dialectic patterns of thought in the questions van Buren asks on page 32 where faith is construed as the acceptance of God's antecedent 'righteous decision'.

Van Buren has rightly shown that in Calvin's thought 'satisfaction cannot imply any opposition between Father and Son', that in its execution the Father was not a mere spectator but the author of salvation (p. 74). And he has not suppressed the implication that 'God poured out His wrath on His Son', an exercise of wrath 'based on His love for us' and 'in no way in conflict with the Father's love for the Son' (p. 59). But it is not apparent that van Buren has sufficiently recognized what, in Calvin's esteem, was the Godward reference of the propitiation and reconciliation when he says merely that 'there is a sense in which Calvin is able to speak of God as the object of reconciliation' and that 'we are the object of reconciliation, not God' (p. 7). It is not difficult to discover in Calvin's exposition the centrality of the wrath and disfavour of God. One quotation will suffice to show this. 'Hence with regard to us, we are always enemies, until the death of Christ interposes in order to propitiate God. And this twofold aspect of things ought to be noticed; for we do not know the gratuitous mercy of God otherwise than as it appears from this – that he spared not his only-begotten Son; for he loved us at a time when there was discord between him and us: nor can we sufficiently understand the benefit brought to us by the death of Christ, except this be the beginning of our reconciliation with God, that we are persuaded that it is by the expiation that has been made, that he, who was before justly angry with us, is now propitious to us. Since then our reception into favour is ascribed to the death of Christ, the meaning is, that guilt is taken away, to which we should be otherwise exposed' (*Comm. ad* Rom. 5:10; E. T., Grand Rapids, 1947).

11

BIBLICAL FOUNDATIONS. *By B. B. Warfield.* Grand Rapids: Wm. B. Eerdmans Publishing Company. 1958. 350.

In Great Britain the published writings of B. B. Warfield are not so readily available as they are in this country. The ten volumes, published by the Oxford University Press from 1927 to 1932, were issued by the American Branch and consequently were not brought to the attention of British readers as they would have been if published in England. The present selection of articles, nine in number, was first published in Great Britain in 1958. The promoters of this publication are to be congratulated on the selection they have made. The articles are all thoroughly representative of Warfield's masterful pen. And for those who do not have access to the ten volumes published by the Oxford University Press or to the volumes being more recently published in this country by The Presbyterian and Reformed Publishing Company the present volume should prove a most valuable 'introduction to the works of the greatest exponent, expounder and defender of the classic Reformed faith in the 20th century' (p. 10).

D. Martyn Lloyd-Jones, from whom I have just quoted, says properly in his 'Introduction': 'No theological writings are so intellectually satisfying and so strengthening to faith as those of Warfield. He shirks no issue and evades no problems and never stoops to the use of subterfuge. One is impressed by his honesty and integrity as much as by his profound scholarship and learning' (p. 9).

In these days when the infallibility of Scripture is so much under attack and when even evangelicals are sometimes unready to contend for this doctrine, it is well to come to grips with the biblical evidence with which Warfield deals in 'The Biblical Idea of Inspiration' (Chapter II). Nothing that Warfield ever wrote excels his treatment of 'Predestination', reproduced in this volume as Chapter VIII. 'The Supernatural Birth of Jesus' (Chapter IV) is a brief article and perhaps not as well known as some of his major articles. But it is one of his most significant contributions because it deals with the *theological* importance of the virgin birth. 'It cannot be denied', Warfield says, 'that the supernatural birth of Jesus enters constitutively into the substance of that system which is taught in the New Testament as Christianity – that it is the expression of its supernaturalism, the safeguard of its doctrine of incarnation, the condition of its doctrine of redemption' (p. 127). This chapter, therefore, along with the three which follow on 'The Person of Christ', 'Christ our Sacrifice', and 'The New Testament Terminology of Redemption' deal with what is central in the Christian faith, namely, the person and work of Christ.

It will illustrate the precision and eloquence of Warfield's writing to give a quotation well worthy of memorization by every Christian. It is from the chapter on 'Faith'. 'The *saving power* of faith resides thus not in itself, but in the Almighty Saviour on whom it rests. It is never on account of its formal nature as a psychic act that faith is conceived in Scripture to be saving. . . . It is not faith that saves, but faith in Jesus Christ. . . . It is not, strictly speaking, even faith in Christ that saves, but Christ that saves through faith' (pp. 330 f.). It is with such definitions as these, unexcelled for competence and compactness, that Warfield's works abound.

12

CHRIST AND ADAM. MAN AND HUMANITY IN ROMANS 5. *By Karl Barth.* New York: Harper & Brothers. 1957. 96.

This is a translation by R. A. Smail of Karl Barth's *Christus und Adam nach Röm. 5* published in 1952 as Heft 35 of *Theologische Studien.* The translation had already appeared in 1956 as *Occasional Papers No. 5* of the *Scottish Journal of Theology.* The present form is more attractive and slight changes have been introduced intended to assist the English reader. The most significant feature of this edition of the translation is the introduction by Wilhelm Pauck in which he summarizes Barth's view of man as found in the *Church Dogmatics.*

The genius of Karl Barth places great demands upon anyone who ventures to review his writings. This brief treatise is no exception. Barth's interpretation of Romans 5 is, as Pauck says, 'an example of Barth's distinctive exegetical method' (p. 6) and it has direct lines of connection with what has come to be known as Barth's theology. An adequate examination would take us, therefore, far beyond Romans 5 and its interpretation as given by Barth. Since the reviewer is compelled to disagree with Barth at pivotal points of his interpretation, it is better to concentrate on these questions rather than to go further afield in evaluation of Barth's theology or in appraisal of Barth himself as a theological genius.

At the outset Barth properly recognizes that the leading theme of the first part of Romans is the revelation of the righteousness of God. This he defines as 'the final righteous decision of God, which, for everyone who acknowledges it in faith, is the power of God unto salvation' (p. 20). This definition in terms of righteous decision (Rechtsentscheidung) is maintained throughout and is determinative of what Barth conceives the blood of Christ to have wrought and justification to be. The definition indicates that justification, in Barth's esteem, is something that occurs in the judgment of God prior to the event of faith. For faith is simply the acknowledgment or grasp of it; by faith it becomes known to believers. 'In believing, they are only conforming to the decision about them that has already been made in Him (Christ)' (p. 24). And that this is applied to justification is made abundantly clear by the following: 'In sovereign anticipation of our faith God has justified us through the sacrificial blood of Christ' (p. 22).

There are at least two respects in which this construction fails to represent Paul's teaching. According to Paul we are justified *by faith* and to apply the terms for justification without discrimination to anything else than to that which is correlative with faith and therefore coincident with it is to deviate radically from the sustained emphasis of the apostle. It is true that there is the once-for-all accomplishment in the blood of Christ which is antecedent to faith. Paul calls it the propitiation, the reconciliation, and redemption. But the all but uniform, if not uniform, use of the term 'justification' and its equivalents is to designate that judgment of God of which faith is the instrument. This act of faith is not directed to the fact that we have been justified but is directed to Christ in order that we may be justified (cf. Gal. 2:16). It is not to be assumed that in the Epistle to the Romans the terms δικαιοσύνη, δικαίωσις, δικαίωμα are used synonymously, as Barth apparently assumes (cf. p. 20). In 5:16 δικαίωμα and in 5:18 δικαίωσις refer to God's justifying act. But exegesis neither requires nor allows identification of this act with the δικαιοσύνη θεοῦ of 1:17; 3:21, 22; 10:3. The latter is the justifying righteousness but is to be distinguished from the justifying act. Secondly, universalism not only in respect of atonement but also of justification is implicit in Barth's construction. Integral to his interpretation of the relation that Christ sustains to Adam is the position that Christ must sustain to mankind as inclusive a relation as Adam. The implications of this will appear later.

It is with Romans 5:12–21 and the parallel between Adam and Christ that Barth is mainly concerned. It should be understood that for Barth Adam is not to be regarded as a single historical personage who as such at the beginning of human history committed a particular sin which is unique in its relationships and effects as the one trespass in which all other members of the race are involved and are therefore related to it as to no other sin. Barth is explicit to the effect that Adam is the typical man and that other men share in his sin because his sin is *repeated* in them and they sin as Adam did. The sins of all other men 'are anticipated' in the sin of Adam and 'the lives of all other men after Adam have only been the repetition and variation of his life, of his beginning and his end, of his sin and his death' (p. 29). 'In v. 12, Paul already has made it clear that "all have sinned", that is to say, that all have repeated Adam's sinful act' (p. 62). Though, then, for Barth Adam is the representative man and though in that sense he can speak of him as the 'responsible representative' of mankind, yet it is not because he accepts the historicity of Genesis 2 and 3 or regards Adam's sin in Eden as a unique sin by reason of its implications and relations, but simply because Adam's sin is repeated and Adam in his sin and death, as *primus inter pares*, is the representative man (cf. pp. 92 f.). 'We are what Adam was and so are all our fellow men. And the one Adam is what we and all men are. Man is at once an individual and only an individual, and, at the same time, without in any way losing his individuality, he is the responsible representative of all men' (pp. 90 f.). Thus the *unique* individuality of Adam and the speciality of his sin by reason of the absolutely distinctive relations which he sustained to all other

men and the distinguishing involvement of other men in his sin are eliminated. We are all Adam.

It cannot be too plainly said that if we adopt this construction of Romans
5:12–19 we must abandon exegesis. If Paul emphasizes one thing it is that
by the one trespass of the one man Adam the many were accounted sinners
and death came to exercise its lordship over all. Paul's sustained emphasis
upon the one trespass and the one man, the one trespass of the one, is just the
very opposite of the idea of *repetition* upon which Barth's construction
hinges. The only exegesis that is compatible with Paul's reiterated emphasis
upon the one trespass is the solidarity of all men in that one trespass in a way
that cannot be equated with the interinvolvements in sin which appear in
our other solidaric relationships. It is this unique character of Adam and this
unique involvement in his trespass that Barth eliminates. For Barth, as he
explains also in his *Church Dogmatics*, it is a case of 'the individual and the
many, each with his own responsibility, each with his own particular form
of pride, each in his own fall, each in his own specific and distinctive way'
(IV, 1, E.T., p. 504).

The most distinctive feature of Barth's interpretation appears in connection
with his view of the identity of ordering principle (Ordnung) underlying the
analogy instituted between Adam and Christ. Since Adam is the *type* of him
who was to come, Barth is insistent that the relationship between Adam and
all of us had not only been ordered so as to correspond to the relationship
between Christ and us, but the latter is the primary anthropological truth
and ordering principle so that 'man's essential and original nature is to be
found, therefore, not in Adam but in Christ. . . . Adam can therefore be
interpreted only in the light of Christ and not the other way round' (p. 29).
Thus 'human existence, as constituted by our relationship with Adam . . .
has no independent reality, status, or importance of its own' and the relationship between Adam and us is 'the relationship that exists originally and
essentially between Christ and us' (p. 30). With respect to this construction
of the analogy and of the ordering principle on which the analogy is based
and in view of the commanding place it occupies in Barth's anthropology as well as soteriology, it is necessary to focus considerable attention
upon it.

(1) As indicated above, this implies that the relation of Christ to men is as
inclusive as the relation of Adam to men and therefore the 'righteous
decision' passes upon all men just as the condemnation passed upon all
through Adam. 'In the existence of the One, there in Christ, the result for
all men is the lordship of grace exercised in the divine righteous decision
and the promise of eternal life' (p. 32). Not only do Barth's repeated expressions in such universal terms (cf. pp. 26, 31, 32, 46, 48, 49, 51, 53, 72, 84, 88,
89) imply this universality, but the priority posited for Christ's relationship

to men, without which the Adamic relationship has no validity or meaning, demands this universal relationship of Christ to man in respect of that which he most characteristically is as representative and revealer (cf. p. 31). And unless exegesis of Paul is evacuated completely at the most vital point this means that all men without exception must be ultimately the beneficiaries of that grace which reigns through righteousness unto eternal life (5:21). Barth cannot hold to universalism at one point in the relationship to Christ without carrying out the implications for the ultimate salvation of all men. For if there is distributive universalism in the apodoses of verses 18 and 19, as Barth's interpretation demands, there must also be in the apodosis of verse 21, and the reign of grace through righteousness unto eternal life must embrace all men without exception.

(2) It cannot be questioned that Adam is the type of Christ (v. 14). There is undoubtedly a similarity of relationship and there is no objection to speaking of the identity of ordering principle. Our relation to Adam in respect of sin, condemnation, and death follows the pattern of our relation to Christ in respect of righteousness, justification, and life. And that it was designed of God to be thus we must recognize. Soteriology is built upon the same kind of relationship as that which is exemplified in our sin and loss. And the ordering principle by which sin, condemnation, and death came to lord it over mankind required that the ordering principle of saving righteousness be of the same kind of pattern. But Paul's teaching in this passage does not establish the primacy or priority which Barth claims for the relationship to Christ. Adam could be the type of Christ, as Paul says, without drawing all the inferences which Barth elicits from this relationship. All that could feasibly be derived from the typological datum mentioned in verse 14 and applied expressly in the succeeding verses is simply that there is an analogy between our relation to Adam in the realm of sin and death and our relation to Christ in the realm of righteousness and life. In the absence of additional data it is an importation adopted on our own responsibility to infer more. And Paul's own teaching in 1 Corinthians 15:45–49 to the effect that Adam was the first man and Christ the second and last Adam, teaching than which nothing is more pertinent to the subject at hand, should at least caution us against a construction in terms of priority and primacy that runs counter to Paul's own express formula in this latter passage. Barth's own treatment of 1 Corinthians 15:45–49 in no way relieves the discrepancy between Paul and Barth. It is true enough that according to Paul's teaching 'Christ is above, Adam is beneath. Adam is true man only because he is below and not above' (p. 34). But it does not help Barth in dealing with the order which Paul establishes in regard to Adam as the first and Christ as the second and last to say that Adam's 'claim to be the "first man" and the head of humanity like Christ is only apparent' (*id.*). Besides, the question is not that of Adam's

claim to be our head and to make us members in his body' (*id.*) but the relationship in respect of order set forth in Paul's statements.

(3) Barth's argument based on the πολλῷ μᾶλλον of verses 15 and 17 illustrates the exegetical method by which he supports his thesis. In Romans 5:9, 10 this same expression occurs in Paul's *a fortiori* argument from reconciliation to the eschatological salvation. And Barth rightly exegetes this to mean that 'it is because we are sure that Christ achieved our reconciliation that we can be "so much more" sure that He has achieved our salvation as well' (p. 45). The same line of thought he applies to the πολλῷ μᾶλλον in verses 15 and 17 and concludes that 'the same Jesus Christ is already involved in the truth in Adam', that 'Jesus Christ suffered and died for the sin of Adam and the sin of all men' and that by the cross 'Adam and all men are reconciled and pardoned' (pp. 47 f.; cf. pp. 43–9). Now it is quite plain that the πολλῷ μᾶλλον of verses 9 and 10 implies that *because* we are reconciled we shall all the more be finally saved – the latter is a necessity arising from the former. But does it therefore follow that πολλῷ μᾶλλον in verses 15 and 17 must have the same effect and establish the same kind of causal relationship between the two elements in the comparison? Does verse 15 mean that, *because* by the trespass of the one the many died, *therefore* the grace of God will abound unto the many? Or verse 17 that *because* death reigned by the trespass of the one *therefore* many will reign in life through Jesus Christ? At the outset it would be preposterous to insist that πολλῷ μᾶλλον must always carry with it the same effect as it has in verses 9 and 10. Language is not so stereotyped as to demand that canon, and particularly is it not so in Paul's usage. What Paul is surely emphasizing in these verses (15, 17) is the superabundance of grace. There is indeed the similitude of *modus operandi*, but the commanding thought is the superabundance of God's judgment of grace in contrast with and in the negation of his condemnatory judgment. It is the unexampled plenitude of grace in its sovereign newness and unexpectedness that the πολλῷ μᾶλλον expresses in each case and, so far from there being either need or warrant for the inferential *a fortiori* of verses 9 and 10, the thought is totally diverse. Paul is saying in effect: from the one trespass of Adam the judgment of God is relentless; it issues in the lordship of death. But how much more efficacious and therefore relentless is the reign of grace! In other words, the πολλῷ μᾶλλον of verses 9 and 10 is the necessity arising from the one manifestation of grace to its fruition in another; if God has done the greater he will surely carry it to its issue in that which is less. But in the πολλῷ μᾶλλον of verses 15 and 17 we can find no such sequence. It is the superabundant freeness and graciousness of God's grace *in contrast* with the processes of punitive judgment. And it is just the relentless logic with which judgment unto death proceeds from *one* trespass that sets off the magnitude and efficacy of grace as brought to bear upon numberless tres-

passes unto pardon, justification, and life. The kind of connection which Barth finds is not only arbitrary but also extraneous and alien to the emphasis of the passage.

There are several other points at which adverse criticism might be offered. But those dealt with will illustrate how divergent from Paul's teaching we deem Barth's interpretation to be. There is much to learn from Barth's treatment and much to challenge renewed and careful examination of this passage. It is also to be appreciated how central for anthropology and soteriology Barth regards this passage to be. But appreciative appraisal must never be allowed to suppress the adverse criticism which divergence from sound exegesis demands.

13

THE BIBLICAL BASIS FOR INFANT BAPTISM. CHILDREN IN GOD'S COVENANT PROMISES. *By Dwight Hervey Small.* Westwood, New Jersey: Fleming H. Revell Company. 1959. 191.

'It cannot be emphasized too strongly that it is unwarrantable to lay down as a principle of Scriptural interpretation that whenever there is no express and explicit injunction requiring a duty to be performed, there is therefore no duty commanded. We have no prerogative to limit God as to the form in which He may be pleased to make known His will in His Word' (p. 9). It is failure to take due account of what is involved in this statement that renders so many immune to the force of the evidence in support of the ordinance of infant baptism. And there is not much hope of making headway with the convinced antipaedobaptist until the validity of this principle in the interpretation and application of Scripture is recognized. There is, however, no subject in Christian theology that illustrates more effectively the propriety and necessity of this principle than the argument for infant baptism. It is the virtue of this book that it establishes infant baptism as a divine institution not from isolated, piecemeal data but from the organism of revelation as a whole. The author shows what the implications are of that covenant institution in terms of which God's saving revelation and action have been operative throughout the history of redemption.

It is futile to adduce the fact of infant circumcision in support of infant baptism unless the relation of circumcision to the Abrahamic covenant and the place of the Abrahamic covenant within the organism of redemptive revelation are properly assessed. It is the significance of the Abrahamic covenant that Small places in the forefront. 'God brought into being a covenant community at that point in the history of redemption, and made Abraham the head of it. God pledged Himself to Abraham and to his posterity in this covenant relation, establishing it on the unalterable promises of God. . . . Progressively through the history of the development of the covenant people of God there is enlargement of understanding and application. But because Abraham was the first person with whom God established the covenant in terms of a distinct covenant community, he is rightly called "the father of all them that believe" (Romans 4:11)' (p. 31). Hence Small is at pains to show that it is this Abrahamic covenant that 'continues on past the dispensation of the Law under Moses and into the present' and is therefore 'the same covenant under which New Testament believers are saved' (p. 34). The evidence in support is adduced in detail in the pages which follow (cf. pp. 35–48). The inferences to be drawn from this thesis respecting infant baptism are apparent.

Small's presentation of the case for infant baptism comes to what is perhaps its most cogent expression in the chapter in which circumcision and baptism are compared (pp. 79–96). Most effective in this chapter is the way he answers the objection that since faith and repentance are required for baptism and, since these are not predicable of infants, they cannot be fit subjects of baptism (pp. 84 ff.).

In Part II Small deals competently with the question of mode and relates the mode to the meaning. The meaning he rightly discovers to be identification. The evidence he adduces in support is both copious and conclusive. It is when viewed in this light that the insistence upon a symbolism which focuses attention upon the one aspect of union with Christ, namely, burial and resurrection, is shown to do prejudice to the inclusiveness and completeness of the identification which baptism represents and seals. 'How inadequate', he says, 'it is to try to equate the meaning of baptism with just one or two facets of this total identification' (p. 166). Although Small is not probably correct in excluding from Romans 6:3 an allusion to the rite of baptism and its significance, yet he is unquestionably correct in saying that 'when ritual baptism is in view . . . it is never some one part of this total identification that is represented by the analogy' (p. 167). This consideration, clearly supported by the other passages with which Small deals in the context, is the decisive answer to the baptist's appeal to Romans 6:3, 4 in the argument for immersion. The examination given in these chapters of classical, Old Testament, and New Testament usage in respect of the relevant terms is one that leaves no reasonable doubt as to the validity of Small's thesis.

Some liabilities, however, call for comment.

Biblico-theological study will show that the traditional formulation of covenant theology, especially that associated with the 17th century, needs modification. This revision does not in the least degree interfere with the centrality of covenant administration in the history of redemption. In fact it only serves to accentuate the significance of the covenant concept. On the whole Small's argument for infant baptism is biblically oriented and is in accord with what the strictly biblical notion of covenant would require. But early in his book (pp. 15–29) he uses the mould of a formulation of biblical data which does not advance the biblico-theological presentation with which the remaining part of the volume is occupied.

The 'principle of presumption' (cf. pp. 64, 80, 87) to which Small appeals in connection with infant baptism is scarcely one that can be biblically supported. It is far better to rest the case upon the divine institution. This is all that is necessary, and to append a questionable inference does not strengthen the argument.

Undoubtedly 'fire' in Scripture is frequently the emblem of judgment. But it is beyond warrant to say in regard to Jesus' baptizing with fire (Matt. 3:11; Luke 3:16) that 'the consistent Biblical reference of fire to judgment makes it reasonably clear that this baptism of fire speaks of the future judgment of the world at the second coming of Christ' (p. 161). Fire has many associations and significations in Scripture and it is more likely that in these references to Jesus' baptizing the thought is that of thorough purification (cf. Zech. 13:9; Mal. 3:2, 3).

Some typographical errors were noted. The most unfortunate is 'blood' in the place of 'Spirit' (p. 88).

Small's book is a commendable contribution to a need which is always with us and several features of biblical teaching are here placed in the forefront that are not elsewhere, at least not in readily available literature, brought to bear upon the questions at issue.

14

STUDIES IN DOGMATICS. DIVINE ELECTION. *By G. C. Berkouwer.* Grand Rapids: Wm. B. Eerdmans Publishing Company. 1960. 336.

In the perspective of historical theology and in the context of present-day debate no undertaking could place greater demands upon the theologian than a monograph on the subject of divine election. And no theologian within the Reformed tradition excels G. C. Berkouwer in the extensive and mature scholarship necessary for such a task. This is not a book to be read at one sitting nor is its argument one to be grasped on one reading. Review is, therefore, more than arduous.

The difficulty just mentioned does not arise from obscurity in Berkouwer's style of writing. It proceeds rather from the complexity of the issues involved, a complexity not always attaching to the mystery of God's counsel but to the aberrations of human thought by which the doctrine has been perplexed and distorted. As a contribution to historical as well as to systematic theology, Berkouwer brings the various facets and currents of thought within his purview. No book on this topic surpasses Berkouwer's in respect of erudition, information, and challenge.

It may not be amiss to suggest that the lay reader should read first of all chapters I, IX, and X. In these chapters the practical and devotional significance of the doctrine of election is brought into focus, and this is particularly true of chapter IX where 'Election and the Certainty of Salvation' is dealt with in admirable fashion. From the beginning of the volume this is the question that Berkouwer poses and it is never far from his interest. At the outset his thesis is: 'In Scripture the certainty of salvation is never threatened or cast in shadows because of the fact of election. Rather, we always read of the joy of God's election and of election as the profound, unassailable and strong foundation for man's salvation, both for time and for eternity' (p. 13). In chapter IX this thesis is vindicated. Here a good deal of space is devoted to the question of the *syllogismus practicus*, to the misinterpretations against which it must be guarded, but particularly to its validity and its consistency with the principle of *sola fide* when it is properly understood as the syllogism of faith. And this means that 'only in the way of sanctification man can be, and remain, certain of his election' (p. 302). 'It is not a connection in which sanctification becomes a compensation whereby man – as a last resort – may deduce his personal election from his sanctification. It is, rather, a connection which originates from the revelation and the reality of election itself' (p. 306). It would have been helpful if some attention had been given in this same discussion to the exposition of Romans 8:16 and to the indispensable complementation of the fruit of the Spirit and the inward witness of the Spirit in the certainty of salvation (cf. p. 301).

In chapter II Berkouwer deals with what in historical perspective has been the crux of debate and division. It is the question :'Where falls the decision of man's redemption?' (p. 28). The whole matter of synthesis 'in which both God's grace and man's decision were given a full place' (p. 29) and that of prescience as conditioning God's election is thoroughly dealt with. Romish, Remonstrant, and Lutheran positions are analysed and the author concludes: 'In no form of synergism is it possible to escape the conclusion that man owes his salvation not solely to God but also to himself' (p. 42). Synergism 'is encountered nowhere in Scripture. For if anything is clear in Scripture, it is that it nowhere presents a human-divine complementary relationship' (p. 44). And, in interpreting Philippians 2:12, 13, a text to which appeal had often been made in the polemics of history, Berkouwer shows that here we do not have 'the idea of a complementary relationship and of co-operation' (p. 45). The human activity is the result of the divine, is created and called forth by the divine; man's act thus receives 'such a form that the nature of his act excludes co-operation' (p. 46).

The necessity of distinguishing between arbitrariness, on the one hand, and the freedom and sovereignty of election, on the other, always rests upon the exponent of the latter. This duty Berkouwer does not evade. One of the difficulties here resides in the use of the term 'arbitrary' in human affairs. The man who is arbitrary is the man who acts 'without taking into account any norm or law above himself' (p. 54). Does this mean, therefore, that since God is not arbitrary he must always act in terms of a law or norm above himself? This is the whole question of the meaning of *exlex* as applied to God. Various positions are passed under review. Of particular interest is the explanation of Calvin's opposition to the idea of God as *exlex* as also to the fiction of *potentia absoluta* (pp. 56 ff.). Berkouwer's own treatment of the question from the biblical point of view (pp. 80 ff.) is eminently valuable.

Much theological discussion has been concerned with the distinction between the secret will of God and the revealed. And closely related to this distinction is the question how, if election belongs to the secret will of God, may we ever attain to the knowledge of our own election? These and related questions are explored in chapter IV. Calvin's concept of Christ as 'the mirror of election', and Luther's of Christ as 'the Book of Life' are adduced to show that in the protestant tradition as opposed to the Romish there is propounded the thesis of 'the knowability, the revelation, of election' (p. 110), so that the certainty of our election is not derived from any special revelation to the individual nor from curious prying into the secret counsel of God but from the revelation in Christ as received by faith. With respect to the distinction between the secret and revealed will, Berkouwer rightly warns against the tendency to construe the revealed will as 'unactual'. When we do this, then 'the will of God in law and gospel is overshadowed and even threatened' by what is supposed to be the only actual will of God, namely, his secret will (p. 117). 'Scripture . . . forbids identification of the will of the ordinance with unactuality' (p. 118).

One of the most difficult questions pertaining to election is the interpretation of Ephesians 1:4 and related texts (cf. 2 Tim. 1:9). It is the question of the relation which Christ sustains to election on the part of God the Father. Berkouwer devotes much illuminating attention to the subject. The discussion is to a considerable extent centred on the question whether Christ should be called the foundation or origin of man's salvation or merely the executor of election (cf. p. 134). We should expect that the Remonstrant view whereby Christ was conceived of as the foundation and cause of election, because election was motivated by Christ's act, and Christ ' "as Mediator is the *causa impulsiva, movens, meritoria* of the decree of election" ' (p. 136) would be rejected. Such a view 'flagrantly contradicts Scripture' (*id.*). On the other hand, it is not sufficient to think of Christ as no more than the executor. Scripture 'speaks not of mere execution but of election in Christ' (p. 137). With the rejection of a false dilemma Berkouwer proceeds with the review of theological discussion, shows that the Reformed rejection of the Remonstrant position did not mean that the notion of 'foundation', when properly understood and clarified, was *per se* unacceptable, exposes the fallacy of J. K. S. Reid's criticism of Calvin, and effectively defends the latter against any such monstrous charge as that election precedes grace (cf. pp. 137 ff.). Berkouwer gives adequate space to the question whether 'in Christ' could be regarded as referring to Christ's participation in election in the eternal counsel, the view propounded by Gomarus (cf. pp. 143 ff.).

The discussion of the *pactum salutis* (pp. 162 ff.) is of particular interest. The author raises some pertinent questions. He is appreciative of the purpose served by this construction, namely, that it was 'employed especially to oppose the idea that election was decreed completely apart from Christ, and that he was nothing but the executor of that decree' (p. 162). But when the idea of 'covenant' is introduced, one comes to entertain suspicion respecting the propriety of such a formulation. And so Berkouwer asks: 'Is it possible to furnish Biblical evidence for such a *pactum* as a real "covenant"? Does not a pact always presuppose an "over against", as in the covenant between God and man?' (*id.*). Bavinck considered that the doctrine was based on 'a Scriptural concept' but nevertheless thought that the formulation was not free from 'scholastic subtleness' and that 'many irrelevant references' have been quoted in its support (pp. 162 f.). Berkouwer defends the doctrine in so far as it indicated the 'depth-aspect' of salvation, that 'eternity does not stand in contrast to what in time becomes historical reality, but rather that the salvation accomplished . . . has its eternal foundation in the love of God'. This is not to 'humanize the counsel of God' but 'to indicate an analogy between what is called a "covenant" or "pact" on earth' (p· 168). However, in the reviewer's judgment, covenant in Scripture always refers to historical administration and it is a deviation from biblical usage to construct the relations which the persons of the Godhead sustained to one another in the counsels of eternity in terms of *covenant*. The *doctrine* of the *pactum* is not thus bereft of any of its significance but it is given a more biblico-theological orientation.

In this chapter one misses a discussion of the correlation that exists between Ephesians 1:4 and Romans 8:29 (cf. p. 151). It would not be feasible to regard predestination to be conformed to the image of God's Son that he might be the firstborn among many brethren as embracing all that is implied in election in Christ. But this is surely a factor that must be given full account in the exegesis of Ephesians 1:4 and particularly when we note that chosen in Christ (Eph. 1:4) and 'in love predestinated' (Eph. 1:5) are most properly taken as parallel to and epexegetical of one another.

I must confess to embarrassment when I read with reference to Ephesians 1:4 the endorsement of Van Leeuwen's remark that ' "the counsel of God is not an immutable and fixed decree" ', and then Berkouwer adds: 'This fixedness and immutability are foreign to Paul's hymn on the love of God. The power and evidence of Paul's testimony have safeguarded the Church and theology at decisive moments against a devaluation of God's election to such a fixedness of decree, which is only later realized in the work of Christ' (p. 149). One is at a loss to understand how the fixedness of the decree could be a devaluation of God's election or how the historical realization of what had been decreed should be prejudicial to the immutability of the decree. Later on Berkouwer repeatedly speaks of the immutability of God's plan when he speaks of 'the foundation of salvation in God's plan as immutable reality' (p. 150) and says that 'the immutability of God's work is based on this plan, which will reach its goal in spite of dangers and weaknesses' (p. 151). Again, 'one may not limit the divine sovereignty or violate the immutability of the counsel of God' (p. 153). The fair construction would be that what Berkouwer is aiming at in the statements quoted from page 149 is the conception of the decree as 'abstract act' or as 'purely formal decree' apart from Christ and detached from those connections which the Scripture itself establishes (cf. p. 153). Of course, the decree of election is never thus abstract or detached. But the statements in question (p. 149) are, to say the least, infelicitous and misleading as a way of guarding election from the abstraction which Scripture does not permit (cf. p. 161). It is without any dissent that we accede to the following: 'God's election is election in Christ. "Not because of works, but because of grace". In this way the tension between sovereignty and grace, which so often became manifest in the thinking of many people, will disappear. For this grace is truly sovereign, and this sovereignty is no longer a hidden menace (the arbitrariness!) which obscures grace. The election of God in Christ is not a violation of the way of salvation, but its proclamation' (p. 162).

As we might expect, the most acute questions arise in connection with election and reprobation (chapter VI). Berkouwer is insistent throughout on the sovereignty of election and the sovereignty of grace in election. This is, indeed, the refrain from start to finish. He will give no quarter to the notion of *praescientia* or *praevisa fides* as the conditioning element in election, explanatory of the differentiation which election involves. 'The essential thing in faith as a gift of God is that it is based on this truly monopleuristic act in the election of God. Faith in its "instrumental" character knows only of this one and sufficient, this absolute and merciful, "causality" ' (p. 179). 'Election is the fountain of all saving good, and out of it flow the fruits of faith, holiness, and other gifts, and finally also life eternal' (p. 180).

It might seem, on occasion, that Berkouwer is not willing to regard the fall and sin as embraced in the counsel of God. Some strange statements appear which might create this impression (cf. pp. 261, 268). But this would be a false inference. Numerous explicit remarks are to the contrary. 'Nothing can be made independent of the counsel of God' (p. 201). It is with approval that he quotes Bavinck to the effect that ' "all of sinful reality, all of world history in the interrelations of its events, does not have its primary cause in itself – how would that be possible? – but beyond itself in the mind and will of God" ' (p. 206; cf. pp. 202 f., 212, 215, 217). Berkouwer's formula is that of Augustine: *contra voluntatem Dei* but not *praeter voluntatem Dei*.

We must also be deeply appreciative of Berkouwer's jealousy in this chapter, as also elsewhere, to avoid fatalistic determinism, on the one hand, and human autonomy, on the other. His discussion is constantly oriented against these fatal aberrations of human thought.

The question of pivotal interest is Berkouwer's polemic against the parallelism or symmetry of election and reprobation. This question has sometimes been expressed in terms of the denial or affirmation of the equal ultimacy of election and reprobation. Against this tenet of equal ultimacy or, as he prefers to call it, the parallelism and symmetry of election and reprobation Berkouwer directs all his polemic resources. The term 'equal ultimacy' in the formula could refer to the ultimacy as it concerns both God's eternal counsel and man's everlasting destiny. But it would appear that in the discussion the former aspect of ultimacy is particularly in view.

It should be recognized at the outset that the issue involved is not the particular terms sometimes used in the debate. The formulae are not themselves sacrosanct. In fact the terms 'reprobation' and 'rejection' are not necessarily the most felicitous or the most biblically accurate to denote the aspect of God's counsel with which the debate is concerned. The Scripture speaks of the determinate counsel of God and there should be no dispute on the biblical doctrine that sin and evil as well as good are embraced in this determinate counsel (cf. Luke 22:22; Acts 2:23; 4:27, 28; 17:26; Eph. 1:11). So it might be well to speak of God's determinate purpose with respect to the non-elect. But in any case, there is predetermination on the part of God with respect to the damnation of those who finally perish. This 'determinism' is real and must not be confused with fatalistic determinism. It is only at the peril of rejecting the witness of revelation that we shy away from the 'determinism' of God's determinate will. Of this Berkouwer is aware. He warns against an 'indeterministic exegesis' of such passages as Romans 9:18, 22 (pp. 213, 215). Hence it is not enough to wave the red flag of 'determinism'; it all depends on the kind of determinism we have in mind. The real issue in this instance is whether in the differentiation that exists among men the pure sovereignty of God's good pleasure and predetermination must be posited in connection with what has been called preterition and reprobation as well as in connection with election. The affirmative would be that in the counsel of God sovereign differentiation is just as ultimate and real in 'reprobation' as in election, understanding reprobation in the sense defined above. This is what the reviewer affirms and it appears to be what Dr Berkouwer denies. It **is** this reviewer's conviction that no other position than that affirmed can be elicited from such passages as Romans 9:10–24; 11:5–10, not to mention other evidence. And I am not persuaded that our author's treatment of Romans 9 (pp. 210 ff.) takes adequate account of Paul's teaching.

Berkouwer devotes much attention to what he regards as implied in parallelism or symmetry, namely, an identity of divine causality. 'Election and rejection', he says, 'do not result from the one "causality" as two parallels in the ways of belief and unbelief. They are not "equivalent-parallel", as is already shown in the fact that belief is from God, while unbelief is not' (p. 178; cf. pp. 194 f. and *passim*). In this connection appeal is made to the 'Conclusion' of the Canons of Dort where it is denied that 'in the same manner (*eodem modo*) in which the election is the fountain and cause of faith and good works, reprobation is the cause of unbelief and impiety' (cf. p. 175). To this pronouncement of Dort the fullest consent must be accorded. In what then does the dispute consist?

This question merits much fuller discussion than this review could reasonably allow. In the matter of distinction between election and what is denoted by 'reprobation', there is not only place but need for careful discrimination. When we deal with election we have to take into account not only the sovereign differentiation which it involves but also the effectuation of the purpose of grace which election contemplates. And when we deal with 'reprobation' we have to take account not only of the sovereign differentiation which is involved but also of the distinct elements comprised in it and of the diverse factors which enter into the final result. There is diversity in the mode of divine operation. Election is the fountain and, in a certain sense, the cause of faith and its various concomitants. But when we deal with sin and unbelief, apart from which reprobation as damnation may never be conceived, we must not say that God is the author or cause of sin as he is of faith and its fruits. We cannot speak of an identity of divine causality. In the language of the Canons of Dort, 'The cause or guilt (*culpa*) of this unbelief, as well as of all other sins, is nowise in God, but in man himself: whereas faith in Jesus Christ, and salvation through him is the free gift of God' (I, 5). Berkouwer's sustained exposition and defence of this distinction must be endorsed (cf. pp. 176 ff.) and it would be improper to speak of the 'two-foldedness of the one divine causality' (p. 194).

The necessary distinctions which must be observed, in respect of *causality*, between election unto life and all that is involved in it and flows from it, on the one hand, and 'reprobation' unto death with all its factors and consequences, on the other, do not in the least interfere with the truth which is the real question at issue, to wit, the pure sovereignty of the differentiation inhering in the counsel of God's will (βουλή, θέλημα, εὐδοκία). The 'equal ultimacy' is here inviolate. God differentiated between men in his eternal decree; *he* made men to differ. And, ultimately, the only explanation of the differentiation is the sovereign will of God. The necessary differentiations in respect of causality in the diverse factors grounding and contributing to the wholly different destinies and outcomes must not be allowed to obscure or prejudice the sovereignty of the counsel of God's will. As far as this aspect is concerned it makes no difference whether a supralapsarian or infralapsarian position is adopted. For, even on the latter premise, the sin of men is not the reason for the differentiation among men but simply and solely the sovereign will of God. Some of Berkouwer's own statements would appear to carry this implication. But the more general thrust is, in the reviewer's judgment, to the opposite effect.

We need not fear that this doctrine is any threat to the gospel of God's grace which it is the glorious privilege of the church to proclaim. It is on the crest of the wave of that sovereignty, exemplified in sovereign discrimination, that the full and free overtures of grace come to a lost world.

Since Berkouwer devotes so much space to the Reformed Confessions, it is surprising that the Westminster Confession should receive such scant attention (cf. p. 22). None of the Reformed Confessions surpasses chapter III of Westminster in finesse of formulation. Here is no imbalance. The caution given in section viii that 'the doctrine of this high mystery of predestination is to be handled with special prudence and care' follows the section dealing with the non-elect which in its import is surely identical with the position of Dort (cf. *contra* p. 181) enunciated some twenty-five years earlier, but sets it forth with incomparable succinctness and precision.

15

THE WITNESS OF THE SPIRIT. AN ESSAY ON THE CONTEMPORARY RELEVANCE OF THE INTERNAL WITNESS OF THE HOLY SPIRIT. *By Bernard Ramm.* Grand Rapids: Wm. B. Eerdmans Publishing Company. 1960. 140.

It would be claiming too much to say that the past decade has witnessed a unique interest in the doctrine of the Holy Spirit. But the number of books published in this period on this subject does show a decided trend in theological thought, and, though not all of this output reflects the viewpoint that devotion to Scripture as the Word of God demands, yet the interest is one that orthodox theology must not ignore. Bernard Ramm's book is one of the most recent in this collection. He writes from an evangelical standpoint. It is with one phase of the Spirit's work that he deals. But it is an all-important phase. If all the talent exemplified in the literature on the Holy Spirit for the last ten years had been guided by the regard for Scripture which Ramm's book reflects, then the church would have made much more progress in the understanding which it is the function of the Holy Spirit to impart.

Though Ramm limits his study very largely to the New Testament, he takes the pains to adduce and examine what the Scripture teaches. This contribution abounds not only in worthy discussion but also in conclusions that are definitive for all sound thinking on this subject. Paragraph after paragraph could be quoted which are unexcelled for clarity, precision, and balance. It is indicative of Ramm's perspective that the three theologians to whom he yields particular esteem are John Calvin, Abraham Kuyper, and B. B. Warfield.

The keynote of the thesis is enunciated when we read as follows: 'The conclusion, then, is that in the Christian religion our certainty is not derived from the rational powers of the human mind, nor from the word of the imperial church, nor from the direct delivery of a revelation within the heart. Rather, it comes only from the *testimonium Spiritus Sancti*' (p. 16).

Ramm does good service to proper understanding when he at an early stage of the discussion and throughout the volume exposes the error of identifying the *testimonium* with religious experience (cf. p. 26). The witness gives experience but does not consist in it. 'A *testimonium* which is not for experience would be meaningless. Nevertheless the *testimonium* is not religious experience *per se*' (p. 104).

One of Ramm's chief emphases is the union of Word and Spirit. 'Revelation is given in two actions: the objective truth as such, and an inward revelation enabling the human mind to grasp revelation as revelation. The objective revelation becomes appropriated by means of an inward revelation. This demands the closest relationship between objective and subjective revelation, which takes concrete form in the doctrine of Word and Spirit' (p. 63). 'To isolate Scripture from the Spirit, or the Spirit from Scripture, is theologically mischievous' (p. 64). In this connection care is taken to show Romish error which either tragically weakens or utterly destroys the union of Word and Spirit, and the autopistic character of Scripture by reason of its intrinsic inspiration is also accorded its rightful place (pp. 63 ff.).

Of equal significance is the insistence that the *testimonium* draws within its scope the divinity of Scripture as a whole. 'Revelation, illumination, and truth are one piece. We cannot think of revelation as untrue, nor of illumination as illuminating a falsehood. Revelation and illumination directly imply the veracity of the contents of the revelation' (pp. 65 f.). 'The *testimonium* becomes anchored in Sacred Scripture, and that is why faith in Jesus Christ is so vitally and indestructibly linked to faith in Sacred Scripture. If it is God who has saved our souls by the preaching of the gospel, it is God who is the author of that Word which contains the gospel' (p. 68).

Other aspects of Ramm's study, too numerous to mention, are similarly worthy of endorsement.

The witness of the Spirit is internal. It is in the heart, in the spirit, in the understanding (cf. p. 75). It does not appear, however, that Ramm always observes this distinction between the objective witness of the Spirit in the Scripture and the internal testimony. When he refers to the word of Scripture, 'Well spake the Spirit through the mouth of the prophet' and then adds, 'what the prophet speaks and what the prophet writes is accomplished by virtue of the indwelling and inward revealing Holy Spirit' (pp. 31 f.), these terms leave the impression that it was by the internal testimony that the prophet spoke, whereas it is surely the theopneustic action of the Spirit that is in view in the text quoted. Although Ramm is quite explicit on the priority of objective revelation (cf. pp. 32 ff.) and insists that 'the *testimonium* lives only by virtue of the previously existing objective revelation' (p. 33), yet the distinction tends to be obscured at certain points, at least for the rapid reader. Without interfering with what Ramm calls 'the double structure of revelation' (*id.*) nor with the place of the internal testimony in the total structure of revelation, this defect could be remedied by a more restricted use of the term 'revelation' and by fuller exegesis of certain passages which are germane to the discussion and to which reference is made (cf. pp. 31, 53 f.).

Ramm is correct in maintaining that the witness to the truth of the gospel and of Scripture is inseparable from the witness to divine adoption. This is the simple truth that the persuasion which the internal testimony produces is inseparable from a state of salvation. But the impossibility of separation does not carry with it the identification of the two. Hence it is pressing the correlativity too far to say that 'the thesis that there are two *testimonia* actually calls for a separation of the *form* of Scripture from the *content* of Scripture' (p. 101). The distinction between that witnessed to in the passages concerned with adoption (Rom. 8:15, 16; Gal. 4:6) and that witnessed to in such passages as 1 Cor. 2:1 ff.; 1 Thess. 1:5 lies on the face of these texts. The interests of exegesis require that full account be taken of the distinct objects in view. No issue is at stake in speaking of two testimonies so long as they are regarded as correlative. And since the witness to adoption is so much more limited in its scope than that which belongs to the *testimonium*, a formulation that would not set off the distinctness would have more liabilities than one that speaks of two *testimonia*. All aspects of the Holy Spirit's saving work are inseparable but they are not to be identified and spoken of as one.

Ramm devotes little space to neo-orthodoxy (cf. pp. 27, 63). This is an omission to be regretted. It is not due to unfamiliarity on Ramm's part with the Barthian theology. Since, as he observes, the neo-orthodox 'doctrine of Scriptural inspiration does not render Scripture suitable for use as the instrument of the Spirit' (p. 63) and since it is the radically different concept of revelation and of revelation to Scripture that makes the neo-orthodox view of the *testimonium* incompatible with the biblical teaching, it would have been a contribution to have had this antithesis developed. One cannot but hope that some of Ramm's expressions and emphases are not due to an infiltration of neo-orthodox patterns of thought. When, for example, he says of fundamentalism that 'it spoke much of the "inspired Word of God" but forgot the priority of the "revealed Word of God" ' and thus 'failed to grasp the truth that inspiration lives on revelation and not vice versa' (p. 124), it is difficult not to suspect a false analysis of the relations of inspiration and revelation. It is true that revelation existed before it took the form of inscripturation. But for us now the only special revelation we possess is that which comes to us by inspiration and so the inspired Word of God and the revealed Word of God are for us identical. In our existential situation to speak of the priority of the latter is a false distinction. Furthermore, it is necessary to bear in mind that Scripture is not simply a record of revelation, nor merely an account of the redemptive acts of God (cf. p. 17). It is itself revelatory, it is itself an act of God, and it is redemptive in its significance and purpose. And the centrality of Christ in the witness of the Spirit (cf. pp. 46, 58) must not be allowed to suppress what Ramm himself elsewhere calls 'the total range of the Christian revelation' (p. 87). In other words, we must not permit the Christological to get out of its proper focus and obscure the finality for us of the inscripturated Word.

There is one aspect of the *testimonium* that calls for a word of concluding comment. It is 'the objectivity of the *testimonium*' (p. 87). It is gratifying and significant that Ramm should have spoken of it thus. It would have been well if this feature had been given greater emphasis so as to be placed in clearer light. Ramm has done good service, as noted, in showing that this testimony is not to be equated with Christian experience, though always operative in the context of Christian experience (cf. pp. 49, 87, 89). And the certainty or persuasion resulting from the testimony receives all due stress (cf. p. 49). But when, in connection with this emphasis upon persuasion, the *testimonium* is said to be a persuasion (cf. p. 18), there is liable to be some confusion. Our certainty is the effect and the *testimonium* consists in the action of the Spirit. Ramm recognizes this when he says that 'the *testimonium* is not a vicarious believing or a vicarious willing or a vicarious thinking' (pp. 87 f.). The main point here is that in the exposition of this doctrine theology needs to observe to an extent greater than has hitherto been the case that the testimony of the Spirit, though internal and to our subjective consciousness and therefore not objective in the sense in which the content of revelation is objective, nevertheless is objective to our consciousness and not to be identified with the effects in our consciousness. Hence greater care will have to be exercised in the use of terms lest this distinction be confused. To this may be added the observation that, however valuable and proper is the term 'illumination' in describing this action of the Spirit, the mere notion of illumination is not sufficient to express or define that in which the internal testimony consists. If it is truly *testimonium* we must also take account of the power and demonstration by which the Spirit seals the veracity and divinity of his own Word.

16

SPECIAL REVELATION AND THE WORD OF GOD. *By Bernard Ramm.* Grand Rapids: Wm. B. Eerdmans Publishing Company. 1961. 220.

The wide reading and research evident in this latest book from Dr Ramm's pen should be the envy of any theologian. Of slightly less than two hundred pages of text, the book is packed with material directly relevant to the theme and with references to literature on the subject. This reviewer cannot suppress the conviction that the book should have been expanded to twice its present size; there is too much for such limited space. And it seems that the author required more mature and critical reflection in order to deal more adequately with certain perspectives and especially with some of the viewpoints alluded to in the course of the discussion.

About half of the volume is devoted to the modalities of special revelation, namely, divine condescension, divine speaking, historical event, and the incarnation. This feature is not out of proportion and the order of treatment is commendable.

Ramm properly lays a great deal of emphasis upon the complementation of redemptive event and revelatory word. A few sample quotations will illustrate. 'An event in itself possesses a certain opacity. When Jesus was crucified some measure of meaning for this event could be deciphered from knowing the Jews, the Romans, and the events leading up to it. But no deeper insight into this event could be so gained. However, this event had an unprecedented weight of meaning for the Jews, the Romans, the disciples, the world, and for God himself. *But only the revelatory word of God rescues the cross from its historical opacity and brings to light its immense weight of meaning*' (pp. 77 f., ital. his). '*The strong event of the cross without an equally strong word of revelation would have lost its power in the Church and then in the world*' (p. 78, ital. his). 'Those theologians who rest the weight of their system upon *events-as-such* have not reckoned adequately with the logical problem of the opacity of historical events' (p. 79). 'The event and the word must be held with equal firmness. . . . The word is the hard datum in the area of truth; the event is the hard datum in the area of history' (p. 82).

A similar insistence appears in connection with the incarnation. 'Christ is both Person and Message. To set up a disjunction forcing us to choose one or the other is theologically wicked' (p. 112). 'Redemption comes therefore as historical, as event, as a particular person in a particular place at a particular time *doing a particular act* (or acts).

'These redeeming acts are not mute events. They are accompanied by a fulness of the divine speaking. . . .

'. . . The death of Christ has a hard locus of fact in space and time, and a hard locus of meaning in the counsels of God' (p. 114). The indispensability of Scripture as the permanent deposit of this revelatory word is likewise stressed. 'The only real Christ is the Christ presented in the Scriptures' (p. 116). 'Christ is the Lord of the Church and of the believer. The sign of saving faith is submission to this lordship. But the only Lord we can truly submit to is the Lord enshrined for us in the pages of the New Testament' (p. 117).

Ramm has hard things to say of the notion that revelation is encounter to the depreciation of truth and doctrine. 'The doctrine of revelation as encounter can be so elaborated as to obscure the nagging and persistent question of truth. And the question of truth is too serious to be buried in a plethora of words about encounter' (p. 152). Equally refreshing and to the same effect is the accent upon the conceptual. 'Without conceptual elements "pure encounter" becomes meaningless encounter' (p. 153, n. 20; cf. also pp. 154–60).

It was suggested earlier in this review that the multiplicity of perspectives and the wide range of literature alluded to required either more mature reflection or expanded critical discussion. Some examples will illustrate.

On the incomprehensibility of God there is lack of precision. The most pervasive use of the term 'incomprehensible' as applied to God in Reformed theology is in the sense 'beyond creaturely comprehension', 'incapable of being comprehensively understood'. This meaning must govern our discussion unless we choose to define the term otherwise. Hence when Calvin says that the essence of God is incomprehensible (cf. pp. 22 f.), study of his usage will show that he means in this instance, as in several others where he deals with God's essence and his secret counsel, that God's essence is 'inapprehensible' and not merely incomprehensible in the sense defined above. Again, Ramm appears to equate the incomprehensibility of God with unknowability (p. 24). This is not correct and hardly consistent with his own position that 'the incomprehensibility of God is always spoken of within the context of the knowledge of God' (p. 21), an eminently correct statement. Furthermore, it was not 'in virtue of the incomprehensibility of God' that man needed special revelation prior to the Fall (p. 22), nor is it fruitful to define incomprehensibility in terms of our inability properly to 'describe God in human language' (p. 21).

Ramm sounds a necessary and all-important note when he says: 'So the word of God once uttered continues as the efficacious word of God by virtue of the magisterial authority of the Speaker' (p. 150). This is in the context of the argument that revelation 'comes as a depositum, as an abiding something', that it takes on substantial form, embodying 'truths' that can be 'repeated – preached! taught! written!' (pp. 150 f.). But justice hardly seems to be accorded to this power and authority belonging to Scripture as the Word of revelation by the *inspiration* of the Holy Spirit when it is said that 'there is an excessive regard for Scripture when the Scripture is given a life or power of its own, as if there were no present Holy Spirit or action in history by the living Christ' (p. 120; cf. p. 44). However much the inward witness of the Holy Spirit must be stressed as indispensable to any saving conviction, the Scripture is not bereft of its intrinsic authority and power when this inward witness is not savingly operative. There are functions which Scripture as the living Word of God performs outside the orbit of salvation, and these we must not underestimate. It could not be otherwise if Scripture is the abiding Word of God. This insistence is not to be identified with the Lutheran doctrine. It is only to recognize the element of truth in that doctrine, and the recognition is not 'bibliolatry' nor an *'excess* regard for Scripture' (p. 120). When properly construed, the letter of Scripture demands veneration because, as Ramm himself shows, 'word' in the biblical conception 'had a dynamic and creative power' (p. 73).

Ramm's discussion of the archetypal and the ectypal (pp. 143 ff.) is a worthy reminder of our dependence upon revelation for our knowledge of God and therefore that *'the datum of theology is not the archetypal knowledge of God but the ectypal'* (p. 145, ital. his). A danger that lurks at this point, not only in Ramm's formulation but also in traditional orthodox theology, needs to be mentioned. While true that we do not study God in himself but God in his revelation (cf. *id.*) and, in this sense, that 'we do not know God in himself' (p. 43), yet it is equally necessary to maintain that we know God as *he truly and really is.* Our knowledge is ectypal but it is not an ectype or analogy of God we know. It is to this great truth that our Lord's own words point (Matt. 11:27; Luke 10:22; John 14:9; 17:3).

The discussion of the anthropic character of revelation and especially the treatment of the way in which revelation comes to us in a great variety of literary forms have many excellent features (cf. pp. 37 ff., 125 ff.). There is, however, one consideration, which Ramm only briefly mentions (p. 127), that ought to be given much more attention. It is that human language rests upon the fact that man is made in the image of God and is patterned after God's speech, particularly God's speech to man. Hence when we are dealing with revelation in human language, we may never overlook the divine exemplar which lies back of all human speech. And our esteem of revelation in speech and of Scripture as inscripturated revelation will be radically affected when we take this fact into account. We shall thus be warned against the tendency to depreciate the Scriptures because they are in the languages of men and against an unwarranted use of the idea of divine accommodation.

It is difficult to understand what purpose can be served by appeal to Barth, for example, in support of the theses Ramm is developing. When Barth is quoted as saying that ' "The Word of God is an act of God which happens *specialissime,* in this way and in no other, to this and that particular man" ' (p. 81), is it not apparent that Barth's view of revelation and of the Word of God is diametrically different from that propounded by Ramm in this book and that the framework within which Barth's statement has meaning is not at all that of Ramm himself? For Barth the Word of God as revelation is not a depositum. Or again, when Ramm contends for verbal inspiration (p. 178), how totally divergent is Barth's version from any historic doctrine of verbal inspiration. This is an uncritical use of authors and, to say the least, misleading.

Exegesis has gone awry when, with reference to 2 Corinthians 3, *gramma* is said to stand for 'the Jewish dispensation in all of its elements' (p. 182). Is not Paul speaking of the law written on tables of stone and therefore of the life-giving impotence of law as mere law (cf. Rom. 8:3)? And surely Paul was aware of writing with the authority of the Holy Spirit when he said, 'And I think that I also have the Spirit of God' (1 Cor. 7:40; cf. Acts 15:22, 25, 28; see Ramm *contra* p. 60). Erroneous exegesis of Philippians 2:7 should not be given the semblance of support by speaking of the Son of God as emptying himself (pp. 33, 186).

Fundamentalism comes in for a good deal of indictment. It 'reads the revelation of God', Ramm says, 'as a transcript without mystery' (p. 24) and 'turns revelation into court-reporting and does not see it as the divine Person in *conversation* with sinners' (p. 26 n.; cf. pp. 55 f., 99, 118 n., 147 n.). Fundamentalism is a rather flexible designation and, even when characterized as 'recent' or 'contemporary', more specification is necessary if the charges are to be understood and properly weighed. This Ramm fails to do except perhaps in the reference to Simon Greenleaf's book on page 99. Since he is liberal with quotations and citations in other instances, this failure is not worthy of his own practice. The jealousy of many fundamentalists for the plenary inspiration and inerrancy of Scripture arises from their recognition that the Bible is the Word of God *written*, a position implicit in Ramm's own theses at numerous points and not to be equated with bibliolatry. Inscripturation is the only mode of special revelation available to us now. It may not be amiss to observe here by way of example that although the 'historical reality of the event [of Pentecost] is not dependent upon its being recorded in Scripture' (p. 121), yet Acts 2 is more than the record of Pentecost. Acts 2 is the Word of God and Pentecost is the theme; it is itself the truth of God and also an 'event of salvation'.

More than one reviewer has said that *Special Revelation and the Word of God* is a 'must' for theological students. To this the present reviewer assents. The perspectives opened up for fruitful study are manifold and the direction mapped out by Ramm is in many areas eminently sound. But the student will have to exercise more discrimination than Ramm shows at this stage of his prolific writing career.

17

WHAT IS THE CHURCH? *By André De Bovis, S.J.* New York: Hawthorn Books. 1961. 160.

Definition is basic to the discussion of any topic. To settle the question of origin is not always indispensable. But in the doctrine of the church this question is all-important. Hence De Bovis properly begins his first chapter by saying: 'The origin of the Church raises a problem. Where did this community come from? How is it to be explained?' (p. 17).

The church is an institution. Any attempt to expound the doctrine that does not take account of the unity and continuity of God's covenantal revelation and institution is disoriented from the outset. It cannot be said that De Bovis' contribution is adequately characterized by this biblico-theological approach. But the Old Testament background is not ignored. 'In a sense that needs to be made clear', he says, 'the Church existed in the Old Testament' (p. 20). Nothing is more central for the appreciation of unity and continuity, as also for definition, than the congregation gathered before the Lord at Sinai. The church is an assembly. De Bovis comes close to this perspective when he says that the Hebrew people 'left Egypt in the name of Yahweh to become the people of God through the Covenant of Sinai. The Twelve at the Last Supper were in a similar position. History was repeating itself and a new Exodus was beginning' (p. 47). The discussion of the relation of the Paschal supper, at which Jesus instituted the Eucharist, to the first Passover and to the New Testament church is suggestive and instructive (pp. 45 ff.).

Here, however, the sacerdotalist view of the Lord's Supper and of the church leaves its impress upon De Bovis' treatment and consequently the continuity arising from the covenantal institution does not receive adequate recognition. Furthermore, a discussion of origin that does not give prominence to the Abrahamic covenant overlooks what is basic to the essence of the church as covenantal institution.

We should expect that much space would be devoted to the subject of the church as the body of Christ. De Bovis rejects the idea of hypostatic union between Christ and the church and will not reduce the concept to 'the status of a mere metaphor'. The 'accurate formula' he propounds is that 'the union between Christ and the Church is a "mystical" union . . . that the identification between Christ and the Church is a unique reality, that it has no equivalent in the rest of our experience' (p. 89). To this formula Protestants will readily accede. Less could not be said: the formula is ecumenical in the truest sense. But at De Bovis' hands the characteristically Roman Catholic accretions are superimposed.

Criticism at this point is not concerned with the denial of the juridical and organizational as such. It is not true to classic Protestant thought to aver that 'the Church of Christ is withdrawn from the earthly plane and has its authentic existence in the mystery of God who calls his elect to himself' (p. 67). And, apart from the Romanist meaning of the term 'hierarchical', it is not a true version of Protestantism to say: 'When the Protestants separated the "Body of Christ" and the hierarchical community ... the Body of Christ became invisible' (p. 91). The Reformers may not have been successful in formulating with sufficient clarity the relations of visibility and invisibility to each other. But there was an undoubted emphasis upon the aspect of visibility and with this the recognition of the organizational structure of the church. Criticism of De Bovis must follow other lines.

Throughout this volume there is what amounts to a refrain. It is to the effect that the church is the prolongation of Christ himself. 'The "Body of Christ" is Christ himself in person, the one Christ who suffered, died, rose again and over whom death has henceforth no dominion' (p. 77; cf. pp. 13, 52, 79, 88, 90, 129, 153, 154). This sustained identification is not relieved of its far-reaching implications by De Bovis' own warning against 'confusion between Christ and the Church' (p. 88). The terms in which the identification is repeatedly stated create the confusion which at this point (pp. 88 f.) De Bovis effectively exposes and thereby shows the fallacy of his own thesis. To mention but one exegetical detail, De Bovis mentions two interpretations of Ephesians 1:23, admits that the first, namely, that the church is the 'space' filled by Christ, is 'more certain from the exegetical point of view' (p. 79 n.) and yet proceeds to say that the '*Ecclesia* which is Christ ... fulfils him, because she is of one nature with her Head and continues Christ throughout time' (p. 79), an example of the precarious exegetical basis on which the doctrine in question rests.

Coordinate with the proposition that the church is the prolongation of Christ and the extension of the incarnation is the perpetuation of the sacrifice of Christ and the continuance of the work of redemption by the *priests* in the sacrifice of the mass (cf. pp. 49 f.). The sacrifice of redemption is thus made 'contemporary with every generation' (p. 65; cf. p. 62). No tenet of Roman Catholic faith more patently contradicts the New Testament witness that by one sacrifice Christ has for ever perfected them that are being sanctified and that once for all in the consummation of the ages Christ has been manifested to put away sin through his sacrifice (cf. Heb. 10:14; 9:26).

De Bovis shows commendable reserve in the matter of papal headship. He indeed calls the pope the 'Vicar of Christ' and the head of the church (cf. p. 131). But he will not allow for any equivalence to Christ's headship. 'The pope does not "take the place" of Christ, as though the Church had two heads, Christ in the past and the pope today. Such a way of presenting the facts would be absurd and blasphemous. Christ alone can be truly called the Head of the Church' (p. 84; cf. p. 112). There is comparable reserve in stating the primacy of Peter as head, for he says that Christ 'conferred this same power of binding and loosing upon the Twelve' (p. 40). The Romanist position, however, is not retracted and this appears particularly in the claim to papal infallibility.

The argument for the primacy of Peter is derived largely from Matthew 16:18–19; John 21:15–18. It would take us too far afield to enter into the exegesis of these passages. Suffice it to say that the imposing superstructure which Rome erects on these passages is as far removed from legitimate inference and application as is the dogmatism of the following on the basis of John 10:3, 15, 16: 'At the same time and in the same words, he [Peter] was given responsibility for the exercise of the magisterium' (p. 108), a magisterium which earlier is stated to be 'the magisterium of Holy Spirit' added to Holy Scripture (p. 95).

It is in connection with papal infallibility that equivocation is most apparent. 'The Vatican Council declared that the Sovereign Pontiff is infallible when he speaks "by virtue of his supreme apostolic authority" as doctor and pastor of the universal Church and defines a doctrine of faith and morals' (p. 109). Yet it is said that 'only the whole episcopal body in communion with the Sovereign Pontiff has received the right to declare authentically and infallibly what truths must be believed' (pp. 113 f.). So 'not every word uttered by the pope is an exercise of the infallible magisterium, even when he is speaking officially' (p. 113). But again we read that 'the extraordinary magisterium . . . is exercised . . . either by the pope alone or by the bishops in communion with the pope' (p. 114) and that when the 'Sovereign Pontiff' proposes truths of faith this he 'does by virtue of his authority, and the approval of the faithful or of the episcopate is not a condition required for the validity of his teaching' (p. 115). Suffice it to ask: when is a pontifical *ex cathedra* declaration infallible?

Exegetical resort is close to desperation when Acts 6:7; 12:24; 19:20 are cited in support of the proposition that the first community of the faithful was called the Word of God. When the Word of God is said to have increased and multiplied, surely the thought is similar to that of Acts 13:49 where the Word of the Lord is said to have been proclaimed throughout the whole region and to Colossians 1:5, 6 where that which is said to *increase* is specified to be 'the word of the truth of the gospel'.

18

INTERPRETING THE BIBLE. *By A. Berkeley Mickelsen.* Grand Rapids: Wm. B. Eerdmans Publishing Co. 1963. xiv, 425.

This is a comprehensive study in the field of biblical hermeneutics, so varied in its contents and showing such wide reading that it could well be considered the product of a life's work.

Professor Mickelsen accepts the Bible as the living and abiding Word of the living and abiding God. But not all who have entertained this view of Scripture have brought to the Scripture the hermeneutics which this estimate requires and which sober study will dictate. Mickelsen devotes much space to the correction of these aberrations. Perhaps the outstanding impression left upon the reader of this volume is the sobriety and sanity of the author's hermeneutics. To sum this up it can be said that he stands in the best tradition of grammatical historical exegesis. Of the allegorical method, for example, he says: 'In the allegorical method a text is interpreted apart from its grammatical historical meaning. What the original writer is trying to say is ignored. What the interpreter wants to say becomes the only important factor' (p. 28). And, respecting the fourfold sense – literal, allegorical, moral, anagogical – he adds: 'Unfortunately, however, this pursuit of multiple meanings is really a magical approach to language' (p. 36).

Mickelsen properly guards against a cold, mechanical abuse of grammatical historical exegesis. Exposition must be joined to exegesis. 'The interpreter is not a spectator. . . . The purpose of exegesis and exposition is to communicate the meaning of an earlier statement to those living at the same time as the interpreter. . . . It is the aim of every faithful interpreter to be involved in what he communicates without expanding or contracting the biblical ideas which he is communicating' (p. 57).

As we would expect, the author gives attention to the existentialist hermeneutic so much in the forefront at the present time. With reference to the 'closed continuum' by which 'history is limited to cause and effect relationships in a time–space framework' he says: 'There is no neutral ground in this controversy' (p. 8). The existential emphasis, exemplified in Bultmann, 'ignores the fact that the one who meets me now has had a specific past history which determines all that he is and can do for me now. . . . The basic convictions of the New Testament writers themselves are ignored even while such interpreters are trying to show the meaning of what the New Testament writers are saying. Such a procedure can bring only distortion' (p. 64; cf. pp. 68–73).

Likewise, in opposition to the current tendency to equate revelation with events in history to the disparagement of the interpretative word it is refreshing to read: 'Interpretation is not by human inference but rather by God's disclosure to particular servants concerning what he has done, is doing, and in some cases of what he will do. . . . The goal of interpreters . . . is to say neither more nor less than the Spirit of God conveyed to those to whom he first disclosed the meaning' (p. 65).

One of the most helpful features of Mickelsen's work is the abundance of examples given to support and illustrate the principles of interpretation enunciated and applied. Much valuable exegesis is hereby provided, with the result that the book is itself a commentary on numerous passages. The impression might at first be left that the author had strayed from his task and had tediously burdened the development with exegesis and exposition. But, as one proceeds, this impression is corrected and what might appear to be a liability proves to be a virtue. His summation of principles at the end of chapters is shown to be the precipitate of what had been demonstrated by the exegesis of selected passages.

The more advanced student will find some of the chapters to be elementary. But these are designed to be of use to those who are beginners, and it is one of the merits of the book that it meets the needs of the layman. Selected lists of tools indispensable for those who use the original languages are given (cf., e.g., pp. 117 ff.). The student who may have spent years in specialized work on exegesis can derive immense profit from such a chapter as that on 'Language' (pp. 114–58). One of the best chapters is on 'Typology' (pp. 236–64). The overall virtue, that of sobriety, is eminently manifest. One quotation will have to suffice. 'The question is often asked: "But how about the Old Testament materials which are not specifically used in the New Testament as types? May not the present-day interpreter follow the example of the New Testament writers and point out the typical significance of other things in the Old Testament?" There are more genuine correspondences than the New Testament writers drew. If treated properly, these could be instructive. But often typology becomes an excuse for sensationalism in interpretation. Such sensationalism must be firmly repudiated by every honest interpreter. But if an interpreter, fully aware of the unity of the people of God, can show historical correlations while being aware of the differences between the type and the antitype, he certainly may observe such historical parallels' (pp. 262 f.). This general statement could, however, be greatly strengthened by observing that not only do we have to take account of the unity of the people of God but also of the organic unity of redemptive history and that the orientation is not merely that of observing parallels but of recognizing the place which the Old Testament occupies in the total structure of that history.

'Biblical Theology' is not properly defined as 'an historical theology of the Old and the New Testaments' (p. 51), if 'historical theology' is understood in the usually accepted sense. It is rather the history of revelation. Mickelsen is not unaware of this definition or of the service this type of study renders to interpretation (cf. pp. 352 f.). But it may be a weakness of his valuable work that the perspectives provided by a true 'Biblical Theology' are not more pervasively applied.

It is true that oftentimes in Scripture we do not have pedantic precision. There are what Mickelsen calls 'approximations, general identifications, and popular descriptions'. It is misleading, however, to speak of these as 'instances where the biblical writers were not as accurate and precise as historians would be today' (p. 93). Historians likewise have their approximations, general identifications, and popular descriptions. There is no need to be notarially exact when this is extraneous to the purpose. The Scripture exhibits the same characteristic. But in the contexts concerned and with the intent of the writers in view one may not speak of a lack of accuracy. The quotations from Calvin (pp. 40 f.) are more fairly construed as referring to errors which, in his esteem, 'crept in' in the transmission of the text.

A few quotations afford samples of Mickelsen's gift for pungent expression and criticism. 'Meaning must be based on usage and context. Without these, brilliant conjectures of etymology should be simply dismissed as "adventurous ingenuity"' (p. 122). 'Beware of fine distinctions of meaning in synonyms that are not supported by the context in which they are found' (p. 129). 'One must never be pedantic about the use of the article. Overrefinements are to be avoided' (p. 147). 'A god who is imprisoned within a pattern laid down by nature, who does not and cannot act apart from it, could hardly be considered a Supreme Being' (p. 267). 'Once lost, a balanced perspective is difficult to regain. Under the illusion of being exhaustive in our study, we "find" what we are looking for in places where no one else has ever seen it' (p. 371).

The 'General Bibliography' (pp. 383–92) is most useful and the three indexes (pp. 393–425) are detailed and competent. Probably the book was well on its way to completion, or completed, before the series *New Frontiers in Theology* began to be published and the *hermeneutic* with which it deals could be properly considered.

19

STUDIES IN DOGMATICS. THE WORK OF CHRIST. *By G. C. Berkouwer.* Grand Rapids: Wm. B. Eerdmans Publishing Company. 1965. 358.

Apology is due to both the author and publishers of *The Work of Christ* for the belated appearance of this review. For the delay the reviewer is responsible. My regret is accentuated by the consideration that no volume I have read from the pen of G. C. Berkouwer has given more pleasure and stimulus than this one and perhaps no other as much. Breadth of erudition and fervent devotion are the characteristics that stand out in Berkouwer's writings. In these respects the present volume excels. It is with massive knowledge of the whole history of debate and in the context of up-to-date discussion that Berkouwer sets forth the various facets of his topic.

The work of Christ can never be properly conceived apart from correct views of his person. This we are reminded of early in this study (cf. p. 11). But we are likewise reminded that we cannot arrive at a 'correct conception of Christ's work merely by drawing logical conclusions from a theory concerning his person' (*ibid.*). So our author warns us at the outset that we must 'hear the testimony of Scripture and thus be safeguarded from the deceitfulness of the human heart' (*ibid.*), a canon constantly exemplified throughout the ensuing chapters.

In this reviewer's judgment one of the most commendable and, in our present situation, most necessary features of Berkouwer's study is the emphasis upon the historical. In dealing with liberal idealism, on the one hand, and Bultmann's demythologizing, on the other, by appeal to the historic progression of Christ's suffering to the glory and light of the resurrection and with incisive frankness he says: 'Whoever tries to find salvation outside of history is only groping in the darkness of the cross. God's activity is one in the midst of history, and is just as historic as man's guilt and lost condition. Idealism denies man's guilt and searches for a therapy which can never heal the damage because it bypasses this historical reality. But Bultmann's representation of God's activity in the cross also simply minimizes the significance of this history. An enormous amount of idealism continues to dominate the entire field, just as, moreover, natural scientific determinism dominates to a large extent the teachings of "demythologizing". The question in all this is not simply a matter of some scientific problems, but we see the battle focusing around the crucial matter of finding God where he *let* himself be found' (p. 51).

Another example appears in the discussion of the place the empty tomb occupies in the resurrection of Jesus. In Berkouwer's esteem, and rightly so, the empty tomb is of the essence of resurrection faith. So with well-conceived appreciation of the relations he says: 'Not the empty grave but the resurrection of Christ is the great soteriological fact, but as such the resurrection is inseparably connected with the empty tomb and unthinkable without it. It is absolutely contrary to Scripture to eliminate the message of the empty tomb and still speak of the living Lord. The Gospels picture his resurrection in connection with historical data, moments, and places of his appearance. Scripture nowhere supports the idea of his living on independently of a corporeal resurrection and an empty tomb' (p. 184). Any contrast between the pneumatic and historic is foreign to the Bible (cf. pp. 184 f.).

The chapter called 'The Great Mystery' (pp. 88–134) is largely devoted to the virgin birth and closely related questions. The same stress upon the historical appears at the outset. 'Not only the birth records, but also the records of his suffering evidence a great difference from all idealism disconnected from history' (p. 93); the issue is history without apocryphal illumination. Relevant and telling criticism is directed against Barth's sign theory and his distinction between the *noetic* and the *ontological*. The bearing of the virgin birth on the sinlessness of Jesus is carefully analysed. The idea, propounded by Brunner, that natural procreation is necessary to the integrity of Christ's human nature, even in the form advocated by Vollenhoven, who accepts the confession of the virgin birth (cf. p. 120), is not for Berkouwer acceptable. 'Certainly at this point', he pleads, 'we must beware of speculation and accept the uniqueness of the incarnation, the miracle of the *assumptio humanae naturae*, without detracting anything from the reality of Christ's human nature' (pp. 120 f.). It is this *uniqueness* that is the answer to other suppositions of preparatory explanations in the births of Isaac, Joseph, Samson, Samuel, and John the Baptist. 'Christ's birth is entirely unique: it is the *mystery* of the incarnation. We are not dealing with a general miraculous power which manifests itself in Mary's life and which is of the same nature as the other manifestations' (p. 133).

It may not be irrelevant to remark that however important is the later text of the so-called Apostles' Creed in respect of the clause 'born of the virgin Mary' (cf. pp. 96 f.), the preceding clause, 'conceived by the Holy Ghost', does not adequately or with sufficient accuracy express the whole truth. Jesus was *begotten* by the Holy Spirit and he was conceived by the virgin (cf. Luke 1:31). The biblical witness requires the fuller statement, 'conceived and born of the virgin Mary'. It was by the overshadowing of the Holy Spirit that Mary conceived. But there should be no suppression of conception on Mary's part. And surely this is significant in relation to various phases of the discussion.

Of particular merit both dogmatically and exegetically in connection with aspects of the work of Christ is Berkouwer's exposition of 'sacrifice' (pp. 294–314) and the substitutionary character belonging to it. He has severe words to say of the Roman Catholic doctrine of the mass as a violation of the 'once-for-all' (cf. p. 302). The Socinian controversy he regards as 'one of the most serious in the history of the Church' (p. 311). The argument was that substitution would be unjust and incompatible with forgiveness. One sentence from Berkouwer sums up the issue and the refutation of the Socinian error. 'God's graciousness and justice are revealed only in the real substitution, in the radical sacrifice, in the reversing of roles' (*ibid.*).

If on page 258 it might appear that Berkouwer is giving countenance to the view that it is not God but man who is reconciled, and though the context might seem to support this interpretation, nevertheless the ensuing discussion shows that this is not the case. He proceeds to expose the fallacy of the idea of *Umstimmung*, namely, 'a doctrine of reconciliation according to which the Father, who was not inclined to reconciliation, *changed his mind* because of the Son's intervention' (pp. 260 f.). Berkouwer defends the church doctrine that the initiative of the reconciliation resides in the Father's love and mercy, that God is indeed the subject of the reconciliation, but at the same time there is the divine *placatio*, that Christ is 'the Lamb of God who has borne the wrath of God' (p. 269), that 'God's wrath and curse were directed against him' (p. 280), that 'according to the biblical teaching man's sin is irreparable and his relationship to God is objectively disturbed' (p. 263), and that 'when theology deals with the *placatio*, it always and emphatically speaks of God as object of reconciliation' (p. 262). This, however, in no way interferes with the correlative truth that God is the subject of the reconciliation nor is the twofold aspect that God is both subject and object (cf. 2 Cor. 5:18, 19) to be confused with the erroneous concept of *Umstimmung*.

One would, nevertheless, appreciate in Berkouwer's *apologia* and exposition a more detailed treatment of the biblical evidence bearing upon both reconciliation and propitiation in the particularity belonging to each as well as in the close relationship they sustain to each other. The final chapter, notwithstanding its length and many excellences, has lacunae on the great subject of the atonement.

It is unfair criticism to indict an author for omissions. Every writer has limitations and these apply to competence as well as to the space allotted to a monograph. There is one omission, however, germane to the subject of the concluding chapter, that it is difficult to excuse. It is the topic of what has been called the extent of the atonement. It is not that the chapter is destitute of allusion to this subject or, at least, to closely related questions. Berkouwer does noble service in pointing out the fallacy in Barth's concept of reconciliation (cf. pp. 291 ff.). In connection with the correlation of reconciliation and mission, for example, he says: 'Those who deny this correlation, making reconciliation an objective fact which is merely announced – Christ died for all and all are elect in Christ – change the *kerygma* into a mere

declaration and rob preaching of its urgency. Such a concept of reconciliation, in principle, opens the way to the *apokatastasis* until the strange discovery
is made that Paul sends out ambassadors with the *word* of reconciliation'
(p. 292). But there is no direct discussion of this much-debated question of
extent. Berkouwer makes frequent appeal to the Confessions of the church.
Indeed this is one of his outstanding and valued contributions. In view of the
crucial significance of the debate in the theology of the 17th century and,
more particularly, the place accorded to the doctrine of limited extent in the
Canons of Dort and the Westminster Confession, we should expect some
explicit reflection on this issue. Furthermore, it cannot be said that the issues
involved have been eclipsed in the intervening centuries or that the Reformed
consciousness can allow this question to recede into the background. Our
present-day situation requires as much as ever renewed appreciation, valida-
tion, and defence of that tenet which Dort and Westminster found it necessary to embody in their confession of faith.

It would have been appropriate, particularly in connection with the discussion of what has been called Christ's 'descent' (cf. pp. 174–80), to make
clearer that the *state* of death for three days and three nights while Jesus,
body lay in the grave was integral to his vicarious undertaking, that not only
did Jesus will to die but also to continue for a period in the state of death
and thus experience the reality and pangs of death. Surely this is that to which
Peter bears express witness when he says that God 'loosed the pangs of death'
(Acts 2:24), and it has its overtones in other passages such as that Jesus 'tasted
death' (Heb. 2:9) and that he 'became dead' (Rev. 1:18).

It is regrettable that the publishers cannot be accorded unqualified con-
gratulation. Typographical errors are too frequent. Perhaps the worst is on
page 178 where, at the end of the text, a line and a half has been shuffled to
the opposite page at the end of the first broken paragraph and at the same
point a line belonging to page 179 has been transposed to page 178. Another
example is that footnote 28 on page 155 appears on page 152.

Berkouwer's study on this central and all-important theme is one to be
read and pondered with the care and gratitude which the work of a master
deserves. Our debt is unmeasured. This is a volume that stands in the front
rank of the contributions with which the church has been blessed on the
subject of the work of Christ.

20

THE FAITH OF THE CHRISTIAN CHURCH. *By Gustaf Aulén.* Philadelphia: The Muhlenberg Press. 1948. viii, 457.[1]

For several years now English readers have had the opportunity to become acquainted with the developments in Swedish theological thought. In addition to Aulén's other books in English, in 1932–1939 Anders Nygren's *Agape and Eros* was published in English in three volumes. In 1939 Nels F. S. Ferré gave us his *Swedish Contributions to Modern Theology* in which he surveyed the movements that provide the background of present-day Swedish theology and also presented this theology 'from its own approach and in the correct proportion of its own emphasis' (p. ix). More recently Edgar M. Carlson in *The Reinterpretation of Luther* (1948) has given us a very illumining and helpful study.

Gustaf Aulén represents the Lundensian school of theology which Ferré tells us is 'the most powerful theological tendency in present-day Sweden' (*op. cit.*, p. 23). Aulén and Nygren, Ferré again informs us, 'are the two co-founders of the Lundensian system' (p. 30). And of Aulén he says, 'Aulén is the intuitive seer of possibilities' (*idem*).

Since *The Faith of the Christian Church* is a work of systematic theology we may regard it as the most comprehensive and representative treatise, emanating from the Lundensian school, that has, up to date, been made available to English readers. Hence our debt to the translators and publishers as well as to Bishop Aulén. 'Systematic theology', Aulén says, 'has as its object of study the Christian faith' (p. 3) and seeks therefore to 'make clear the meaning and significance of the Christian faith by the use of all available resources' (p. 5). Its task is to 'unveil and reveal everything that is essential, to brush aside all nonessential and foreign elements, to remove all unnecessary accretions, and to bring out clearly the very heart of the matter' (*idem*). One is constrained to ask immediately: in what sense is the word 'faith' used in this definition? Is it *fides qua creditur* or *fides quae creditur*? But Aulén does not regard it necessary or feasible to draw such a distinction or to attach to the word 'faith' one of these senses rather than the other. In fact he regards the distinction as obscure and misleading. 'The content of faith cannot be separated from faith itself' (p. 92). 'The divine revelation and faith are . . . correlative concepts' (p. 22). Many readers will probably experience not a little bewilderment as they read Aulén just because the distinction between the faith that believes and the faith that is believed is not maintained. However, one does get the distinct impression that very frequently, if not per-

---

[1] This and the following review appeared in 1949 and 1957 respectively but became known to the Publishers only after volumes 3 and 4 had been typeset.

vasively, the word 'faith' is used throughout the discussion in the subjective sense of 'the religious self-consciousness' (cf. p. 276). This does not mean that, for Aulén, systematic theology is simply the exposition of the Christian religious self-consciousness. He is very insistent upon what he calls objectivity and reality (cf. p. 21) and therefore insists that 'from the religious point of view the divine revelation is primary in relation to faith' (p. 22).

What then is this faith which systematic theology studies? Faith, Aulén maintains, is 'the expression of the Christian relationship between God and man' (*idem*) and all definitions are 'statements of that which is implied in the fellowship with God' (p. 26). In other words, faith implies our being subdued and dominated by God, on the one hand, and our commitment to God, on the other, both of which are accomplished by the act of God in Christ. This faith is grounded in divine revelation. For when we are confronted with the divine revelation we are captivated and overwhelmed, that is to say, subdued and dominated (cf. pp. 27, 29). We are laid under divine compulsion. The fundamental fact of Christian faith is the act of God in Christ and all other affirmations of faith are validated when they are shown to stand in an inner organic relation to what is the fundamental fact. It is the conception or series of conceptions implicit in this summary that governs the whole of Aulén's systematic treatise. The ever-recurring formula, 'foreign to faith' is to be understood in this light and means simply that what does not stand in inner organic connection with the act of God's love in Christ does not find a place in the affirmations of Christian faith – they do not 'correspond to the judgment of the religious self-consciousness' (p. 276). It is apparent, therefore, that the all-determining criterion for inclusion or exclusion is consonance or lack of consonance with the reconciling and redemptive act of God's sovereign love in Christ Jesus.

There is a series of questions which cannot be evaded at this point. What is the source and norm of our knowledge with reference to that fundamental fact to which everything that belongs to Christian faith sustains an organic relation? What is to be our criterion of judgment when we ask the question whether or not a particular statement sustains this organic relation to the fundamental fact? What precisely is the nature and character of that source and norm? In other words, since faith is grounded on revelation, where is that revelation? It is when we ask and press such questions that the opaqueness of Aulén's theological position becomes apparent. To put the matter very bluntly: to what purpose are Aulén's ever-recurring insistences upon the central fact of Christian faith and upon the necessity of relating all the other statements of faith to this central fact if he does not adequately validate the proper source of knowledge and the proper criterion of judgment? It is perfectly true that everything that belongs to our Christian faith stands organically related to what is fundamental and central. It is true that revelation is the basis of faith. But there is a more ultimate question. How do we come into contact with divine revelation? In what is it embodied? What is the character of that medium by which it is conveyed to us?

It is not by any means to be supposed that Aulén is not insistent upon the need and the primacy of divine revelation. 'In the sphere of history,' he says, 'the Christian faith finds that revelation which is decisive' (p. 32), a revelation which is indeed an 'unveiling of God's "essence"' (p. 31), a revelation which is *completed* in Christ and yet is never an isolated act of God. Christ is the 'absolute centre' but he always stands in a larger context 'which extends from him both back into ancient history and forward into the future' (p. 33). Furthermore, Aulén frequently appeals to Scripture. At one point he claims that the evangelical principle that Scripture is ' "the only infallible rule of faith and life" ' is for ever valid' (p. 91). He maintains that in the midst of New Testament diversity the message is an 'indivisible unity' (pp. 58 f.). Notwithstanding all of this and much more that might be quoted along these lines, our criticism is still valid that Aulén does not undertake to show the precise relation that this revelation sustains to Scripture and that Scripture sustains to it. Neither does he validate the propriety of his own rather facile and confident appeal to Scripture in support of his statements and conclusions. Aulén has no right of such appeal to Scripture unless he can validate the legitimacy and necessity of such appeal by formulating a doctrine of Scripture that will demonstrate its propriety. This he has not done. Instead, he criticises, perhaps we should say dismisses, that view of Scripture which, after all, is the only proper basis for appeal to it as the infallible rule of faith and life. He regards the doctrine of verbal inspiration as a 'mechanical objectivizing' of the Word of God, 'contrary to the actual attitude of faith and to the real character of the Word' (pp. 364 f.). On what he calls 'the theory of verbal inspiration' he thinks the Christian teachings could be validated by reference to any passage whatsoever – a very easy method, he says, nullified however by the simple fact that the Bible does not possess the uniformity supposed (p. 82).

It may be that orthodox traditionalists in Scandinavian countries, as well as in others, have sometimes made use of the doctrine of verbal inspiration in such a way as to merit something of Aulén's criticism. But Aulén's construction of the meaning and consequence of the classic protestant doctrine of plenary inspiration is one mixed with grave misconception and caricature.

It is true indeed that all Scripture is of divine origin and authority, and there are no differing degrees of divine authority. Therefore all Scripture is authoritative. The rich multiformity of the counsel of God can be elicited only as we take account of the whole of Scripture. But that this view is to be equated with 'uniformity' is completely devoid of truth. Verbal inspiration is not incompatible with the recognition of the fullest variety. The imprecatory portions of Scripture, to which apparently Aulén alludes when he speaks of 'the "prayers "of hate and vengeance in the Old Testament' (p. 82), have the deepest significance for that with which they deal. Divine wrath and vengeance cannot be eliminated. To do so would eviscerate the Christian doctrine of God. And to recognize that God's servants are sometimes the mouthpieces of this divine wrath is not something to which the Old Testament alone constrains us. Aulén would have to engage in some radical emendation of the New Testament also if he is to eliminate that fact. The very witness the New Testament bears to Christ would have to be revised. It becomes only too apparent how easy it is to impugn the doctrine of plenary inspiration by talking of ' "prayers" of hate and vengeance', when more careful consideration will disclose that what underlies such portions of Scripture is something that belongs to the very integrity of the Christian revelation. Scripture is an organism with closely knit and interwoven organic unity. In this unity there is that which is central and that which is more peripheral. But in that which is more peripheral we can discover that which belongs to the perfected unity and completeness of the whole. This the doctrine of verbal inspiration recognizes and also validates.

The inadequacy and falsity of Aulén's concept of Scripture and of the relation Scripture sustains to revelation appears at many points in his exposition of the content of the Christian faith. Aulén protests against any arbitrary selection of the materials which comprise the content of the Christian revelation. In voicing such protest he is right, and he provides us with much useful criticism of the old liberal theology. But we cannot but be impressed with the arbitrariness of Aulén's own procedure. When, for example, he maintains that love is the 'dominant centre of the Christian conception of God', that the 'inmost character of the conception of God is love' and that 'every affirmation about God becomes an affirmation about divine love' (pp. 130 f.), we cannot but wonder if there is not here arbitrary simplification and reduction. As we proceed this suspicion is confirmed. For we find that the various attributes of God are construed in terms of love. God's omnipotence is the sovereignty of love; God's eternity is the sovereignty of love in relation to time; God's unchangeableness is an expression of love's sovereign stedfastness; omnipresence is the sovereignty of love in relation to space; and omniscience is love's sovereign and penetrating eye (p. 143). Aulén says some fine things regarding God's love, especially as love manifests itself in the sacrifice of Christ and in the divine act of forgiveness. What he says regarding the sovereignty of the latter is at many points superb. And that the love of God stands in the innermost relation to the other attributes no one should deny. God is one in all the perfections which constitute His glory. But Aulén's analysis only serves to show how arbitrary are his inferences if we are to be guided by the total witness of Scripture. 'God is love' – the Scripture says so. But it also says that 'God is light' and that 'God is spirit'. These patent simplicities of Scripture expression should guard us against the arbitrariness of Aulén's simplification. And we find that this simplification is more than arbitrary selection. It leads to devastating conclusions with reference to our conception of the living God.

Two respects in which this becomes particularly conspicuous may be mentioned – the relation of God to creation and God's final judgment. With reference to the former Aulén says, 'If God is love, then by inner necessity he is the creating God. Faith cannot think of God as existing in lonely separation "before the world", before creation; it cannot, if God really is love, think of him except as creating' (pp. 183 f.). We are compelled to ask: what conception of the triune God, of his eternity, of his self-sufficiency, of his sovereignty, and of his creative work underlies such a statement? It is neither biblical nor Christian. With reference to the latter – God's final judgment – he says, that the judgment of God must be 'understood in the final analysis as an expression of his love. For the only really radical judgment of sin is that of pure love' (p. 170). The judgment of God is 'finally, simply an expression of his benevolence' (p. 171). It is no wonder, therefore, that the boundary line of faith which Aulén's view of revelation constrains him to draw leads him to the following dictum: 'The result of God's final judgment cannot be made the object of any definite statement of faith' (p. 169).

Another example of the way in which Aulén's view of revelation reacts on his exposition of Christian doctrine is his treatment of the will of God in relation to evil. At the outset it is necessary to note the confusion by which he associates evil, in the sense of what he calls 'physical evil', with the fact that 'human life is subject to finiteness and corruption'. Here he is thinking 'especially of physical suffering and death' (p. 193). By what warrant may we suppose that what is connected with man's finiteness is in any way included in evil or that evil in any sense has its origin in finiteness? And to associate death with finiteness is flat contradiction of an elementary principle of the Christian revelation.

Aulén does, however, recognize that there is also 'physical evil' which is 'the result of the corrupting and destructive power of sin' (p. 194), and he rightly distinguishes between this kind of evil and sin itself. Furthermore, he emphatically maintains that sin 'under all circumstances stands in a radical antithesis to the will of God' (p. 193). His concentration on this point is certainly to be commended. But it is here that his failure to make the proper distinctions in reference to the will of God leads him into a position that conflicts with Christian revelation. The following quotations will bring this into focus. 'Faith does not perceive the course of events in its entirety as a realization of the divine will, nor does it identify God's will with the course of nature. . . . If God's will were comprehended in everything that happens, there would be no need of a "revelation" ' (p. 196). 'God does not will everything that happens, but he wills something *in* everything that happens' (p. 197; cf. pp. 193–206). And so he says that 'the desolation and nameless suffering which follow sin are as far from God's will as the blackest darkness is from the brightest sunshine' (p. 196).

There are two distinctions which are necessary if we are to assess such statements in Christian light. The first is that while sin is the contradiction of God's perfection and therefore of his will and while God is not the author or agent of sin, yet the *consequences* of sin, including death and 'nameless suffering', are the results of God's will in curse and condemnation. They are the expressions of his wrath. In their essence they are the divine judgments upon sin, and to remove his judgment upon sin from his agency and will is to deny the reality of his judgment. Though God uses many agencies as the instruments of his displeasure yet the very essence of sin's penal consequence is the curse of God, and that curse is a positive infliction executed in accordance with his will. The second distinction is that between the decretive and pre-ceptive will of God. Whatever language may be used to express this distinction – theology has used a variety of terms – the distinction itself is indispensable if we are to be faithful to the whole counsel of God. Aulén does not think in terms of this distinction and, consequently, he makes sweeping statements which are partly true and partly false. If we are thinking of God's revealed and preceptive will it is perfectly true to say that 'actual existence is not in every respect a reflection of the divine will' and that 'God does not will everything that happens' (pp. 196 f.). But that Aulén means simply this is not by any means apparent. For he says: 'faith in providence does not mean that the course of events is mapped out beforehand by God' (p. 200). And to aver that anything which happens is not embraced in God's decree and therefore in his decretive will is to curtail that sovereignty without which God is not God. And to curtail it is really to deny it.

Aulén's work abounds in much that is instructive and stimulating. His criticisms of various systems are oftentimes discriminating and thoroughly helpful. He shows his wide scholarship without obtruding it. Particularly valuable are his critiques of metaphysical idealism and metaphysical dualism. In the field of theology his analyses of Schleiermacher and Ritschl, as well as of 'liberal' theology in general, are cogent and valid. The volume abounds in references to Luther and quotations from his works. From his more positive exposition of doctrine we can learn a great deal. His discussion of the holiness of God, for example, is an eloquent exposition of the majesty of God. Yet we do not find in *The Faith of the Christian Church* what would warrant the judgment that here we have an exposition of the Christian faith. On such a basic question as revelation and inspiration we do not find what corresponds to the witness of the only inspired revelation we possess but something very different. On such a subject as the trinity, notwithstanding Aulén's sustained protest against any conception of Christ as an intermediary being and against humanistic notions of his person, we are not able to discover the most essential marks of the Christian doctrine. Though Aulén affirms that Christ is of one substance with the Father and that the substance of the Father is incarnate in Christ, we are not assured even then that we have the Christian doctrine of the incarnation (cf. p. 211). For, in this regard, it is not sufficient to say that Christian faith speaks of 'the incarnation of the divine "essence", the divine love, in Christ' (p. 208) or that 'the "essence" of God, or in other words the divine and loving will, "dwells" in Christ' (p. 211). Though Aulén has done so much to bring to the forefront the triumphant aspect of Christ's redeeming work in victory over the powers of darkness and death, yet we cannot discover in this volume the Christian doctrine of reconciliation. And while Aulén has much to teach us on the significance of the forgiveness of sins, the complementary and more inclusive truth of justification does not determine his concept of established fellowship with God. For such reasons we are compelled to say that we do not find in this volume the most essential lineaments that would identify it as the faith of the Christian church.

21

WHEN THE TIME HAD FULLY COME: STUDIES IN NEW TESTAMENT THEOLOGY. *By Herman N. Ridderbos.* Grand Rapids: Wm B. Eerdmans Publishing Co. 1957. 104.

This is one of a series of 'Pathway Books' being currently published by the Wm. B. Eerdmans Publishing Company and 'designed to help teachers, students, preachers, and laymen keep themselves informed on the important subjects and the crucial problems which confront the Christian church today' (p. 5). Dr Ridderbos is well qualified to deal with the subject discussed in this volume. The treatment of these topics is unavoidably brief, but within the space allotted to him the author has provided us with a thoroughly competent and biblically oriented direction of thought on problems which are at the centre of New Testament studies. Ridderbos is abreast of the debates going on in the field of New Testament studies, and it is in relation to the demands of the present hour that he, as a scholar in the Reformed tradition and maintaining the doctrine of plenary inspiration, presents the findings of careful and reverent reflection.

Every student of the New Testament knows how central is the concept of the kingdom of God. What is this concept? How is it to be related to the present and to the future? In what relation does the kingdom of God stand to the church? In the first chapter Ridderbos deals with these and related questions as they are to be answered by the witness of the synoptic Gospels. In relation to the 'spiritual concept' of the liberal theology and the eschatologism of Schweitzer, to give but examples, Ridderbos maintains that 'the concept of the Kingdom in the Synoptic Gospels . . . is one of presence as well as of futurity, of both secrecy and revelation. The rising of Christ marks the boundary' (p. 17). This is saying that the kingdom of God has entered this world and it is, at the same time, yet to come. Because it has entered, 'this world is full of the redemptive power of God' (p. 18), and the parables of the mustard seed and the leaven point respectively to the 'expansive power' and the intensive penetration of the kingdom. 'That is why eschatologism . . . is as unbiblical as the connection of the Kingdom with the immanence philosophy. Eschatologism misjudges the resurrection, and the power of the exalted Lord through His Word and Spirit' (p. 19). Since Christ's resurrection is pivotal and is the point of coincidence of the two aeons it casts 'its light in two directions. It is the proof of what has happened, and the guarantee or pledge of what will happen' (p. 20).

After surveying the various interpretations of the sermon on the mount and discussing the question of the place that its ethic occupies in the kingdom of God, Ridderbos' own position is clearly stated and is to the effect that the sermon has the closest bearing upon the life of the disciples 'amidst the different connections and relationships in the world'. This means that 'the children of the Kingdom ought to ask for the Kingdom and God's righteousness in all the sectors of life and that they have to do that in the light of the whole revelation of God to which the Sermon on the Mount refers' (p. 42).

Ridderbos devotes a good deal of attention specifically to the teaching of the apostle Paul. This is as we might expect. One of his main concerns is the point of view from which Paul's preaching may be approached, and here we have a discriminating analysis of the question as it relates to justification by faith. The latter is not, in Ridderbos' judgment, the main entrance in Paul's preaching of the gospel. Justification is of central importance. But 'the central motive of justification by faith can be understood in its real, pregnant significance' only from, what Ridderbos calls, the 'redemptive-historical viewpoint' (p. 49) which is to the effect that 'in the crucified and risen Saviour the great turning-point in God's times has come' (p. 48). The main theme of Paul's ministry is that what has been promised of old has *now* been fulfilled and manifested. Paul's kerygma was the '*now* of the day of salvation' (*idem*). And so 'the starting-point of Paul's preaching of justification by faith is to be found in the great turning-point in the *historia salutis*' (p. 49). It is in this same connection that Ridderbos shows the significance of the identification of the believer with Christ in his death and resurrection if we are to understand the redemptive-historical character of Paul's preaching (cf. pp. 54 ff.).

Ridderbos declares in favour of the doctrine of plenary, verbal inspiration. In his concluding chapter he shows the relation of this view of Scripture to the history of redemption. This view of Scripture, he says, lays 'all its stress on the authority of the Scriptures as the word of God. It does not allow man to make a qualitative distinction between the Scriptures and the word of God'. It is this position that guards against subjectivism and 'without this principle of the Scriptures as the expressed word of God . . . there is no possibility', he thinks, 'of sufficient theological resistance against subjectivism in its various forms and against the assaults upon the absoluteness of the Christian faith' (p. 81). It is in this connection that Ridderbos develops admirably, though only briefly in this book, the place which the apostolate occupies in the institution of Christ and, more particularly, the New Testament concept of tradition. The latter is not 'a purely human tradition of the revelation of God' but represents 'an authoritative, personal institution' which is only another word for 'the authoritative preaching of the apostles . . . and is identified with the teaching to which the community has to submit in obedience' (p. 86). The canonicity belonging to this tradition is but 'the canonicity which Jesus Christ Himself conferred on His apostles' (p. 87).

It is, of course, by the inspiration of the Holy Spirit that the apostles were able to exercise this authority vested in them by Christ. 'We need not fear that in the formation of the Scripture some things have escaped the supervision of the Holy Spirit' (p. 93). Ridderbos is aware of the limitations under which we are placed. The Gospels, for example, do not provide us with all the details whereby we can make 'a fine map of all the journeys of Jesus' (*idem*). And Ridderbos is sensitive to the danger of artificial harmonization. It would appear, however, that he is disposed to exercise undue restraint at this point. While arbitrary harmonizing must be avoided, we are nevertheless oftentimes placed under the necessity of showing that apparent discrepancy can readily be resolved. If one evangelist informs us that there were two blind men at Jericho when Jesus passed (Matt. 20:30), we have no reason to remain in doubt as to whether there were one or two (cf. p. 94). Reserve can become pedantic as surely as can artificial harmonistics.

This is a well-written book. Perspectives of far-reaching significance on central questions of New Testament theology are opened up for the reader and at every point these perspectives are made relevant to the exigencies placed upon the believing scholar by the most recent developments of New Testament criticism.

Bibliography

The following Bibliography lists all the published writings of John Murray known to the present publishers. Further information on published work will be welcomed by them at the Edinburgh address.

The titles of books and booklets are printed in capital letters.

Material appearing in the *Collected Writings of John Murray* is identified by volume and page number in square brackets at the end of the citation.

John Murray served on numerous committees of the Orthodox Presbyterian Church, and was author, *or principal author*, of a number of Reports which appeared in the published *Minutes* of the General Assembly of the Church. These items are also included in the Bibliography. The publishers are indebted to the Revd. Arthur W. Kuschke, Librarian Emeritus of Westminster Theological Seminary, for supplying these details.

1931

'The Christian Doctrine of Vicarious Atonement: The Origin of the Idea of Vicarious Atonement, II',[1] *The Homiletic Review*, 102:2, p. 93.

1932

'The Confessional Statement of the United Presbyterian Church', *Christianity Today*, II:9, p. 7.

'The Proposed Doctrinal Basis of Union', *Christianity Today*, II:10, p. 8.

1934

Review of Bryden: *Apologia, Christianity Today*, V:5, p. 115.

1935

'The Sanctity of the Moral Law'. An address published by the League of Evangelical Students [i:193].

---

[1] The second part only of this article was written by John Murray.

Sunday School Lessons, *Christianity Today*, V:11, p. 262; V:12, p. 289; VI:1, p. 15.

'The Reformed Faith and Modern Substitutes', *The Presbyterian Guardian*, I, p. 88 (part I); p. 142 (part II); p. 163 (part III); p. 200 (part IV).

1936

'The Reformed Faith and Modern Substitutes', *The Presbyterian Guardian*, II, p. 27 (part V); p. 77 (part VI); p. 210 (part VII).

'Eschatological Freedom', an editorial, *The Presbyterian Guardian*, II, p. 44.

'Shall we include the Revision of 1903 in our Creed?', *The Presbyterian Guardian*, II, p. 249.

'A Calvinistic Exposition of the Atonement', a review of L. Berkhof, *Vicarious Atonement Through Christ*, *The Presbyterian Guardian*, III, p. 52.

'The Westminster Confession of Faith and the Salvation of Infants', *The Presbyterian Guardian*, III, p. 120.

1937

'The "Kingdom of Heaven" and the "Kingdom of God"', *The Presbyterian Guardian*, III, p. 139.

'Dr Machen's Hope and the Active Obedience of Christ', *The Presbyterian Guardian*, III, p. 163.

'Dr Buswell's Premillennialism', a review of J. O. Buswell: *Unfulfilled Prophecies*, *The Presbyterian Guardian*, III, p. 206.

'What is Amillennialism?', *The Presbyterian Guardian*, III, p. 242.

'The Propagation of the Reformed Faith in New England', *The Presbyterian Guardian*, IV, p. 24 [i:135].

1938

'Why we Baptize Infants', *The Presbyterian Guardian*, V, p. 143.

'Proposed Confessional Revision in the Presbyterian Church in U.S.A.', *The Presbyterian Guardian*, V, p. 207.

'Is Infant Baptism Scriptural?', *The Presbyterian Guardian*, V, p. 227.

1939

Review of S. W. Carruthers, *The Westminster Confession of Faith*, *Westminster Theological Journal*, II:1, p. 50 [iii:291].

Introduction to David Freeman, *The Bible and Things to Come* (Zondervan, Grand Rapids).

1940

'The Inspiration of Scripture', *Westminster Theological Journal*, II:2, p. 1. [iv:30].

Contributor to: *The Sovereignty of God*, ed. J. T. Hoogstra (Zondervan, Grand Rapids), pp. 25–44, reprinted in revised form in 1943 as a booklet.

Review of J. Baillie: *Our Knowledge of God*, *Westminster Theological Journal*, III:1, p. 49 [iii:295].

1941

'Who Raised up Jesus?' *Westminster Theological Journal*, III:2, p. 113 [iv:82].

'The Necessity of Scripture', *The Presbyterian Guardian*, IX (6), p. 90.

'The Inspiration of Scripture', *The Presbyterian Guardian*, IX (7), p. 108.

'The Authority of Scripture', *The Presbyterian Guardian*, IX (8), p. 121.

'The Sufficiency of Scripture', *The Presbyterian Guardian*, IX (9), p. 137.

'The Fourth Commandment', *The Calvin Forum*, VI (10), p. 204.

'Is the Decalogue Abrogated?', *The Calvin Forum*, VI (11–12), p. 236.

'The Sabbath Symposium', *The Calvin Forum*, VII (4), p. 70.

Report of the Committee on Texts and Proof-Texts of the Confession of Faith and the Catechisms, *Minutes* of the 8th General Assembly of the Orthodox Presbyterian Church, pp. 26–29.

1942

'God and the War' (1), *National Republic Magazine*, December [i:344].

'Common Grace', *Westminster Theological Journal*, V:1, p. 1 [ii:93].

'The Calling of the Westminster Assembly', *The Presbyterian Guardian*, XI (2), p. 26.

'The Work of the Westminster Assembly', *The Presbyterian Guardian*, XI (3), p. 37.

Review of J. S. Whale: *Christian Doctrine*, *Westminster Theological Journal*, IV:2, p. 174 [iii:301].

Review of F. E. Hamilton: *The Basis of Millennial Faith*, *Westminster Theological Journal*, V:1, p. 129 [iii:304].

1943

THE SOVEREIGNTY OF GOD (Committee on Christian Education, Orthodox Presbyterian Church).

'God and the War' (II), *National Republic Magazine* (January) [i:344].

'A Notable Tercentenary', *The Presbyterian Guardian*, XII (11), p. 161 [i:312].

'The Calling of the Westminster Assembly', *The Presbyterian Guardian*, XII (13), p. 195.

'The Work of the Westminster Assembly', *The Presbyterian Guardian*, XII (16), p. 254.

'The Christian World Order', *The Presbyterian Guardian*, XII (18), p. 273 [i:356].

'The Catechisms of the Westminster Assembly', *The Presbyterian Guardian*, XII (23), p. 362.

Review of W. E. Sangster: *The Path to Perfection*, *Westminster Theological Journal*, VI:1, p. 58, [iii:307].

Review of S. W. Carruthers: *The Everyday Work of the Westminster Assembly*, *Westminster Theological Journal*, VI:1, p. 106, [iii:317].

1944

'The Banner of Westminster Seminary', *The Presbyterian Guardian*, XIII (13), p. 197 [i:99].

'The Light of the World', *The Presbyterian Guardian*, XIII (17), p. 263.

'The Theology of the Westminster Standards', *The Calvin Forum*, IX, p. 111.

Review of G. F. Hershberger: *War, Peace and Nonresistance*, *Westminster Theological Journal*, VII:2, p. 188 [iii:320].

Review of H. W. Clark: *The Cross and the Eternal Order*, *Westminster Theological Journal*, VII:1, p. 72 [iii:324].

The Message of Evangelism: part of a Report by the Committee on Local Evangelism, *Minutes* of the 11th General Assembly of the Orthodox Presbyterian Church, pp. 26–31 [i:124].

1945

'The Study of the Bible', *The Presbyterian Guardian*, XIV (4), p. 53 [i:3].

The Responsibility of the Church in the Matter of Theological Education: Report to the 12th General Assembly of the Orthodox Presbyterian Church, *Minutes*, pp. 77–81.

1946

'The Attestation of Scripture' in N. B. Stonehouse, P. Woolley, eds., *The Infallible Word* (The Presbyterian Guardian Publishing Co., Philadelphia; revised edition, Presbyterian and Reformed Publishing Co., 1967), pp. 1–52.

'Divorce', part I,[1] *Westminster Theological Journal*, IX:1, p. 31.

Review of Athanasius: *The Incarnation of the Divine Word* (translated by a C.S.V.M.), *Westminster Theological Journal*, VIII:2, p. 254 [iii:336].

Review of S. G. Craig: *Christianity Rightly So Called*, *Westminster Theological Journal*, IX:1, p. 87 [iii:329].

Minority Report of the Committee elected by the 12th General Assembly to consider the doctrinal part of the complaint of certain members of the Presbytery of Philadelphia, *Minutes* of the 13th General Assembly of the Orthodox Presbyterian Church, pp. 68–81.

The Teaching of our Standards respecting the Songs that may be sung in the Public Worship of God: Report to the 13th General Assembly of the Orthodox Presbyterian Church, *Minutes*, pp. 101–107.

1947

'Tradition: Romish and Protestant' (I), *The Presbyterian Guardian*, XVI (9), p. 133 [iv:264].

'Tradition: Romish and Protestant' (II), *The Presbyterian Guardian*, XVI (10), p. 150.

'The Redeemer of God's Elect', *The Presbyterian Guardian*, XVI (20), p. 309 [i:29].

'Divorce', part II, *Westminster Theological Journal*, IX:2, p. 181.

'Divorce', part III, *Westminster Theological Journal*, X:1, p. 1.

Review of G. F. Nuttall: *The Holy Spirit in Puritan Faith and Experience*, *Westminster Theological Journal*, X:1, p. 74 [iii:324].

Minority Report of the Committee on Song in the Public Worship of God, *Minutes* of the 14th General Assembly of the Orthodox Presbyterian Church, pp. 58–66.

---

[1] This and the succeeding articles in the series were later published as *Divorce* in 1953.

Collected Writings

1948

'Divorce', part IV, *Westminster Theological Journal*, X:2, p. 168.

Review of Geerhardus Vos: *Biblical Theology*, *The Presbyterian Guardian*, XVII (16), p. 274.

Review of E. L. Mascall: *Christ, the Christian and the Church*, *Westminster Theological Journal*, V:2, p. 199 [iii:333].

Review of John Calvin: *Commentary on the Epistle to the Romans*, *Westminster Theological Journal*, X:2, p. 226 [iii:337].

The Incomprehensibility of God: Report to the 15th General Assembly of the Orthodox Presbyterian Church, *Minutes*, Appendix, pp. 2–29.

The Free Offer of the Gospel: A Report to the 15th General Assembly of the Orthodox Presbyterian Church, *Minutes*, Appendix, pp. 51–63 [iv:113].

1949

'Unbelief in the Presbyterian Church in U.S.A.', *The Presbyterian Guardian*, XVIII (2), p. 32.

'Divorce', part V, *Westminster Theological Journal*, XI:2, p. 105.

'Divorce,' part VI, *Westminster Theological Journal*, XII:1, p. 30.

Review of B. B. Warfield: *The Inspiration and Authority of the Bible*, *Westminster Theological Journal*, XI:2, p. 200 [iii:339].

Review of D. M. Baillie: *God was in Christ*, *Westminster Theological Journal*, XI:2, p. 224 [iii:346].

Review of Gustav Aulén: *The Faith of the Christian Church*, *Westminster Theological Journal*, XII:1, p. 81 [iv:349].

1950

'The Weak and the Strong', *Westminster Theological Journal*, XII:2, p. 136 [iv:142].

'That they all may be one', *The Presbyterian Guardian*, XIX (3), p. 45.

Review of A. Lecerf: *An Introduction to Reformed Dogmatics*, *Westminster Theological Journal*, XII:2, p. 134 [iii:345].

Review of A. Booth: *The Reign of Grace from its Rise to its Consummation*, *Westminster Theological Journal*, XII:2, p. 231 [iii:349].

Review of A. Nygren: *Commentary on Romans*, *Westminster Theological Journal*, XIII:1, p. 43 [iii:350].

Review of H. Thiessen: *Introductory Lectures in Systematic Theology*, *Westminster Theological Journal*, XIII:1, p. 97 [iii:356].

The Relation of Church and State: part of a Report to the 17th General Assembly of the Orthodox Presbyterian Church, *Minutes*, pp. 60–62 [i:253].

Minority Report, Committee on Ecumenicity, *Minutes* of the 17th General Assembly of the Orthodox Presbyterian Church, pp. 66–68.

1951

'Christian Baptism', part I,[1] *Westminster Theological Journal*, XIII:2, p. 105.

'Christian Baptism', part II, *Westminster Theological Journal*, XIV:1, p. 1.

Review of W. C. Dickinson: *John Knox's History of the Reformation in Scotland*, *Westminster Theological Journal*, XIV:1, p. 84 [iii:361].

Review of J. M. Bates: *A Manual of Doctrine*, *Westminster Theological Journal*, XIII:2, p. 212 [iii:362].

1952

CHRISTIAN BAPTISM (Presbyterian & Reformed Publishing Co., New Jersey).

'Corporate Responsibility', *The Presbyterian Guardian*, XXI (2), p. 25 [i:273].

'Ministers, Members of Local Congregations', *The Presbyterian Guardian*, XXI (5), p. 85.

'The Application of Redemption: The Order of Application' (1),[2] *The Presbyterian Guardian*, XXI (10), p. 188.

'The Order of Application' (2), *The Presbyterian Guardian*, XXI (11), p. 207.

'The Effectual Calling', *The Presbyterian Guardian*, XXI (12), p. 228.

Review of Alan Richardson, ed.: *A Theological Word Book of the Bible*, *Westminster Theological Journal*, XIV:2, p. 169 [iii:367].

Review of L. Hodgson: *The Doctrine of the Atonement*, *Westminster Theological Journal*, XIV:2, p. 203 [iii:371].

---

[1] This and the succeeding article were published as *Christian Baptism* in 1952.
[2] This series was later published in 1955 as the second part of *Redemption – Accomplished and Applied*.

Review of G. Vos: *The Teaching of Jesus Concerning the Kingdom and the Church*; L. Berkhof: *The Kingdom of God*, *Westminster Theological Journal*, XIV:2, p. 230 [iii:375].

Review of B. B. Warfield: *Biblical and Theological Studies*, *Westminster Theological Journal*, XV:1, p. 77 [iii:376].

1953

DIVORCE (Committee on Church Education of the Orthodox Presbyterian Church) French Edition, LE DIVORCE (translated by E. Trocmé and L. Turner), published in *La Revue Reformée*, (IV:15–16), 1953.

THE SABBATH INSTITUTION (The Lord's Day Observance Society, London).

'Regeneration' (1), *The Presbyterian Guardian*, XXII (1), p. 9.

'Regeneration' (2), *The Presbyterian Guardian*, XXII (2), p. 28.

'Faith', *The Presbyterian Guardian*, XXII (3), p. 48.

'Repentance', *The Presbyterian Guardian*, XXII (4), p. 68.

'Justification' (1), *The Presbyterian Guardian*, XXII (5), p. 88.

'Justification' (2), *The Presbyterian Guardian*, XXII (6), p. 109.

'Justification' (3), *The Presbyterian Guardian*, XXII (7), p. 128.

'Justification' (4), *The Presbyterian Guardian*, XXII (9), p. 168.

'Adoption' (1), *The Presbyterian Guardian*, XXII (10), p. 192.

'Adoption' (2), *The Presbyterian Guardian*, XXII (11), p. 213.

'Sanctification', *The Presbyterian Guardian*, XXII (12), p. 232.

Review of E. A. Dowey, Jr.: *The Knowledge of God in Calvin's Theology*, *Westminster Theological Journal*, XV:2, p. 64 [iii:377].

Review of S. Barabas: *So Great Salvation*, The History and Message of the Keswick Convention, *Westminster Theological Journal*, XVI:1, p. 78.

1954

THE COVENANT OF GRACE (Tyndale Press, London), Spanish Edition EL PACTO DE GRACIA, published by Fundación Editorial de Literatura Reformada, 1967.

'Sanctification' (2), *The Presbyterian Guardian*, XXIII (1), p. 15.

'Perseverance' (1), *The Presbyterian Guardian*, XXIII (2), p. 33.

'Perseverance' (2), *The Presbyterian Guardian*, XXIII (3), p. 54.

'Union with Christ' (1), *The Presbyterian Guardian*, XXIII (4), p. 71.

'Union with Christ' (2), *The Presbyterian Guardian*, XXIII (5), p. 94.

'Union with Christ' (3), *The Presbyterian Guardian*, XXIII (6), p. 110.

'Glorification' (1), *The Presbyterian Guardian*, XXIII (7), p. 131.

'Glorification' (2), *The Presbyterian Guardian*, XXIII (8), p. 154.

'The Revision of the Form of Government', *The Presbyterian Guardian*, XXIII (9), p. 171.

Review of C. Welch: *In This Name*, *Westminster Theological Journal*, XVI:2, p. 197 [iv:277].

Review of A. Fridrichsen *et al.*: *The Root of the Vine*, *Westminster Theological Journal*, XVI:2, p. 238 [iv:286].

'Calvin's Doctrine of Creation', *Westminster Theological Journal*, XVII:1, p. 21.

Review of G. C. Berkouwer: *Faith and Justification*, *Westminster Theological Journal*, XVII:1, p. 53 [iv:288].

Review of J. C. Wenger: *An Introduction to Theology*, *Westminster Theological Journal*, XVII:1, p. 74 [iv:292].

1955

REDEMPTION – ACCOMPLISHED AND APPLIED (Eerdmans, Grand Rapids; U.K. Edition, Banner of Truth, 1961; Japanese Edition, 1970).

'The Ordination of Elders, Arguments against Term Eldership', *The Presbyterian Guardian*, XXIV (2), p. 23 [ii:351].

Review of E. Brunner: *Eternal Hope*, *Westminster Theological Journal* XVII:4, p. 169 [iv:298].

1956

'The Imputation of Adam's Sin', part 1,[1] *Westminster Theological Journal*, XVIII:2, p. 166.

'The Imputation of Adam's Sin', part 11, *Westminster Theological Journal*, XIX:1, p. 25.

1957

PRINCIPLES OF CONDUCT (Eerdmans, Grand Rapids; Tyndale Press, London).

---

[1] This and the following articles in the series were later published in 1959.

'The Imputation of Adam's Sin', part III, *Westminster Theological Journal*, XIX:2, p. 141.

'The Imputation of Adam's Sin', part IV, *Westminster Theological Journal*, XX:1, p. 1.

Review of F. C. Jansen: *Calvin's Doctrine of the Work of Christ*, Westminister *Theological Journal*, XIX:2, p. 235 [iv:302].

Review of H. N. Ridderbos: *When the Time had Fully Come*, Westminster *Theological Journal*, XX:1, p. 104 [iv:355].

1958

THE HEAVENLY, PRIESTLY ACTIVITY OF CHRIST. The Campbell Morgan Memorial Lecture for 1958 [i:44].

The Presbyterian Form of Church Government, Evangelical Presbyterian Fellowship, 1958 [ii:345 partial reprint].

Foreword to reprint of C. Hodge: *Princeton Sermons* (Banner of Truth Trust, London), pp. v–vi.

Foreword to reprint of H. Martin: *Jonah* (Banner of Truth Trust, London), p. v.

Review of K. Barth: *Christ and Adam in Romans 5*, *Westminster Theological Journal*, XX:2, p. 198.

Review of H. Buis: *The Doctrine of Eternal Punishment*, *Westminster Theological Journal*, XXI:1, p. 98 [iv:304].

1959

THE IMPUTATION OF ADAM'S SIN (Eerdmans, Grand Rapids).

'Co-operation in Evangelism', *The Presbyterian Guardian*, XXVIII (5), p. 67; also in *The Bible Times*, vol. viii, 5 [i:152].

'The Christian Reformed Church and the Orthodox Presbyterian Church', *The Presbyterian Guardian*, XXVIII (8), p. 123.

Review of C. K. Barrett: *A Commentary on the Epistle to the Romans*, *Westminster Theological Journal*, XXI:2, p. 182 [iv:306].

Review of P. van Buren: *Christ in our Place*, *Westminster Theological Journal*, XXII:1, p. 55 [iv:310].

Review of B. B. Warfield: *Biblical Foundations*, *Westminster Theological Journal*, XXII:1, p. 99 [iv:314].

1960

THE EPISTLE TO THE ROMANS, Volume 1, Chapters 1–8 (Eerdmans, Grand Rapids; Marshall, Morgan & Scott, London).

CALVIN ON SCRIPTURE AND DIVINE SOVEREIGNTY (Baker Book House, Grand Rapids) [iv:158].

Contributor to: E. F. Harrison, ed., *Baker's Dictionary of Theology* (Baker Book House, Grand Rapids):

Adoption, pp. 25–6
Divorce, pp. 169–171
Elect, Election, pp. 179–80.

Review of P. N. Small: *Biblical Basis for Infant Baptism*, *Westminster Theological Journal*, XXII:2, p. 214 [iv:321].

Review of G. C. Berkouwer: *Divine Election*, *Westminster Theological Journal*, XXIII:1, p. 39 [iv:323].

1961

'Pictures of Christ', *The Reformed Herald* (February).

Review of B. Ramm: *The Witness of the Spirit*, *Westminster Theological Journal*, XXIII:2, p. 194 [iv:331].

Report of the Committee on Relations with the Christian Reformed Church, *Minutes* of the 28th General Assembly of the Orthodox Presbyterian Church, pp. 90–92.

1962

Contributor to: J. D. Douglas, ed., *The New Bible Dictionary* (Tyndale Press, London; Eerdmans, Grand Rapids):

Adam (in the N.T.), p. 14.
Covenant, pp. 264–268
Ethics, Biblical, pp. 394–397
Law (in the N.T.) pp. 721–723
Mediator, pp. 802–4
Repentance, pp. 1083–4
Sin, pp. 1189–1193.

'Sanctification' in C. F. Henry, ed., *Basic Christian Doctrines* (Baker Book House, Grand Rapids), pp. 227–233.

'Funeral Message for Dr Stonehouse (Heb. 9:27–8)', *The Presbyterian Guardian*, XXXI (11), p. 167.

Review of B. Ramm: *Special Revelation and the Word of God*, *Westminster Theological Journal*, XXIV:2, p. 205 [iv:334].

Review of A. De Bovis: *What is the Church?*, *Westminster Theological Journal*, XXV:1, p. 81 [iv:339].

1963

'The Last Things'. Supplement to *Acts of the Reformed Ecumenical Synod*, 1963 [ii:401].

'Systematic Theology' part I, *Westminster Theological Journal*, XXV:2, p. 133. [iv:1].

'Systematic Theology', part II, *Westminster Theological Journal*, XXVI:1, p. 33.

'The Infallibility of Scripture', *The Banner of Truth*, 30, p. 8.

1964

'Calvin as Theologian and Expositor' (Annual Lecture of The Evangelical Library, London, 1964) [i:305].

Contributor to: E. H. Palmer, ed., *The Encyclopaedia of Christianity*, vol. I (The National Foundation for Christian Education, Delaware):

Abstinence, pp. 37–9

Adoption, pp. 70–4

Atonement, pp. 465–80

Review of A. B. Mickelsen: *Interpreting the Bible*, *Westminster Theological Journal*, XXVII:1, p. 31 [iv:342].

1965

THE EPISTLE TO THE ROMANS, Volume II, Chapters 9–16 (Eerdmans, Grand Rapids; Marshall, Morgan & Scott, London).

'The Free Offer of the Gospel and the Extent of the Atonement', *The Torch and Trumpet* (now *The Outlook*): I, 15:3, p. 185; II, *The Torch and Trumpet*, 15:5, p. 14; III *The Torch and Trumpet*, 15:9, p. 5 [i:59].

Foreword to British Edition of J. G. Machen: *The Christian View of Man* (The Banner of Truth, London), pp. 7–10.

1966

'The Reconciliation', *Westminster Theological Journal*, XXVIII:2, p. 1 [iv:92].

'The Creedal Basis of Union in the Church', *The Banner of Truth*, 40, p. 14 [i:280].

Report on the Question: 'Does the Constitution of the Orthodox Presbyterian Church permit Church Sessions to receive into communicant membership those who refuse to present their children for baptism on account of scruples concerning infant baptism?', *Minutes* of the 33rd General Assembly of the Orthodox Presbyterian Church, pp. 92–96.

1967

'Definitive Sanctification', *Calvin Theological Journal*, II:1, p. 5 [ii:277].

Review of G. C. Berkouwer: *The Work of Christ, Westminster Theological Journal*, XXXI:1, p. 59 [iv:345].

1968

'Edward J. Young: An Appreciation', *The Banner of Truth*, 54, p. 1 [i:113].

'Calvin, Dordt and Westminster on Predestination – A Comparative Study', in P. Y. de Young, ed., *Crisis in the Reformed Churches*, Essays in Commemoration of the Great Synod of Dordt, 1618–19 (Reformed Fellowship, Inc., Grand Rapids) [iv:205].

Foreword to R. B. Kuiper: *The Bible Tells Us So* (The Banner of Truth, London), pp. 7–9.

1969

Contributor to: M. C. Tenney, ed., *The Zondervan Pictorial Bible Dictionary* (Zondervan, Grand Rapids):

Baptism (Reformed View), Vol. 1: 468–69
Elect, Election, Vol. 2:270–74
The Fall, Vol. 2:492–94
Foreknow, Foreknowledge, Vol. 2:590–93
Foreordain, Foreordination, Vol. 2:594
Intercession of Christ, Vol. 3:294–95

1970

'The Advent of Christ', *The English Churchman* (August 1970).

part 1 issue 6656, p. 5;
part 2 issue 6657, p. 5;

part 3 issue 6658, p. 5;
part 4 issue 6659, p. 5; [i:86].

1972

Contributor to: P. E. Hughes, ed., *The Encyclopaedia of Christianity*, III (The National Foundation for Christian Education, Delaware):
Covenant Theology, pp. 199–216 [iv:216].
Divorce, pp. 421–4.
'The Origin of Man' in J. H. Skilton, ed., *The Law and the Prophets* (Presbyterian and Reformed Publishing Co., New Jersey), [ii:3].
'The Theology of the Westminster Confession of Faith' in J. H. Skilton, ed., *Scripture and Confession* (Presbyterian and Reformed Publishing Co., New Jersey, [iv:241].
Foreword to George P. Hutchinson: *The Problem of Original Sin in American Presbyterian Theology* (Presbyterian and Reformed Publishing Co.), pp. vii–viii.

1973

THE PATTERN OF THE LORD'S DAY (The Lord's Day Observance Society, London).

POSTHUMOUSLY PUBLISHED FROM LITERARY REMAINS
March 1976 'Abounding Hope', *The Banner of Truth*, 150, p. 1.
December 1976 'Love and its Correlatives', *The Banner of Truth*, 159, p. 13.
January 1978 'Memory and Prospect', *The Banner of Truth*, 172, p. 1.
May 1979 'The Coming of the Spirit', *The Banner of Truth*, 188, p. 9.
July 1980 'Love to Christ: The Supreme Necessity', *The Banner of Truth*, 202, p. 1.
February 1982 'Christ our Sin Bearer', *The Banner of Truth*, 221, p. 13.
July 1982 'Situation Ethics', *The Banner of Truth*, 226, p. 7.
November 1982 'The Unity of the Body of Christ', *The Banner of Truth*, 231, p. 10.

COLLECTED WRITINGS

1976   Vol. 1: *The Claims of Truth* (The Banner of Truth).

1977   Vol. 2: *Select Lectures in Systematic Theology* (The Banner of Truth).

1982   Vol. 3: *Life (by Iain H. Murray), Sermons and Reviews* (The Banner of Truth).

1983   Vol. 4: *Studies in Theology* (The Banner of Truth).

Indexes

Index of Names

Index of Subjects

(Volume number is indicated by Roman numerals)

Adam: historical fact i.331–2
  his creation ii.4–13
  made in image of God ii.34–41
  the Adamic administration ii.47–59
  free agency of man before Fall ii.60–6
  Fall of man ii.67–76
Advent (second) of Christ i.86–95; *see also* Eschatology
Aeons of first and second Adam iii.352–4
Adoption: linked with God's Fatherhood ii.223–6, 230–3
  how described in Bible ii.226
  its nature ii.227–9
  the Spirit of adoption ii.229–30
  as explained in Westminster Confession iv.259
Amyraldianism iv.256
Anabaptists iv.293, 294, 295
Arminianism i.130–2; iii.58, 59, 131–2; iv.400
Assurance (of Faith): its nature and meaning ii.264–7
  the duty and privilege of ii.267–70
  its grounds ii.270–4
  its cultivation ii.274

Atonement, The, of Christ i.59–85; ii.142–3; iii.129, 147, 340–5
  limited i.127–9, 285
  the love of God its source ii.143–7
  characterized by inter-Trinitarian co-operation ii.147–50
  its cosmic significance iii.311–17, 324
  its doctrine iii.371–4
  its extent iii.129; iv.256, 311–13, 347–8
  Calvin's doctrine of its extent iv.311–13
Auburn Affirmation (1924) i.99, 194

Baptism (Christian) iii.135
  not regeneration ii.181–2
  its place, import, mode, subjects, efficacy ii.370–5
  of infants iv.239–40, 321–3
Bible, The, its study i.3–8
  its organic unity i.5, 23–6
  its infallibility and inerrancy i.9–15; iv.22–9
  its uniqueness i.11–12
  its witness i.12–15
  its inspiration, authority, utility, and purpose i.14; ii.249–51;

Collected Writings